Bibliography of
Georgia Authors
1949-1965

Bibliography of Georgia Authors
1949-1965

By
JOHN WYATT BONNER, JR.

UNIVERSITY OF GEORGIA PRESS
ATHENS

Paperback edition, 2010
© 1966 by the University of Georgia Press
Athens, Georgia 30602
www.ugapress.org
All rights reserved
Printed digitally in the United States of America

The Library of Congress has cataloged the hardcover edition of this book as follows:
Library of Congress Cataloging-in-Publication Data

LCCN Permalink: http://lccn.loc.gov/66023074
Bonner, John Wyatt.
Bibliography of Georgia authors, 1949–1965.
vii, 266 p. 24 cm.
1. American literature—Georgia—Bibliography. 2. Georgia—In literature—Bibliography.
I. Georgia authors, 1949–1965.
Z1273 .B6
013'.9758   66-23074

Paperback ISBN-13: 978-0-8203-3526-1
ISBN-10: 0-8203-3526-6

Contents

PREFACE   vii

BIBLIOGRAPHY OF GEORGIA AUTHORS

    1949-1950 _____ 1

    1950-1951 _____ 17

    1951-1952 _____ 29

    1952-1953 _____ 43

    1953-1954 _____ 53

    1954-1955 _____ 67

    1955-1956 _____ 83

    1956-1957 _____ 97

    1957-1958 _____ 113

    1958-1959 _____ 129

    1959-1960 _____ 149

    1960-1961 _____ 173

    1961-1962 _____ 187

    1962-1963 _____ 203

    1963-1964 _____ 219

    1964-1965 _____ 237

INDEX _____ 257

Preface

BIBLIOGRAPHIES are compiled for people interested in either a small facet of human knowledge or for those who want to compass the whole spectrum of a subject. It is impossible to make the perfect, all inclusive bibliography and this one of Georgia Authors is no exception. The task of finding, identifying, and obtaining copies of the books included is a never ending one. Authors have been omitted through oversight or because I had no way of identifying them. The criterion for inclusion of material is printed in detail elsewhere and I will not repeat it. Herein the yearly bibliographies, 1949-1965, are reprinted by photo offset from Winter issues of the *Georgia Review*. An index of the authors has been added.

It has been the belief and policy of the University of Georgia to serve as custodian of the literary, historical, and cultural history of the state. This bibliography is an outgrowth of my effort to build and strengthen the Georgiana Collection in the Special Collections Division of the University of Georgia Libraries. I hope that this compilation, with all its imperfections, will aid students, librarians, and scholars in their study and collecting of Georgia literature.

I am greatly indebted to many friends for their help, their interest, their time, and most of all, their encouragement. First and foremost I am grateful to Dr. J. O. Eidson, former editor, and to Mr. W. W. Davidson, present editor of the *Georgia Review*, who saw the need for the *Bibliography* and refused to let me give it up; and to the personnel of the book stores throughout the state who have allowed me to browse among their collections. I also am indebted to the staff of the Special Collections Division of the University of Georgia Libraries for clerical assistance.

JOHN W. BONNER, JR.

Bibliography of Georgia Authors
1949-1950

This annotated bibliography aims to be a complete and accurate record of books published by Georgia authors for the period January 1, 1949- November 1, 1950. The annotations are descriptive, not critical; intended to place, not to judge the book. U. S., State, County, and City Documents, parts of books, brief analytics, and pamphlets of less than 25 pages have been omitted. Prices are given except when not supplied by publisher or when book is obtainable only on specific request, in which cases the word "apply" is used.

As a basis for determining those entitled to be called Georgia authors, the compiler has used the criteria established by the Junior Members Round Table of Atlanta in their Bibliography of Georgia Authors published in 1942: authors born in Georgia and claiming Georgia as their native state and those who have lived in Georgia for a period of five years and who did their writing here.

The compiler realizes the impossibility of making such a list as this absolutely complete, and he will both welcome and appreciate any additions and corrections. They may be sent to him at any time in care of the GEORGIA REVIEW. Since this Bibliography will appear annually, any books which have been inadvertently omitted will be incorporated in the list for 1951.

Acknowledgement is made to Mrs. Raymond Massey, President of the Georgia Writers Association, and Mrs. Betty Anne Morgan, member of the University of Georgia Library Staff, for their help and encouragement.

ADAMS, CARSBIE C. *The Cure, the Story of an Alcoholic.* New York, Exposition Press, 1950. 143p. $3.00.
    An attempt to bring about a better understanding of the causes of chronic alcoholism — its treatment and cure.

AIKEN, CONRAD P. *The Divine Pilgrim.* Athens, University of Georgia Press, 1949. 288p. $4.50.
    A series of long philosophical poems, published separately over the years, is brought together in this single work. The poems are subtitled "Symphonies," and the central theme is the problem of personal identity.

AIKEN, CONRAD P. *The Short Stories of Conrad Aiken.* New York, Duell, Sloan & Pearce, 1950. 416p. $5.00.

A collection of 29 short stories by a writer perhaps better known for his poetry. The book represents work of the last 28 years.

ANDREWS, MARSHALL. *Disaster Through Air Power.* New York, Rinehart, 1950. 143p. $2.00.

A denunciation of the Air Force faith in strategic bombing and the B-36 as expressed in the recent airing of inter-service disputes.

BAYNE, CHARLES J. *Coming of the Crow's Feet.* Atlanta, Tupper & Love, 1949. 415p. $3.50.

Reminiscences of a veteran newspaperman well acquainted with Baltimore, Washington, Atlanta, Macon, and other Southern cities.

BIXLER, HAROLD H., and SIMMONS, ERNEST P. *The New Standard High School Spelling Scale.* Atlanta, Turner E. Smith, 1949. 66p. $1.00.

This is a revised and enlarged edition of an earlier work by the same authors. The book includes 72 lessons in spelling for Junior and Senior High Schools.

BLACKSTOCK, WALTER. *The West Wind Blowing.* Mill Valley, Calif., The Wings Press, 1950. 48p. $2.00.

A wide range of subjects is covered in this collection of poems by a graduate of the University of Georgia. Many of the poems included have appeared in various national publications.

BOLAND, FRANK KELLS, M.D. *The First Anesthetic; the Story of Crawford W. Long.* Athens, University of Georgia Press, 1950. 160p. $3.00.

A biographical sketch of a 19th century Georgia doctor who was the first to use ether as a surgical anesthetic.

BOWEN, ELIZA A. *The Story of Wilkes County, Georgia.* Marietta, Ga., Continental Book Co., 1950. 192p. $7.50.

A reprint edition of newspaper articles from the Washington (Georgia) *Gazette and Chronicle*, 1886-1897, edited, annotated, and indexed by Louise Frederick Hays, State Historian of Georgia.

BROOKES, STELLA BREWER. *Joel Chandler Harris—Folklorist.* Athens, University of Georgia Press, 1950. 182p. $4.00.

A detailed study of the writing and publication of the Uncle Remus books and a critical analysis of the folklore which abounds in them.

BROWN, MAREL. *The Greshams of Greenway.* Atlanta, Home Mission Board, Southern Baptist Convention, 1950. No Paging. $.40.

A story of home life centered around the rural church in which junior boys and girls take an active part.

CALDWELL, ERSKINE. *Episode in Palmetto.* New York, Duell, Sloan & Pearce, 1950. 252p. $2.75.

The story of a young schoolteacher in a small Southern town who discovers that her beauty has so upset the male population of the town that she decides after one week to abandon teaching and run away with one of her many admirers.

CALDWELL, ERSKINE. *Place Called Estherville.* New York, Duell, Sloan & Pearce, 1949. 244p. $2.75.

One crisis after another characterizes this story of a mulatto brother and sister as they move from the country to Estherville in search of an honest living.

CAMPBELL, ALICE (ORMOND) *Veiled Murder.* New York, Random House, 1949. 279p. $2.50.

An American girl married to a Royal Air Force pilot is suspect number one when he is mysteriously murdered.

CAMPBELL, MARIE. *A House With Stairs.* New York, Rinehart, 1950. 245p. $2.50.

The story of two little girls — one white and one black — who live on a plantation in southern Alabama. It opens in 1863, the year of the emancipation, and follows the two children raised "separate—together," until marriage separates them.

CANDLER, CHARLES HOWARD. *Asa Griggs Candler.* Atlanta, Emory University Press, 1950. 502p. Apply.

Biography of the man behind the spectacular building of the nation's leading soft drink industry. A revealing account of how Candler, Coca-Cola, and Atlanta achieved world-wide fame and recognition.

CASH, GRACE. *Pattern for Living and Other Poems.* Philadelphia, Dorrance, 1950. 123p. $2.00.

A collection of 100 religious poems arranged by subject classification.

CHANDOS, DANE (pseud. of PETER LILLEY and NIGEL STANSBURY-MILLET). *House in the Sun.* New York, G. P. Putnam's Sons, 1949. 240p. $3.00.

The authors weave a vivid Mexican tapestry of the same charm, color, humor, and veracity as they did in *Village in the Sun.* An interesting presentation of the major differences between life and attitudes south of the Rio Grande and those in the U. S. A.

CHAPMAN, PAUL W. *Occupational Guidance.* Revised Edition. Atlanta, Turner E. Smith, 1950. 635p. $3.30.

A high school textbook reviewing the opportunities in many different job fields, and listing the necessary qualifications and training for each type of work. The book has been completely re-written and is profusely illustrated.

CHAPMAN, PAUL W., VEATCH, C. L., and FITCH, FRANK W. JR., *Conserving Soil Resources*. Atlanta, Turner E. Smith, 1950. 355p. $4.10.

A study dealing with the basic and fundamental problems of the U. S conservation program.

CLAY, LUCIUS DUBIGNON. *Decision in Germany*. New York, Doubleday, 1950. 522p. $4.50.

General Clay's story covers his four years in Germany — two as deputy military governor under Gen. Eisenhower and Gen. McNarney, and two as military governor. It is the candid account of the establishment and breakdown of the quadripartite government in Berlin, the blockade, and the establishment of a West German government as a political fact. The book is illustrated and indexed.

CLAY, LUCIUS DUBIGNON. *Germany and the Fight for Freedom*. Cambridge, Mass., Harvard University Press, 1950. 83p. $2.00.

A report of General Clay's administration of Germany with emphasis on the series of incidents with Russia during that period. The General declares that U. S. foreign policy should be aimed at a United Western Europe, in which Germany should have a place.

COOPER, GEORGE W., M.D. *Poems for Peace*. Philadelphia, Dorrance, 1949. 143p. $2.00.

A collection of poems written by a veteran of both world wars who parades one soldier's opinions and reactions to war through all the poems. The author is a physician and teacher on the faculty of Loyola University in New Orleans.

COOPER, JAMES B. *Poultry for Home and Market*. Atlanta, Turner E. Smith, 1950. 487p. $2.96.

A practical guide book to efficient poultry management for either the family with a small backyard flock or the large producer. Details are given concerning necessary equipment, with instructions for building, maintaining good health in the flock, breeding and marketing. Illustrated and indexed.

COPE, CHANNING. *Front Porch Farmer*. Atlanta, Turner E. Smith, 1949. 171p. $2.75.

The Atlanta *Constitution's* popular writer on things agricultural tells his personal story of how he learned to make eroded, gullied, and impoverished land live again, and, as a result, created a new farm. The introduction is by Louis Bromfield, and the book is illustrated with photographs.

COPELAND, EDNA ARNOLD. *Nancy Hart: The War Woman*. Elberton, Ga., Published by the Author, 1950. 48p. $3.00.

A collection of incidents and anecdotes from the life of Nancy Hart, this is the first work to be devoted completely to the brave deeds of this unique Revolutionary War heroine.

COULTER, ELLIS MERTON. *Confederate States of America, 1861-1865.* Baton Rouge, Louisiana State University Press, 1950. 644p. $7.00.

This is the fourth published volume in the proposed series of ten, which will cover the history of the South. This volume treats of the Civil War as an aspect of the life of a people. Mr. Coulter tells his story in a vivid style, and the boon of humor proves a great help to the layman following so formidable a subject. This book was the selection of the History Book Club for September, 1950.

COULTER, ELLIS MERTON, and SAYE, ALBERT BERRY. *A List of the Early Settlers of Georgia.* Athens, University of Georgia Press, 1949. 103p. $4.00.

The book contains a list of 2,979 settlers of Georgia from the founding of the colony until 1741, as well as such pertinent information as their age, occupation, date of embarkation, date of arrival, lots in Savannah, lots in Frederica, and a column entitled "Dead, Quitted, Run Away." The material is taken from manuscripts located in the University of Georgia Libraries in Athens.

CRAIG, GEORGIA, pseud. See: Gaddis, Peggy

DANIELS, MOSE. *Marshes of Glynn, photographs by Mose Daniels.* New York, Duell, Sloan & Pearce, 1949. 48p. $3.00.

A photographic impression of Sidney Lanier's famous poem in its original setting.

DERN, MRS. JOHN SHERMAN. See: Gaddis, Peggy

DERN, PEGGY. See: Gaddis, Peggy

DREWRY, JOHN E., ed. *Contemporary Journalism.* Athens, University of Georgia Press, 1949. 122p. $2.00.

This book edited by Dean Drewry is made up of press, radio, and specialized publications as seen through the institutes at the University's School of Journalism during 1948-49.

DREWRY, JOHN E., ed. *Journalism at the Mid-Century.* Athens, University of Georgia Press, 1950. 124p. $2.00.

This book edited by Dean Drewry is made up of press, radio, and specialized publications as seen through the institutes at the University's School of Journalism during 1949-50.

DUNCAN, AMON O. *Food Processing; a Guide to Selecting, Producing, Preserving and Storing the Family Food Supply.* Atlanta, Turner E. Smith, 1949. 564p. $3.28.

This study discusses in detail the various methods of food processing — curing, canning, freezing, dehydrating — their advantages and disadvantages. The book is illustrated.

ELLIOT, CHARLES N., and MOBLEY, MAJOR D. *Southern Forestry*. Atlanta, Turner E. Smith, 1949. 494p. $2.96.

A textbook for use in schools of vocational agriculture and other schools offering a course in practical forestry. Chief emphasis is placed on Southern problems and their relation to the nation as a whole.

ETHRIDGE, WILLIE SNOW. *Going to Jerusalem*. New York, Vanguard Press, 1950. 313p. $3.50.

As wife of the American representative on the United Nations Palestine Commission, Mrs. Ethridge accompanied her husband to Jerusalem. This is her informal story of the complexities of the many problems faced by Arabs and Jews in a land familiar to all through Bible history.

FLEMING, BERRY, compiler. *199 Years of Augusta's Library*. Athens, University of Georgia Press, 1949. 96p. $3.00.

A compilation of data relating to the history of the library and the cultural life of Augusta and vicinity.

GADDIS, PEGGY. *Back Home*. New York, Arcadia House, 1950. 238p. $2.00.

The story of how a young actress saves her old South Carolina home by turning it into a guest house and restaurant.

GADDIS, PEGGY (pseud. PERRY LINDSAY). *Brief Pleasure*. New York, Phoenix, 1949. 256p. $2.00.

A novel concerning the trials, tribulations, and disappointments of young lovers.

GADDIS, PEGGY. *Come into My Heart*. New York, Arcadia House, 1950. 235p. $2.00.

A career girl accepts a position on the ranch of the man who caused her to lose her job back East.

GADDIS, PEGGY (pseud. Gail Jordan). *Dark Passion*. New York, Phoenix, 1950. 236p. $2.00.

The story of a sedate New England schoolmistress on tour in the Carolina mountains. She was storm-bound in the isolated cabin of a man she learned to love.

GADDIS, PEGGY (pseud. Peggy Dern.). *Doctor Christopher*. New York, Arcadia House, 1949. 254p. $2.00.

Julie, a shy, retiring girl, wins the affections of a young doctor in spite of the schemes of her glamorous foster sister.

GADDIS, PEGGY. *Girl Next Door*. New York, Arcadia House, 1949. 255p. $2.00.

A girl in love with her childhood sweetheart has a hard time convincing him of her love when he returns from the war blinded.

GADDIS, PEGGY (pseud. PERRY LINDSAY). *Impatient Lovers.* New York, Phoenix, 1949. 254p. $2.00.
  The story of a girl whose marriage for spite backfires in a most unusual way.

GADDIS, PEGGY (pseud. GAIL JORDAN). *Love Slave.* New York, Phoenix, 1949. 255p. $2.00.
  A wealthy young socialite falls in love with the mechanic who repaired her car.

GADDIS, PEGGY (pseud. GAIL JORDAN). *The Other Dear Charmer.* New York, Arcadia House, 1949. 255p. $2.00.
  A widower and his daughter buy a plantation in the South only to find that they are scorned by their neighbors. The daughter's charms, however, help to break down the neighbors' prejudices.

GADDIS, PEGGY (pseud. GEORGIA CRAIG). *Perry Kimbo, R. N.* New York, Phoenix, 1950. 239p. $2.00.
  The romantic convalescence of a girl in white.

GADDIS, PEGGY. *Suddenly It's Love.* New York, Arcadia House, 1949. 256p. $2.00.
  Story of the havoc created by a meek, mild, and mousey orphan in the family that so warmly welcomed her on the death of her parents.

GADDIS, PERRY (pseud. PERRY LINDSAY). *Swamp Girl.* New York, Phoenix, 1950. 237p. $2.00.
  The appearance in New York of the girl who rescued a wealthy young sportsman from a plane crash in Florida upsets his carefree life.

GADDIS, PEGGY (pseud. GEORGIA CRAIG). *This Too Is Love.* New York, Phoenix, 1949. 249p. $2.00.
  This novel is about the life and loves of Louella Hargroves in the little town of De Kalb.

GARRETT, CONSTANCE. *Growth in Prayer.* New York, Macmillan, 1950. 156p. $2.00.
  The basic theme of this book is to teach a greater appreciation of prayer as a communion with God rather than as a vehicle for getting wishes granted. The author discusses the deeper reaches of prayer—the kind that transforms and activates every phase of life.

GODLEY, MARGARET WALTON, and BRAGG, LILLIAN CHAPLIN. *Stories of Old Savannah: Second Series.* (Savannah?) Privately Printed, 1950. 47p. $.50.
  Murder, intrigue, religion, ghosts, Indians, and Sherman's occupation of the city are some of the subjects covered in this collection of nine stories about old Savannah. The cover drawing is by Elizabeth O'Neill Verner.

GORDON, ARTHUR. *Reprisal.* New York, Simon and Schuster, 1950. 310p. $3.00.

　The story of a Negro's revenge against a Southern town which has let the men who lynched his wife go free.

GRAHAM, LORAH HARRIS. *Inspirations: Radio Talks and Travel Sketches.* Ringgold, Ga., Ringgold Bible Club, 1950. 270p. Apply.

　A collection of 40 inspirational radio programs given by the founder and director of the Ringgold Bible Club over a period of three years.

GREEN, GARDNER LELAND. *These Will Remain.* Boston, Bruce Humphries, 1949. 64p. $2.50.

　A group of inspirational poems seeking for the permanent values which should come out of death, devastation, and confusion of war.

HARWELL, RICHARD B. *Confederate Music.* Chapel Hill, N. C., University of North Carolina Press, 1950. 184p. $3.50.

　The first work devoted to the music of the Confederacy is not only an extensive bibliography of the music written, published, sung, and played in the South during the sixties, but also an account of the composers and publishers in this region during the War.

HENDERSON, LEGRAND (pseud. LE GRAND). *Here Come the Perkinses!* Indianapolis, Bobbs-Merrill, 1949. 183p. $2.50.

　The adventures of a sea-going family, complete with villains, complications, and data on seamanship.

HENDERSON, LE GRAND (pseud. LE GRAND). *The Puppy Who Chased the Sun.* New York, Grosset & Dunlap, 1950. 44p. $.25.

　A story for young children about the puppy who thought he chased the sun up every morning until a rainy day made him see the error of his ways.

HENDERSON, LE GRAND (pseud. LE GRAND). *Why Cowboys Sing in Texas.* Nashville, Tenn., Abingdon-Cokesbury Press, 1950. 40p. $2.00.

　How "Slim Jim Bean," the "silentest" cowboy in all Texas, in the days before cowboys sang on the range, was the first to discover the kind of music cows like best.

HENSON, JEAN. *Time for Reflection.* Paris, France, A. Somogy, 1949. 250p. $4.00.

　Autobiography of a native of Cartersville, Ga., who left the U. S. to live the life of an expatriate in France. The book traces the author's life from the mountains of North Georgia to a German prison camp in World War II.

HERVEY, HARRY. *Barracoon.* New York, G. P. Putnam's Sons, 1950. 275p. $3.00.

The 12th novel by Savannah's Harry Hervey is about the emotional anguishes of a sensitive and beautiful woman caught in the foul life of a slave-trading post in Portuguese Guinea in the 1850's.

HOFFMAN, JOHN LEON. *The South, the Land of Flowers.* Forsyth, Ga., Hoffman Publications, 1949. 113p. $2.00 paper, $3.50 cloth.

A list and description of all trees and shrubs of ornamental value in the Southeast. Mr. Hoffman gives instructions on such matters as collecting, transplanting, fertilizing, pruning, mulching, and general care of plants.

HOFFMAN, JOHN LEON. *365 Happy Days in the Garden.* Forsyth, Ga., Hoffman Publications, 1950. 95p. $1.50 paper, $2.50 cloth.

Day to day instructions on what to do in a garden and what flowers to expect on trees, shrubs, perennials, and bulbs in the various seasons. Blank pages are included for notes and a diary of the garden.

HOLLAND, LYNWOOD MATHIS. *Direct Primary in Georgia.* Urbana, Ill., University of Illinois Press, 1949. 125p. $3.00.

This is the first full-length study of the direct primary as it operates in a predominantly one-party state. The study includes a descriptive analysis of the primary, development of the primary from reconstruction days, and a discussion of the power of the rural vote. This expanded doctoral dissertation is also Volume 30, No. 4, of the *Illinois Studies in the Social Sciences.*

JENKINS, SARA. *The Lost Lamp.* New York, Crowell, 1950. 244p. $3.00.

Story of a Georgia Methodist minister and his ecclesiastical travels from one charge to another and his learning to blend tolerance with righteousness.

JOHNSTON, EDITH DUNCAN. *The Houstouns of Georgia.* Athens, University of Georgia Press, 1950. 430p. $5.00.

A study of a colonial family of Georgia, a father and five sons, who all took prominent part in the political, economic, and civic life of Savannah from 1733 to 1836. The descendants of the original family are traced to almost every state in the union.

JORDAN, GAIL, pseud. See: Gaddis, Peggy

KAYE, JACK. *Honey Shops.* Philadelphia, Dorrance, 1949. 259p. $2.50.

The book is a story of chain store buying methods, merchandising, and also the loves, frustrations, and failures of its personnel. The author is a resident of Albany, Georgia.

LEDBETTER, ELIZABETH O'CONNOR. *Out of the South.* Boston, Bruce Humphries, 1950. 84p. $2.50.

The poems are tributes to the beauty, traditions, and customs of the South. The book is illustrated with the drawings of Eileen A. Soper.

LEE, EDNA L. (MOONEY). *Queen Bee.* New York, Appleton-Century-Crofts, 1949. 295p. $3.00.

The story concerns a beautiful, selfish, ruthless woman who considers it her royal prerogative to rule her husband and family. The setting of this novel is Atlanta, Georgia.

LE GRAND, pseud. See: Henderson, Le Grand

LIGHTLE, BURNETTE. *St. Simons Island.* Decatur, Ga., Bowen Press, 1950. 31p. $1.50.

In prose, poetry, and pictures the author has caught the romance and loveliness of one of Georgia's "Golden Isles."

LINDSAY, PERRY, pseud. See: Gaddis, Peggy

LONG, MARGARET. *Louisville Saturday.* New York, Random House, 1950. 278p. $2.75.

An episodic novel about eleven women living in Louisville, Kentucky, on a Saturday afternoon in the fall of 1942, and the way they react to the pressure of love and life.

MCGILL, RALPH. *Israel Revisited.* Atlanta, Tupper & Love, 1950. 116p. $2.00.

A Southern newspaperman tells what he saw in Israel in 1946 when he visited the new nation, and reports of the great improvements observed on his second visit in 1950.

MACKAY, ROBERT. *The Letters of Robert Mackay to His Wife;* edited by Walter C. Hartridge. Athens, University of Georgia Press, 1949. 325p. $4.00.

The letters in this volume were written from ports in America and England by a Savannah merchant and cover the period 1795-1816. The book was issued under the auspices of the Georgia Society of Colonial Dames.

MCMAHAN, CHALMERS A. *The People of Atlanta; a Demographic Study of Georgia's Capital City.* Athens, University of Georgia Press, 1950. 257p. $4.00.

Analysis and organization of data on the factors of race, nativity, age, sex, marital condition, education, occupation, mortality, religion, and migration of the people of Atlanta, Georgia. The author is Associate Professor of Sociology at the University of Georgia.

MALOOF, LOUIS J. *Truth About China's Crisis.* Huntington, Ind., Our Sunday Visitor Press, 1949. 143p. $ .75.

The book is a revelation of what is happening in China and an impassioned appeal to the forces of Christianity and democracy to combat communistic inroads.

MARSHALL, EDISON. *Gypsy Sixpence.* New York, Farrar, Straus, 1949. 371p. $3.00.
   A story of love, hate, compassion, and revenge laid in India and Zanzibar of the 1830's when Victoria's armies were carving an empire for England.

MARSHALL, EDISON. *The Infinite Woman.* New York, Farrar, Straus, 1950. 374p. $3.00.
   A novel based on the life of the exotic dancer, Lola Montaro, whose daring full-blooded life made her a 19th century headliner. The locale moves from India across all Europe to England.

MARSHALL, EDISON. *Love Stories of India.* New York, Farrar, Straus, 1950. 307p. $3.00.
   Fifteen romantic stories laid in India, Indo-China, and China. Each tale is prefaced with a brief notation concerning its history and how it came to be written.

MARTIN, SIDNEY WALTER. *Florida's Flagler.* Athens, University of Georgia Press, 1949. 280p. $4.00.
   Biography of the fabulous figure who gave the better part of his life and fortune to the development of Florida.

MAXWELL, EDNA STEPHENS. *She Says.* Boston, Baker's Plays, 1949. 110p. $1.00.
   A humorous collection of 12 monologues about the American clubwoman.

MAXWELL, GILBERT. *Sleeping Trees.* Boston, Little, Brown, 1949. 285p. $3.00.
   A story of Southern life in a small town, told warmly and with rare understanding as it probes into the complicated lives of its characters. The author is a native of Washington, Georgia.

MAXWELL, JAMES QUILLIAN. *Birth of a Salesman.* Atlanta, Stein Printing Co., 1950. 154p. $2.00.
   A practical working guide for the neophyte salesman with many helpful suggestions for the more experienced salesman. The foreword is by Harold J. Bean.

MAXWELL, SUE, and O'CALLAGHAN, GOLDA LARKIN. *South American Fiesta.* Boston, Bruce Humphries, 1950. 110p. $2.75.
   A book of life and travel in South America based on the four year sojourn of the O'Callaghan family.

MAYNARD, LOUISE, and AULTMAN, RUTH W. *Our Georgia.* Austin, Texas, The Steck Co., 1950. 160p. $2.50. Text ed. $1.90.
   A collection of stories about Georgia—people, places, and events—for elementary school children. The book is illustrated by Elizabeth Rice.

MEANS, ALEXANDER. *Diary for 1861*, edited by Ross H. McLean. Emory University, Ga., Emory Sources and Reprints, 1949. 46p. $ .75.

Diary of a Methodist minister active in state politics and a non-secessionist member of the Georgia Secession Convention. Means was also a professor of natural history at Emory University.

MENABONI, ATHOS and SARA. *Menaboni's Birds*. New York, Rinehart, 1950. 132p. $10.00; Deluxe ed. $25.00.

Sara Menaboni has written the text to accompany the extraordinary bird portraits by her husband. The book contains 32 plates in full color, 13 pages in black and white, and numerous small illustrations.

MILLER, PAUL W. *Atlanta, Capital of the South*. New York, Oliver Durrell, 1949. 318p. $3.75.

This volume of the American Guide Series has been completely revised and brought up-to-date. The book is divided into four parts and covers all phases of life in Atlanta and the metropolitan area. Illustrated with photographs.

MITCHELL, ADDIE STOKES. *Flashlights*. Boston, Bruce Humphries, (c. 1948) 1949. 63p. $2.50.

A collection of poetry dealing with the subjects of religion, philosophy, and children. The book contains five poems written by the author's sister, Miss Estelle Mitchell.

MONTGOMERY, HORACE. *Cracker Parties*. Baton Rouge, La., Louisiana State University Press, 1950. 278p. $4.00.

This study of the "golden era" of Georgia politics, 1845-1861, traces Georgia's break with the Whig Party and her subsequent assumption of leadership in the Democratic Party.

MONTGOMERY, JAMES STUART. *The Incredible Cassanova*. New York, Doubleday, 1949. 437p. $3.95.

This biography, subtitled "The Magnificent Follies of a Peerless Adventurer, Amorist and Charlatan," is based upon Cassanova's own memoirs, which in the original filled twelve volumes.

MOREHOUSE, WARD. *Matinee Tomorrow; Fifty Years of Our Theatre*. New York, Whittlesey House, 1949. 340p. $5.00.

An informal, inclusive, and anecdotal chronicle of the New York stage from 1899 to 1948 by one of the nation's outstanding dramatic critics.

ORR, DOROTHY. *A History of Education in Georgia*. Chapel Hill, N. C., University of North Carolina Press, 1950. 463p. $6.00.

A history, 1733 to 1943, of the continuing struggle for free public schools and creditable colleges in Georgia. This study, including an appendix, bibliography, and index, is an enlargement of a Master's Thesis written in 1933.

OSBORN, STELLANOVA. *Balsam Boughs.* Cedar Rapids, Iowa, Torch Press, 1949. 64p. Apply.
A collection of 52 nature poems.

OUTLAW, NELL WARREN. *Voiceless Lips.* Nashville, Tenn., Broadman Press, 1949. 141p. $2.00.
A book of 25 devotional essays suggested by the silent blossoms of your garden favorites. The book is illustrated by Novie Moffat Ahrenhold.

PARKS, AILEEN W. *Davy Crockett: Young Rifleman.* Indianapolis, Bobbs-Merrill, 1949. 194p. $1.75.
This is another in the popular Childhood of Famous Americans Series. It tells the story of the boyhood days of the young Tennesseean who became a famous hunter and died in the Alamo, the cradle of Texas liberty. The book is illustrated by Charles V. John.

PARKS, EDD WINFIELD. *Little Long Rifle.* Indianapolis, Bobbs-Merrill, 1949. 139p. $2.00.
The locale of this adventure story is Tennessee in the early 1800's. The action, suspense, and excitement will appeal to young people of both sexes. The story is illustrated by Bob Myers.

PATTEN, MAXIE SNEED. *Youth, the Miracle Age.* Adel, Ga., Adel *News,* 1949. 288p. Apply.
This book contains stories and lessons for the guidance of young people.

POETRY SOCIETY OF GEORGIA, compiler. *25th Anniversary Volume.* Athens, University of Georgia Press, 1949. 69p. $2.00.
This collection of selected poems commemorates 25 years of continuous activity of the Poetry Society of Georgia.

POUND, JEROME B. *Memoirs.* (Miami Beach?), Fla., Privately printed, 1949. 340p. $5.50.
Recollections of a well known Georgia hotel man with histories of the Pound, Murphy, Willingham, Palmer, and Pitts families.

REECE, BYRON HERBERT. *Better a Dinner of Herbs.* New York, Dutton, 1950. 220p. $3.00.
A novel based on the conflicts, the repressions, the thwarted desires, and the hunger for vengeance of several people in a Southern rural district.

REECE, BYRON HERBERT. *Bow Down in Jericho.* New York, Dutton, 1950. 160p. $2.75.
A book of poems, dealing with Biblical themes, made up of ballads, lyrics, and sonnets. The book derives its title from the first ballad in the volume.

REECE, BYRON HERBERT. *Remembrance of Moab.* Cleveland, Ohio, American Weave Press, 1949. 28p. $ .50.

Seven ballads gathered under the title of "Remembrance of Moab" and written in the same style as the author's first collection, "Ballad of the Bones." This book won the American Weave Publication Award for 1949.

ROGERS, ERNEST. *The Old Hokum Bucket.* Atlanta, Tupper & Love, 1949. 250p. $2.50.

A compilation of the best columns written during the last six years by a veteran Atlanta newspaperman. The collection is a gay, pungent commentary on our times with a foreword by H. Allen Smith.

SAYE, ALBERT BERRY, POUND, MERRITT B., and ALLUMS, JOHN F. *Principles of American Government.* New York, Prentice-Hall, 1950. 451p. $5.00.

The principles, organization, and functions of American government are presented in a concise, straightforward account.

SELL, EDWARD SCOTT. *Geography of Georgia.* Oklahoma City, Harlow Pub. Corp., 1950. 126p. $2.00.

A detailed geographic study of the state of Georgia for use in elementary and junior high schools. The book is illustrated with charts, maps, and photographs. Dr. Sell is Professor Emeritus of Geography at the University of Georgia.

SMITH, LILLIAN E. *Killers of the Dream.* New York, Norton, 1949. 256p. $3.00.

Using the Freudian method the author lays bare the weaknesses of the South, dwelling on the triangulation of sin, sex, and race segregation. This book received the 1950 Southern Authors' Award as the outstanding publication by a Southern author about the South among the 1949 publications.

STEWARD, DAVENPORT. *No Time for Fear.* Atlanta, Hale Pub. Co., 1950. 314p. $3.00.

South Carolina's low country during the Revolutionary period is the locale of this story of Francis Marion, the celebrated "Swamp Fox," who dealt death and misery to the British.

STEVENSON, ELIZABETH. *Crooked Corridor: a Study of Henry James.* New York, Macmillan, 1949. 172p. $2.75.

An analysis of Henry James, the man and the literary genius, revealing his breadth, depth, and craftsmanship. This book was the recipient of the Georgia Writers Association's Annual Literary Achievement Award for 1950.

VINSON, DORA. *Shamrock, the Tennessee Walking Horse.* Atlanta, Williams Printing Co., 1950. 32p. $1.00.

Illustrated with photographs, this book tells the story of a champion walking horse from his birth to his first blue ribbon in the show ring. A book for children and horse-lovers.

WIGGINTON, BROOKS E., *Trees and Shrubs for the Southern Piedmont.* Athens, University of Georgia Press, 1949. 126p. $1.50.

Selected lists, primarily for the Southern Piedmont, of the best dozen or so plants within several different classifications for use in landscaping.

WILLIAMS, ELEANOR. *Ivan Allen, A Resourceful Citizen.* Atlanta, Allen-Marshall, 1950. 273p. $3.00.

A profusely illustrated biography of a self-made man who left the hills of North Georgia more than fifty years ago to make his fortune in Atlanta.

WILLIAMS, PRESTON H. *Bits of Beauty.* Emory University, Ga., Banner Press, 1949. 115p. $2.50.

A collection of 61 poems on nature, philosophy, and life in Georgia. The author is a native of Winder, Georgia.

WILLINGHAM, CALDER. *Geraldine Bradshaw.* New York, Vanguard, 1950. 415p. $3.50.

The story of a bellhop at a luxurious hotel in wartime and his struggles to seduce a neurotic elevator operator.

WINDHAM, DONALD. *The Dog Star.* New York, Doubleday, 1950. 221p. $2.50.

Blackie Pride, lonely and unhappy after the suicide of his best friend, drifts further along the path of juvenile delinquency. Tormented by conflicts and confusion about his own future, he finally kills himself in the same way. The setting of this story is Atlanta, Georgia.

WYNN, WILLIAM T. *Smile With Me.* Milledgeville, Ga., The Author, 1950. 83p. $1.50.

The book contains 143 "story incidents" gathered by the author during his experiences as a boy in Henry County, Georgia, a public school teacher, professor, college president, church leader, and traveler.

YERBY, FRANK GARVIN. *Floodtide.* New York, Dial Press, 1950. 342p. $3.00.

An attractive and ambitious man climbs from the slums to the wealthy hills of Natchez in the 1850's. His climb is helped by a lovely Cuban girl and impeded by a beautiful woman.

YERBY, FRANK GARVIN. *Pride's Castle.* New York, Dial Press, 1949. 342p. $3.00.

The story of Pride Dawson, who arrived in New York penniless, became one of the robber barons of the 1870's and 80's and died a suicide victim, after discovering that he was no longer needed.

Bibliography of Georgia Authors
1950-1951

THE second of the REVIEW's annual "Bibliographies of Georgia Authors," this annotated bibliography is, as nearly as the compiler could make it, a complete and accurate record of books published by Georgia authors from November 1, 1950, to November 1, 1951. The annotations are descriptive, not critical; intended to place, not to judge the book. U. S., State, County, and City Documents, parts of books, brief analytics, and pamphlets of less than 25 pages have been omitted. Prices are given except when not supplied by publisher or when book is obtainable only on specific request, in which cases the word "Apply" is used.

In determining whom to call Georgia authors, the compiler has used the following criteria: authors born in Georgia and claiming Georgia as their native state and those who have lived in Georgia for a period of five years and who did their writing here.

The compiler will welcome and appreciate readers' sending to him any additions or corrections. They may be sent to him at any time in care of the GEORGIA REVIEW. Several books inadvertently omitted from the Bibliography for 1949-1950 are listed here. Any books omitted from the present Bibliography will be included in the list for 1951-1952.

ABRAHAM, JOSEPH L. *Handbook for Real Estate Contracts.* Georgia Edition. Emory University, Ga., Clifton Press, 1951. 32p. $2.00.

    A practical guide to be used in the preparation of real estate contracts, it contains a checklist of what both parties should bring to the title closing. Sample forms are included.

ALEXANDER, THOMAS B. *Political Reconstruction in Tennessee.* Nashville, Tenn., Vanderbilt University Press, 1950. 292p. $4.00.

    An analysis of the political factors influencing post-Civil War reconstruction in Tennessee, the division between elements of the population, the men who rose to power, and the conflict between radicalism and the more conservative leaders.

ALLEN, CHARLES L. *Roads to Radiant Living*. New York, Fleming H. Revell Co., 1951. 157p. $2.00.

    A collection of 53 "heart-side" talks, liberally sprinkled with common sense and designed to give spiritual comfort to people in a troubled world.

BARKER, LILLIAN. *The Dionne Legend: Quintuplets in Captivity*. New York, Doubleday, 1951. 269p. $3.00.

    Writing as a friend of the Dionne family, the author tells the story of the birth of the quintuplets, their separation from their parents and Mr. and Mrs. Dionne's long legal and personal struggle to regain their children and live as a private family.

BENFIELD, LOWELL VANCE. *Poems*. Atlanta, Parks Printing Co., 1951. 100p. Apply.

    A veteran of World War II records in this book of poems his impressions of nature, life, and foreign countries.

BRANNEN, JOHN R. *Rogue Country*. Boston, Chapman & Grimes, Inc., 1951. 123p. $2.50.

    A romance of the Old South depicting the love of a poor sharecropper for the daughter of a plantation owner.

BROACH, CLAUDE U., D.D. *Dr. Frank*. Nashville, Tenn., The Broadman Press, 1950. 152p. $2.25.

    An informal biography of Frank H. Leavell, organizer and director of the Baptist Student Union, who died in 1949.

BRYANT, ALLEN. *Hence These Tears*. Atlanta, Keelin Press, 1950. 47p. $2.00.

    A collection of love lyrics. The author is a native Atlantian.

CALDWELL, ERSKINE. *Call It Experience*. New York, Duell, Sloan & Pearce, 1951. 239p. $3.50.

    The famous novelist reminisces with frankness and humor on the parts of his life which contributed most to his skill and career as a writer.

CALDWELL, ERSKINE. *Humorous Side: Erskine Caldwell Anthology*. New York, Duell, Sloan & Pearce, 1951. 286p. $3.50.

    This anthology, edited by Robert Cantwell, contains selected short stories of Caldwell and episodes from "Tobacco Road," "God's Little Acre," and others of his novels.

CAMPBELL, ALICE ORMOND. *The Corpse Had Red Hair*. London, Collins, 1950. 256p. $2.00.

    A volume in the Crime Club Series concerned with solving the murder of the beautiful corpse with red hair.

CANNON, WILLIAM R. *The Redeemer: The Work and Person of Jesus Christ*. Nashville, Tenn., Abingdon-Cokesbury Press, 1951. 224p. $2.75.

An attempt to explain the personality and spirit of Jesus Christ from a study of His role as a man, prophet, judge, priest, teacher, and leader. Dr. Cannon is Professor of Church History at Emory University.

COLEMAN, LONNIE (COLEMAN, WILLIAM LAURENCE). *The Sound of Spanish Voices*. New York, Dutton, 1951. 252p. $3.00.

An approaching revolution in a Central American country forms the background for this love story of a North American author and an Indian servant girl.

CLECKLEY, HERVEY M., M.D. *Mask of Sanity*. Second Edition. St. Louis, C. V. Mosby, 1950. 576p. $6.50.

This attempt to clarify some of the issues involved in the "psychopathic personality" will aid physicians, educators, lawyers, and social workers who are seeking a solution to this distressing social disease. This is a new edition of a study that appeared in 1941. Dr. Cleckley is Professor of Psychiatry and Neurology, University of Georgia School of Medicine.

COULBORN, WILLIAM A. L. *A Discussion of Money*. New York, Longman's, Green & Co., 1950. 384p. $3.50.

A detailed study principally devoted to the British monetary system and the effect which World War II had on economics throughout the world. Illustrated with maps and tables. Dr. Coulborn is Head of the Division of Citizenship, Oglethorpe University.

COULTER, ELLIS MERTON. *College Life in the Old South*. Reprint Edition. Athens, University of Georgia Press, 1951. 333p. $4.50.

The effects of the social life, political development, and general temperament of the Old South are reflected in this lively account of the University of Georgia from 1785 to the 1870's. Formerly published by Macmillan and now re-published with slight corrections and revisions in connection with the University of Georgia's Sesquicentennial celebration.

DAVIS, WILLIAM COLUMBUS. *The Columns of Athens; Georgia's Classic City*. Atlanta, Foote & Davies, Inc., 1951. 80p. $2.75.

An album containing photographs of the homes and public buildings in the city and on the University of Georgia campus. Comments and photographs are by Dr. Davis, member of the History Department, University of Georgia.

DAVIS, WILLIAM COLUMBUS. *The Last Conquistadores; The Spanish Intervention in Peru and Chile, 1863-1866.* Athens, University of Georgia Press, 1950. 395p. $5.00.

An account of the 19th century conquistadores, who, three centuries after their predecessors, set out to reconquer for Spain a part of her lost empire in South America.

DAY, ENID. *Adventures of a Nurse's Aide.* New York, Woman's Press, 1951. 116p. $2.50.

A humorous and poignant human interest story of the adventures of an Atlanta woman as a wartime nurse's aide. The foreword is by Bob Hope and the introduction is by E. Roland Harriman.

DESOSA, MARGARET OHLMAN. *Love Songs.* San Antonio, Texas, Carleton Pub. Co., 1951. 61p. $2.00.

A collection of 43 poems dedicated to friendship, love, nature, and mankind. Margaret DeSosa, a native Georgian, is a resident of Atlanta.

DERN, MRS. JOHN SHERMAN, and DERN, PEGGY. See: Gaddis, Peggy

DREWRY, JOHN E., editor. *Journalism Enters A New Half-Century.* Athens, University of Georgia Press, 1951. 170p. $2.50.

This book edited by Dean Drewry is composed of addresses delivered at the institutes conducted by the University's School of Journalism during 1950-51.

DYER, JOHN PERRY. *The Gallant Hood.* Indianapolis, Bobbs-Merrill, 1950. 383p. $3.50.

The biography of a noted and daring Confederate general, who expended all his energies for the Southern cause and emerged from the Civil War crippled but undaunted in spirit. Illustrated with maps and half-tones.

EIDSON, JOHN OLIN. *Charles Stearns Wheeler: Friend of Emerson.* Athens, University of Georgia Press, 1951. 129p. $3.00.

A study of the life and work of a young man who was a friend of Emerson, Thoreau, Carlyle, Tennyson, and other literary men of his age.

ELLIOT, CHARLES NEWTON. *Conservation of American Resources.* Revised Edition. Atlanta, Turner E. Smith & Co., 1951. 438p. $3.39.

An inclusive text designed to show the relationship of one natural resource to another and the importance of each in the life of our country and its people. Illustrated and indexed.

EUBANKS, JOHN EVANS. *Ben Tillman's Baby; The Dispensary System of South Carolina.* Limited Edition. Augusta, Ga., Tidwell Printing Supply Co., 1950. 213p. $3.50.

A full account of South Carolina's experiences with state monopoly of the sale of alcoholic beverages, 1892-1915.

FORT, JOHN. *Make Way for the Great.* Nashville, Tenn., Benson Printing Co., 1951. 174p. $3.00.

An adventure tale of post-Revolution days involving a young man's attempt to wrest land from hostile Creek and Cherokee Indians in the Nickajack area of Georgia, Alabama, and Tennessee.

FORT, TOMLINSON. *Calculus.* Boston, D. C. Heath, 1951. 572p. $4.75.

Fundamentals of calculus for college students. Dr. Fort is Professor of Mathematics at the University of Georgia.

FOSTER, MARIAN CURTIS (pseud. Mariana). *Miss Flora McFlimsey's Easter Bonnet.* New York, Lothrop, Lee, & Sheppard Co., 1951. 40p. $1.00.

When all the other dolls get new spring hats Miss Flora McFlimsey feels most unhappy because she doesn't have one. Her friend, Peterkins, the rabbit, comes to the rescue with a beautiful bonnet that wins Miss Flora a prize.

GABRIELSEN, BRAMWELL W.; KIEFER, ADOLPH; and GABRIELSEN, MILTON. *Learning to Swim.* New York, Prentice-Hall, 1951. 117p. $3.00.

Self-instruction for adults and methods of instruction for adults to use in teaching children how to swim in twelve lessons.

GADDIS, PEGGY. *Dr. Jerry.* New York, Arcadia House, 1951. 224p. $2.00.

An attractive school teacher's romance with the new doctor in a small rural community is shattered by the glamorous appeal of one of his patients and the evil gossip of an old herb doctor.

GADDIS, PEGGY (pseud. Gail Jordan). *Innocent Wanton.* New York, Phoenix Press, 1950. 220p. $2.00.

The story of a romance between a Broadway producer and a student nurse.

GADDIS, PEGGY (pseud. Peggy Dern). *Where Love Is.* New York, Arcadia House, 1951. 224p. $2.00.

An eccentric young lawyer selects a charming employee of an advertising agency as the secretary for his client, and immediately, romantic complications set in.

GOSNELL, CULLEN B., and HOLLAND, LYNWOOD M. *State and Local Government in the United States.* New York, Prentice-Hall, 1951. 635p. $6.65. Text ed. $5.00.

This book describes the various systems of state and local governments and the functioning of intergovernmental relations. The authors are Professors of Political Science at Emory University.

GRIFFITH, LOUIS T., and TALMADGE, JOHN E. *Georgia Journalism, 1763-1950.* Athens, University of Georgia Press, 1951. 423p. $6.00.
A history of journalism in Georgia sponsored by the Georgia Press Association. The introduction is by Dean John E. Drewry.

GROVE, DOROTHY HAVERTY, editor. *Cultural Atlanta at a Glance.* Atlanta, The Junior League of Atlanta, Inc., 1950. 85p. Apply.
A survey of the cultural resources of Atlanta.

HARDMAN, THOMAS COLQUITT. *History of Harmony Grove-Commerce, Jackson County, Georgia, 1810-1949.* Commerce, Ga., T. C. Hardman, 1949. 219p. $3.50.
The story of the agricultural, industrial, religious, and educational development of Harmony Grove, a community which grew into Commerce, Georgia. Illustrated.

HARGRETT, LESTER. *Oklahoma Imprints, 1835-1890.* New York, Published for the Bibliographic Society of America by R. R. Bowker Co., 1951. 284p. $7.50.
This is the fourth in a series of Bibliographies of American Imprints published by the Bibliographic Society. It begins with the forced Cherokee migration from Georgia to the Oklahoma "Indian Territory," and ends after Oklahoma was thrown open to white settlers.

HARRIS, LUCIEN, JR. *The Butterflies of Georgia.* Revised Edition. Atlanta, Georgia Society of Naturalists, 1950. 41p. $1.00.
A series of life histories and descriptions of specimens of butterflies found in Georgia—with date and place of capture—and the months during which the various specimens are most likely to be found. The foreword and bibliography are by Austin H. Clark, of the U. S. National Museum, Washington, D. C.

HARWELL, RICHARD B., editor. *Songs of the Confederacy.* New York, Broadcast Music, Inc., 1951. 112p. $3.95.
A compilation of 38 significant "songs that stirred the South" reproduced in their original form with historical text and illustrations.

HEWLETT, JOHN HENRY. *The Blarney Stone.* New York, Appleton-Century-Crofts, 1951. 370p. $3.50.
An illustrated history of the famous Blarney Stone, and the Irish superstitions, legends, and folklore that go with it, as well as anecdotes of the men and women who have traveled many miles to win the gift of eloquence with a kiss.

HICKY, DANIEL WHITEHEAD. *Never the Nightingale.* Atlanta, Tupper & Love, Inc., 1951. 62p. $3.00.
   A collection of 56 poems of the Georgia countryside, children, and flowers. Illustrated by Athos Menaboni.

HOLCOMB, WALT. *Sam Jones—An Ambassador of the Almighty* Nashville, Tenn., Methodist Publishing House, 1951. 192p. $2.00.
   A biography of the great Methodist preacher by one of his last co-workers.

HOLCOMB, WALT, editor. *Best Loved Sermons of Sam Jones.* Nashville, Tenn., Methodist Publishing House, 1951. 192p. $2.00.
   A collection of the sermons that Sam Jones loved best to preach and people loved best to hear.

HOLLAND, LYNWOOD M. *State Administrative Agencies in Georgia.* Emory University, Ga., Banner Press, 1950. 153p. Paper, $1.00, cloth, $2.00.
   This book, divided into twelve parts, deals with the thirty-odd existing commissions, committees, bureaus, and departments of the State. It explains their authorization, duties, personnel, methods of appointment and removal, and compensation.

HUDSON, CHARLES J., JR. *Hudson's Garden Scrapbook.* Atlanta, Twentieth Century Enterprises, Inc., 1951. 96p. Paper, $1.00.
   A chronological collection of 55 garden articles which appeared in Atlanta newspapers for the period April 1, 1950 to April 1, 1951. It contains a subject index.

JACOBS, THORNWELL. *When for the Truth.* Charleston, S. C., Walker, Evans, and Cogswell, 1950. 587p. $3.75.
   A novel of the Reconstruction Period in South Carolina.

JENKINS, SARA. *The Brand New Parson.* New York, Crowell, 1951. 246p. $3.00.
   A story of a young unordained Methodist minister in his first church and how he finds love and faith in a Georgia mill town.

JOHNSON, MALCOLM. *Crime on the Labor Front.* New York, McGraw-Hill, 1950. 254p. $3.50.
   A report on scandals involving certain union leaders and racketeers. The author, winner of the 1949 Pulitzer Prize for a series on crime along New York City's waterfront, again surveys this area and also turns his attention to notorious cases involving the movie industry, building trades, and other labor unions.

JONES, CLAYTON. *The Spirit of the Fountain.* New York, Vantage Press, 1951. 90p. $2.50.

The love story of Florence Vernon and John Delamer is the subject of this narrative poem based partly on the life of Florence Martus, "The Waving Girl" of the Savannah River. Clayton Jones is City Judge of Albany, Georgia.

JORDAN, G. RAY. *You Can Preach.* New York, Fleming H. Revell Co., 1951. 256p. $2.50.

In this book, Dr. Jordan explains the art and science of preaching successfully. With effective illustrations and stories, he shows, in a practical way, how it can be accomplished.

JORDAN, GAIL, pseud. See: Gaddis, Peggy

KELLY, GEORGE LOMBARD, M.D. *Sex Manual, for Those Married or About to Be, Written for the Layman.* 5th Revised Edition. Augusta, Ga., Southern Medical Supply Co., 1950. 88p. $1.00.

A simple, direct, and authoritative book containing the forthright answers to those questions most frequently asked on all aspects of sex. Restricted distribution.

KEYES, KENNETH S., JR., *How To Develop Your Thinking Ability.* New York, McGraw-Hill, 1950. 246p. $3.50.

A formula for using common sense and taking a scientific attitude toward personal and business problems. Illustrated with cartoons by Ted Key.

KILPATRICK, WILLIAM HEARD. *Philosophy of Education.* New York, Macmillan, 1951. 475p. $4.75.

A critical consideration of the principal problems of general educational theory, the book is written for both educators and laymen.

LAMKIN, AUGUSTUS F. *Songs at Sunset.* Emory University, Ga., Banner Press, 1951. 85p. $2.00.

Hope, faith, beauty, friendship, nature, and truth are the subject of these 103 poems. This volume is published as a memorial to the Augusta poet, who died before its publication.

LOBSENZ, AMELIA FREITAG. *Kay Everett Calls CQ.* New York, Vanguard Press, 1951. 220p. $2.50.

Four teen-age girls use their knowledge of amateur radio operations to trap a jewel thief. The author is a former resident of Atlanta.

McCullers, Carson. *The Ballad of the Sad Cafe.* Boston, Houghton Mifflin Co., 1951. 791p. $5.00.

    A representative collection of Carson McCullers' work including seven short stories, the title novelette, and three novels, "The Heart Is a Lonely Hunter," "Reflections in a Golden Eye," and "The Member of the Wedding."

McCullers, Carson. *The Member of the Wedding, A Play.* New York, New Directions, 1951. 118p. $3.00.

    The complete acting version of the Broadway production based on the author's novel of the same title.

McMurray, J. Max. *The Far Bayou.* New York, Rinehart, 1951. 186p. $2.50.

    A portrait of life in a small Southern bayou community where a close-knit existence draws the inhabitants together in happiness and tragedy.

Mariana, pseud. See: Foster, Marian Curtis

Marshall, Edison. *The Viking.* New York, Farrar, Straus, & Young, 1951. 380p. $3.50.

    The adventurous wanderings of Ogier the Viking, who escapes from a slave pen in Denmark, encounters new and old enemies in Europe and England, and finally sets out with the beautiful daughter of the King of Wales in search of a fabled island.

Millis, Walter, editor. *The Forrestal Dairies.* New York, Viking, 1951. 605p. $5.00.

    A selection of the diary notes which James Forrestal, first Secretary of Defense, kept from his appointment as Secretary of the Navy in 1944 till his death in 1949. Walter Millis is a native of Atlanta, Georgia.

Moore, Mavis Garey. *Pony for a Prize.* New York, Macmillan, 1951. 210p. $2.50.

    A boy in a Georgia village wins a pony in a contest, only to have it stolen, and an exciting chase takes place before it is found. The book is illustrated by William Moyers.

Moore, Walter Lane. *Courage and Confidence from the Bible.* New York, Prentice-Hall, 1951. 383p. $2.75.

    Bible quotations, prayers, and meditations for each day of the year. There is an index for locating those passages of particular help in certain problems. Dr. Moore is pastor of the First Baptist Church of Waycross, Georgia.

ODUM, HOWARD WASHINGTON. *American Sociology; The Story of Sociology in the United States Through 1950.* New York, Longman's Green & Co., 1951. 507p. $5.00.

    A comprehensive study of the background, heritage, and promise of American sociology, with material and information on the development of schools, societies, and journals devoted to the subject.

PARKS, EDD WINFIELD, editor, in collaboration with Olive Shaw and Michael Keller. *A Modern American Sampler.* Rio de Janeiro, Instituto Brasil-Estados Unidos, 1950. Two vols., xi, 240p.; xi, 235p. For sale only in Latin America.

    An anthology of contemporary American prose and poetry, prepared especially for use as a text in Latin American schools and colleges.

PIERCE, ALFRED MANN. *Lest We Forget; The Story of Methodism in Georgia.* Atlanta, Georgia Methodist Information, 1951. 206p. Paper, .75.

    A history of the cradle of Methodism from 1736 to 1950 told through the story of the lives of the outstanding personalities in Georgia Methodism. The introduction is by Bishop Arthur J. Moore, and the book contains a bibliography and index.

POUND, MERRITT B. *Benjamin Hawkins: Indian Agent.* Athens, University of Georgia Press, 1951. 279p. $4.00.

    The life of a North Carolina congressman who became a friend, protector, and government agent for the Indians of the frontier in the period between the close of the Revolutionary War and the War of 1812.

PUCKETT, JAMES. *Silver Scepters.* Emory University, Ga., Banner Press, 1950. 80p. $2.00.

    A collection of poems on nature, beauty, and truth. The author is a native of Winder, Georgia.

QUATTLEBAUM, M.M. *Quattlebaum Family History.* Savannah, Ga., The Author, 1950. 280p. Apply.

    A comprehensive history of one of the pioneer families of Georgia and South Carolina. Index of names only. Mimeographed.

RUTHERFORD, VADA. *This Eager Pace.* Boston, Bruce Humphries, Inc., 1951. 310p. $3.00.

    This novel, with a Southern locale, begins at the close of World War I and ends during World War II. The plot concerns the life and loves of a girl named Lynlie.

SEARS, WILLIAM. *Excavations of Kolomoki, Nos. 1 & 2.* Athens, University of Georgia Press, 1951. 48p. Paper, $1.50 each.

    Illustrated reports of the intensive excavations carried on at the Kolomoki mounds located in Early County, Georgia.

SCRUGGS, ANDERSON M. *What Shall the Heart Remember?* Athens, University of Georgia Press, 1951. 78p. $2.50.
   A collection of 69 poems dealing with life, love, music, nature, and destiny—by a native Georgian, who is Professor of Dentistry in the Emory University School of Dentistry.

STOKES, THOMAS L. *The Savannah.* New York, Rinehart, 1951. 401p. $4.00.
   From the Appalachians to the sea the story of the Savannah River is the romance and history of gold, debtors, King Cotton, Sherman's march to the sea, and the wide harbors of today. This 43rd volume in the *Rivers of America Series* is illustrated by Lamar Dodd and contains a bibliography and index.

SMITH, NANNETTE CARTER. *Lines for Lindsey and Cutouts for Carter.* East Point, Ga., Martin Johnson Co., 1950. Apply.
   A book of poems for the child of "in-between" age. The volume is illustrated with silhouettes by George Hitt of Toccoa, Georgia.

STUCKEY, H. P. *Southern Horticulture.* Revised Edition. Atlanta, Turner E. Smith & Co., 1951. 688p. $3.39.
   This completely revised edition gives indispensable information on the fruit and vegetable crops which can be successfully cultivated in the Southern region. Illustrated.

SUDDETH, RUTH ELGIN; OSTERHOUT, ISA LLOYD; and HUTCHESON, GEORGE LEWIS. *Empire Builders of Georgia.* Austin, Texas, The Steck Co., 1951. 482p. $1.89.
   Designed for the general public as well as students, this book is divided into two parts: Georgia's Role in History and the Treasures of Georgia. The book is illustrated and designed by Warren Hunter.

TANKERSLEY, ALLEN P. *College Life at Old Oglethorpe.* Athens, University of Georgia Press, 1951. 197p. $3.00.
   The early days, 1835-1873, of Oglethorpe University, a Presbyterian school and the first chartered denominational educational institution in Georgia.

TANKERSLEY, CHARLES W. *Genealogy of the Tankersley Family in the United States.* Atlanta, Privately Printed, 1950. 30p. $6.00.
   A re-issue of the Tankersley family history which originally appeared in 1895. Mrs. Rachel Peeples Rogers has added additional notes and data concerning the Tankersley and Peeples families.

WARE, LOUISE. *George Foster Peabody: Banker, Philanthropist, Publicist.* Athens, University of Georgia Press, 1951. 289p. $4.00.
   The biography of the noted Georgia-born businessman, banker, philanthropist, and educator, 1852-1938.

WILLIAMS, PRESTON H. *Said in Sonnets.* Emory University, Ga., Banner Press, 1950. 139p. $3.00.

A collection of 94 sonnets that describe love, neighbors, roads, snow, sunsets, and the fading summer.

WILLIAMS, PRESTON H. *The Tillers.* Emory University, Ga., Banner Press, 1951. 102p. $3.00.

This book of songs of the soil contains poems on rocks and rivers, trees and skies, growing crops and the men who till them.

WILLIAMS, NELLIE LOWMAN. *Songs in the Night.* Emory University, Ga., Banner Press, 1951. 65p. $3.00.

A volume of poems, by a widely known poet and teacher, that deal with many of the facets of life, beauty, and truth.

WILLINGHAM, CALDER. *The Gates of Hell.* New York, Vanguard Press, 1951. 190p. $2.50.

Twenty-five short stories in varied moods—ranging in subject from violence in a Southern town to sophisticated love in New York.

WILSON, PAULINE PARK. *College Women Who Express Futility; A Study Based on Fifty Selected Life Histories of Women College Graduates.* New York, Bureau of Publications, Teachers College, 1950. 179p. $2.75.

An analysis of the feelings of futility expressed by fifty college graduates living in Detroit. The purpose of the study was to determine the effectiveness of education in encouraging a positive attitude toward life. This is number 956 in the *Contributions to Education Series.*

YERBY, FRANK. *A Woman Called Fancy.* New York, Dial Press, 1951. 340p. $3.00.

The story of a beautiful carnival girl from the Carolina hill country who bewitched, outraged, and nearly conquered the aristocracy of Georgia in the turbulent years after the South's defeat.

YOUNG, ELEANOR M. *Forgotten Patriot: Robert Morris.* New York, Macmillan, 1950. 292p. $4.00.

The biography of the Revolutionary businessman who poured his own money and time into the Revolution, and later ruined himself by his own land speculation. The author, a former resident of Atlanta, Athens, Decatur, and Forsyth, now resides in Denver, Colorado.

YOUNG, IDA; GHOLSON, JULIUS; and HARGROVE, CLARA NELL. *History of Macon, Georgia, 1823-1949.* Macon, Ga., Lyon, Marshall & Brooks, 1950. 728p. $10.00.

This history, sponsored by the Macon Woman's Club, is based primarily upon local newspaper files. Events of public importance take precedence over family lore. The book is indexed and contains biographical sketches of prominent Macon citizens.

Bibliography of Georgia Authors
1951-1952

THE third of the REVIEW's annual "Bibliographies of Georgia Authors," this annotated bibliography is, as nearly as the compiler could make it, a complete and accurate record of books published by Georgia authors from November 1, 1951, to November 1, 1952. The annotations are descriptive, not critical; intended to place, not to judge the book. U. S., State, County, and City Documents, parts of books, brief analytics, and pamphlets of less than 25 pages have been omitted. Prices are given except when not supplied by publisher or when book is obtainable only on specific request, in which cases the word "Apply" is used.

In determining whom to call Georgia authors, the compiler has used the following criteria: authors born in Georgia and claiming Georgia as their native state and those who have lived in Georgia for a period of five years and who did their writing here.

The compiler will welcome and appreciate readers' sending to him any additions or corrections. They may be sent to him at any time in care of the GEORGIA REVIEW. Several books inadvertently omitted from the Bibliography for 1950-1951 are listed here. Any books omitted from the present Bibliography will be included in the list for 1952-1953.

AIKEN, CONRAD P. *Ushant.* New York, Duell, Sloan & Pearce, 1952. 365p. $4.50.
    The poet's self-analytical autobiographical record in which the author is both the man on the couch talking and the observer listening to the man. Mr. Aiken is Consultant in English Poetry in the Library of Congress.

ALLEN, CHARLES L. *In Quest of God's Power.* Westwood, N. J., Fleming H. Revell Co., 1952. 191p. $2.50.
    A collection of Sunday night sermons on problems inherent in human life delivered by the pastor of the Grace Methodist Church, Atlanta, Georgia.

ANDERSON, THOMAS, D.D. *Estate of Glory.* Atlanta, Tupper & Love, 1951. 104p. $2.75.
    Brief inspirational articles by an Atlanta Congregational minister, taking their point of reference from Biblical quotations.

BIXLER, HAROLD HENCH, and MEADE, RICHARD H. *Spelling for Everyday Life.* Atlanta, Turner E. Smith, 1952. 7 vols. $1.76 each.
  Illustrated spellers designed to be used in grades two through eight in the public schools.

BLAKE, WILLIAM MORGAN. *A Sports Editor Finds Christ.* Atlanta, Hale Pub. Co., 1952. 192p. $3.00.
  Reminiscences of evangelistic activities by a former sports editor and editorial columnist of the Atlanta *Journal.*

BROOKS, ROBERT PRESTON. *The Financial History of Georgia, 1732-1950.* Athens, Institute for the Study of Georgia Problems, 1952. 85p. $1.00.
  A brief financial history of Georgia from 1732 to 1950 with particular emphasis on the revolution in Georgia finances from 1915 to 1951. During this period the state government has increased its expenditures by 2,211 per cent.

BROOKS, ROBERT PRESTON. *Georgia Studies: Selected Writings of Robert Preston Brooks; Edited and with an Introduction by Gregor Sebba.* Athens, University of Georgia Press, 1952. 321p. $3.50.
  This volume, edited for the general reader, contains the essence of Professor Brooks' work of forty-five years at the University of Georgia, in the fields of education, economics, government, and history.

BROWN, CALVIN S. *Repetition in Zola's Novels.* Athens, University of Georgia Press, 1952. vi, 124p. Paper, $1.75.
  This monograph is concerned with the formal rather than the accidental repetitions in Zola's novels. The repetitions range from the use of key words and phrases to sentences, and occasionally passages of more than a page, repeated either identically or with variations.

CALDWELL, ERSKINE. *The Courting of Susie Brown.* New York, Duell, Sloan & Pearce, 1952. 202p. $3.00.
  A dozen short stories on a variety of subjects—love, murder, traveling salesmen, and race violence. All but one have appeared in magazines.

CALDWELL, ERSKINE. *A Lamp for Nightfall.* New York, Duell, Sloan & Pearce, 1952. 211p. $3.00.
  A mean and miserly man, Thede Emerson, is left alone on his desolate Maine farm when his daughter escapes by marrying one of the "Canucks" Thede hates. His son commits suicide and his philandering wife leaves him.

CASH, GRACE. *Blueprint for Abundant Living: Twenty Guides to Happiness.* New York, Exposition Press, 1952. 104p. $2.50.
  A collection of twenty essays on character building and guidance in the following of religious precepts.

CODINGTON, ARTHUR. *Jest About Georgia.* Atlanta, Printed by Longino & Porter, Inc., 1952. 36p. $1.00.

A limerick cycle about Georgia, illustrated by Garland M. Wheeler.

COLEMAN, LONNIE (COLEMAN, WILLIAM LAURENCE). *Clara.* New York, Dutton, 1952. 285p. $3.00.

A small town Southern woman engages in a bitter, long drawn out feud with Clara, her husband's mistress and the mother of his child. Troubles and tragedies touch their lives during the passing years, and at the close, with their loved ones gone, both women find themselves in a close bond of understanding and friendship.

COTSAKIS, ROXANE. *The Wing and the Thorn.* Atlanta, Tupper & Love, 1952. 356p. $3.75.

A conflict between the Old World and the New is set up in the life of John Pantellis, a young Greek immigrant who came to America in the early part of this century. Greek customs, cookery, and pageantry highlight a tender love story, and the final resolution for John is to recognize a new era or be lost.

CRANFORD, MARY POOLE. *When Cometh Peace?* New York, Pageant Press, 1952. 200p. $3.00.

This novel with a Georgia locale is the courageous story of Margaret Warren's struggle to keep her family of nine children together despite various economic setbacks and an unhappy second marriage.

CRAIG, GEORGIA, pseud. See: Gaddis, Peggy.

DAVIES, GENEVA. *Whence the Wind.* Emory University, Ga., Banner Press, 1952. 63p. $2.00.

A collection of more than a hundred short poems about nature and experiences common to man. Mrs. Davies is a resident of Decatur, Georgia.

DEGIVE, MARY L., and CUSSLER, MARGARET. *'Twixt the Cup and the Lip.* New York, Twayne Publishers, 1952. 262p. $3.95.

A psychological and socio-cultural study of the factors affecting food habits and the diet pattern of several areas of the rural South.

DERN, MRS. JOHN SHERMAN. See: Gaddis, Peggy.

DEWEY, MAYBELLE JONES. *Push the Button.* Atlanta, Tupper & Love, 1951. 180p. $2.75.

The reminiscences of the wife of Dr. Malcom H. Dewey, Head of the Fine Arts Department of Emory University and director of the famous Emory Glee Club. The author tells about her childhood in Cartersville, Georgia, of her school days, her marriage to the Professor, and her domestic, intellectual, and social life in Atlanta.

DONALDSON, GEORGE WARREN. *School Camping.* New York, Association Press, 1952. 140p. $2.25.

An explanation of the growing movement for school-sponsored, year-round camps, at both elementary and high school levels, throughout the United States, showing how meaningful work, social living, nature and conservation study help children and adolescents approach maturity. The introduction is written by Ernest O. Melby.

DOWELL, SPRIGHT. *Columbus Roberts: Christian Steward Extraordinary.* Nashville, Tenn., Broadman Press, 1951. xiv, 171p. $3.00.

The life of a Southern farmer and businessman who rose from poverty to material success, retaining and amplifying his Christian faith. The book is illustrated.

DRAKE, JULIAN R. *Look to the Dawn.* New York, Vantage Press, 1952. 401p. $3.50.

The successes and failures of Roland Droch, a young Southerner, in the years before the First World War and continuing until 1945. The story deals with the problems that confronted the South when factories began to dot the cotton fields and sharecroppers became members of labor unions.

DREWRY, JOHN E., ed. *New Horizons in Journalism.* Athens, University of Georgia Bulletin, 1952. x, 155p. Paper, $1.50, Cloth, $2.50.

This book is composed of nineteen addresses on journalistic subjects which were delivered at the several institutes, conventions, and special occasions sponsored by the University of Georgia's Henry W. Grady School of Journalism during the 1951-52 session.

EDWARDS, LILLIE TRICE. *Beauty Parlor Girl.* New York, Vantage Press, 1952. 169p. $3.00.

Debbie, an orphan, adopted by the Grant family, gives an account of her young life and her ambition to make women beautiful. Debbie becomes a beautician who gets to know all the whims and fancies of women in beauty salons.

ELTON, MAUDE LAY, ed. *Blended Voices.* Emory University, Ga., Banner Press, 1952. 103p. $3.00.

A collection of the poems of more than fifty of Georgia's leading poets.

ETHRIDGE, WILLIE SNOW. *Let's Talk Turkey.* New York, Vanguard Press, 1952. 252p. $3.00.

The irrepressible Mrs. Ethridge invades Turkey, "by accident," with her husband and twelve-year-old son, "Mr. Big." One or the other is in trouble, it seems, most of the time. Mr. Big is arrested for driving a taxi; his parents wander into a fortified zone. Yet all in all, the Ethridges and Turkey have a good time together.

FLEMING, BERRY. *The Fortune Tellers.* Philadelphia, Lippincott, 1951. 442p. $3.75.

A moving, dramatic story describing a great flood, fear, and a tense human struggle as a small community fights a rising river and a family scandal threatens to ruin the town's leading citizen. This book was the Literary Guild selection for December, 1951.

FORT, MARIE JOHNSON, *Flower Arrangements for All Occasions.* New York, Rinehart, 1952. 237p. $8.50.

Thirty-two full page plates in color and sixty-four black and white gravure plates illustrate this comprehensive book dealing with period arrangements, arrangements for the home, for flower shows, for church, for holidays, etc. The book is edited by Robert Sommerville.

FOSTER, MARIAN CURTIS (pseud. Mariana). *Miss Flora McFlimsey and the Baby New Year.* New York, Lothrop, Lee, and Sheppard Co., 1951. 26p. $1.00.

Illustrated in color by the author, this little story for ages four to eight finds Miss McFlimsey and the Pookoo Cat in the doll house to welcome the Baby New Year when he blows in with the snow as the old year ends.

FOSTER, MARIAN CURTIS (pseud. Mariana). *Miss Flora McFlimsey's Birthday.* New York, Lothrop, Lee, & Sheppard Co., 1952. 34p. $1.25.

Birthdays are important, and it is no wonder that Miss McFlimsey ran away from the Doll House when she decided that everyone had forgotten hers. After many adventures she gets back home just in time for her birthday supper. Illustrated by the author.

FOSTER, MARIAN CURTIS (pseud. Mariana). *Miss Flora McFlimsey's Christmas Eve.* New York, Lothrop, Lee, & Sheppard Co., 1949. 40p. $1.25.

The wistful heroine of this little book is an old doll, long since abandoned in an attic. She steals downstairs on Christmas Eve to peek at the tree and Santa Claus surprises her and substitutes her for a doll he has lost. Water-color illustrations are by the author.

FOSTER, EDITH. *To Wind a Chain.* New York, Exposition Press, 1952. 64p. $2.00.

A collection of seventy-six poems of love and nature by the director of the West Georgia Regional Library at Carrollton. The book is dedicated to Miss Foster's brother, Kerry, who died a prisoner of the Nazis.

GADDIS, PEGGY (pseud. Georgia Craig). *A Husband for Jennie.* New York, Arcadia House, 1951. 224p. $2.50.

When the man she loves wants to marry her after he has been jilted by another girl, Jennie Mayson accepts, not knowing how difficult her role will be.

GARRISON, KARL CLAUDIUS. *Growth and Development.* New York, Longman's, Green, 1952. 559p. $5.00.

A summary of data relating to the physical and psychological development of infants and children, and their interpersonal relations.

GARRISON, KARL CLAUDIUS. *The Psychology of Adolescence.* New York, Prentice-Hall, 1951. 4th edition. xxii, 510p. $6.00. School ed. $4.50.

This new edition includes enlarged material drawn from recent selected studies of adolescents, their physiological changes, peer relations, attitudes and beliefs, and moral and spiritual development. It covers the ages ten to nineteen.

GASSMAN, McDILL McCOWN. *Daddy Was an Undertaker.* New York, Vantage Press, 1952. 249p. $3.00.

The humorous account of the trials and tribulations of a small town undertaker. Mrs. Gassman is a resident of Rome, Georgia. Illustrations by John V. Graven.

GOVAN, GILBERT E., and LIVINGWOOD, JAMES W. *The Chattanooga Country: 1540-1951, From Tomahawks to TVA.* New York, Dutton, 1952. 509p. $5.00.

The long history of Chattanooga, from its days as a frontier town, neighbor to the Cherokee Nation, through its emergence as a river port, its violent part in the Civil War, and its present importance as a power station of the TVA.

GRAY, JOHN STANLEY. *Psychology in Industry.* New York, McGraw-Hill, 1952. 401p. $5.00.

Psychological principles and statistical data used in the analysis of the various factors which affect work production and employee morale in industry. Dr. Gray is Professor of Psychology at the University of Georgia.

HAMMER, JANE ROSS, ed. *Logic for Living: Lectures of 1921-22 by Henry Horace Williams.* New York, Philosophical Library, 1951. xix, 281p. $3.75.

This book is a statement of idealistic non-symbolic logic and its application to the problems of action in the modern world. Based on stenographic notes of actual classroom discussions, it has been edited in dialogue form by Jane Ross Hammer to convey the teaching methods successful in dialectic development of ideas.

HARRIS, PIERCE. *Spiritual Revolution,* New York, Doubleday, 1952. 191p. $2.75.

A plea for a moral and Christian renaissance in America. The author is pastor of the First Methodist Church in Atlanta, Georgia.

HARWIN, BRIAN, pseud. See: Henderson, LeGrand.

HENDERSON, LEGRAND (pseud. Brian Harwin). *Home Is Upriver.* New York, Macmillan, 1952. 224p. $3.00.
    A novel of family life among the "river-rats," the aquatic migratory workers of the Mississippi River. The plot revolves around the relations between a daughter and the adopted son, a fight with river bandits, and the struggle against the storms and floods of the river.

HENDERSON, LEGRAND (pseud. LeGrand). *When the Mississippi Was Wild.* Nashville, Tenn., Abingdon-Cokesbury Press, 1952. Unpaged. $2.00.
    An amusing, fable-like story of the Mississippi in the wild days and of why the West was settled by brave men. Predominant episodes concern Old Al, the alligator who whipped up storms on the Mississippi with his tail, and Mike Fink, and a hound dog who put a damper on Old Al's activities. Illustrated by the author.

HOLLERAN, CECIL JAMES. *Know Your Georgia.* Atlanta, Tupper & Love, 1951. 94p. $1.50.
    One hundred cartoons and stories of little known events in the history of the State of Georgia under three flags. The stories are reprinted from the "Know Your Georgia" series published in the Atlanta *Constitution.*

JENKINS, SARA LUCILLE. *Year in Paradise.* New York, Crowell, 1952. 244p. $3.00.
    Janet Brownlee, daughter of a famous concert singer, learns to stand on her own two feet during a year as teacher in drab Paradise, Florida, and finds a new love in the principal of the school.

KELLY, GEORGE LOMBARD, M.D. *Manual de Educacion Sexual, para Casados o Proximos a Contraer Matrimonio; Dedicado al Publico en General.* (1. ed. española) traducido de la 5. ed. Mexico, Exportadora de Publicaciones Mexicanas, 1950. 166p. Apply.
    The first Spanish edition of Dr. Kelly's authoritative book on all aspects of sex. This edition has a preface written by Robert B. Greenblatt.

KELLY, GEORGE LOMBARD, M.D. *Sexual Feeling in Married Men and Women.* New York, Greystone Press, 1951. 186p. $2.50.
    Portions of this book are taken from the author's "Sex Manual" and "Sexual Feeling in Women." The book is illustrated by H. L. Treusch, M.D.

LAMAR, DOLLY BLOUNT. *When All Is Said and Done.* Athens, University of Georgia Press, 1952. xii, 286p. $3.75.
    The long and eventful life of Mrs. Lamar, who after eighty-odd years still continues an active interest in the affairs of her town, Macon, and

her state and country. A daughter of a member of the House of Representatives from 1872-1892, she recalls life in the Capital City, and activities as a member of the United Daughters of the Confederacy. There are also many personal remembrances—school, debut, courtship and marriage, and travel.

LAWRENCE, ALEXANDER A. *Storm Over Savannah: The Story of Count d'Estaing and the Siege of the Town in 1779.* Athens, University of Georgia Press, 1951. 224p. $3.50.

The history of the French attempt to aid the American cause by laying siege to the British-held city of Savannah during the Revolutionary War—an attempt which ended in failure.

LEE, EDNA L. MOONEY, and LEE, HARRY. *All That Heaven Allows.* New York, G. P. Putnam's Sons, 1952. 312 p. $3.50.

An attractive widow of forty falls in love with a younger man, a gardener, outside her comfortable suburban circle; and the opposition of her family and friends and her own self-doubt almost make her lose him.

LOWANCE, KATHLEEN. *Much Ado About Music.* Atlanta, Tupper & Love, 1952. 241p. $3.50.

Two teen-agers visit their uncle in New York, where the glamour and fascination of music is unfolded to them with the help of the uncle's best girl, a Metropolitan opera singer. The book is illustrated by John Anderson.

MCALLISTER, ELVA SINCLAIR. *Poems.* Atlanta, Parks Printing Co., 1952. 148p. $3.00.

A book of 127 poems dealing with friendship, love, and nature. The author is a resident of Atlanta.

MARIANA, pseud. See: Foster, Marian Curtis.

MARSHALL, EDISON (pseud. Hall Hunter). *The Bengal Tiger: a Tale of India.* Garden City, N.Y., Doubleday, 1952. 319p. $3.50.

The adventures and the love affairs of a young Englishman in mid-nineteenth century India, a man born to money but suddenly deprived of his inheritance and forced to earn his living, which he does as a tiger hunter.

MARTIN, EDWIN THOMAS. *Thomas Jefferson: Scientist.* New York, Henry Schuman, Inc., 1952. x, 289p. $4.00.

For a man who labored for his state and country so long and faithfully, Jefferson's outlook and scientific attainments were truly remarkable. He had an extraordinary range of interests over such fields as meteorology, paleontology, ethnology, archaeology, astronomy, chemistry, agriculture, geology, history, medicine, and botany. The author is a member of the English faculty at Emory University.

MEADOWS, JOHN C. *Modern Georgia.* Athens, University of Georgia Press, 1951. 368p. Paper, $3.75. Cloth, $4.75.

This textbook, used in a number of Georgia colleges, contains a wealth of information about the State of Georgia; its geography and history, culture, population, education, health, public welfare, agriculture, industry, government, income and expenditures.

MILLS, CHARLES. *The Alexandrians.* New York, G. P. Putnam's Sons, 1952. 675p. $4.00.

The panoramic story of Alexandria, a fictional town in Georgia, during a hundred years of its history, 1839-1939. Though Anna Anderson Redding, who lives through this period, is the central figure, the novel is made up of the loves, envies, tendernesses, and fears of the town folk. Their sins and their nobilities, their clandestine loves and their dark violence have a cumulative effect.

MOORE, ARTHUR JAMES. *The Mighty Savior; The Hope That Is Ours Through Faith in Christ.* Nashville, Tenn., Abingdon-Cokesbury Press, 1952. 154p. $2.00.

Messages to strengthen the faith and brighten the hopes of man with the familiar truths of the old, old story. The author is the resident Bishop of the Atlanta area of the Methodist Church.

MORGAN, MARY FRANCES. *Teacher Lady.* Garden City, N. Y., Doubleday, 1952. 250p. $3.00.

The heroine of this story is Bruce Sheehan, a graduate of Louisiana State University with a penchant for getting herself in and out of embarrassing situations. The setting is Louisiana's bayou country.

NORRIS, ROBERT A. *Distribution and Population of Summer Birds in Southwestern Georgia.* Athens, University of Georgia Press, 1951. vi, 67p. $1.25.

This is an analysis of the geographical and ecological distribution of summer birds in an eight-county region of the Upper Coastal Plain. The study is divided into three parts: an annotated list of species; a summary and discussion of distributional data; and the summer bird population of three major habitats. This is Occasional Publication No. 3 of the Georgia Ornithological Society.

O'CONNOR, FLANNERY. *Wise Blood.* New York, Harcourt, Brace, 1952. 232p. $3.00.

The story of a primitive fanatic from Tennessee, a self-made preacher who believed fervidly in his mission to preach the "Church without Christ" on street corners in Georgia.

OUTLAW, NELL WARREN. *For Love—For Life: The Presence of Christ in Human Experience.* Westwood, N. J., Fleming H. Revell Co., 1952. 160p. $2.50.

An earnest and challenging discussion of the place and power of God's love in human living by the wife of a prominent Atlanta business man.

PARKS, AILEEN WELLS. *Bedford Forrest: Boy on Horseback.* Indianapolis, Bobbs-Merrill, 1952. 192p. $1.75.

General Bedford Forrest's boyhood in Tennessee and Mississippi, his early training in judging horses, his interest in figures, and his enforced self-reliance explain how he was able to rise from private to lieutenant general. This is another in the Childhood of Famous Americans Series and is illustrated by Paul Laune.

PARKS, EDD WINFIELD, and SMITH, JAMES HARRY. *The Great Critics: An Anthology of Literary Criticism.* New York, Norton, 1951. 3rd rev. ed. xx, 952p. $5.90.

The first part of this anthology contains thirty masterpieces of critical literature from Aristotle's "Poetics" to John Crowe Ransom's "Poetry: A Note in Ontology." The second, supplementary section contains works of lesser importance which give expansion to numerous ideas which appear in the greater criticisms.

PERKERSON, MEDORA FIELD. *White Columns in Georgia.* New York, Rinehart, 1952. 382p. $7.95.

A record in text and photographs of the old houses of Georgia, their history, legend, and romance in antebellum days. In addition to being interesting to the general reader, this book has particular interest for architects, designers, and antiquarians.

PETERS, HAROLD SEYMOUR, and BURLEIGH, THOMAS D. *The Birds of Newfoundland.* Boston, Published in Association with the Department of Natural Resources, Province of Newfoundland, by Houghton Mifflin, 1951. xix, 431p. $6.00.

Detailed accounts, with brief descriptions and many drawings, of the 227 birds which have been recorded in Newfoundland. Introductory chapters provide background information on Newfoundland and the study of birds there. Illustrated by Roger Tory Peterson.

POUND, MERRITT B., and SAYE, ALBERT B. *Handbook on the Constitutions of the United States and Georgia.* Athens, University of Georgia Press, 1951. xi, 160p. Paper, $1.00.

This handbook contains the text of both Constitutions, with discussions of the historical background and analyses of the articles and amendments.

PUTNAM, PETER. *"Keep Your Head Up, Mr. Putnam!"* New York, Harper, 1952. xi, 171p. $2.50.

Blinded by a shooting accident while he was a junior at Princeton, Peter Putnam took the twenty-six day "Seeing Eye" course at Morristown, then resumed his education. He marries, has three children, teaches, writes, and translates. His account of his re-learning to live is cheerful and encouraging, and it offers inspiration to troubled or afflicted people.

PUTNAM, PETER, ed. *Seven Britons in Imperial Russia, 1698-1812.* Princeton, N. J., Princeton University Press, 1952. xxiv, 424p. $7.50.

This study is volume seven of the Princeton Studies in History. Illustrated with maps and portraits. A bibliography is included.

PYRON, JOSEPH H., and MCVAUGH, ROGERS. *Ferns of Georgia.* Athens, University of Georgia Press, 1951. 210p. $5.00.

This illustrated volume describes seventy-nine ferns which have been found growing wild in Georgia. The authors traveled more than 6,000 miles within the state, observing and collecting specimens. This study, sponsored by the Garden Clubs of Georgia, will be useful to both professional and amateur botanists, gardeners, students, or those who love plants for their own sake.

RANGE, WILLARD. *The Rise and Progress of Negro Colleges in Georgia, 1865-1949.* Athens, University of Georgia Press, 1951. 254p. $3.75.

A history of the three phases of higher education for Negroes in Georgia: the Northerners' first efforts on the freedmen's behalf, after 1865; the more thoughtful and effective work of philanthropic foundations later; and the modern trends and activities.

REECE, BYRON HERBERT. *A Song of Joy and Other Poems.* New York, Dutton, 1952. 125p. $2.75.

A new volume of ballads, lyrics, and sonnets, many with a strong religious motif, by the author of *Bow Down in Jericho*.

RESPESS, JOHN L., JR., comp. *Wit and Wisdom of Georgia Law.* Atlanta, Privately Printed, 1952. 92p. $3.00.

Short excerpts, of particular aptness, wittiness, or wisdom, from decisions handed down by the Appellate Courts of Georgia.

STACY, JAMES. *History of the Midway Congregational Church, Liberty County, Georgia. . . .* Reprint ed. New York, Privately Printed, 1951. 723p. $10.00.

This book is a processed reprint of the two original volumes with different paging and with new illustrations. The inclusion of addenda by Mrs. Elizabeth Walker Quarterman, of Flemington, Georgia, brings the history up to date.

STEWARD, DAVENPORT. *They Had a Glory.* Atlanta, Tupper & Love, 1952. 311p. $3.75.

A story of pioneer heroes and heroines at constant war with the forces of nature, disease, famine, fear, and Indians, as they sought the fabulous land of Kaintuck on the westward movement through the Cumberland Gap.

SYDNOR, CHARLES SACKETT. *Gentlemen Freeholders: Political Practices in Washington's Virginia.* Chapel Hill, University of North Carolina Press, 1952. 189p. $3.50.

An examination of eighteenth century Virginia's social climate and political practices, which produced, among other great men, Washington, Jefferson, Madison, and Monroe. The author is the Dean of the Duke University Graduate School.

THOMPSON, THELMA. *Make Haste, My Beloved.* New York, Austin-Phelps, 1952. 327p. $3.00.

Leprosy and its relation to the conflict between religion and science, since the development of sulfa, is the theme of this dramatic story about an atheistic woman surgeon in a small Georgia textile community who finds faith through working with the Catholic Sisters of Charity and through her love for a minister.

TYRE, NEDRA. *Mouse in Eternity.* New York, Alfred A. Knopf, 1952. 215p. $2.50.

A Social Service Bureau in Atlanta serves as a hiding place for a killer. The murder of a hateful Mrs. Patch, tyrannical department head, is soon followed by a suicide and a confession. Jane Wallace, who narrates the story, does not believe the confession, says so, and pays for her suspicion in terror.

WALKER, GEORGE FULLER. *Persons Lineage.* Atlanta, Conger Printing Co., 1952. xi, 192p. $20.00.

This book, printed in a limited edition of 300 copies, deals with the genealogy of one of the South's leading families, and covers the period from 1630 to date. The author is a member of the faculty of the Georgia Institute of Technology.

WASSON, WOODROW WILSON. *James A. Garfield: His Religion and Education.* Nashville, Tenn., Tennessee Book Co., 1952. 155p. $2.50.

The story of the religious and educational thought and activity of one who became prominent as an American soldier, a congressman, and President of the United States.

WEST, LULAMEADE. *The Isle of Me.* Emory University, Ga., Banner Press, 1952. 61p. $2.00.

A collection of sixty-four poems written over a period of nearly thirty years. The book is dedicated to the author's twin sister, Lila McIntyre, who died while serving as a missionary to China.

WILEY, BELL IRVIN. *The Life of Billy Yank: The Common Soldier of the Union.* Indianapolis, Bobbs-Merrill, 1952. 454p. $6.00.

A companion volume to *The Life of Johnny Reb.* From thousands of soldiers' letters, diaries, and official reports, Dr. Wiley has built up a biography of the Union soldier of the Civil War. He reveals what sent Billy Yank to war, what he thought about it, what he ate, etc. The book has twenty-eight halftone illustrations.

WILLINGHAM, CALDER. *Natural Child.* New York, Dial Press, 1952. 289p. $3.50.

A portrait of a Bohemian group on Manhattan's 57th Street and of a naive and tempestuous Southern girl suddenly introduced into their midst.

WILLINGHAM, CALDER. *Reach to the Stars.* New York, Vanguard, 1951. 223p. $3.00.

A novel relating the experiences of Richard Davenport, a bellhop, in a California luxury hotel.

WOOD, VIRGINIA L. *Due Process of Law, 1932-1949; The Supreme Court's Use of a Constitutional Tool.* Baton Rouge, Louisiana State University Press, 1951. 445p. $6.00.

A review of attitudes taken by recent Supreme Court Justices in applying the "due process of law" requirements of the Constitution to actual cases.

WORSLEY, ETTA BLANCHARD. *Columbus on the Chattahoochee.* Columbus, Ga., Columbus Office & Supply Co., 1952. 513p. $10.00.

A detailed account of the Columbus section's ascent to the metropolitan area of today. Chapters are devoted to the development of the cotton industry, plantation life, the War Between the States, Reconstruction, Fort Benning, education, and social and economic life.

YERBY, FRANK. *The Saracen Blade.* New York, Dial Press, 1952. 406p. $3.50.

The story of a young Sicilian peasant named Pietro, who, in the thirteenth century, became a great lord and the confidant of the colorful Frederick the Second of Hohenstaufen, Holy Roman Emperor.

Bibliography of Georgia Authors
1952-1953

THE fourth in the REVIEW's series of annual "Bibliographies of Georgia Authors," this annotated bibliography is, as nearly as the compiler could make it, a complete and accurate record of books published by Georgia authors from November 1, 1952, to November 1, 1953. The annotations are descriptive, not critical; intended to place, not to judge the book. U. S., State, County, and City Documents, parts of books, brief analytics, and pamphlets of less than 25 pages have been omitted. Prices are given except when not supplied by publisher or when book is obtainable only on specific request, in which cases the word "Apply" is used.

In determining whom to call Georgia authors, the compiler has used the following criteria: authors born in Georgia and claiming Georgia as their native state and those who have lived in Georgia for a period of five years and who did their writing here.

The compiler will welcome and appreciate readers' sending to him any additions or corrections. They may be sent to him at any time in care of the GEORGIA REVIEW. Several books inadvertently omitted from the Bibliography for 1951-1952 are listed here. Any books omitted from the present Bibliography will be included in the list for 1953-1954.

ABERCROMBIE, THOMAS FRANKLIN. *History of Public Health in Georgia.* Atlanta, Longino & Porter, 1953. 228p. Available on request at the Georgia Health Department.
    The history of the growth of Georgia's public health program from 1733 to date. The book is illustrated with charts and graphs.

AIKEN, CONRAD POTTER. *Collected Poems.* New York, Oxford Press, 1953. 907p. $10.50.
    This volume contains all that Mr. Aiken has chosen to retain from forty years of writing poetry, including "The Morning Song of Senlin" and "At a Concert of Music."

ALCIATORE, JULES. *Stendhal et Helvétius; les Sources de la Philosophie de Stendhal.* Genève, E. Droze, 1952. vi,301p. $3.75.
    A chronological study of the ideas and principles borrowed by Stend-

hal from Helvétius that shows how Stendhal applies these principles in his works of criticism and in his novels.

ASHER, ERNA FROMME. *This Journey and Other Poems.* Atlanta, Privately Printed, c.1951. 66p. Apply.

A collection of sonnets and lyric poems concerned with life and its many ramifications.

BEARD, DONALD E., M.D., GOODYEAR, WILLIAM E., M.D., and WEENS, H. STEPHEN, M.D. *Radiologic Diagnosis of the Lower Urinary Tract.* Springfield, Ill., Charles C. Thomas, 1953. 150p. $6.50.

This atlas for roentgenologists contains carefully selected materials from some 2000 urologic cases. It is illustrated with approximately three hundred photographs and drawings. The authors are members of the faculty of the Emory University School of Medicine.

BELL, ALICE. *Beauty Can Be Fun.* Atlanta, Alice Bell Publications, 1953. 84p. $2.50.

An illustrated account of how to remain beautiful without the usual rigorous routine.

BLACKSTOCK, WALTER, JR. *Call Back the Swallows, and Other Selected Poems.* Mill Valley, Calif., The Wings Press, 1953. 117p. $2.00.

A collection of one hundred and thirty-five lyric poems. Dr. Blackstock is Assistant Professor of English at Florida State University.

BOYLSTON, ELSIE REID. *Creative Expression with Crayons.* Worcester, Mass., Davis Press, 1953. 98p. $3.95.

A book for teachers and others interested in fostering art work in the primary and junior high grades, it covers methods of stimulating the child's interest and creative abilities through art work with crayons. Illustrated.

BROWN, CALVIN S. *Tones into Words: Musical Compositions as Subjects of Poetry.* Athens, University of Georgia Press, 1953. 171p. $3.50.

This book is a study of the methods, the types of approach, the problems involved, and the techniques used in transposing musical works into verse. The work is based on three hundred poems from the French, German, and English.

BROWN, MAREL. *Fence Corners.* Nashville, Tenn., Broadman Press, 1952. 103p. $1.50.

A collection of fifty-one poems and fourteen informal essays reflecting the author's spiritual faith found in the various aspects of nature.

BRYAN, THOMAS CONN. *Confederate Georgia.* Athens, University of Georgia Press, 1953. x,299p. $4.50.

A study of the political, military, economic, and social history of Georgia from 1860 to 1865.

BUNTING, JAMES WHITNEY, ed. *Ethics for Modern Business Practice.* New York, Prentice-Hall, 1953. 269p. $5.15. Text Edition, $3.85.

An historical and analytical consideration of business ethics, showing the growth of ethical practices in various business operations and indicating the trend of business ethics in general as illustrated by possible business professionalization and collegiate programs of business training.

BUSBEE, JAMES, JR. *Son of Egypt.* New York, Avon, 1953. 319p. 35 cents.

A paperback original that details the fortunes and escapades of one Aahmes, an Egyptian soldier in the days of the Black Land's glory.

CALDWELL, ERSKINE. *Soleil du Sud (Southways);* Nouvelles, traduit de l'Américain par Max Morise. Paris, Gallimard, 1952. 249p. 500 francs.

A translation into French of the sixteen stories that first appeared in print in 1938.

CALDWELL, ERSKINE. *We Are the Living.* New York, Duell, Sloan and Pearce, 1953. 264p. $3.00.

A reissue of twenty Caldwell short stories first published in 1933. Some of them are laid in the South; others are in New England, and all of them are full of the pungency and realism found in *Tobacco Road* and *God's Little Acre.*

CAMPBELL, WILLIAM T. *Big Beverage.* Atlanta, Tupper & Love, 1952. 429p. $3.95.

A novel about the building of a soft drink empire in the South.

CENTER, STELLA STEWART. *The Art of Book Reading.* New York, Scribner's, 1952. xix, 208p. $3.50.

Director of the Reading Institute of New York University from 1936 to 1950, the author presents a method of approach to the problem of teaching reading. The book is based on the author's experience in teaching reading to people of all ages.

CHAPMAN, PAUL WILBUR, and DINSMORE, WAYNE. *Livestock Farming.* Atlanta, Turner E. Smith, 1953. 503p. $3.39.

After an introductory section on animal husbandry in general, there are sections on dairy and beef cattle, swine, sheep, horses, and mules, with particular reference to farming in the South.

CHAPMAN, PAUL WILBUR, and THOMAS, ROY HILMAN. *Southern Crops.* Atlanta, Turner E. Smith, 1953. 503p. $3.39.

An agricultural text, the first part presenting basic material on soil, water, and plants, and the second dealing with the production of different types of field crops cultivated throughout the South. The book is illustrated with photographs, maps, and diagrams.

CLARK, FAYE. *I Married a Preacher.* New York, Vantage Press, 1953. 51p. $2.00.

Behind-the-scene views of weddings, church people and preachers—those high lights of humor that break the tension of religious work are included in this collection.

COLEMAN, LONNIE (COLEMAN, WILLIAM LAWRENCE). *Adam's Way.* New York, Dutton, 1953. 252p. $3.00.

A solitary and eccentric man in his sixties, living on the edge of a Southern town, becomes a social outcast by choice, and strong feeling is aroused when he tries to mold a young Negro girl into a cultured lady.

DERN, MRS. JOHN SHERMAN. See: Gaddis, Peggy.

DERN, PEGGY, pseud. See: Gaddis, Peggy.

DREWRY, JOHN E. *Advancing Journalism: Press, Radio, Television, Periodicals, Public Relations, and Advertising, As Seen through Institutes and Special Occasions of the Henry W. Grady School of Journalism, 1952-53.* Vol. LIV, No. 2. Athens, University of Georgia Bulletin, 1952. x,157p. Paper, $2.00. Cloth, $3.00.

A compilation of addresses on journalistic subjects which were delivered at the several institutes, conventions, and special occasions sponsored by the University of Georgia's School of Journalism during the 1952-53 session.

ELLIOTT, CHARLES NEWTON. *Gone Fishin'.* Harrisburg, Pa., Stackpole Co., 1953. 291p. $5.00.

Fishing experiences of nearly fifty years set down by the field editor of *Outdoor Life.* Illustrated by Jack Hogg.

ENGLISH, THOMAS H. *Memory Book; Thirty-Five Years of Occasional Verse.* Atlanta, The Library of Emory University, 1953. 64p. $1.25.

This collection of forty-nine verses reflects the various chapters in the life of Dr. English, such as his travels and his experiences in World War I.

FAY, ELIOT. *Lorenzo in Search of the Sun; D. H. Lawrence in Italy, Mexico and the American Southwest.* New York, Bookman Associates, 1953. 147p. $2.75.

A chronicle of the main episodes and influences in the life of D. H. Lawrence from 1920 to 1930, years in which he spent much time in the American Southwest. Dr. Fay is Associate Professor of Romance Languages at Emory University.

FLEMING, BERRY. *Carnival.* Philadelphia, Lippincott, 1953. 189p. $3.00.

A symbolic novel in which the whole sequence of a man's life from boyhood to death unfolds as a succession of episodes at a carnival.

FORD, MARCIA. *Dixie Nurse.* New York, Bouregy & Curl, 1953. 255p. $2.50.

Nancy Craig, a young nurse, happy in her work with children and in her love of Dr. Terry Fenton, finds herself the victim of the spite of a tyrannical supervisor.

FORD, MARCIA. *The Sycamores.* New York, Bouregy & Curl, 1952. 255p. $2.50.

An impoverished old Southern plantation is an important element in a modern love story.

FOSTER, MARIAN CURTIS (pseud. Mariana). *Hotspur.* New York, Lothrop, Lee, & Sheppard Co., 1953. 48p. Boards, $1.25. Cloth, $1.60.
The creator of Flora McFlimsey has invented a new character, Hotspur, the little red horse. This is his first adventure outside of Mr. Twiddletwitch's toy shop. Illustrated by the author.

GADDIS, PEGGY. *Eileen Duggan.* New York, Arcadia House, 1952. 220p. $2.50.
A native Floridian, who finds a scarcity of eligible males in her neighborhood, falls in love with a young real estate salesman for whom her boss also has an eye.

GADDIS, PEGGY (pseud. Peggy Dern). *Nora Was a Nurse.* New York, Arcadia House, 1953. 223p. $2.50.
A young nurse falls in love with the doctor who takes her uncle's place when the latter goes on his vacation. The doctor, however, has eyes only for a local belle.

GANN, ERNEST KELLOGG. *The High and the Mighty.* New York, William Sloane Associates, 1953. 342p. $3.50.
Caught in a tropical storm, an airplane bound from Honolulu to San Francisco is in danger of crashing into the sea at any moment. For each passenger and member of the crew the imminent threat of death becomes something to be faced according to his own needs.

GIBBONEY, CHARLES H. *Frontiers of Hope.* Atlanta, Presbyterian Board of Church Extension, 1953. 214p. $1.00.
This book tells of the worthwhile developments of the Presbyterian Church and points out the opportunities for growth and service which are knocking at the door of the Church in the South.

HAM, TOM. *Give Us This Valley.* New York, Macmillan, 1952. 304p. $3.50.
The marriage of Lizzie Weldon and Wash Stonecypher begins as a matter of convenience, but by the time they have traveled by wagon to the Blue Ridge Mountains of Georgia and founded a home there, love has entered the bargain.

HARRIS, KATHLEEN, pseud. See: Humphries, Mrs. Adelaide.

HARWELL, RICHARD BARKSDALE. *Cornerstones of Confederate Collecting.* Charlottesville, University of Virginia Press for the Bibliographical Society of the University of Virginia, 1953. Second Edition. 35p. $2.50.
This new edition, revised by Clifford Dowdy, contains twenty facsimiles of title pages and a history of printing in the Confederacy.

HAWES, LILLA M., ed. *Collections of the Georgia Historical Society, Vol. X.* Savannah, Georgia Historical Society, 1952. 147p. $3.00.
Published from manuscript records of "The Proceedings and Minutes

of the Governor and Council, from October 4, 1774, through November 7, 1775, and from Spetember 6, 1779, through September 20, 1780." These manuscripts are in the library of the Georgia Historical Society.

HOLDEN, GENEVIEVE. *Killer Loose*. New York, Doubleday, 1953. 189p. $2.50.

    A young woman and her nephew, alone in a Southern farmhouse, are warned by the sheriff that a psychopathic killer is on the loose, but before they can get away, the man appears on the scene.

HUDSON, CHARLES. *Hudson's Southern Gardening*. Atlanta, Tupper & Love, 1953. 464p. $4.95.

    Covering soil types, plant materials, and cultural handling of many plants not generally included in existing works, this book is a comprehensive guide for Southern flower and vegetable gardens for the beginner as well as the expert.

HUMPHRIES, MRS. ADELAIDE. *Home Front Nurse*. New York, Bouregy & Curl, 1952. 253p. $2.50.

    An Army nurse who is engaged to a man back home finds herself falling in love with the surgeon with whom she works.

HUMPHRIES, MRS. ADELAIDE (pseud. Kathleen Harris). *Let Love Alone*. New York, Arcadia House, 1951. 224p. $2.00.

    The story of the romance of a young girl with an aeroplane pilot who was her flying instructor.

HUMPHRIES, MRS. ADELAIDE (pseud. Kathleen Harris). *No Other Love*. New York, Arcadia House, 1952. 222p. $2.50.

    A girl decides that her eight-year engagement is too long, and turns from her fiancé to another man.

HUMPHRIES, MRS. ADELAIDE. *Nurse Lady*. New York, Bouregy & Curl, 1953. 253p. $2.50.

    A Virginia nurse falls in love with a wealthy young man whom she meets when he is involved in a hit-and-run automobile accident.

HUMPHRIES, MRS. ADELAIDE. *Nurse Landon's Challenge*. New York, Bouregy & Curl, 1952. 253p. $2.50.

    A spoiled rich girl is attracted to a young doctor and decides to become a nurse at the hospital at which he works. During her training she learns to respect the profession of nursing and also gets her doctor.

HUMPHRIES, MRS. ADELAIDE. *Nurses Are People*. New York, Bouregy & Curl, 1951. 255p. $2.50.

    A Georgia nurse finds herself an heiress when a wealthy patient dies and leaves her all his money, much to the annoyance of his rich relatives.

HUMPHRIES, MRS. ADELAIDE (pseud. Kathleen Harris). *Rehearsal For Love*. New York, Arcadia House, 1953. 221p. $2.50.

    A career woman, the main support of her eccentric family, chooses between two suitors: a wealthy lawyer and a young Texas newspaperman.

HUMPHRIES, MRS. ADELAIDE (pseud. Kathleen Harris). *Stand by for Romance.* New York, Arcadia House, 1952. 224p. $2.50.
   The romance of a fashion model with a wealthy playboy is disapproved by both of their families.

HUMPHRIES, MRS. ADELAIDE. *The Nurse Knows Best.* New York, Bouregy & Curl, 1953. 254p. $2.50.
   The pretty young nurse in the office of a Park Avenue psychiatrist takes an interest in the case of a mentally disturbed Korean War veteran.

JENKINS, SARA LUCILLE. *The Happy People.* New York, Crowell, 1953. 246p. $3.00.
   Stephen Elliott, a young Methodist minister, torn between devotion to his church and love of a divorcee finds understanding and an inner peace when he subordinates personal problems to those of his community.

KEELER, O. B. *The Bobby Jones Story: From the Writings of O. B. Keeler.* Compiled by Grantland Rice. Atlanta, Tupper & Love, 1953. 304p. $3.95.
   This story of an all-time golfing master was assembled by Mrs. Eleanor Keeler from Keeler's writings in books, magazine articles, and news reports from golf tournaments in which Jones played. Illustrated with photographs.

KENNEDY, JOSEPH A. *Relax and Live.* New York, Prentice-Hall, 1953. 205p. $3.95.
   A system of relaxation both passive and rhythmic, which the author has taught at Bill Brown's health camp in New York State.

LEE, MRS. EDNA L. MOONEY. *The Southerners.* New York, Appleton-Century-Crofts, 1953. 407p. $3.75.
   With the background of the South during the post-Reconstruction period, Jess Kildare, an illegitimate child, grows from childhood into womanhood. After her marriage to Wes Carrabee, she becomes involved in a struggle for control of the Carrabee cotton mill, and Jess comes closer to the secret of her birth.

LONG, MARGARET. *Affair of the Heart.* New York, Random House, 1953. 376p. $3.50.
   Returning to her Georgia home town after the breakup of her marriage, newspaper woman Carter Kelly joins a small group of friends to found a liberal weekly newspaper that will work for Negro rights. As prejudice mounts in the town and the Ku Klux Klan acts, Carter's estranged husband comes back to edit the new paper and win back her love.

LONG, NATHANIEL GUY. *Goal Posts.* Atlanta, Tupper & Love, 1953. 162p. $2.75.

Twenty-three talks to young people on building a sound successful life in today's troubled world.

McALLISTER, MRS. ELVA SINCLAIR. *Poems.* Atlanta, Parks Printing Co., 1952. 148p. $3.00.
A collection of inspirational poems.

McLEMORE, HENRY. *One of Us Is Wrong!* New York, Holt, 1953. 242p. $3.00.
An Atlanta-born newspaperman's reminiscences of an unorthodox and lively career that has taken him in and out of unpredictable situations from a B and G Sandwich Shop in New York to Peiping, Hawaii, and the Taj Mahal. Illustrated by the Strimbans.

MARIANA, pseud. See: Foster, Marian Curtis.

MARSHALL, EDISON. *Caravan to Xanadu.* New York, Farrar, Straus & Young, 1953. 371p. $3.50.
The story of the great adventurer of the thirteenth century, Marco Polo, the hardships that beset him, the deadly hatred that pursued him, and the passionate devotion that brought him triumphant to the palace of the Khan.

MASON, LUCY RANDOLPH. *To Win These Rights; A Personal Story of the CIO in the South.* New York, Harper, 1952. 222p. $3.00.
Miss Mason, a great-great-granddaughter of the man who wrote the Virginia Bill of Rights, became an organizer for the CIO in the South in 1937. This is her account of the growth of the movement and of the social changes it has brought about in those fifteen years. The foreword is by Eleanor Roosevelt.

MOORE, ARTHUR JAMES. *Immortal Tidings in Mortal Hands.* Nashville, Tenn., Abingdon-Cokesbury, 1953. 128p. $1.75.
The meaning of Christianity as expressed by an evangelical Methodist bishop.

MOORE, MAVIS GAREY. *Whale Mountain.* New York, Macmillan, 1953. 234p. $2.75.
In a small Southern town, Sledge Beston, the town bully, and a group of small boys hunt and finally find a lost companion and also a new source of water to help the drought-stricken town. Illustrated by John Moore.

MOREHOUSE, WARD. *Just the Other Day; From Yellow Pines to Broadway.* New York, McGraw-Hill, 1953. 240p. $4.00.
The variegated life of Mr. Morehouse, from his childhood and early journalistic career in the South, through his long intimacy with "Broadway After Dark."

NEFF, LAWRENCE WILSON. *The Quest.* Emory University, Ga., Banner Press, 1953. 240p. $2.50.
Laid in the years following Christ's death, this novel presents a thought-

ful, human account of the work and personalities of St. Paul and his followers.

OLNEY, CLARKE. *Benjamin Robert Haydon: Historical Painter.* Athens, University of Georgia Press, 1952. 309p. $5.00.

The biography of a colorful nineteenth century English painter and writer who was a friend to many of the literary figures of his day.

PARKS, EDD WINFIELD. *Safe on Second, The Story of a Little Leaguer.* Indianapolis, Bobbs-Merrill, 1953. 199p. $2.00.

Tom Winton has an uphill fight to become second baseman on his Little League team, and in order to win the acceptance of the boys, he learns to play with headwork and teamwork and becomes a leader.

PARKS, EDD WINFIELD. *Teddy Roosevelt, All-Round Boy.* Indianapolis, Bobbs-Merrill, 1953. 192p. $1.75.

The amazing story of an active boy who, in happy triumph over physical handicaps, became the famous Rough Rider, President of the United States, and builder of the Panama Canal. This is another in the Childhood of Famous Americans Series and is illustrated by Sandra James.

POSEY, WALTER BROWNLOW. *The Presbyterian Church in the Old Southwest, 1778-1838.* Richmond, Va., John Knox Press, 1952. 192p. $2.50.

Presbyterian church history in the area of Mississippi, Alabama, Tennessee, and Kentucky, in an era when the church was largely a missionary and frontier organization, and when its members were deeply concerned about the slavery question.

POU, GENEVIEVE LONG. See: Holden, Genevieve.

RADFORD, RUBY. See: Ford, Marcia.

SEARS, WILLIAM. *Excavations at Kolomoki, Seasons III & IV, Mound D.* Athens, University of Georgia Press, 1953. 94p. $2.00.

An illustrated paper-bound report on the excavation techniques and findings at the Kolomoki mounds located in Early County, Georgia. Maps, charts, and photographs show burials, artifacts, ceramics, and textiles.

STEWARD, DAVENPORT. *Rainbow Road.* Atlanta, Tupper & Love, 1953. 283p. $3.75.

The story of love, violence, and greed in the gold camps of northern Georgia, where white men came in 1820 to take away wealth from the land belonging to the Cherokee Nation.

SUDDETH, RUTH ELGIN, and MORENUS, CONSTANCE GAY, compilers. *Tales of the Western World; Folk Tales of the Americas.* Austin, Texas, The Steck Co., 1953. 281p. $2.50.

A collection of thirty-eight stories from the folklore treasury of the Western Hemisphere reflecting its history, heritage, and charm. The illustrations are by Warren Hunter.

SUGGS, LOUISE. *Par Golf for Women.* New York, Prentice-Hall, 1953. 128p. $2.95. School Edition, $2.20.

Golf from the woman's angle by one of the country's foremost women golfers. Foreword by Ben Hogan and illustrated with photographs by Paul Siegel and diagrams by Al Papas.

TATE, WILLIAM, ed. *Documents and Memoirs, Genealogical Tables, The Tates of Pickens County.* Marietta, Ga., The Continental Book Co., 1953. 94p. $3.00.

This book, mimeographed in a limited edition, deals with the genealogy of one of the South's leading families, and covers the period from 1830 to date. The editor is Dean of Men at the University of Georgia.

TYRE, NEDRA. *Death of an Intruder: A Tale of Horror in Three Parts.* New York, Alfred A. Knopf, 1953. 181p. $2.50.

The hard-won contentment of a timorous spinster is challenged in a terrific fashion by another woman who takes over her house and her life and, finally, destroys her sanity.

WHITE, HELEN CHAPPELL. *With Wings as Eagles.* New York, Rinehart, 1953. 246p. $2.75.

A mother's personal account of her journey through the valley of the shadow of death and of how she succeeded in overcoming grief and fear when her son's plane was shot down over the Baltic Sea in 1944. The introduction is written by Dr. Ralph W. Sockman.

WHITE, ROBB. *Our Virgin Island.* New York, Doubleday, 1953. 284p. $3.50.

The story of how the author and his wife built a new existence for themselves, amid great difficulties, on a lonely island in the Caribbean.

WHITTEMORE, MYRTLE. *Flute Concerto of Sidney Lanier.* New York, Pageant Press, 1953. 301p. $3.50.

A biography of Lanier, this book makes use of some newly discovered letters and poems, and stresses the importance of music in Lanier's life.

WILLIAMS, NELLIE LOWMAN. *Sincerely Yours.* Emory University, Ga., Banner Press, 1953. 55p. $2.00.

A collection of fifty-five poems dealing with faith, hope, and the many facets of everyday life.

WOOD, MARIE STEVENS. *Flower Arrangements Judged and Point Scored.* Macon, Ga., Merriewood Press, 1952. 177p. $3.50.

Photographs of thirty-two of the author's flower arrangements with the point scoring by which they won prizes and with brief sketches of the judges who awarded the prizes.

YERBY, FRANK. *The Devil's Laughter.* New York, Dial Press, 1953. 376p. $3.50.

The adventures of a hot-headed, amorous lawyer who rises to become a leader in the French Revolution.

Bibliography of Georgia Authors
1953-1954

THE fifth in the REVIEW's series of annual "Bibliographies of Georgia authors," this annotated bibliography is, as nearly as the compiler could make it, a complete and accurate records of books published by Georgia authors from November 1, 1953, to November 1, 1954. The annotations are descriptive, not critical; intended to place, not to judge the book. U. S., State, County, and City Documents, parts of books, brief analytics, and pamphlets of less than 25 pages have been omitted. Prices are given except when not supplied by publisher or when book is obtainable only on specific request, in which cases the word "Apply" is used.

In determining whom to call Georgia authors, the compiler has used the following criteria: authors born in Georgia and claiming Georgia as their native state and those who have lived in Georgia for a period of five years and who did their writing here.

The compiler will welcome and appreciate readers' sending to him any additions or corrections. They may be sent to him at any time in care of the GEORGIA REVIEW. Several books inadvertently omitted from previous Bibliographies are listed here. Any books omitted from the present Bibliography will be included in the list for 1954-1955.

Acknowledgement is made to Mrs. William Tate, member of the University of Georgia Library staff, for her assistance in the preparation of this Bibliography.

ALCIATORE, JULES C. *Stendahl et Maine de Biran.* Genève, E. Droz, 1954. 46p. $1.00.
    An analysis of the influence of Maine de Biran's famous treatise on habit on Stendhal's novels and critical works.

ALLEN, CHARLES L. *12 Ways to Solve Your Problem.* Atlanta, Privately Printed, 1954. 30p. $1.00.
    This is the fourth of a series of inspirational works by Dr. Allen, pastor of Atlanta's Grace Methodist Church and columnist for the Atlanta *Constitution*. It is brief, readable, and spiritually uplifting.

ALLEN, CHARLES L. *God's Psychiatry; the Twenty-third Psalm, the Ten Commandments, the Lord's Prayer, the Beatitudes.* Westwood, N. J., Fleming H. Revell Co., 1953. 159p. $2.00.

A prescription written by a minister of the Gospel for people who are distressed and confused, for people whose lives have become drab and flat.

ALLEN, ROSSIE C. *Today, We're Free!* New York, Pageant Press, 1954. 59p. $2.50.

A man, caring for his child after its mother had apparently died in a German concentration camp, finally comes out of his shell and builds a new life.

BARRAGAN, MAUDE. *John Howard Payne, Skywalker.* Richmond, Va., Dietz Press, 1953. 376p. $3.00.

A biographical novel about the flamboyant life of John Howard Payne, actor and writer, who was bound up closely with the American theatrical and literary scene in the early nineteenth century.

BLACKFORD, LAUNCELOT MINOR. *Mine Eyes Have Seen the Glory.* Cambridge, Mass., Harvard University Press, 1954. 293p. $5.00.

The life of a remarkable Southern gentlewoman, Mary Berkley Minor Blackford (1802-1896), who taught her sons to hate slavery and to love the Union. Her five sons fought for the Confederacy, but Mary Blackford stuck to her fight against slavery and sin.

BOLES, PAUL DARCY. *The Beggars in the Sun.* New York, Macmillan, 1954. 217p. $3.00.

A Southern folk singer gets mixed up with the wife of a wealthy and influential man and seems headed for trouble. Despite all that happens he remains true to his own nature, however, and comes out of the experience a little wiser than before.

BOLES, PAUL DARCY. *The Streak.* New York, Macmillan, 1953. 218p. $3.00.

A gripping account of a few months in the life of a European sport car racer riding hard on a winning streak over continental closed-circuit courses.

BOVEE, ARTHUR GIBBON, and CARNAHAN, DAVID HOBART. *Lettres de Paris.* Boston, D. C. Heath, 1954. xii, 228p. $2.60.

A beginning French grammar for use in colleges, this text presents lessons and exercises designed to make the student need and want to use the language.

BRAMBLETT, AGNES COCHRAN. *My Brother, Oh, My Brother.* New York, Pageant Press, 1954. 255p. $3.00.

The impact of two world wars on a Southern family is the theme of this first novel by a distinguished poet of Forsyth, Georgia.

BUNTING, JAMES WHITNEY. *Essentials of Retail Selling.* New York, Bookman Associates, 1954. 147p. $2.50.
   An introduction to the basic principles of selling written for the retail salesman by the President of Oglethorpe University.

CALDWELL, ERSKINE. *The Complete Stories.* New York, Duell, Sloan & Pearce, 1953. 664p. $5.00.
   A collection of ninety-six short stories, all of which had been previously published.

CALDWELL, ERSKINE. *Love and Money.* New York, Duell, Sloan & Pearce, 1954. 244p. $3.50.
   A writer's pursuit of a "cocktail girl" who drifts from one plush bar to another, from Sarasota to Colorado Springs.

CAYLOR, JOHN, ed. *A Path of Light.* Atlanta, Home Mission Board, Southern Baptist Convention, 1950. 118p. 50 cents.
   Biographical sketches of eight Baptist missionaries who have reached the age of retirement or have passed on to their rewards.

CAYLOR, JOHN. *Christ for Our Cities.* Atlanta, Home Mission Board, Southern Baptist Convention, 1951. 60p. 50 cents.
   A resource book on the 1951 graded series of Baptist Home Mission studies entitled, "The Urban Church Serving Its Community." Dr. Caylor is secretary of education for the Baptist Home Mission Board.

CAYLOR, JOHN. *In Evangeline's Country.* Atlanta, Home Mission Board, Southern Baptist Convention, 1954. 101p. 50 cents.
   A study of the work of Baptist missionaries among the 700,000 people of French extraction living in southern Louisiana.

CAYLOR, JOHN. *Our Neighbors of Many Tongues.* Atlanta, Home Mission Board, Southern Baptist Convention, 1954. 69p. 50 cents.
   A source book for the teacher of the 1954 graded series of Baptist Home Mission Studies.

CHAMBLISS, ROLLIN. *Social Thought, From Hammurabi to Comte.* New York, Dryden Press, 1954. 477p. $5.00.
   Summaries and explanations of some ideas which constitute an important part of the intellectual heritage of mankind. Dr. Chambliss is professor of sociology at the University of Georgia.

CHIVERS, THOMAS HOLLEY. *Life of Poe.* New York, Dutton, 1952. 127p. $5.00.
   The text here presented is an assemblage, an arrangement, and a pruning from the several manuscripts among the Poe-Chivers Papers in the Henry E. Huntington Library. The explanatory notes and introduction are by Richard Beale Davis. The edition is limited to 1500 copies.

CHRISTIAN, MARY. *Home Missions Meeting Spiritual Needs.* Atlanta,

Home Mission Board, Southern Baptist Convention, 1952. 52p. 50 cents.

A teachers' source book for a Baptist study series on home missions. The author is a native of Elberton, Georgia.

COTTLE, CHARLES SIDNEY, AND WHITMAN, WILLIAM TATE. *Investment Timing: the Formula Plan Approach.* New York, McGraw-Hill, 1953. 200p. $5.00.

Not for the novice or superficial student of investments, this volume presents in a concise form a highly informative and penetrating analysis of investment formula plans. The approach is the analytical and the critical. The authors are professors at Emory University.

CRANFORD, MARY POOLE. *From My Window; to Shut-ins All Over the World.* New York, Pageant Press, 1953. 146p. $2.50.

An illustrated collection of inspirational essays and meditations based on Biblical texts. The author is a resident of Macon, Georgia.

DERN, MRS. JOHN SHERMAN. See: Gaddis, Peggy.

DERN, PEGGY. See: Gaddis, Peggy.

DODD, ROBERT L. *Bobby Dodd on Football.* New York, Prentice-Hall, 1954. 344p. $4.50.

Illustrated with pictures and diagrams this account covers every phase of football from its early history to helpful hints for the spectator. The coach of Georgia Tech gives a complete analysis of the plays that have made his team great.

DREWRY, JOHN E. *Journalism is Communications: Press, Radio, Television, Periodicals, Public Relations, and Advertising, As Seen through Institutes and Special Occasions of the Henry W. Grady School of Journalism, 1953-1954.* Vol. LV, No. 1. Athens, University of Georgia Bulletin, 1954. 193p. Paper, $2.00. Cloth, $3.00.

A compilation of addresses on journalistic subjects which were delivered at the several institutes, conventions, and special occasions sponsored by the University of Georgia's School of Journalism during the 1953-54 session.

EDWARDS, H. GRIFFIN. *Specifications.* New York, Van Nostrand, 1953. 311p. $5.00.

The book is a primer of good specification writing designed to serve as a guide to the student and young architect, as well as an aid to the more experienced.

ELLIOTT, CHARLES NEWTON. *Gone Huntin'.* Harrisburg, Pa., Stackpole Co., 1954. 279p. $5.00.

Reminiscences of the author's big game hunting in various parts of America.

EVERETT, EDWIN M., WALL, CHARLES A., JR., AND DUMAS, MARIE. *Correct Writing, Form B.* Boston, D. C. Heath, 1952. 243p. $1.75.

A revised and enlarged edition of *Freshman Workbook for Correct Writing*, which appeared in 1948. Combining the best features of a book of exercises and a handbook of composition, this workbook is noteworthy for its clarity and simplicity.

EVERETT, EDWIN M., WALL, CHARLES A., JR., AND DUMAS, MARIE. *Correct Writing, Form A.* Boston, D. C. Heath, 1954. 243p. $1.75.

This workbook includes the same grammatical rules and explanations as *Correct Writing, Form B*, but it has an entirely different set of exercises.

FERSEN, NICOLAS. *Tombolo.* Boston, Houghton Mifflin, 1954. 241p. $3.00.

Tombolo is a wild unapproachable island set in the salt marshes near Pisa. In his novel, Mr. Fersen describes life on this island during the Italian campaign of World War II—when the island became the refuge for dregs of all armies.

FORD, MARCIA. *Peacehaven.* New York, Bouregy & Curl, 1954. 252p. $2.50.

A Southern girl returns home to South Carolina after a year in New York to find the family plantation about to be lost, a mentally ill brother, and romantic problems of her own.

FOSTER, MARIAN CURTIS (pseud. Mariana). *Miss Flora McFlimsey and Little Laughing Water.* New York, Lothrop, Lee, & Sheppard Co., 1954. 30p. Paper, $1.25. Cloth, $1.60.

Miss Flora McFlimsey makes a new friend in this latest adventure, and visits an Indian Village on Running River. Water-color illustrations are by the author.

FULLER, ELLIS ADAMS. *Evangelistic Sermons.* Nashville, Tenn., Broadman Press, 1953. 144p. $1.75.

Ten evangelistic sermons based on a sound interpretation of the Bible by the late Dr. Ellis A. Fuller. These sermons were selected by Mrs. Fuller for their direct and simple appeal for all ages.

GADDIS, PEGGY. *A Guest in Paradise.* New York, Arcadia House, 1954. 221p. $2.50.

Celia Judson, in love with her young employer, finds her way through conflict to happiness on a luxurious estate on an island off the Georgia coast.

GADDIS, PEGGY. *Moon of Enchantment.* New York, Arcadia House, 1953. 224p. $2.50.

A Florida nurse is hired to take care of a young man who has suffered a severe beating and finds herself drawn into the mystery surrounding him.

GADDIS, PEGGY. *Oleander Cove.* New York, Arcadia House, 1954. 224p. $2.50.

A country school teacher in the South falls in love with a Korean veteran and then worries about a beautiful heiress who is stealing him away from her.

GARRETT, FRANKLIN M. *Atlanta and Its Environs: A Chronicle of Its People and Events.* New York, Lewis Historical Publishing Co., 1954. Two volumes. 2000p. $48.50.

Mr. Garrett's work is based on twenty-five years of research and presents a detailed account of Atlanta's history from the early 1800's to the present. The edition is limited to 1500 copies sold on a subscription basis.

GINSBERG, PAUL. *Wake Up, America.* New York, Vantage Press, 1954. 154p. $3.00.

An illustrated report on the author's world tour in 1952, made in his capacity as National Commander of Jewish War Veterans of the U.S.A.

GORDON, HUGH H., JR. *A Letter to My Sons About Their Forebears.* Athens, Privately Printed, 1954. 34p. Apply.

A history of the Gordons, Haralsons, Howards, Williamses, and allied families.

GRAY, JOHN STANLEY. *Psychology Applied to Human Affairs.* New York, McGraw-Hill, 1954. Second edition. 581p. $6.00.

This edition incorporates new studies and interpretations, with an added chapter on wage determination. New tables, diagrams, and graphs are included. Dr. Gray is professor of psychology at the University of Georgia.

HANSON, WESLEY TURNELL, JR., and others. *Principles of Color Photography.* New York, Wiley, 1953. 709p. $11.00.

Basic theory of color photography, with sections on vision and sensitometry, and with a description of methods of obtaining colorant images and combining them to obtain color processes. The authors are scientists associated with Eastman Kodak.

HARRIS, JOEL CHANDLER. *The Complete Uncle Remus.* Boston, Hougton Mifflin, 1954. 800p. $5.00.

Joel Chandler Harris's beloved, comical tales that have given humor and pathos to succeeding generations of children for over seventy years are now available in one volume. This edition was compiled by Richard Chase and is illustrated by A. B. Frost and Frederick Church.

HARRIS, JOEL CHANDLER. *Uncle Remus.* London, Gawthorn Press, 1953. 144p. 12s 6d.

An English edition of the folktales of Joel Chandler Harris adapted for British readers by Robert Harding and illustrated by Neave Parker.

HARWELL, RICHARD BARKSDALE, ed. *Three Months in the Confederate Army*. University, Ala., University of Alabama Press, 1952. 38p. $1.00.

Facsimile reprint of articles by Henry Hotze originally published in the London *Index*, interpreting the Confederacy to British readers.

HARWELL, RICHARD BARKSDALE, ed. *Stonewall Jackson and the Old Stonewall Brigade*. By John Esten Cooke. Charlottesville, University of Virginia Press, 1954. 76p. $3.50.

This is the first separate printing of Cooke's life of Jackson which originally appeared as a series of articles in the *Southern Illustrated News* in 1863.

HENDERSON, LEGRAND. *Tom Benn and Blackbeard, The Pirate*. Nashville, Tenn., Abingdon, 1954. 64p. $2.00.

The amazing story of how Blackbeard the Pirate was captured off Ocracoke Island, North Carolina, with the help of Tom Benn and an old wooden washtub.

HOLDEN, GENEVIEVE. *Sound an Alarm*. New York, Doubleday, 1954. 189p. $2.75.

Hired as governess by a wealthy Southern family, Linda Stanley joins police, a private detective, and another girl in an attempt to find her young charge who has been kidnapped and perhaps murdered.

HOLLINGSWORTH, CLYDE DIXON. *The Hollingsworth Family of Screven County, Georgia*. Sylvester, Ga., Privately Printed, 1952. 46p. Apply.

An illustrated family history of one branch of the Hollingsworth family in Georgia.

HUMPHRIES, MRS. ADELAIDE. *Navy Nurse*. New York, Bouregy & Curl, 1954. 254p. $2.50.

A Navy nurse stationed on a hospital ship off San Diego straightens out her romantic entanglements.

HUMPHRIES, MRS. ADELAIDE. *Nurse Barclay's Dilemma*. New York, Bouregy & Curl, 1950. 251p. $2.50.

A physical therapist falls in love with her patient, a former prisoner of war with many emotional as well as physical problems.

HUMPHRIES, MRS. ADELAIDE. *Ocean Wedding*. New York, Arcadia House, 1953. 220p. $2.50.

A girl who is taking a Jamaica cruise to forget a false lover accepts, on board ship, an offer of marriage which is made as a strictly business proposition.

HYMAN, MAC. *No Time for Sergeants.* New York, Random House, 1954. 214p. $2.95.

A draftee from the Southern hill country makes a big impact on the army, emerging intact from a wild and hilarious series of misadventures. This book was the Book-of-the-Month Club selection for October, 1954.

JORDAN, ARNA R. *Dreams Come True: Being a Biography of Gov. Herman E. Talmadge and a Pictorial Record of Achievements During His Administration as Governor of Georgia.* Atlanta, Privately Printed, 1954. 53p. $3.50.

A record, in words and pictures, of Governor Talmadge's administration as told by a former school teacher and administrator.

KILLENS, JOHN O. *Youngblood.* New York, Dial Press, 1954. 566p. $3.95.

A few years in the life of a Negro family living in a Georgia factory town in the 1920's and '30's. Through their relations with their friends and neighbors Negro and white, a better pattern of racial understanding begins to emerge at last.

LECKIE, GEORGE G., ed. *Georgia: A Guide to Its Towns and Countryside.* Atlanta, Tupper and Love, 1954. 457p. $6.00.

A survey of Georgia's agriculture, industry, religion, education, arts, history, press, government, folklore, traditions, and legends. This is a revised and expanded edition, with a foreword by Ralph McGill.

LEGRAND, pseud. See: Henderson, LeGrand.

LEMLY, JAMES HUTTON. *The Gulf, Mobile and Ohio.* Homewood, Ill., Richard D. Irwin, 1953. 347p. $6.65.

The fascinating story of the growth of the Gulf, Mobile and Ohio Railroad during the period from 1920 to the present.

MCCLUNG, BARBARA ADAIR. *The Hidden Self.* New York, Exposition Press, 1954. 64p. $2.50.

A collection of inspirational poems dealing with life in its many ramifications.

MCGILL, RALPH. *The Fleas Come With the Dog.* Nashville, Tenn., Abingdon, 1954. 128p. $2.00.

Mr. McGill's comments on modern America and the South and the problems that come with urbanization. The book contains many interesting personal anecdotes, and opinions based on his daily column in the Atlanta *Constitution.*

MCKINNEY, CHARLES D., SR. *Local Government in DeKalb.* Decatur, Ga., Decatur News Publishing Co., 1954. 71p. Gratis.

A series of factual and informative articles on the pattern of local government in DeKalb County.

MANN, LUCILE ABBEY. *Precious in His Sight.* Atlanta, Home Mission Board, Southern Baptist Convention, 1951. 43p. 50 cents.

Incidents related in *Precious in His Sight* are actual experiences of the author in her work as a Sunbeam leader. Mrs. Mann is a native of Atlanta.

MARSHALL, EDISON. *American Captain.* New York, Farrar, Straus & Young, 1954. 407p. $3.95.

Centered around an American sailor of the last century, this adventure story of love lost, treachery at sea, eighteen years dedicated to revenge, and love regained.

MELL, EDWARD BAKER. *A Short History of Athens Baptist Church, Now The First Baptist Church of Athens, 1830-1953.* Athens, Speering Printing Co., 1954. 28p. Gratis.

A short, fact-filled history giving in a simple form some of the highlights in the growth and development of the First Baptist Church of Athens.

MEADOWS, JOHN CASSIUS. *Modern Georgia.* Athens, University of Georgia Press, 1954. Revised Edition. 352p. Paper, $4.00. Cloth, $5.00.

This textbook, used in a number of Georgia colleges, contains a wealth of up-to-date material about Georgia's geography, history, culture, population, education, health, public welfare, agriculture, industry, government, and finance.

MELTON, JAMES, and PURDY, KEN. *Bright Wheels Rolling.* Philadelphia, Macrae Smith Co., 1954. 188p. $4.50.

An account of the world's great antique cars and an almost forgotten era of brocaded elegance on wheels, taken from America's most famous collection, the James Melton Autorama. Mr. Melton was born in Moultrie, Georgia.

MITCHELL, MARGARET. *Gone With the Wind.* Garden City, N. Y., Garden City Books, 1954. 689p. $1.98.

The first reprint edition of the famous Georgia historical novel.

MITCHELL, MARGARET. *Gone With the Wind.* Garden City, N. Y., Permabooks, 1954. 862p. Paper, 75 cents.

An inexpensive reprint of a great fiction classic.

MORRIS, JOSEPH SCOTT, JR. *The Genealogy of the Allen Family.* Macon, Ga., J. W. Burke Co., 1951. 132p. Apply.

A detailed study of one branch of the Allen family in Georgia.

MOSTELLER, JAMES D. *History of the Kiokee Baptist Church in Georgia.* Ann Arbor, Mich., Edwards Brothers, 1952. 275p. $5.00.

A definitive history of the First Baptist church organized in Georgia. Out of Kiokee grew the first association and in turn the first state convention of Georgia Baptists.

NORRIS, JACK CLAYTON, M.D. *Gleanings From a Doctor's Eye.* Atlanta, Higgins-McArthur Co., 1953. 120p. $2.75.
    An account of the author's experiences and observations both as a Naval medical officer in World War II and as a peacetime medical practitioner.

ODUM, EUGENE PLEASANTS. *Fundamentals of Ecology.* Philadelphia, Saunders, 1953. 384p. $6.50.
    A concise and simplified study of the principles of ecology designed for the college student and the layman desiring an introduction to the subject.

ODUM, MAMIE OZBURN. *Heart Leaves.* Emory University, Ga., Banner Press, 1954. 60p. $2.00.
    A collection of poems dealing with subject matter familiar to every Southern home—reflecting a genuine warmth and appreciation of Southern life in its many aspects.

OSBORN, STELLANOVA. *Jasmine Springs.* Lancaster, Pa., Business Press, 1953. 47p. Apply.
    A collection of seventy-seven poems about Georgia, nature, and religion.

OUTLER, ALBERT C. *Psychotherapy and the Christian Message.* New York, Harper, 1954. 286p. $3.50.
    The viewpoints of psychotherapy and of Christian thought are examined, to define the problems of alliance and conflict between the two and to analyze four of the basic issues that lie between them.

PARK, HUGH. *Street Scenes.* Atlanta, Privately Printed, 1954. 112p. $1.75.
    A compilation of the best of 10,000 "Street Scenes" published on page one of the Atlanta *Journal* in the last ten years. The illustrations are by Lou Erickson.

PARKS, AILEEN WELLS. *Bedford Forrest: Boy on Horseback.* Indianapolis, Bobbs-Merrill, 1954. 192p. $1.48. School Edition.
    A new edition of the boyhood life of General Bedford Forrest, which first appeared in 1952. It is in the Childhood of Famous Americans Series and is illustrated by Paul Laune.

PENDLEY, EVELYN HOGE. *Mountain Top Moments.* Emory University, Ga., Banner Press, 1953. 91p. $2.50.
    Approximately a hundred lyric poems recording the many facets of the author's busy life and wholesome philosophy.

PFUETZE, PAUL E. *The Social Self.* New York, Bookman Associates, 1954. 392p. $4.50.
    A full scale exposition, comparison, and criticism of the concept of the social self in the writings of George Herbert Mead and Martin

Buber. Dr. Pfuetze is professor of philosophy at the University of Georgia.

POATS, RUTHERFORD M. *Decision in Korea.* New York, McBride, 1954. 340p. $4.75.

An account of the origin and events of the war in Korea, and of the objectives it served. The author is at present United Press chief correspondent and manager for Japan.

POU, GENEVIEVE LONG. See: Holden, Genevieve.

POUND, MERRITT B., and SAYE, ALBERT B. *Handbook on the Constitutions of the United States and Georgia.* Athens, University of Georgia Press, 1954. Fourth Edition. 165p. $1.00.

Contains the text of both constitutions along with discussion of historical background and analyses of the articles and amendments.

RADFORD, RUBY. See: Ford, Marcia.

RANGE, WILLARD. *A Century of Georgia Agriculture: 1850-1950.* Athens, University of Georgia Press, 1954. 333p. $5.00.

A comprehensive study of the changing pattern of Georgia agriculture from the rich ante-bellum years through a long period of depression to the modern era of scientific planting.

SAYE, ALBERT B., POUND, MERRITT B., and ALLUMS, JOHN F. *Principles of American Government.* New York, Prentice-Hall, 1954. Second Edition. 442p. $6.35.

The principles, organization, and functions of American government are presented in a concise, straightforward account.

SCOTT, COL. ROBERT LEE, JR. *Between the Elephant's Eyes!* New York, Dodd Mead, 1954. 243p. $3.75.

Col. Scott recounts the realization of a lifelong ambition to hunt the Sambur elephant in the wilds of Africa. Illustrations were drawn by Frank Hubbard.

SCOTT, COL. ROBERT LEE, JR. *God Is My Co-Pilot.* Garden City, N. Y., Doubleday, 1951. xiv, 277p. $1.95.

Col. Scott's best selling book on combat flying and religion in the Far East has been re-edited for the Young Modern Series.

SHERROD, ROBERT LEE. *History of Marine Corps Aviation in World War II.* Washington, D. C., Combat Forces Press, 1952. 496p. $6.50.

A review of the history of Marine Corps aviation back to its beginnings in 1912, and a full account of the combat activity of Marine aviation in World War II. Illustrated.

SHERROD, ROBERT LEE. *Tarawa: The Story of a Battle; 10th Anniversary Edition.* Boston, Little, Brown, 1954. 164p. $3.50.

This edition has a new preface by the author and an appendix containing reflections by a number of officers who fought at Tarawa.

SHULER, EDWARD LEANDER. *Blood Mountain: A Historical Story About Choestoe and Choestoeans.* Jacksonville, Fla., Convention Press, 1953. 147p. Apply.

A description of Choestoe's pretty valley and mountains, as well as an account of the lives of the sturdy people who have lived in that small district in the Blue Ridge Mountains of Georgia. The book is dedicated to Dr. M. D. Collins.

SMITH, LILLIAN EUGENIA. *The Journey.* Cleveland, World Publishing Co., 1954. 256p. $3.50.

A retrospective view of the moments in the author's life when her philosophy of living became clear and her understanding of herself and of other people deepened.

STANDARD, DIFFEE WILLIAM. *Columbus, Georgia, In the Confederacy; The Social and Industrial Life of the Chattahoochee River Port.* New York, William-Frederick Press, 1954. 77p. $2.00.

A study of the changes in the social and industrial life of Columbus, Georgia, as a result of the War Between the States.

STEWARD, DAVENPORT. *Sail the Dark Tide.* Atlanta, Tupper & Love, 1954. 310p. $3.75.

A novel of Confederate blockade-running in the Atlantic, to supply the Army of Northern Virginia in the last desperate days of the Civil War.

STROBEL, P. A. *The Salzburgers and Their Descendants.* Athens, University of Georgia Press, 1953. 318p. $3.00.

A facsimile reprint of a book originally published in 1855, giving the history of the colony of Lutheran Protestants that emigrated to Georgia in 1734 and settled at Ebenezer, near Savannah. Mr. Edward D. Wells of Savannah has prepared a foreword and index for the book.

TYRE, NEDRA. *Journey to Nowhere.* New York, Alfred A. Knopf, 1954. 209p. $2.75.

On a flight to London a girl whom tragedy had pursued throughout her life succumbs to a new terror when mysterious persons seem to be pursuing her.

VANDIVER, JEWELL. *Soundings.* Emory University, Ga., Banner Press, 1954. 80p. $2.00.

A collection of poems by an Atlanta school teacher concerning beauty, truth, and the many facets of everyday living.

WATT, NELL HODGSON. *Ball of Southern Yarns.* Greenville, S. C., Hiott Press, 1953. 54p. $2.00.

A series of short rhymed narratives about people and events in Athens, Georgia.

WHITE, ROBB. *Midshipman Lee of the Naval Academy.* New York, Random House, 1954. 216p. $2.75.

Midshipman Courtney Lee gets through his first two years at Annapolis but worries about the time he will have to go up in a plane again and face the fear that has haunted him ever since the airplane crash he experienced as a child.

WILCOX, GERALD ERASMUS (pseud. Thomas G. E. Wilkes). *Hell's Cauldron.* Atlanta, Stratton-Wilcox Co., 1953. 278p. $3.75.

A former captain in the combat engineers tells his story of confinement as a neuropsychiatric patient in army hospitals, delivers an indictment of the conditions and most of the personnel in the hospitals, and relates how he obtained his release.

WILKES, THOMAS G. E., pseud. See: Wilcox, Gerald Erasmus.

WINGO, CAROLINE ELIZABETH. *The Clothes You Buy and Make.* New York, McGraw-Hill, 1953. 270p. $4.00.

A comprehensive treatment of the complete problem of women's clothes designed as a textbook for the basic clothing course in college. Miss Wingo is a member of the faculty of Georgia Teachers College, Statesboro, Georgia.

YERBY, FRANK. *Bride of Liberty.* Garden City, N. Y., Doubleday, 1954. 219p. $2.50.

Polly Knowles, whose father is a New York Tory, remains true to the young man she loves who has joined Washington's army. This story is written for teen-agers.

Bibliography of Georgia Authors
1954-1955

THE sixth in the REVIEW's series of annual "Bibliographies of Georgia Authors," this annotated bibliography is, as nearly as the compiler could make it, a complete and accurate record of books published by Georgia authors from November 1, 1954, to November 1, 1955. The annotations are descriptive, not critical; intended to place, not to judge the book. U. S., State, County, and City Documents, parts of books, brief analytics, and pamphlets of less than 25 pages have been omitted. Prices are given except when not supplied by publisher or when book is obtainable only on specific request, in which case the word "Apply" is used.

In determining whom to call Georgia authors, the compiler has used the following criteria: authors born in Georgia and claiming Georgia as their native state and those who have lived in Georgia for a period of five years and who did their writing here.

The compiler will welcome and appreciate readers' sending to him any additions or corrections. They may be sent to him at any time in care of the GEORGIA REVIEW. Several books inadvertently omitted from previous Bibliographies are listed here. Any books omitted from the present Bibliography will be included in the list for 1955-1956.

Acknowledgement is made to Mrs. William Tate, member of the University of Georgia Library staff, for her assistance in the preparation of this Bibliography.

AIKEN, CONRAD POTTER. *A Letter from Li Po and Other Poems.* New York, Oxford Press, 1955. 93p. $3.50.

    The title poem in this collection states the function of poetry and the poet in society. The other six poems, also the work of the last five years, are related to the major work. They are available boxed with a Caedmon recording of Aiken reading the title poem and others, for $10.00.

ALEXANDER, HENRY AARON. *Notes on the Alexander Family of South Carolina and Georgia, and Connections.* Atlanta, Privately Printed, 1954. 142p. $5.00.

A profusely illustrated history of the Alexander family and allied branches, of Georgia and South Carolina. The book is available from Goodspeed's Bookshop, Boston, Massachusetts.

ALLEN, CHARLES L. *When the Heart Is Hungry; Christ's Parables for Today.* Westwood, N. J., Fleming H. Revell, 1955. 159p. $2.00.

Inspirational messages based on twenty-two of the parables for today's Christian living. Dr. Allen is pastor of Grace Methodist Church in Atlanta.

BENTON, BONNIE HIGDON. *The Sonnie by Bonnie.* Philadelphia, Dorrance, 1954. 137p. $3.00.

A collection of original, semi-free verse on the realm of reality. The author is a native of Higdon, Georgia.

BIRDSONG, GEORGE L. F. *Sporting Sketches from The Countryman, 1863-1864.* Emory University, Ga., Emory University Library, 1955. 34p. 75 cents.

Three selections of Birdsong's sketches reprinted with notes and introduction by Ward Pafford, Head of the Department of English at Emory University.

BLACKSHEAR, PERRY LYNNFIELD. *Blacksheariana: Genealogy, History, Anecdotes; A Compilation.* Atlanta, Privately Printed, 1954. 476p. $15.00.

An illustrated history of one of the pioneer families of Georgia and the South. This edition is limited to 300 copies.

BLACKSTOCK, WALTER. *The Deeper Bond.* Mill Valley, Calif., The Wings Press, 1955. 61p. $2.00.

A collection of thirty-nine sonnets and lyric poems on a variety of subjects. The author is Assistant Professor of English at Florida State University.

BRAY, COLQUITT C. *The Third Sunday Singing.* Decatur, Ga., William C. Bray Enterprises, 1954. 616p. $5.50.

A novel based on the annual Sunday singings in the rural South and the myriad activities surrounding them.

BROWN, INEZ MARGUERITE. *Will-o'-the-Wisp, and Other Poems.* New York, Pageant Press, 1955. 85p. $2.50.

A wide range of subjects is covered in this collection of poems by an Associate Professor of English on the staff of Middle Georgia College, Cochran, Georgia.

BROWN, WENDELL H. *The Long View.* Atlanta, Foote and Davies, 1954. 228p. Apply.

A classroom text edition of a study of some of the Hebrew prophets. Professor Brown teaches at Oglethorpe University.

BRUNETTI, GEORGE. *The Bawl Game.* Chamblee, Ga., Brunetti and Worrill, 1954. 40p. $1.00.

A pictorial account, with appropriate baseball captions, of episodes before and after the baby's arrival.

BRYAN, FERREBEE CATHERINE. *At the Gates.* Nashville, Broadman Press, 1949. 374p. $3.75.

A biographical account of the lives of Matthew Tyson and Eliza Moring Yates, Baptist missionaries in China. Dr. Bryan, a retired missionary, lives in Atlanta.

BYRON, DORA. *Bishop of Heard County.* Atlanta, Church and Community Institute, 1955. 120p. Cloth, $2.00. Paper, $1.00.

The biography of a circuit-riding Methodist preacher, Dr. J. C. Adams, telling of his fifty years of service to rural people of North Georgia.

CALDWELL, ERSKINE. *Gretta.* Boston, Little, Brown, 1955. 242p. $3.50.

A novel about the life and loves of a secretary in a Midwestern town who sought security through the use of her body.

CALLAWAY, TIMOTHY WALTON. *Callaway Baptist Preachers.* LaGrange, Ga., Fuller E. Callaway Foundation, 1953. 72p. Apply.

An illustrated collection of short biographies of the thirty-one Baptist preachers in the Callaway family, 1789-1953.

CATE, MARGARET DAVIS. *Early Days of Coastal Georgia.* St. Simons, Ga., Fort Frederica Association Publication, 1955. 236p. $6.00.

One hundred and seven photographs with textual descriptions of ancient historical landmarks of coastal Georgia. The concluding section of the book is devoted to descendants of plantation slaves and to some of their cemeteries. The photographs are by Dr. Orrin Sage Wightman. This book is distributed by the University of Georgia Press.

CHRISTOPHER, THOMAS WELDON, and DUNN, C. W., editors. *Special Federal Food and Drug Laws.* New York, Commerce Clearing House, 1954. 1334p. $17.50.

A compilation of statutes, regulations, legislative history, and annotations of Federal food and drug laws. Professor Christopher is Assistant Dean of the Emory University School of Law.

CLECKLEY, HERVEY M., M.D. *The Mask of Sanity.* St. Louis, C. V. Mosby, 1955. Third Edition. 596p. $9.50.

This is a new edition of a study that appeared first in 1941 and again in 1950. This attempt to clarify some of the issues involved in the "psychopathic personality" will aid all those who are seeking a solution to this distressing social disease.

COLEMAN, LONNIE. See: Coleman, William Laurence.

COLEMAN, WILLIAM LAURENCE. *Ship's Company.* Boston, Little, Brown, 1955. 229p. $3.50.

Life aboard the *U.S.S. Nellie Crocker* during the last two years of the Second World War—presented in a series of self-contained stories about members of her crew.

COLLINGS, HENRIETTA, comp. *Georgia's Heritage of Song.* Athens, University of Georgia Press, 1955. 87p. $1.50.

A compilation of fifty songs pertaining to the state of Georgia for use in the public schools. Miss Collings is supervisor of elementary school music, Bibb County, Georgia. The illustrations are by Virginia B. Hall.

CORDER, LOYD. *The New Orleans Story.* Atlanta, Home Mission Board, Southern Baptist Convention, 1954. 95p. 50 cents.
A study of the Baptist missions at work in the metropolitan area of New Orleans.

COULTER, ELLIS MERTON. *Wormsloe: Two Centuries of a Georgia Family.* Athens, University of Georgia Press, 1955. 337p. $5.00. Limited Edition.
The history of one of Georgia's most famous families and its contributions to the life of the state from colonial times to the present. This is number one of the Wormsloe Foundation Publications. Dr. Coulter is Head of the History Department at the University of Georgia.

COULTER, ELLIS MERTON, KING, SPENCER B., JR., and SAYE, ALBERT BERRY. *History of Georgia.* New York, American Book Co., 1954. 448p. $2.66.
A history of Georgia designed for use in the public schools of the state. The book is profusely illustrated and is edited by W. W. Livengood.

CUTTINO, GEORGE PEDDY, translator. *I Laugh Through Tears; the Ballades of Francois Villon.* New York, Philosophical Library, 1955. 79p. $3.50.
Thirty-two ballads of the fifteenth century French poet, twenty-four of them accompanied by historical and explanatory notes. Dr. Cuttino is Associate Professor of History at Emory University.

DAMERON, MRS. W. C. *The History of Fossett, Sudduth, and Montgomery Families.* Atlanta, Privately Printed, 1954. 100p. Apply.
An illustrated family history of several prominent Georgia families.

DERN, MRS. JOHN SHERMAN. See: Gaddis, Peggy.

DODD, ED. *Mark Trail's Book of North American Mammals.* New York, Hawthorn Books, 1955. 242p. $1.95.
A field guide with pictures of the most important of the larger mammals of North America, as seen in their native habitats by the creator of the comic strip "Mark Trail."

DREWRY, JOHN E. *Dimensional Journalism: Press, Radio, Television, Periodicals, Public Relations, and Advertising, As Seen Through Institutes and Special Occasions of the Henry W. Grady School of Journalism, 1954-1955.* Vol. LVI, No. 1. Athens, University of Georgia Bulletin, 1955. 179p. Paper, $2.00. Cloth, $3.00.
A compilation of addresses on journalistic subjects which were delivered at the several institutes, conventions, and special occasions sponsored by the University of Georgia's School of Journalism during the 1954-1955 session.

EDGE, SARAH SIMMS. *Joel Hurt and the Development of Atlanta.* Kingsport, Tenn., Kingsport Press, 1955. 345p. $5.00. Issued as Atlanta Historical Bulletin No. 37.
A biographical account of a nationally recognized financier, builder of skyscrapers, residential developer, and builder of the first successful electric street-railway in the world. The author is the granddaughter of Joel Hurt.

EVERETT, EDWIN M., BROWN, CALVIN S., and WADE, JOHN D., editors. *Master-

works of World Literature. New York, Dryden Press, 1955. **Revised Edition.** Two volumes, v.1 1024p.; v.2 983p. $4.90 each.

A revised and enlarged edition of a popular college anthology of world literature. Each work appears in complete or unitary form.

FAY, ELIOT GILBERT. *Lorenzo in Search of the Sun.* London, Vision, 1955. 148p. 12s 6d.

The English edition of the study of the life of D. H. Lawrence in Italy, Mexico, and the American Southwest. The late Dr. Fay was a staff member at Emory University.

FENSTER, SAMUEL BENJAMIN. *Outline of Georgia Criminal Law.* Atlanta, John Marshall Law School Press, 1951. 76p. $2.65.

An outline of all phases of criminal law in Georgia, prepared by the Dean of the John Marshall Law School.

FLANDERS, BERTRAM HOLLAND. *A New Frontier in Education; The Story of the Atlanta Division, University of Georgia.* Atlanta, Atlanta Division, University of Georgia, 1955. 169p. $2.00.

An illustrated account of the unique development of an institution devoted to educating young men and women who earn their living while attending college.

FORBES, WILLIAM STANTON. *Monologue.* Los Angeles, Privately Printed, 1954. 6p. 25 plates. $100.00. Limited Edition.

A dream sequence of twenty-five original etchings. The edition is limited to forty copies.

FORD, MARCIA, pseud. See: Radford, Ruby Lorraine.

FOSTER, MARIAN CURTIS (pseud. Mariana). *Doki, The Lonely Papoose.* New York, Lothrop, Lee, & Sheppard Co., 1955. 27p. $2.50.

The story of a tiny Indian who wanders off by himself into the woods. Watercolor illustrations are by the author.

GADDIS, PEGGY. *The Joyous Hills.* New York, Arcadia House, 1955. 221p. $2.50.

A rest and romance for a harried department store executive in the Georgia mountains.

GARNETT, CHRISTINE. *Through a Cuban Window.* Atlanta, Home Mission Board, Southern Baptist Convention, 1954. 93p. 50 cents.

An account of young people converted, trained, and serving as Christian leaders in Cuba. The author is a native of Sylvania, Georgia.

GARRISON, KARL C., AARON, IRA E., and BLEDSOE, JOSEPH C. *Workbook in Educational Psychology.* New York, Appleton, 1955. 102p. $1.60.

The twenty units that comprise this workbook are designed to be used in conjunction with any recent textbook in educational psychology. The authors are members of the staff of the College of Education, University of Georgia.

GARRISON, KARL C., and GRAY, JOHN STANLEY. *Educational Psychology.* New York, Appleton, 1955. 524p. $5.00.

A textbook for use in basic courses preparing students to become classroom teachers.

GORDON, HUGH H., JR. *The Family of Edward Reginald Hodgson and Mary Virginia Strahan.* Athens, Privately Printed, 1953. 32p. Apply.
An illustrated history of the Hodgson and Strahan families of Athens, Georgia.

GOSNELL, CULLEN BRYANT, LANCASTER, LANE W., and RANKIN, ROBERT S. *Fundamentals of American National Government.* New York, McGraw-Hill, 1955. 497p. $5.00.
A description of the actual way our national government operates, including the theories and principles which form its basis.

HARRIS, KATHLEEN, pseud. See: Humphries, Adelaide.

HARRIS, SEALE, M. D. *Death of National Democratic Party; The Truth About Truman.* Birmingham, Ala., Privately Printed, 1952. 141p. Apply.
A discourse on the passing of the National Democratic Party, by a prominent Alabama physician. Dr. Harris is a native of Cedartown, Georgia.

HARRIS, SEALE, M.D. *Woman's Surgeon: Life Story of J. Marion Sims.* New York, Macmillan, 1950. 432p. $5.00.
The remarkable life of a nineteenth century doctor who drifted into medicine, discovered his gifts as a surgeon, became a pioneer in the field of gynecology. The book is written in collaboration with Frances Williams Browin.

HART, JOHN FRASER. *The British Moorlands.* Athens, University of Georgia Press, 1955. 106p. Paper, $2.00.
A study in land utilization that examines the area and location of the moorlands and their relation to the remainder of the island. Twenty-five maps illustrate the text.

HARWELL, RICHARD B., editor. *Destruction and Reconstruction by Richard Taylor.* New York, Longmans, Green & Co., 1955. 412p. $7.50.
Memoirs of a Confederate general; originally published in 1879 and long out of print. The editor is a former assistant librarian at Emory University and is now Director of the Southeastern Inter-library Research Facility.

HARWELL, RICHARD B. *Research Resources in the Georgia-Florida Libraries of SIRF.* Atlanta, Southern Regional Educational Board, 1955. 241p. $2.50.
A survey of research resources in the Georgia and Florida libraries of the Southeastern Inter-library Research Facility.

HARWELL, RICHARD B., compiler. *A Union List of Serial Holdings in Chemistry and Allied Fields.* Atlanta, Southern Regional Education Board, 1955. 99p. $1.50.
A compilation of the holdings at Emory University, Georgia Institute of Technology, University of Georgia, Florida State University, University of Florida, and University of Miami for the Georgia-Florida Committee for Planning Research Library Cooperation.

HAWES, LILLA M., editor. *Collections of the Georgia Historical Society,* Vol. XI, Savannah, Georgia Historical Society, 1955. 110p. $3.00.

A collection of the papers of James Jackson (1757-1806), Revolutionary soldier, Governor of Georgia, and United States Senator, the collection covers the years 1781-1798 and is in the library of the Georgia Historical Society.

HAYES, JOHN ALEXANDER. *How Red This Dust.* New York, Pageant Press, 1955. 250p. $3.00.

Chronicle of events in a small, smoldering Southern town, as reflected in the lives of a curiously diverse group of local citizens.

HOLCOMB, WALT. *The Gospel of Grace.* Emory University, Ga., Town and Country Church Book Club, 1955. 144p. $2.50.

A series of lectures first prepared and delivered to young preachers at seminars at Emory University. The book is a distillation of the humor, piety, and faith of a man who has preached the Gospel for fifty years in Georgia and all the corners of the earth.

HOUSER, HARRIET H. *Hentz: Of Things Not Seen.* New York, Macmillan, 1955. 248p. $3.50.

An account of the faith of the Houser family and the courage of their son who was injured in a diving accident in 1951. Mrs. Houser is a native of Perry, Georgia.

HOWARD, ANNIE HORNADY. *Simplified Lessons in Parliamentary Law.* Atlanta, R. C. Smith Printing Co., 1955. 32p. $1.00.

This pocket-sized book giving simplified rules on how to conduct meetings properly is designed primarily for use by clubwomen.

HUMPHRIES, ADELAIDE (pseud. Kathleen Harris). *Jane Arden: Student Nurse.* New York, Bouregy and Curl, 1955. 256p. $2.50.

A student nurse, during her first year in training, falls in love with a handsome doctor and develops romantic problems.

HUMPHRIES, ADELAIDE. *Nurse with Wings.* New York, Bouregy and Curl, 1955. 254p. $2.50.

A flight nurse in Japan gains one romantic attachment as she loses another.

HUMPHRIES, ADELAIDE. *Orchids for the Nurse.* New York, Bouregy and Curl, 1955. 256p. $2.50.

A romance about a nurse in New England who has her choice of men.

HUXFORD, FOLK. *Pioneers of Wiregrass, Georgia.* Adel, Ga., The Patton Publishers, 1954. Vol. II, 384p. $6.00.

A biographical account of some of the early settlers of that portion of Wiregrass, Georgia, embraced in the original counties of Irwin, Appling, Wayne, Camden, and Glynn.

JACOB, PEYTON. *The Behavior Cycle.* Ann Arbor, Mich., Edwards Brothers, 1954. 126p. $2.50.

An interpretation of behavior from the standpoint of an educationist by the late President Emeritus of Georgia Southwestern College.

JACOBS, THORNWELL. *For Heretics Only.* Atlanta, Westminster Publishers, 1954. 293p. $3.75.

A discussion of controversial Christian literature.

JENKINS, WILLIAM FRANKLIN. *Afterthoughts.* Atlanta, Foote and Davies, 1955. 22p. Apply.
 A collection of inspirational poems covering the many facets of life. The author is Associate Justice Emeritus of the Georgia Supreme Court.

JESSUP, RICHARD. *The Cunning and the Haunted.* New York, Fawcett Publications, Inc., 1954. 270p. 35 cents.
 A novel about a Savannah boy who lived in the swamps and of his assistance to two men escaping from a chain gang.

JESSUP, RICHARD. *A Rage to Die.* New York, Fawcett Publications, Inc., 1955. 287p. 35 cents.
 Two strange partners try to take over a corrupt and vice-ridden Southern city.

JORDAN, GERALD RAY. *Beyond Despair.* New York, Macmillan, 1955. 166p. $2.50.
 A guide to developing spiritual capacities so that one may move beyond despair to Christian confidence. Dr. Jordan is Professor of Homiletics and the Chapel Preacher at the School of Theology, Emory University.

KEARNS, WILLIAM H., JR., and BRITTON, BEVERLY. *The Silent Continent.* New York, Harpers, 1955. 237p. $3.50.
 A collection of actual adventure stories about the Antarctic regions and the explorers who have tried to conquer it. The authors are residents of Atlanta.

KELLY, GEORGE LOMBARD, M.D. *Sex Manual, for Those Married or About to Be, Written for the Layman.* Seventh Revised Edition. Catholic Edition. Augusta, Southern Medical Supply Co., 1954. 91p. $1.00.
 A special edition prepared for Catholic laymen on all aspects of sex. Restricted distribution.

KELLY, GEORGE LOMBARD, M. D. *Sex Manual, for Those Married or About to Be, Written for the Layman.* Seventh Revised Edition. Augusta, Southern Medical Supply Co., 1954. 92p. $1.00.
 A simple, direct, and authoritative book containing the forthright answers to those questions most frequently asked on all aspects of sex. Restricted distribution.

KELLY, GEORGE LOMBARD, M. D. *Sexual Relations in Marriage.* London, Torchstream Books, 1954. 127p. 8s 6d.
 A British edition based on the author's authoritative book on all aspects of sex.

KNOX, JAMES. *Sunday's Children.* Boston, Houghton Mifflin, 1955. 186p. $2.75.
 A story of the author's childhood days in a small Shenandoah Valley town forty years ago. The plot centers around the rivalry between the two local churches. The book is illustrated by David Hendrickson.

LAWRENCE, JOHN BENJAMIN. *Holy Spirit in Evangelism.* Grand Rapids, Mich., Zondervan Publishing House, 1954. 88p. $1.50.

A discussion of the need and the necessity of the Holy Spirit in successful evangelism. The author is a resident of Atlanta.

LAWRENCE, JOHN BENJAMIN. *Kindling for Revival Fires.* Westwood, N. J., Fleming H. Revell Co., 1950. 187p. $2.25.
A series of rousing, yet reverent sermons on the "lost art" of evangelism.

LONGSTREET, AUGUSTUS BALDWIN. *Address Delivered at His Inauguration, 10th February, 1840,* by Augustus B. Longstreet, President of Emory College. Edited by Judson C. Ward, Jr. Emory University, Ga., Emory University Library, 1955. 31p. Paper, 75 cents. Emory Publications, Sources and Reprints, Ser. 9, No. 2.
The inaugural address of A. B. Longstreet edited by Judson C. Ward, Jr., Dean of the College of Arts and Sciences at Emory University.

LOWMAN, MRS. GEORGE S., and BOYKIN, MRS. B. M. *Leaders in Georgia in Education, in Business, and in the Arts.* Atlanta, Curtis Printing Co., Inc., 1955. 121p. $10.00.
Illustrated biographies of leaders from all sections of the state in various fields of endeavor.

MCCULLERS, CARSON SMITH. *Die Mär von der Glucklosen Scheneke.* Stuttgart, Reclam, 1954. 95p. Paper, DM1.30.
A translation of *The Ballad of the Sad Cafe* into German by Wolfgang von Einsiedel.

MACRAE, KEVIN. *Nikki.* New York, Vantage Press, 1955. 134p. $2.75.
A novel of "bachelor girls," attempting to understand the problems of Lesbians. The author is a resident of Savannah, Georgia.

MALONE, EVA EARNSHAW. *Jeremiah Dumas Malone.* Wilmington, Del., Charles L. Story Co., 1949. 159p. Apply.
A genealogical outline of the descendants of Jeremiah Dumas Malone and Mary Hale Malone. It is primarily factual, without personal histories other than short biographical sketches. The author was born near Marietta, Georgia.

MALOOF, LOUIS J., editor. *Medical Education in the University.* Gainesville, Fla., University of Florida Press, 1955. 176p. $1.50.
A selective catalog of teaching and research units of the University of Florida, grouped for their potential contribution to medical education and research. The editor is a native of Rome, Georgia.

MARIANA, pseud. See: Foster, Marian Curtis.

MORRIS, JOE LAWRENCE. *Modern Manufacturing Processes.* New York, Prentice-Hall, 1955. 542p. $9.35.
A survey of the principles and processes of manufacturing, explained at a fundamental level. The author is Associate Professor of Mechanical Engineering at Georgia Institute of Technology.

MORRIS, JOE LAWRENCE. *Welding Principles for Engineers.* New York, Prentice-Hall, 1951. 511p. $8.00. Text Edition $6.00.
Welding processes explained for engineering college students rather than for vocational and trade school groups.

Morris, Joe Lawrence. *Welding Processes and Procedures.* New York, Prentice-Hall, 1954. 255p. $5.00.
  History, description, details of use, and information concerning the application and limitations of the more important welding processes—intended for use in colleges, technical institutions, and advanced vocational schools.

O'Connor, Flannery. *A Good Man Is Hard to Find and Other Stories.* New York, Harcourt, Brace, 1955. 251p. $3.50.
  A collection of ten short stories with a bit of Faulkner regional color. The author lives in Milledgeville, Georgia.

Ogburn, Charlton, and Ogburn, Dorothy S. *The Renaissance Man of England.* New York, Coward McCann, 1955. 57p. $1.50. Revised Edition.
  A digest of the authors' work entitled *This Star of England.*

Ogburn, Charlton, and Ogburn, Dorothy S. *This Star of England.* New York, Coward McCann, 1952. 1297p. $10.00.
  A book of monumental research designed to prove that Edward de Vere, Earl of Oxford, wrote the works attributed to Shakespeare.

Ogburn, William Fielding. *Social Change with Respect to Culture and Original Nature.* New York, Viking Press, 1950. 401p. $2.50.
  New 1950 edition with supplementary chapter referring to more recent developments of thought with regard to man's cultural evolution.

Ogburn, William Fielding. *Technology and the Changing Family.* Boston, Houghton Mifflin, 1955. 329p. $3.75.
  An analysis of the relationship between technological developments and changes in the family, using the methodological approach. The author is a native of Butler, Georgia. Meyer F. Nimkoff is co-author of this study.

Ogburn, William Fielding. *Sociology.* Boston, Houghton Mifflin, 1950. Revised Edition. 619p. $5.00.
  A new chapter on war and international relations has been added as well as one on science and sociology. Other changes include the adaptation of statistics and text to the latest sociology developments. Meyer F. Nimkoff is co-author of this study.

Ogburn, William Fielding, editor. *Technology and International Relations.* Chicago, University of Chicago Press, 1949. 208p. $4.00.
  A collection of studies on the world importance of new inventions, scientific discoveries, and technological approaches, and their effect on international relations.

O'Quinn, Allen, pseud. See: Quinter, Al.

Osborn, Stellanova. *Polly Cadotte.* New York, Exposition Press, 1955. 48p. $2.50.
  A tale in verse of Duck Island and the Chippewa Indians.

Outler, Albert Cook, editor and translator. *Augustine: Confessions and Enchiridion.* Philadelphia, Westminster Press, 1955. 423p. $5.00.
  A new edition and translation of two well known works of St. Augustine. This is Volume VII in the Library of Christian Classics.

OUTLER, ALBERT COOK. *Psychotherapy and the Christian Message.* New York, Harpers, 1954. 286p. $3.50.
   The problems of alliance and conflict between the viewpoints of psychotherapy and of Christian thought are examined, defined, and analyzed. The author is a native of Thomasville, Georgia.

PALMER, CHARLES F. *Adventures of a Slum Fighter.* Atlanta, Tupper & Love, 1955. 272p. $4.00.
   The author's personal account of his fight for slum clearance in a campaign that began in the early 1930's, when he organized and directed the clearance of the Techwood slum area in Atlanta.

PARKS, EDD WINFIELD. *Teddy Roosevelt, All-Round Boy.* Indianapolis, Bobbs-Merrill, 1955. 192p. $1.48. School Edition.
   A new edition of the boyhood life of President Theodore Roosevelt, which first appeared in 1953. It is in the *Childhood of Famous Americans Series* and is illustrated by Sandra James.

PAULK, WILLIAM E., JR. *Green Jade Bowl.* Rebecca, Ga., The Persimmon Hill Press, 1955. Limited Edition. 66p. Apply.
   A collection of fifty sensitive lyric poems on nature, love, death, and the many facets of life. The author is a native of Rebecca, Georgia.

PEPPER, HENRY C. *Legal Handbook for County Commissioners.* Atlanta, Association County Commissioners of Georgia, 1955. 103p. $2.00.
   A useful guide prepared for County Commissioners, County Attorneys, and others interested in the office and duties performed by County Commissioners.

PEPPER, HENRY C. *Legislative Process in Georgia.* Atlanta, School of Business Administration, Atlanta Division, University of Georgia, 1955. 70p. 50 cents.
   A study of the legislative processes and committee procedures, and of action taken on bills by committees in the Georgia House of Representatives.

PEPPER, HENRY C. *Sheriff's Handbook.* Atlanta, School of Business Administration, Atlanta Division, University of Georgia, 1953. 111p. $4.00.
   A practical guide for Georgia sheriffs, their deputies, other officials whose knowledge of the duties of the sheriff is useful, and for the citizen who is interested in the duties of the sheriff.

POPE, EDWIN. *Football's Greatest Coaches.* Atlanta, Tupper & Love, 1955. 334p. $3.95.
   The executive sports editor of the *Atlanta Journal* selects twenty-eight famous football coaches and tells their stories. The author is a native of Athens, Georgia.

QUINTER, AL. *Swamp Brat.* New York, Fawcett Publications, Inc., 1953. 180p. 25 cents.
   The complicated love affairs of three people in a small Southern town is the subject of this novel by a resident of Winder, Georgia. This is an original Gold Medal novel—not a reprint.

RADFORD, RUBY LORRAINE. *Dixie Doctor*. New York, Bouregy and Curl, 1955. 255p. $2.50.
   A young doctor tracks down a Communist spy on a hospital staff, and also eventually wins the nurse he loves.

REDFEARN, DANIEL H. *Alexander McDonald of New Inverness, Georgia, and His Descendants*. Miami, Fla., Privately Printed, 1954. 194p. Apply.
   An illustrated history and list of the descendants of Alexander McDonald, who settled in Georgia in 1736.

REDFEARN, DANIEL H. *History of the Redfearn Family*. Miami, Fla., Privately Printed, 1954. 378p. Apply.
   A revised and illustrated account of the descendants of James Redfearn, who settled in Johnson County, North Carolina, in 1763.

REECE, BYRON HERBERT. *The Hawk and the Sun*. New York, Dutton, 1955. 192p. $3.00.
   A novel of violence and the lynching of an innocent man in a Southern town.

REECE, BYRON HERBERT. *The Season of Flesh*. New York, Dutton, 1955. 96p. $2.75.
   A book of poems, dealing with Biblical and regional themes, made up of ballads, lyrics, and sonnets.

ROGERS, RACHAEL EMMELINE (Peeples). *Our Peeples Family*. Atlanta, Privately Printed, 1953. 154p. Apply.
   A comprehensive history of the descendants of William Peeples and his wife Rebecca Johnson.

SCOTT, COL. ROBERT LEE, JR. *Look of the Eagle*. New York, Dodd Mead, 1955. 278p. $3.50.
   A story of a U. S. Air Force jet pilot and his last dangerous mission, against the Chinese Communists.

SEBBA, GREGOR. *Displaced Persons in Georgia*. Athens, 1954. 293p. $3.00. Distributed by University of Georgia Press.
   This report to the Georgia Displaced Persons Committee covers an investigation of 1,200 persons resettled in Georgia under the Displaced Persons Act. Dr. Sebba is Professor of Economics at the University of Georgia.

SMITH, LILLIAN EUGENIA. *Now Is the Time*. New York, Viking Press, 1955. 126p. $2.00.
   The author discusses the immediate meaning of the Supreme Court decision on segregation, the questions that still stand in the way of implementing the decree, and some answers to these questions.

STEELE, HAROLD CLYDE. *I Was a Stranger: the Faith of William Booth, Founder of the Salvation Army*. New York, Exposition Press, 1954. 183p. $3.00.
   A biography of the founder of the Salvation Army and an analysis of his social thinking. The author is an instructor in biology at the Georgia Teachers College. Dr. B. O. Williams, University of Georgia, wrote the foreword.

SWEIGERT, RAY LESLIE, and GOGLIA, MARIO J. *Thermodynamics.* New York, Ronald Press, 1955. 355p. $6.50.
A book for engineering students who, at the beginning of their junior year, have completed courses in college physics and calculus. Dr. Sweigert is Dean of the Graduate Division at the Georgia Institute of Technology, and Dr. Goglia is Professor of Mechanical Engineering there.

TALMADGE, HERMAN EUGENE. *You and Segregation.* Birmingham, Ala., Vulcan Press, 1955. 79p. Paper, $1.00. Cloth, $2.00.
The former governor of Georgia discusses the Supreme Court's segregation decision and its various effects on Georgia, the South, and the nation.

TANKERSLEY, ALLEN P. *John B. Gordon: A Study in Gallantry.* Atlanta, The Whitehall Press, 1955. 400p. $5.00.
A biography of John Brown Gordon, covering the many aspects of the life of this distinguished Confederate general, United States Senator, and Governor of Georgia.

TUCKER, GLENN. *Poltroons and Patriots.* Indianapolis, Bobbs-Merrill, 1954. Two Volumes. 812p. $10.00.
An account of the War of 1812, dwelling not just on the military events but on the thoughts and feelings of the people, and on much biographical and episodic anecdote. The author drew especially on contemporary periodical sources.

VAN ROYEN, RUSSELL G. and VAN ROYEN, EDITH. *Tabo in Panama.* Atlanta, Home Mission Board, Southern Baptist Convention, 1954. 55p. 50 cents.
A picture storybook on missions in Panama and the Canal Zone operated by the Southern Baptist Convention.

VINSON, JOHN CHALMERS. *The Parchment Peace; The United States Senate and the Washington Conference, 1921-1922.* Athens, University of Georgia Press, 1955. 270p. $4.50.
A study of the important role of the Senate in shaping American foreign policy in the years following World War I. The author is Associate Professor of History at the University of Georgia.

WALKER, DANTON M. *Danton's Inferno.* New York, Hastings House, 1955. 312p. $3.95.
Autobiography of a New York newspaperman and Broadway columnist who was born in Marietta, Georgia.

WARE, SARAH POLLARD. *Faith Makes the Difference.* New York, Greenwich Book Publishers, Inc., 1955. 63p. $2.50.
An anesthetist, who has devoted her life to the sick, relates her personal experiences and proves that faith does make a difference both in the sickroom and elsewhere.

WEST, JOHN QUINN. *Mirror of Human Nature American Style.* Fort Lauderdale, Fla., Privately Printed, 1953. 74p. Apply.
Observations on the basic truths and fundamentals of life written by the late John Q. West of Georgia and Florida.

WEST, ROBERT HUNTER. *Milton and the Angels.* Athens, University of Georgia Press, 1955. 240p. $4.50.

John Milton's treatment of angels, together with an analysis of seventeenth century angelology, written by a professor of English at the University of Georgia.

WHITE, HELEN CHAPPELL. *This Is the Life.* New York, Doubleday, 1955. 254p. $3.50.

A collection of ten short stories based on the television series of the same title. Mrs. White is the wife of the president of Emory University.

WHITE, MARY CULLER. *Just Jennie.* Atlanta, Tupper & Love, 1955. 103p. $1.00.

An illustrated account of the life of Virginia M. Atkinson. The author is a retired Methodist missionary to China.

WHITE, WALTER FRANCIS. *How Far the Promised Land?* New York, Viking Press, 1955. 256p. $3.50.

A report on the Negro problem during the last fifteen years by the late leader of the National Association for the Advancement of Colored People. The author was a native of Atlanta.

WILEY, BELL IRVIN, editor. *Confederate Letters of John W. Hagan.* Athens, University of Georgia Press, 1954. 55p. $1.50.

A collection of letters by a Confederate enlisted man to his wife and relatives gives a personalized account of the War as it affected the common soldier. Dr. Wiley is a professor of history at Emory University.

WILEY, BELL IRVIN, editor. *Fourteen Hundred Days in the Confederate Army by W. W. Heartsill.* Jackson, Tenn., McCowart-Mercer Press, 1954. 332p. $6.00.

A journal of camp life in the Confederate army from April 19, 1861, to May 20, 1865.

WILEY, BELL IRVIN, editor. *Rebel Private Front and Rear, by William Andrew Fletcher.* Austin, University of Texas Press, 1954. 162p. $3.75.

Private Fletcher, a Texan, describes in a homespun and colorful manner his encounters during the Civil War. Dr. Wiley has written a preface for this volume.

WILKINS, BOBBY E. *Random Thoughts.* Dallas, Texas, The Story Book Press, 1953. 48p. $2.50.

A collection of forty poems on religion, nature, life, and Georgia. The author is a native of Cobb County, Georgia.

WILLIAMS, NELLIE LOWMAN. *The Golden Circle.* Macon, Ga., J. W. Burke Co., 1954. 36p. Apply.

A collection of spiritual, philosophical, and inspirational poems by a native of Fitzgerald, Georgia.

WILLIAMS, RALPH ROGER, editor. *Standard Georgia Practice with Forms.* Rochester, New York, Lawyers Cooperative Publishing Co., 1955. Vols. I and II. $15.00 each.

A comprehensive text statement of pleading and practice in civil cases in Georgia, together with appropriate forms, including a treatment of evidence and matters of trial and appellate procedure. These are two volumes of a proposed set of six.

WILLINGHAM, CALDER. *To Eat a Peach.* New York, Dial, 1955. 247p. $3.00.
Madeline Jerome is a beautiful instructor at a boys' camp in the South. Her effect on the otherwise male population of Camp Walden results in some amusing and startling incidents, interwoven with a love story.

WOOD, WILLIAM THOMAS and WOOD, MARIE STEVENS. *Flower Show Know-How.* Macon, Ga., Merriwoode Press, 1954. 71p. $2.75; paper $1.00.
An illustrated booklet on how to stage a flower show, how to conduct a flower show, and how to win blue ribbons with flowers.

YERBY, FRANK. *Benton's Row.* New York, Dial, 1954. 346p. $3.50.
The story of four brawling generations of the Bentons of Louisiana. Marriage, love, death, and war, with an historical background climaxing in World War I, are presented in this tremendous span of a Delta family.

YERBY, FRANK. *Treasure of Pleasant Valley.* New York, Dial, 1955. 348p. $3.50.
An historical novel of gold rush days in California and a hero from the South who seeks a good living, happiness, and love in existence as a farmer rather than as a prospector.

Bibliography of Georgia Authors
1955-1956

THE seventh in the REVIEW's series of annual "Bibliographies of Georgia Authors," this annotated bibliography is, as nearly as the compiler could make it, a complete and accurate record of books published by Georgia authors from November 1, 1955, to November 1, 1956. The annotations are descriptive, not critical; intended to place, not to judge the book. U. S., State, County, and City Documents, parts of books, brief analytics, and pamphlets of less than 25 pages have been omitted. Prices are given except when not supplied by publisher or when book is obtainable only on specific request, in which case the word "Apply" is used.

In determining whom to call Georgia authors, the compiler has used the following criteria: authors born in Georgia and claiming Georgia as their native state and those who have lived in Georgia for a period of five years and who did their writing here.

The compiler will welcome and appreciate readers' sending to him any additions or corrections. They may be sent to him at any time in care of the GEORGIA REVIEW. Several books inadvertently omitted from previous Bibliographies are listed here. Any books omitted from the present Bibliography will be included in the list for 1956-1957.

Acknowledgement is made to Mrs. William Tate, member of the staff of the University of Georgia Library, for her assistance in the preparation of this Bibliography.

ALLEN, CATHERINE LOUISE. *Fun for Parties and Programs*. Englewood Cliffs, N. J., Prentice-Hall, 1956. 157p. $3.95. Text Edition, $2.95.
    An inclusive guide book for the social recreation leader, it tells how to lead any type of group in games, stunts, and activities, and it gives instructions on how to plan parties. The author is a native of Columbus, Georgia.

BAKER, WOOLFORD BALES, HARRIS, LUCIEN, JR., and ROGERS, WALLACE. *Southern Nature Stories*. Atlanta, Turner E. Smith, 1956. Three volumes, v.1 244p.; v.2 256p.; v.3 280p. $2.96 each.
    A series of three books in natural science designed to acquaint pupils in the fourth grade and above with facts about nature which they may verify by personal observation and experience.

BARBER, SADIE PIKE. *Beverly Butterfly.* New York, Comet Press Books, 1955. Unpaged. $2.00.

The adventures, told in verse, of a little butterfly which travels from one end of the country to the other. Mrs. Barber is the mother of four young children and lives in LaGrange, Georgia.

BARROW, ELFRIDA DeRENNE and BELL, LAURA PALMER. *Anchored Yesterdays.* Darien, Ga. Printed by the Ashantilly Press for the Little House, Savannah, 1956. Second Edition. 135p. $3.50.

A new edition of the history of Savannah, Georgia, written in the form of a log book recording the city's voyage across a Georgia century, in ten watches. The authors are residents of Savannah.

BEESON, LEOLA SELMAN. *Historical Sketch of the First Presbyterian Church of Milledgeville, Georgia.* Milledgeville, Ga., First Presbyterian Church, 1955. 151p. $2.00.

An illustrated account of the 120-year history of the First Presbyterian Church of Milledgeville, Georgia.

BOLES, PAUL DARCY. *Glenport, Illinois.* New York, Macmillan, 1956. 424p. $4.50.

The story of a town as seen through the eyes of a twelve-year-old boy, Tone Grayleaf, who moves there with his parents in 1929, then grows to manhood and dies in World War II.

BOWERS, EDGAR. *The Form of Loss.* Denver, Colo., Allen Swallow, 1956. 48p. $2.00.

A brief collection of poems by a young Georgia poet.

BROOKS, ROBERT PRESTON. *The University of Georgia Under Sixteen Administrations, 1785-1955.* Athens, University of Georgia Press, 1956. 260p. $4.50.

A detailed history of the University of Georgia, emphasizing all phases of the University's growth, including changes in the curriculum as they have come about from the early years to the present administration of President O. C. Aderhold.

BROWN, CALVIN S., editor. *The Reader's Companion to World Literature.* Mentor paper-bound edition. New York, New American Library, 1956. 493p. 50 cents. Hard-cover edition: New York, Dryden Press, 1956. 493p. $3.50.

This reference book contains information on authors, individual works, literary terms, mythological figures, and literary periods. Edited by Dr. Brown, Professor of English at the University of Georgia, it is the work of eight scholars at the Universities of Georgia, Indiana, Miami, Arizona, Washington, New York, and Howard.

BROWN, ROBERT HENRY. *Farm Electrification.* New York, McGraw-Hill, 1956. 367p. $7.00.

This college-level text on farm electrification is designed for the agricultural student who wishes to acquire a good general knowledge of electricity and its application to farm electrical systems and equipment.

The author is an Associate Professor of Agricultural Engineering at the University of Georgia.

BRYAN, MARY G., and HAWES, LILLA M., editors. *Georgia Date Book, 1957.* Boston, Colonial Publishing Co., 1956. 54p. $1.50.

An illustrated, annotated calendar and date book compiled in collaboration with the State Department of Archives and History and the Georgia Historical Society; with Margaret Davis Cate, Bessie Lewis, and Lewis Larsen, Jr., as contributors. The subject matter of this first issue is Georgia colonial history.

CALDWELL, ERSKINE. *Erskine Caldwell's Gulf Coast Stories.* Boston, Little, Brown, 1956. 248p. $3.50.

Short stories set in varying Southern locales. The moods range from lighthearted comedy to bitter tragedy.

CARTER, VIRGINIA L., and WHITTLE, CONNIE R. *Happy Scrappy.* New York, Vantage Press, 1956. 47p. $2.00.

Happy Scrappy, a mischievous squirrel, creates quite a problem as the result of his many pranks. The book is illustrated by Ray A. Duttry of Atlanta. The book, based on fact, was written by two nurses at the Emory University Hospital.

COLLINS, THOMAS. *The Golden Years: An Introduction to Retirement.* New York, John Day, 1956. 251p. $3.75.

A practical guide to retirement at the age of sixty-five. The author, who conducts a syndicated newspaper column under the same title as the book, has given many examples of actual cases of his readers' retirement problems and how they solved them.

COLQUITT, JOSEPH C. *The Art and Development of Freight Classification.* Washington, D. C., National Motor Freight Traffic Association, 1956. 423p. $6.00.

The book presents the history, development, and techniques of freight classification. The author is a member of an old Savannah, Georgia, family.

COULTER, ELLIS MERTON. *Auraria: The Story of a Georgia Gold-mining Town.* Athens, University of Georgia Press, 1956. 160p. $3.00.

A close-up view of an exciting period of gold-mining history in the South ante-dating by almost two decades the mining booms in the West. Auraria, the first gold-mining town in America, is located in north Georgia, and today is one of Georgia's famous "dead towns."

COULTER, ELLIS MERTON. *Lost Generation: The Life and Death of James Barrow, C. S. A.* Tuscaloosa, Ala., Confederate Publishing Co., 1956. 118p. $4.00.

The life and letters of a young Confederate officer typifying a generation denied, by death in battle, the chance of future greatness. This is the first in a series of Confederate Centennial Studies. Dr. Coulter is Head of the History Department at the University of Georgia.

DAVIS, WILLIAM E. *Fleetfoot, and Other Stories.* New York, Vantage Press, 1956. 114p. $2.00.

A collection of short stories about animals and life in the South. Mr. Davis is a native of Jesup, Georgia.

DERN, MRS. JOHN SHERMAN. See: GADDIS, PEGGY.

DODD, HUBERT. *The Weeping God.* New York, Vantage Press, 1956. 70p. $2.00.

The author tells in poetic symbols his own search for God and religion. The Reverend Dodd, a native of Bartow County, Georgia, is the minister of the Forsyth, Georgia, Methodist Church.

DOKOS, COSMAS J. *The Common Touch.* New York, Vantage Press, 1956. 109p. $3.00.

A book of poems dealing with life and nature and their many ramifications. The author lives in Columbus, Georgia.

DONAHUE, CHENEY BRADSHAW. *My Children's Stories.* New York, Pageant Press, 1955. 47p. $2.00.

A collection of four bedtime stories for children between the ages of three and six. Mrs. Donahue lives in Rome, Georgia. The illustrations are by Dave Lyons.

DREWRY, JOHN E., editor. *Communication Problems and Progress: Press, Radio, Television, Periodicals, Public Relations, and Advertising As Seen Through Institutes and Special Occasions of the Henry W. Grady School of Journalism, 1955-1956.* Vol. LVII, No. 2. Athens, University of Georgia Bulletin, 1956. 179p. Paper, $2.00. Cloth, $3.00.

A compilation of addresses on journalistic subjects which were delivered at the several institutes, conventions, and special occasions sponsored by the University of Georgia's School of Journalism during the 1955-1956 session.

EDMONDS, RICHARD W. *Young Captain Barney.* Philadelphia, Macrae-Smith Co., 1956. 248p. $2.75.

An historical novel based on the life of young Joshua Barney, an eighteenth century American seaman who, at the tender age of fifteen, became the captain of a sailing ship with a crew of full grown men.

ETHRIDGE, WILLIE SNOW. *Nila.* New York, Simon and Schuster, 1956. 241p. $3.50.

An account of Mrs. Robert Magidoff's life in Russia, her exile in Siberia, and her marriage to a correspondent for the National Broadcasting System, which brought her to America in 1941.

FINCH, MILDRED AUSTIN, editor. *Poetry Prisms, Anthology of the Manuscript Club of Atlanta, Georgia.* Emory University, Ga., Banner Press, 1956. 71p. $2.00.

A collection of poems by Atlanta poets, reflecting the emotions of the heart.

FOLGER, JOHN K. *Future School and College Enrollments in the Southern Region.* Atlanta, Southern Regional Education Board, 1954. 34p. Apply.

A study of the problems arising from the increased enrollment in schools and colleges in the South. It is illustrated with statistical tables.

FORD, MARCIA, pseud. See: RADFORD, RUBY LORRAINE.

FOWLER, GRADY. *Three Races Under God.* New York, Vantage Press, 1956. 172p. $2.75.

A LaGrange, Georgia, businessman has drawn on an estimated 20,000 hours of Bible study to write this study giving his proposals for an approach to the solution of the race problem.

GADDIS, PEGGY. *City Nurse.* New York, Arcadia House, 1956. 224p. $2.50.

A young private nurse caring for a crotchety old man has to defend herself against the jealousy of his sister-in-law.

GADDIS, PEGGY (pseud. PEGGY DERN). *County Nurse.* New York, Arcadia House, 1956. 224p. $2.50.

Beth Mason, a nurse in a small backwoods community, finds herself working with a doctor who resents his obligation to work in so isolated an area.

GADDIS, PEGGY. *Magic in May.* New York, Arcadia House, 1956. 223p. $2.50.

A registered nurse, Sally Sinclair, turns what she thought was to be a vacation on the Georgia coast into days of work for young children.

GADDIS, PEGGY (pseud. PEGGY DERN). *Nurse Ellen.* New York, Arcadia House, 1956. 222p. $2.50.

Nurse Ellen Burke dedicates her work and love to Doctor Henry Griswold, a widower who is afraid to acknowledge his love for her.

GADDIS, PEGGY. *Roses in December.* New York, Arcadia House, 1955. 219p. $2.50.

A novel set in North Georgia and telling of the happenings when a summer theatre group offers to pay handsome rent for an old barn.

GAILLARD, PEYRE. *The Amazing Mr. Mocker.* New York, Comet Press Books, 1955. 65p. $2.50.

A definitive study of the most intriguing and talented of American birds—*mimus polyglottus*, more commonly known as the Mockingbird. The author is a native of Savannah, Georgia.

GARRISON, KARL C. *The Psychology of Adolescence.* Englewood Cliffs, N. J., Prentice-Hall, 1956. Fifth Edition. 529p. $6.00.

This new edition, using the biological concept of individual development, pictures the adolescent as a unified personality growing and developing in accordance with his genetic constitution and the environmental forces that have affected him from birth.

GIBSON, ROBERT E. *The Office of the Justice of the Peace in Georgia.* Athens, Institute of Law and Government, School of Law, University of Georgia, 1956. 136p. Paper, $2.00. Cloth, $2.50.

A study of the statutory provisions and common law rules applicable to the office of justice of the peace in Georgia and to practice in the justice court. Mr. Gibson is an attorney in Athens.

GILDEA, FLORENCE. *Kathy.* New York, Vantage Press, 1955. 300p. $3.50.

A novel about a girl who becomes involved in the activities of a Communist spy ring. The author is a native of Savannah, Georgia.

GILMAN, GLENN. See: GILMAN, GLENDELL WILLIAM.

GILMAN, GLENDELL WILLIAM. *Human Relations in the Industrial Southeast: A Study of the Textile Industry.* Chapel Hill, N. C., University of North Carolina Press, 1956. 339p. $5.00.

A sociological and psychological study of the regeneration of industry in the South from the end of the Civil War until the present. Taking the cotton textile industry and its mill communities as an example, it stresses local, regional, and national influences on the development of a pattern of human relations in industry. The author is an Associate Professor of Industrial Management at the Georgia Institute of Technology.

GNANN, PEARL RAHN, compiler and editor. *Georgia Salzburgers and Allied Families.* Macon, Ga. Published by Pearl R. Gnann, Genealogist, Georgia Salzburger Society, 1956. Printed by J. W. Burke & Co., 537p. $12.50.

A compilation of data concerning Georgia Salzburgers from records in courthouses, churches, family Bibles, cemeteries, books, documents, and family papers. This book may be obtained from Mrs. W. G. Gnann, 425 Bull Street, Savannah, Georgia.

GODFREY, CAROLINE HARDEE. *Home in the Orange Grove.* Nashville, Tenn., Benson Publishing Co., 1956. 76p. $3.00.

A collection of poems concerning religion, nature, and life as seen from the dormer windows at the author's plantation home. Mrs. Godfrey lives in Covington, Georgia.

GOSNELL, CULLEN BRYANT, and ANDERSON, C. DAVID. *The Government and Administration of Georgia.* New York, Thomas Y. Crowell Co., 1956. 422p. $4.95.

A college textbook on the structure, functions, and problems of government at both state and local levels in Georgia. Dr. Gosnell is Professor of Political Science at Emory University, and Mr. Anderson is Instructor of Social Studies at Emory-at-Oxford.

GOVAN, GILBERT E., and LIVINGOOD, JAMES W. *A Different Valor: The Story of General Joseph E. Johnston, C. S. A.* Indianapolis, Ind., Bobbs-Merrill, 1956. 412p. $6.00.

This biography of General Johnston is also a study of the South and the Civil War and of Jefferson Davis, with whom the General was often in disagreement. Mr. Govan was born in Atlanta and is now Librarian at the University of Chattanooga.

GRANT, DANIEL T. *When the Melon Is Ripe.* New York, Exposition Press, 1955. 174p. $3.50.

The autobiography of a Negro High School Principal and Minister who lives in Americus, Georgia.

GUTZKE, MANFORD GEORGE. *John Dewey's Thought and Its Implications for Christian Education.* New York, Kings Crown Press, 1956. 270p. $4.00.

A discussion of processes involved in education, to show that the method of education now used in schools can also be used in Christian education. Dr. Gutzke is Professor of English Bible and Christian Education at Columbia Theological Seminary in Decatur, Georgia.

HARRIS, KATHLEEN, pseud. See: HUMPHRIES, ADELAIDE.

HARWELL, RICHARD BARKSDALE, editor. *The Committees of Safety of Westmoreland and Fincastle.* Richmond, Va., Virginia State Library, 1956. 127p. $1.00.

Proceedings of two Virginia county committees covering the years 1774-1776. The editor, a native of Washington, Georgia, is director of publications at the Virginia State Library.

HAYGOOD, WILLIAM CONVERSE. *The Ides of August: A Novel.* Cleveland, Ohio, World Publishing Co., 1956. 376p. $4.75.

A humorous view of expatriate life on the Spanish isle of Mallorca, where some arty Americans and English intellectuals exchange culture with the down-to-earth natives. Mr. Haygood is a native of Atlanta.

HENDERSON, LEGRAND (Pseud. LeGrand). *Matilda.* Nashville, Tenn., Abingdon Press, 1956. 63p. $2.00.

The story of a goat who, when she isn't eating, helps Columbia University's football team win games. The illustrations are by the author.

HENRY, INEZ, and KANE, HARNETT. *Miracle in the Mountains.* New York, Doubleday, 1956. 320p. $3.50.

A full-length biography of Martha Berry and the story of the Berry Schools in the North Georgia mountains.

HINMAN, DOROTHY. *Reading Made Easy—for Johnny, for Teacher, for Mother.* New York, Bookman Associates, 1956. 96p. $1.50.

A workbook for teaching reading by phonetics. This book has been written after years of study and teaching reading. The author is the director of the Hinman School in Atlanta.

HOLDEN, GENEVIEVE. *The Velvet Target.* Garden City, N. Y., Doubleday, 1956. 192p. $2.75.

Eve Halsey believes her aunt has married a fortune hunter and prospective murderer and enlists police aid to prove her point. This is a Crime Club selection. The author lives in Atlanta.

HOLLEY, JOSEPH WINTHROP. *Education and the Segregation Issue.* New York, William-Frederick Press, 1956. 62p. $3.00.

A plan for integration and better race relations set forth by the President Emeritus of Albany State College, a unit of the University System of Georgia.

HOLLEY, JOSEPH WINTHROP. *Regnum Montis.* New York, William-Frederick Press, 1954. 112p. $3.00.

The author is convinced that scriptural and historical evidence indicates that the age of the Regnum Montis is now upon us, and that the social and economic destiny of the South is interwoven with the Second Advent of Christ.

HUMPHRIES, ADELAIDE (pseud. KATHLEEN HARRIS). *Jane Arden, Registered Nurse.* New York, Bouregy and Curl, 1956. 224p. $2.50.

When her fashion-model sister invites her to visit Palm Beach and see about accepting a nursing position in Florida, Jane Arden is thrown into a glamorous new world where all the people she knew from back home seem strangers.

HUMPHRIES, ADELAIDE. *New England Nurse*. New York, Bouregy and Curl, 1956. 224p. $2.50.

Judy Andrews, an expert skier but a novice at romance, almost loses her heart to the wrong man.

HUMPHRIES, ADELAIDE. *Park Avenue Nurse*. New York, Avalon Books, 1956. 222p. $2.50.

The life and loves of a small town girl who is a nurse in the plush office of a New York City doctor.

ISLEY, DORIS NATELLE. *Bibliography of the Control of Roadside Development*. Atlanta, School of Architecture, Georgia Institute of Technology, 1955. 35p. Apply.

This bibliography compiled by the Librarian of the School of Architecture at Georgia Tech includes references to court cases and judicial decisions as well as book and periodical material.

JESSUP, RICHARD. *Cry Passion*. New York, Dell, 1956. 224p. 25 cents.

A young police lieutenant investigates the murder of wealthy K. T. Mcduff's loose-living wife. The story has a Georgia setting.

JESSUP, RICHARD. *Night Boat to Paris*. New York, Dell, 1956. 158p. 25 cents.

A former war hero becomes involved with a gang of thieves, gamblers, and blackmailers over some microfilm that he has been sent to France to obtain for a charity organization in America.

JONES, HOUSTON G. *Bedford Brown: State Rights Unionist*. Carrollton, Ga., Privately Printed, 1955. 54p. Apply.

An account of the political life of Bedford Brown of North Carolina, one of the best known leaders of the Democratic Party in the South during the period 1830-1870. The author is Chairman of the Division of Social Sciences at West Georgia College, Carrollton, Georgia.

JONES, WILLIAM POWELL. *James Joyce and the Common Reader*. Norman, Okla., University of Oklahoma Press, 1955. 179p. $3.00.

This study provides an analysis and an evaluation of the complete works of this artistic revolutionary, James Joyce. The author is a native Georgian and at present is Chairman of the English Department at Western Reserve University in Cleveland, Ohio.

KEELER, CLYDE E. *Land of the Moon-Children: The Primitive Culture of the San Blas Indians*. Athens, University of Georgia Press, 1956. 236p. $4.00.

A firsthand account of the traditions, rituals, religious beliefs, and way of life of the San Blas Indians off the coast of Panama. Illustrated. The author is a member of the Biology Department at Georgia State College for Women, Milledgeville, Georgia.

KIMBALL, GARNET DAVIS. *Poems*. Atlanta, Privately Printed, 1956. 90p. $2.50.

A collection of poems dealing with the many facets of life.

KING, FRANK P., and HARDIN, L. S. *Better Farm Management*. Atlanta, Turner E. Smith, 1956. 436p. $3.95.

This text, designed primarily for students and young farmers, is mainly an evaluation of problems which face the farmer and suggested courses of action for solving those problems. Dr. King is the Director of the Georgia Coastal Plain Experiment Station at Tifton, Georgia.

KNIGHT, HENRY. *One God, One Country, One Church.* New York, Vantage Press, 1956. 116p. $2.50.

An impassioned plea, by a resident of Columbus, Georgia, for mankind to get back on the road, to follow the true way—the path started in the Bible.

LEGRAND, pseud. See: HENDERSON, LEGRAND.

LEMLY, JAMES H. *Economic Consequences of Highways By-Passing Urban Communities.* Atlanta, Bureau of Business and Economic Research, Georgia State College of Business Administration, 1956. 53p. Apply.

This survey of the existing studies pertaining to the economic effects of by-passes upon nearby urban areas has been undertaken to provide information on one segment of the highway construction problem. The author is Chairman of the Department of Transportation and Public Utilities at the Georgia State College of Business Administration.

LERCHE, CHARLES O., JR. *Principles of International Politics.* New York, Oxford University Press, 1956. 441p. $5.00.

An introduction to international politics, the fundamental principles of the subject and their applications to actual situations existing in the modern world. Written for the student or general reader by an Associate Professor of Political Science at Emory University.

LOCHRIDGE, BETSY HOPKINS. *Blue River.* New York, Macmillan, 1956. 124p. $2.75.

A collection of sixteen short stories depicting life in a small Southern town, called Blue River. Mrs. Lochridge is a native of Atlanta.

LUNCEFORD, ALVIN MELL, JR. *Early Records of Taliaferro County, Georgia.* Crawfordville, Ga., Privately Printed, 1956. 126p. $7.50.

A compilation of the militia, lottery, marriage, and will records of this Georgia county from its founding in 1825 to the present. It is intended as a reference work for the historian and genealogist. The author is a native of Crawfordville, Georgia.

MALONE, HENRY THOMPSON. *Cherokees of the Old South: A People in Transition.* Athens, University of Georgia Press, 1956. 238p. $4.00.

This is the story of a social transformation of the Cherokee Nation which resulted in an odd culture, a red-white amalgam, during the early nineteenth century. The invasion of the Cherokee lands by white men, in the 1830's, rudely shattered their dreams of greater progress. The author is Professor of History at the Georgia State College of Business Administration.

MARSHALL, EDISON. *The Gentleman.* New York, Farrar, Straus, & Cudahy, 1956. 406p. $3.95.

A Southerner's search for respectability leads him to a gambler's life and new adventures in South Carolina, the Caribbean, and Africa. The setting is in the mid-nineteenth century.

MARSHALL, EDISON. *The Heart of the Hunter*. New York, McGraw-Hill, 1956. 328p. $4.75.

Memoirs of the author's experiences as a big game hunter in Canada, Africa, and Asia.

MARTIN, HAROLD H. *Soldier: The Memoirs of Matthew B. Ridgway*. New York, Harpers, 1956. 361p. $5.00.

Memoirs of the former Supreme Commander of S H A P E and Chief of Staff of the U. S. Army. They deal with his whole life but emphasize his army career during and after World War II. Harold Martin is a native of Commerce, Georgia.

MARTOF, BERNARD S. *Amphibians and Reptiles of Georgia*. Athens, University of Georgia Press, 1956. 94p. $2.00.

The first comprehensive account of the herpetofauna of Georgia, it is designed to be used by students, sportsmen, Boy Scouts, and others interested in outdoor life. The author is a member of the Zoology Department at the University of Georgia.

MIZE, LEILA RITCHIE, and MIZE, JESSIE JULIA. *Threads of Ancestors—Telford, Ritchie, Mize*. Athens, University of Georgia Printing Department, 1956. 281p. $6.00.

A genealogy of the Telford, Ritchie, and Mize families, with historical references to war services and records of migration of people through the Southeast. Mrs. Leila Mize is a retired member of the faculty of the Agricultural Extension Department, and her daughter, Dr. Jessie Mize, is an Associate Professor in the School of Home Economics at the University of Georgia.

MOBLEY, M. D., and HOSKINS, ROBERT N. *Forestry in the South*. Atlanta, Turner E. Smith, 1956. 448p. $3.95.

A comprehensive study of the latest information on forestry practices, including drawings and illustrations on how to plant and heel-in seedlings, and how to perform numerous other jobs related to this field.

MONSEES, CASEY F. *At Last I Am Free*. Atlanta, Broadwell Press, 1956. 74p. $2.00.

A testimony of how God changed a life, bound by the chains of sin, and made it useful. The author lives in Atlanta.

MOORE, HARRIET MAHAFFEY. *Dixie Is My Home*. Charlotte, N. C., Morehead Press, 1955. 71p. $2.75.

A collection of poems with a distinctive Southern flavor written by an Elberton, Georgia, newspaper columnist. The poems concern the seasons, nature, and home.

PAULK, WILLIAM E., JR. *Earth-Chant, a Litany*. Rebecca, Ga., The Persimmon Hill Press, 1956. Limited edition. 26p. Apply.

An antiphonal chant of a psalm of love and devotion. The author is a member of the English Department at the University of Georgia.

POPE, CLIFFORD HILLHOUSE. *The Reptile World: A Natural History of the*

Snakes, Lizards, Turtles, and Crocodilians. New York, Knopf, 1955. 324p. $7.50.

General accounts of each reptile group and descriptions of its species with special attention to the reptiles of the United States and adjacent countries and with emphasis on function and distribution rather than anatomy and structure. Profusely illustrated. The author is a native of Washington, Georgia.

POSNER, JACK. *Nothing Goes to Waste.* New York, Pageant Press, 1956. 261p. $3.50.

A story about a young woman's attempt to learn the meat-packing business, and of her adventures in trying to save her company from the grip of gamblers. The author lives in Cumming, Georgia.

RADFORD, RUBY LORRAINE. *Kathy Phillips, Scriptwriter.* New York, Bouregy and Curl, 1956. 222p. $2.50.

Kathy and a handsome member of the art department of the local TV station work out a puppet show and then look for a sponsor.

RADFORD, RUBY LORRAINE. *Nurse in the Pinelands.* New York, Bouregy and Curl, 1955. 252p. $2.50.

The romance of a young nurse in the foothills of South Carolina.

RECE, ELLIS HEBER, and BEARDSLEE, WILLIAM A. *Reading the Bible: A Guide.* Englewood Cliffs, N. J., Prentice-Hall, 1956. 200p. $3.75. Text edition, $2.25.

A new study-guide to the Bible containing information on how to read the Bible, a short history of the English Bible, a selection of passages, questions, and suggested readings in a number of interpretive books.

RIDGE, JOHN ROLLIN. *The Life and Adventures of Joaquin Murieta, the Celebrated California Bandit.* Norman, Okla., University of Oklahoma Press, 1955. 159p. $2.00.

An account—which first appeared in print in 1854—of the deeds of a California outlaw in the early days of the gold rush. The author, John Rollin Ridge, or Yellow Bird, was a Cherokee Indian born in Georgia in 1827. This edition has an introduction by Joseph Henry Jackson, Literary Editor of the San Francisco *Chronicle.*

ROGERS, ERNEST. *Peachtree Parade.* Atlanta, Tupper and Love, 1956. 221p. $3.00.

Recollections of a beloved Atlanta citizen and a staff member of the Atlanta *Journal* for more than thirty-five years.

SCOTT, HAROLD GEORGE. *Epithalamion.* Atlanta, Foote & Davies, 1955. 33p. $2.00.

A tribute of love and devotion, by the author, to his wife.

SEARS, WILLIAM H. *Excavations at Kolomoki: Final Report.* Athens, University of Georgia Press, 1956. 120p. $3.50.

The fifth and final report presenting an overall synthesis and interpretation of five years of archeological excavations at the Kolomoki Indian mounds located in South Georgia.

SMITH, C. JAY, JR. *The Russian Struggle for Power: 1914-1917.* New York,

Philosophical Library, 1956. 568p. $4.75.

A study of Russian foreign policy during the First World War, including the alliances, entanglements, treaties, and the collapse of Russia as a great power. The author is an Assistant Professor of History at the University of Georgia.

SMITH, VIRGINIA FIELD. *Women at Work*. Denver, Colo., Colorado State Federation of the National Federation of Business and Professional Women's Clubs, 1955. 82p. Apply.

This study points up a plan to meet the challenge of women workers to parents, schools, and employers to insure saving the talents of youth, and the future labor supply. Dr. Smith is Director of Guidance in the Richmond County, Georgia, schools.

STEPHENS, LEILA. *Enthralled*. Emory University, Ga., Banner Press, 1956. 76p. $2.50.

A collection of inspirational poems written by a resident of Fitzgerald, Georgia.

STEVENSON, ELIZABETH. *Henry Adams: A Biography*. New York, Macmillan, 1955. 439p. $6.00.

This full-length biography is the first comprehensive account of Adams' life, thought, and personality that has been written. It won the 1955 Bancroft Prize given by Columbia University for distinguished writings in American history.

STEVENSON, MARY B. *Latchkeys to the Heart*. Birmingham, Ala., Vulcan Press, 1956. 68p. $2.50.

A collection of 145 inspirational poems by the wife of an Atlanta, Georgia, Methodist minister. The poems deal with nature, travel, religion, and the sympathetic understanding of the human heart.

STEWARD, DAVENPORT. *Way of a Buccaneer*. New York, Dutton, 1956. 320p. $3.95.

Wayne Thorpe, a handsome young Englishman, enslaved by the Spanish soldiers in Panama, escapes and joins the crew of pirate Henry Morgan. Thorpe's buccaneer activities are filled with bloody land and sea fighting and tempestuous love affairs.

SURRENCY, ERWIN CAMPBELL, editor. *The Marshall Reader*. New York, Oceana, 1956. 256p. $3.50.

Carefully chosen excerpts from the mass of material about Chief Justice John Marshall point up the far-reaching consequences of his decisions. This compilation is primarily for students of law and constitutional history. The editor is a native of Jesup, Georgia.

SWANSON, ERNST, and GRIFFIN, JOHN, editors. *Public Education in the South Today and Tomorrow*. Chapel Hill, N. C., University of North Carolina Press, 1956. 137p. $5.00.

This study brings together in a statistical manner some of the basic data through which Southern schooling must be seen if a proper understanding of the problems of desegregation are to be understood. Mr. Swanson is Professor of Economics at Emory University, and Mr. Griffin is an Associate Professor of Economics and Director of Community Educational Services at Emory University.

THOMPSON, CICERO L. *Sands of Time*. New York, Pageant Press, 1956. 77p. $2.50.

A group of sensitive poems dealing with the elemental experiences of man. The author lives in Thomasville, Georgia.

TRAVIS, ROBERT JESSE. *The Travis (Travers) Family and Its Allies*. Decatur, Ga., Bowen Press, 1954. 194p. $10.00.

A genealogical history of the Travis, Darracott, Lewis, Livingston, Nicholson, McLaughlin, Pharr, Smith, and Terrell families. The book was compiled by Major General Robert Jesse Travis, a native of Conyers, Georgia, now a resident of Savannah.

TUCKER, GLENN. *Tecumseh—Vision of Glory*. Indianapolis, Ind., Bobbs-Merrill, 1956. 399p. $5.00.

A biography of the famous Chief of the Shawnee who attempted to unite all the Indian tribes in order to prevent white settlers from invading the Northeast in the early 1800's. The author is a part-time resident of Georgia whose North Georgia farm is named "Filibuster Hill."

VANCE, HENRY C. *Day Before Yesterday*. Birmingham, Ala., Vulcan Press, 1956. 121p. $2.50.

Life in a small Southern community fifty years ago, as told in chapters, each dealing with an individual citizen and his inter-relationships, by a Birmingham newsman who was born in Georgia.

VANSTORY, BURNETTE. *Georgia's Land of the Golden Isles*. Athens, University of Georgia Press, 1956. 202p. $3.75.

A history of the coastal islands of Georgia from early days to the present. In addition to the islands, the book contains material on Darien, Brunswick, St. Marys, and several coastal plantations. The author lives in Atlanta.

WALKER, DANTON MACINTYRE. *Spooks Deluxe*. New York. Franklin Watts, 1956. 187p. $3.95.

A look-behind-you collection of things that could not possibly happen, but did, to various celebrated men and women, who afterward confided in Danton Walker, New York *Daily News* Broadway columnist. The author is a native of Marietta, Georgia.

WHITE, ROBB. *Up Periscope!* Garden City, New York, Doubleday, 1956. 251p. $2.75.

Designed for boys fourteen to eighteen, this is an action story of Navy warfare in the Pacific during World War II.

WILEY, BELL IRVIN, editor. *Reminiscences of Big I by William Nathaniel Wood*. Jackson, Tenn., McCowart-Mercer Press, 1956. 138p. $3.95.

A new edition of a rare personal narrative of a Confederate company officer from Albemarle County, Virginia. Of particular interest is Lieutenant Wood's firsthand account of the Battle of Gettysburg.

WILEY, BELL IRVIN. *The Road to Appomattox*. Memphis, Memphis State College Press, 1956. 121p. $4.00.

Dr. Wiley, Professor of History at Emory University and an authority on the 1861-65 conflict, presents the reasons why the South lost the Civil War.

WILLIS, AUBREY. *I Was an Alcoholic.* New York, Vantage Press, 1956. 132p. $2.75.

The story of an alcoholic—from his first drink, through the years of "social" drinking, to the final phase, when he became powerless to function without the aid of liquor, and finally how he found help in God to break away from the disease. The author lives in Tifton, Georgia.

WINTERS, MARGARET CAMPBELL. *Protective Body Mechanics in Daily Life and Nursing.* Philadelphia, W. B. Saunders, 1952. 150p. $3.50.

Designed primarily for students and instructors in nursing, this illustrated manual has as its aim the preparation of nurses for giving better care to patients. The author is a native of Athens, Georgia.

WOODALL, BESS GREY. *Beauty—God's Gift.* New York, Pageant Press, 1956. 128p. $2.50.

A collection of lyric poems based on a strong religious faith. The author lives in Thomaston, Georgia.

WOODALL, BESS GREY. *My Yoke Is Easy and There Is Life Everlasting.* New York, Pageant Press, 1956. 128p. $3.00.

The inspirational story of a true conversion to a complete Christian faith is combined with thoughtful essays on a religious theme.

YERBY, FRANK. *Captain Rebel.* New York, Dial, 1956. 343p. $3.50.

Set against a Civil War background, this is the story of a bold, rebellious Confederate blockade runner and the two women who love him.

Bibliography of Georgia Authors
1956-1957

THE eighth in the REVIEW's series of annual "Bibliographies of Georgia Authors," this annotated Bibliography is, as nearly as the compiler could make it, a complete and accurate record of books published by Georgia authors from November 1, 1956, to November 1, 1957. The annotations are descriptive, not critical; intended to place, not to judge the book. U. S., State, County, and City Documents, parts of books, brief analytics, and pamphlets of less than 25 pages have been omitted. Prices are given except when not supplied by publisher or when book is obtainable only on specific request, in which case the word "Apply" is used.

In determining whom to designate as Georgia authors, the compiler has included authors born in Georgia and claiming Georgia as their native state and those who have lived in Georgia for a period of five years and who did their writing here.

The compiler will welcome and appreciate readers' sending to him any additions or corrections. They may be sent to him at any time in care of the GEORGIA REVIEW. Several books inadvertently omitted from previous Bibliographies are listed here. Any books omitted from the present Bibliography will be included in the list for 1957-1958.

Acknowledgment is made to members of the staff of the Special Collections Division of the University of Georgia Library for their assistance in the preparation of this Bibliography.

AIKEN, CONRAD POTTER. *Mr. Arcularis; a Play*. Cambridge, Harvard University Press, 1957. 83p. $2.75.

Conrad Aiken's short story first put into play form by Diana Hamilton has now been dramatized by the author himself. Mr. Arcularis, its protagonist, while undergoing a heart operation, dreams of taking a recuperation voyage, which is actually his journey to death, for on the trip he finds reality and is able to face death.

ALLEN, CHARLES L., and WALLIS, CHARLES L. *Christmas in Our Hearts*. Westwood, N. J., Revell, 1957. 64p. $1.00.

A gift edition of an inspirational book on the real meaning of Christmas for the season and for all the years. Charles Allen is a Methodist minister in Atlanta, Georgia; Charles Wallis, a Baptist, is Professor of English at Keuka College, Keuka Park, New York.

ALLEN, CHARLES L. *Touch of the Master's Hand; Christ's Miracles for Today*. Westwood, N. J., Revell, 1956. 158p. $2.00.

Discusses the miracles of Christ and their relationship to present-day religion. The author is Pastor of Grace Methodist Church, Atlanta, Georgia.

BEALOR, ALEX W., III. *The Picture-Skin Story*. New York, Holiday House, 1957. Unpaged. $2.75.

An authentic story of a Sioux Indian boy. Illustrated by the author. Mr. Bealor is a resident of Atlanta, Georgia.

BLANKENSHIP, GEORGE H. *Tootsie Toots*. New York, Comet Press, 1957. 32p. $2.00.

A seven-year-old girl, her devoted Pekingese dog, and her silver horn become involved in a strange kidnapping in Haiti and a smashing tropical hurricane. The author, a native of Columbus, Georgia, now resides in Atlanta, Georgia.

BOLES, PAUL DARCY. *Deadline*. New York, Macmillan, 1957. 254p. $3.75.

After four indecisive and soul-searching days, the liberal editor of an influential Southern newspaper takes a definite stand about desegregation.

BOYCE, KATHRYN. *You Can Master Yourself and Your Problems*. Privately printed, 1956. 131p. $2.00.

A study outlining the author's beliefs in the power of the metaphysical in meeting everyday problems. Miss Boyce is co-founder and minister of the Three-fold Truth Foundation in Atlanta.

BRAGG, LILLIAN CHAPLIN. *Old Savannah Ironwork*. Savannah, The Pigeonhole Press, 1957. 46p. $1.25.

An account of the lacy wrought-iron balconies, winding stairs, window grilles, and elaborate lamp posts that grace the old homes in Savannah, Georgia.

BROWN, MAREL. *The Cherry Children*. Atlanta, Home Mission Board, Southern Baptist Convention, 1957. 73p. 50 cents.

Episodes in the life of the Cherrys, a Negro family living in Florida, are used to illustrate the ideals of Christian living.

BRYAN, MARY G., and HAWES, LILLA M., editors. *Georgia Date Book, 1958*. Boston, Colonial Pub. Co., 1957. 92p. $1.50.

An illustrated, annotated calendar and date book compiled in collaboration with the Department of Archives and History and the Georgia Historical Society; with Carroll Hart and Mrs. Philip W. Bryant as contributors.

BURGESS, JACKSON. *Pillar of Cloud*. New York, Putnam, 1957. 254p. $3.50.

The story of an assorted group of people making their way West in 1858 under the leadership of a man who was trying to prove there was a new, more practical way across the plains. The author was born in Atlanta, Georgia.

CALDWELL, ERSKINE. *Certain Women.* Boston, Little, Brown, 1957. 249p. $3.75.
   The dingy mill town of Claremore is the setting for this novel in which the love-focused lives of seven young women are examined—a reluctant bride, a prostitute, a victim of town gossip, a wife pursued by a vicious lover, and others.

CANTEY, ROBERT C. *The Law of Search and Seizure.* Athens, Georgia. Institute of Law and Government, University of Georgia, 1957. 43p. Paper $1.50. Cloth $2.50.
   A guide for peace officers published by the Institute of Law and Government as a part of its program of continuing legal education for public officials in Georgia. Mr. Cantey is an Assistant in the Institute of Law and Government, School of Law, University of Georgia.

CHARLES, A. ALDO. *College Law.* Cincinnati, South-Western Pub. Co., 1957. Fifth edition. 538p. $2.70.
   This revised edition of a textbook on law has been brought up to date by including changes in public welfare laws, and supplementary questions and case problems have been added at the end of each chapter. Dr. Charles is Professor of Business Law at the University of Georgia.

CHEATHAM, ELLIOTT EVANS. *Cases and Materials on the Legal Profession.* Second edition. Brooklyn, N. Y., The Foundation Press, 1955. 585p. $7.50.
   A textbook designed for the members of the law profession, to give an understanding of the legal profession as an institution and to encourage an appraisal of its work and organization in the light of its social functions and of the conditions under which it operates. Mr. Cheatham is a native of Savannah, Georgia.

CLECKLEY, HERVEY M., M.D. *The Caricature of Love; A Discussion of Social, Psychiatric, and Literary Manifestations of Pathologic Sexuality.* New York, Ronald Press, 1957. 329p. $6.50.
   Critically examines some concepts of sexuality common today and discusses sexual disorder and its influences. Dr. Cleckley is Professor of Psychiatry and Neurology at the University of Georgia School of Medicine.

COCHRAN, LEONARD H. *Man at His Best.* Nashville, Abingdon Press, 1957. 174p. $2.50.
   Thoughts on great doctrinal themes of the Christian religion. The author is the minister of the Mulberry Street Methodist Church in Macon, Georgia.

COOPER, J. WESLEY. *Natchez: A Treasure of Ante-Bellum Homes.* Philadelphia. Printed optakrome by E. Stern, 1957. 159p. $10.00.
   A collection of thirty-two color photographs of the ante-bellum mansions that have made Natchez famous. A short historical sketch accompanies each photograph. The author is a native of Tifton, Georgia.

COUEY, ELIZABETH D., and STEPHENSON, DIANE D. *The Field of Private Duty Nursing.* Montgomery, Ala., Cadden Advertising Agency, 1955. 363p. $3.00.

A study of the functions of the private duty nurse in the hospital environment, conducted by a firm of educational consultants for the Georgia State Nurses Association under a grant from the American Nurses Association.

COUEY, FRED, and COUEY, ELIZABETH D. *Human Relations in Private Duty Nursing.* Atlanta, Georgia, Georgia State Nurses Association, 1957. 155p. $3.00.

An experimental research methodology for studying the dynamics of critical functions connected with the nursing profession. The survey was conducted by Couey and Couey, educational consultants, for the Georgia State Nurses Association.

DERN, MRS. JOHN SHERMAN. See: Gaddis, Peggy.

DERN, PEGGY. See: Gaddis, Peggy.

DOUGHTIE, BEATRICE MACKEY. *The Mackeys (variously spelled) and Allied Families.* Decatur, Georgia, Bowen Press, 1957. 1002p. $10.00.

A comprehensive study of the Mackey family in America and its numerous allied families. The compiler is a resident of Atlanta, Georgia.

DREWRY, JOHN E., editor. *Communications: Key to So Much: Press, Radio, Television, Periodicals, Public Relations, and Advertising as Seen through Institutes and Special Occasions of the Henry W. Grady School of Journalism, 1956-1957.* Vol. LVIII, No. 1. Athens, University of Georgia Bulletin, 1957. 183p. Paper $2.00. Cloth $3.00.

A compilation of addresses on journalistic subjects which were delivered at the several institutes, conventions, and special occasions sponsored by the University of Georgia's School of Journalism during the 1956-1957 session.

DYKES, NOBIE BEALL. *Not I But Christ.* Lithonia, Georgia, Stone Mountain Litho. Co., 1957. 56p. Apply.

A group of inspirational poems expressing the author's strong religious faith.

EQUEN, MURDOCK, M.D. *Magnetic Removal of Foreign Bodies.* Springfield, Ill., Charles C. Thomas, 1957. 94p. $4.50.

An account, written for doctors, of the use of the Alnico magnet in the recovery of foreign bodies from the air passages, the esophagus, stomach, and duodenum. Dr. Equen is founder and Chief of Staff of the Ponce de Leon Infirmary in Atlanta, Georgia.

FARBER, EVAN IRA. *Classified List of Periodicals for the College Library.* Fourth edition. Boston, F. W. Faxon Co., 1957. 144p. $5.00.

A selected list of journals by college professors and librarians for the college library. The listings are arranged by subject, and many of the descriptive notes have been rewritten. The author is a member of the Emory University library staff.

FORD, MARCIA, pseud. See: Radford, Ruby Lorraine.

FLEMING, BERRY, comp. *Autobiography of a Colony: The First Half-Century of Augusta, Georgia.* Athens, University of Georgia Press, 1957. 204p. $4.00.

The story of Augusta, Georgia, from its beginning to 1791, told in diary form. Mr. Fleming is a resident of Augusta, Georgia.

FOSTER, MARIAN CURTIS (pseud. Mariana). *Miss Flora McFlimsey and the Little Red Schoolhouse.* New York, Lothrop, Lee & Sheppard Co., 1957. Unpaged. $1.50.

The little world of Miss Flora McFlimsey is widening, and now there is added to its miniature landscape a tiny red schoolhouse for dolls. The water-color illustrations are by the author.

GADDIS, PEGGY. *Flight from Love.* New York, Arcadia, 1957. 224p. $2.75.

Nurse Brooke must choose between a handsome, wealthy suitor who can offer her a life of luxury, and a homely, hard working young doctor.

GADDIS, PEGGY. *Lady Doctor.* New York, Arcadia House, 1956. 224p. $2.50.

Dr. Ruth Prescott, disappointed in love, leaves the Grace Memorial Hospital to take over a general practice in an isolated town along the coast only to be snubbed by the local citizens.

GADDIS, PEGGY (pseud. Peggy Dern). *Nurse in the Tropics.* New York, Arcadia House, 1957. 223p. $2.75.

Black magic and romance impinge upon nurse Martie Howell's professional work and make her visit to Haiti a most memorable one.

GIBSON, COUNT DILLON. *Figures in the Straw.* New York, Exposition Press, 1957. 204p. $3.00.

An allegorical novel concerning the influence an older man wields in the life of a widow and her eight-year-old son. The story takes place on a Georgia plantation.

GIBSON, FRANK K., and HAMMOCK, TED L. *Forms of City Government in Georgia.* Athens, Bureau of Public Administration, The University of Georgia, 1957. 46p. $1.50.

A discussion of the various types of municipal government found in Georgia today which presents to the citizens of Georgia some of the basic facts concerning the forms of government available to them.

GODFREY, CAROLINE HARDEE. *God's Christmas Trees.* Atlanta, Harper Printing Co., 1957. 40p. $1.00.

A collection of inspirational essays in which the author relates the characteristics of twelve trees to certain spiritual qualities in mankind. Copies may be obtained from P.O. Box 347, Decatur, Georgia. Mrs. Godfrey lives in Covington, Georgia.

GOSNELL, CULLEN B., LANCASTER, LANE W., and RANKIN, ROBERT S. *Fundamentals of American National Government; National, State, and Local.* New York, McGraw-Hill, 1957. 603p. $6.00.

A text designed to include the theory and the actual mechanism of government, and also to balance the study of the federal government with an examination of state and municipal organizations. Dr. Gosnell is a Professor of Political Science at Emory University.

GRAY, MACY BISHOP. *Through the Years.* Americus, Ga., Americus Printing Co., 1957. 48p. $1.00.

A brief and informal record of Georgia Southwestern College for the years 1908-1957. Miss Gray is Librarian at Georgia Southwestern College, Americus, Georgia.

GREEN, CLAUD B. *John Trotwood Moore: Tennessee Man of Letters.* Athens, University of Georgia Press, 1957. 189p. $4.00.

A biography of a Southern author whose writings were greatly influenced by the grass roots and traditions of Tennessee. Dr. Green, a native of Clayton, Georgia, is Professor of English at Clemson College.

GREEN, THOMAS F. JR., and HARPER, CARL H. *The Georgia Law of Evidence.* Atlanta, The Harrison Co., 1957. 667p. $20.00.

The material in this work has been carefully authenticated by reference to Georgia Code Sections and the case law of the State in both civil and criminal cases. Approximately two thousand cases are cited. Dr. Green is a Professor of Law at the University of Georgia Law School, Athens, Georgia, and Mr. Harper is Regional Attorney, U. S. Department of Health, Education, and Welfare in Atlanta, Georgia.

HARLEY, WILLIAM MCDONALD. *Thomas Jane Shepard of Liberty County, Georgia and His Descendants.* St. Simons Island, Ga., Privately printed, 1957. 25p. Apply.

A genealogical record of the Shepard and allied families.

HARRIS, JOEL CHANDLER. *Uncle Remus Stories.* Mount Vernon, N. Y., Peter Pauper Press, 1957. 106p. $2.50.

A new edition of the folk stories of Joel Chandler Harris. The illustrations in black and color are by Fritz Eichenberg.

HARRIS, KATHLEEN, pseud. See: Humphries, Adelaide.

HARWELL, RICHARD B., editor. *The Confederate Reader; As the South Saw the War.* New York, Longmans, Green, 1957. 217p. $7.50.

This is the story of the Confederacy, told in the words of Southern soldiers and civilians. Arranged chronologically, the book touches on all aspects of Confederate life. There is a generous sampling of battle reports and general orders, Confederate sermons, songs, humorous sketches, novels, prison narratives, and travel observations.

HARWELL, RICHARD B. *More Confederate Imprints.* Richmond, Va., The Virginia State Library, 1957. Two parts. 345p. $2.50 each.

These volumes are the first supplements to Marjorie Lyle Crandall's *Confederate Imprints* published by the Boston Athenaeum in 1955. They record 1773 additions to the record of Confederate printing and publishing, many of routine interest only, but some of primary importance to an understanding of Confederate history.

HAWES, LILLA M., editor. *Collections of the Georgia Historical Society*, Vol. XII. Savannah, Georgia Historical Society, 1957. 176 p. $3.00.
A collection of the papers of Major-General Lachlan McIntosh (1727-1806) for the period 1774-1779. These manuscripts are in the library of the Georgia Historical Society.

HORKAN, NELLE IRWIN. *The Awakening and Other Poems*. Philadelphia, Dorrance, 1957. 51p. $2.00.
A collection of poems written during a long convalescence about a variety of subjects close to the heart of the poet—nature, family, and God. Mrs. Horkan is a resident of Gainesville, Georgia.

HUMPHRIES, ADELAIDE. *Case for Nurse Marian*. New York, Avalon Books, 1957. 224p. $2.75.
Marian Cooper, a nurse at an atomic energy plant near the Mexican border, is dangerously ill—and romantically involved in a case of espionage and murder.

HUMPHRIES, ADELAIDE (pseud. Kathleen Harris). *Jane Arden, Staff Nurse*. New York, Thomas Bouregy and Co., 1957. 223p. $2.75.
The romances of two nurses on the staff of a large university hospital in Tennessee.

HUMPHRIES, ADELAIDE. *Nurse Laurie's Cruise*. New York, Avalon Books, 1957. 222p. $2.50.
Laurie Fielding goes on a Caribbean cruise as a nurse-companion for a husband-hunting woman. The cruise results in both romance and danger for Laurie.

HUTCHINGS, FLORENCE SHEAVER. *A Litany of Love*. New York, Fine Editions Press, 1956. 66p. $3.00.
A collection of sonnets that reflect an ageless concern with life and love and grapple with the problems of the embattled human spirit. Mrs. Hutchings lives in Atlanta, Georgia.

JESSUP, RICHARD. *Cheyenne Saturday*. Greenwich, Conn., Fawcett Publications, 1957. 125p. 25 cents.
A story about Indians fighting with the men building the Union Pacific Railroad across Nebraska.

JESSUP, RICHARD. *Comanche Vengeance*. Greenwich, Conn., Fawcett Publications, 1957. 126p. 25 cents.
The self-appointed guardian of a young widow, whose husband and children have been murdered by Comanches, joins her in a search of vengeance.

JOHNSON, HAROLD L. *Piggyback Transportation: An Economic Analysis*. Atlanta, Division of Business Research, School of Business Administration, Georgia State College of Business Administration, 1956. 54p. $1.00.
An economic study of transportation coordination between the railroads and the motor carriers in America—especially the movement of

truck trailers on railroad flatcars, or so called "piggy-back" service. The author is Associate Professor of Economics at Georgia State College of Business Administration, Atlanta, Georgia.

JONES, WILBUR DEVEREUX. *Lord Derby and Victorian Conservatism.* Athens, University of Georgia Press, 1957. Oxford, England, Basil Blackwell, 1956. 367p. $5.00 (37s 6d).

A political biography of Great Britain's first three-term Prime Minister, discussing his work in the House of Lords, his leadership of the Conservative Party, and his relations with the dominating political figures of the nineteenth century, Palmerston, Gladstone, and Disraeli. The author is a member of the History Department of the University of Georgia.

KELLEY, EVELYN OWENS. *Seeded Furrows.* Daytona Beach, Fla., College Pub. Co., 1957. 297p. $3.95.

An historical novel about the Reconstruction Era in Georgia. The action centers around Irwinsville, Georgia, where President Davis of the Confederacy was captured. The author is a resident of Fitzgerald, Georgia.

KENNEDY, HARVEY J. *Murder and the Shocking Miss Williams.* New York, Vantage Press, 1957. 185p. $2.95.

Two confessions of murder complicate the solution of this mystery story that reaches its climax in a dramatic trial scene. The author is a resident of Barnesville, Georgia.

KIKER, DOUGLAS. *The Southerner.* New York, Rinehart, 1957. 314p. $4.00.

Jess Witherow, the key figure, is a reporter on a Southern paper who becomes embroiled in a race situation when a Negro child tries to register in a white school. The author was born and raised in Griffin, Georgia.

LAWRENCE, ALEXANDER A. *James Johnston: Georgia's First Printer.* Savannah, The Pigeonhole Press, 1956. 54p. $3.00.

A biographical sketch of James Johnston, Georgia's first printer, who established the first newspaper in Georgia in 1763. Mr. Lawrence is a resident of Savannah, Georgia.

LEVERETT, E. FREEMAN, HALL, ROBERT H., CHRISTOPHER, THOMAS W., DAVIS, WILEY H., and SHULMAN, ARNOLD. *Georgia Procedure and Practice.* Atlanta, The Harrison Co., 1951. 889p. $20.00.

This volume, prepared under the auspices of the Bureau of Legal Research, Emory University Law School, is designed to serve as an aid in research, and often as the initial step in such research. This study, based on a 1948 publication of Davis and Shulman entitled "Georgia Practice and Procedure," has treated a number of new subjects, such as pre-trial proceedings, new trial, trover, garnishment and attachment. All of the authors are members of the Georgia Bar.

LIPSCOMB, LAMAR RUTHERFORD. *Essays Wise and Otherwise.* Brussels, Belgium, Mildred Seydell Publishing Co., 1957. 100p. $2.00.

A collection of essays that originally appeared in the *Athens Banner-Herald*, Athens, Georgia. The author is a native of Athens, Georgia.

McClain, Roy O. *This Way, Please: Facing Life's Crossroads.* Westwood, N. J., Revell, 1957. 389p. $3.00.

A book of sermons in which the author singles out practically all of the faults of society and the church and brands them as sins. Dr. McClain is Pastor of the First Baptist Church of Atlanta, Georgia.

Macon, Alethea Jane. *Gideon Macon of Virginia and Some of His Descendants.* Macon, Georgia, J. W. Burke Company, 1956. 267p. $10.00.

A compilation of records, from many sources, relating to the numerous descendants of Col. Gideon Macon of Virginia. Miss Macon is a resident of Brunswick and Clayton, Georgia.

McCumber, W. E. *Our Sanctifying God.* Kansas City, Mo., Beacon Hill Press, 1956. 124p. $1.50.

A study that considers the experience of holiness in its New Testament significance through an examination of the tri-personal activity in sanctification and the means by which the Triune God sanctifies His believers. The author is a pastor in Thomasville, Georgia.

Marshall, Edison. *The Inevitable Hour.* New York, Putnam, 1957. 320p. $3.95.

An historical romance set on the island of Martinique before and during the great disaster caused by the eruption of Mt. Pelee in 1902.

Morgan, Beatrice Payne. *Ophar's Child.* Richmond, Va., The Dietz Press, 1951. 34p. Apply.

A narrative poem concerning the love, life, and problems of Nilla, Ophar, and their child, Ilna. Mrs. Morgan is a resident of Savannah, Georgia.

Murphey, Arthur G., Jr. *The Law of Criminal Arrest in Georgia.* Athens, Georgia, Institute of Law and Government, University of Georgia, 1957. 70p. Paper $1.50. Cloth $2.00.

A manual designed for use by peace officers and others who may be concerned with the law of criminal arrest. Mr. Murphey is an Assistant in the Institute of Law and Government, School of Law, University of Georgia.

Nadler, Charles Elihu. *Georgia Corporation Law; Practice, Form.* Atlanta, The Harrison Company, 1950. 726p. $17.50.

This one-volume work on the law of corporations, geared directly to Georgia statutes and Georgia law, has been prepared to serve as an aid and a guide to the general practitioner in meeting the ever increasing demands of his client for his services in "business."

Nadler, Charles Elihu. *The Law of Creditor and Debtor Relations: Cases, Text, Procedure, Forms.* St. Paul, Minn., West Publishing Co., 1956. 698p. $11.00.

A law textbook designed to fit the needs of fundamental courses in debtor-creditor relations. The author is Professor of Law at the Walter F. George School of Law, Mercer University.

NADLER, CHARLES ELIHU. *The Law of Debtor Relief; Bankruptcy and Non-Bankruptcy Devices; Arrangements, Assignments, Compositions, Extensions, Equity Receiverships, and Corporate Reorganizations.* Atlanta, The Harrison Company, 1954. 1117p. $25.00.

A one-volume work designed to serve the general practitioner as a practical and helpful aid in the law relating to bankruptcy and non-bankruptcy devices available for the relief of a financially distressed debtor.

NEWTON, LOUIE DEVOTIE. *Why I Am a Baptist.* New York, Thomas Nelson and Sons, 1957. 306p. $2.75.

Testimony of a religious training and background in the faith of the Baptist denomination, with an examination into its teachings. The author is Pastor of the Druid Hills Baptist Church in Atlanta, Georgia.

NICHOLSON, MRS. MADISON G. *Ladies' Garden Club.* Athens, University of Georgia Printing Department, 1957. 28p. Apply.

An historical sketch of the first Garden Club in America. Mrs. Nicholson is a resident of Athens, Georgia.

OLIVER, VIRGINIA KATHERINE. *The Children's Magic Corner.* New York, Vantage Press, 1957. 40p. $2.00.

An illustrated collection of poems and stories for children. The author lives in Atlanta, Georgia.

OSBORN, STELLANOVA B. *Beside the Cabin.* Sault Ste. Marie, Michigan, Northwoods Press, 1957. 41p. Apply.

A collection of inspirational poems about nature, people, places, and things.

OUTLAW, NELL WARREN. *This Is the Day.* Grand Rapids, Mich., Zondervan, 1957. 160p. $2.50.

A series of essays on the outstanding days of our lives. The origin, history, significance, and manner of observance are given for each of these days. Mrs. Outlaw is a resident of Atlanta, Georgia.

PARKS, EDD WINFIELD. *Backwater.* New York, Twayne Publishers, 1957. 188p. $3.00.

An account of what happens to the Camerons and other families of a small Tennessee town when the Mississippi overflows, destroying their farms, homes, and livelihoods. Dr. Parks is a Professor of English at the University of Georgia.

POPE, CLIFFORD HILLHOUSE. *Reptiles Round the World.* Knopf, N. Y., 1957. 219p. $3.50.

A simplified natural history of snakes, lizards, turtles, and crocodilians. Designed for ages 10-14, this is an illustrated review of the types and habits of reptiles. The author is a native of Washington, Georgia.

PIERCE, ALFRED M. *A History of Methodism in Georgia, February 5, 1736-June 24, 1955.* Atlanta, Georgia, North Georgia Conference Historical Society, 1956. 345p. $3.75.

An historical account of the founding and growth of the Methodist Church in Georgia by a retired Methodist minister.

POSEY, WALTER B. *The Baptist Church in the Lower Mississippi Valley, 1776-1845.* Lexington, Ky., University of Kentucky Press, 1957. 176p. $5.00.

A study of the development of the early Baptist Church—how its evangelism and aggressiveness produced a phenomenal membership in the lower Mississippi Valley. Dr. Posey is Head of the Department of History at Agnes Scott College.

RADFORD, RUBY LORRAINE (pseud. Marcia Ford). *Anne Fuller, Librarian.* New York, Avalon Books, 1957. 220p. $2.75.

Anne's first job lands her in a political fight over raising funds for a new library, and she is ably assisted by a cub reporter who is interested in both the library and the librarian.

RADFORD, RUBY LORRAINE. *The Enchanted Cove.* New York, Avalon Books, 1957. 223p. $2.75.

When her mother travels to Europe, Eileen goes to the country with her father, and finds not only inspiration to paint, but a romantic adventure.

RADFORD, RUBY LORRAINE. *Pamela Lee, Home Economist.* New York, Avalon Books, 1956. 224p. $2.50.

Pamela Lee and her brother Rod are kept busy trying to renovate a run-down farm, and Pam finds more excitement in supervising 4-H Club juniors.

RADFORD, RUBY LORRAINE. *Tomorrow's Promise.* New York, Avalon Books, 1956. 224p. $2.50.

Jean Dawson agrees to help Dan Hampton, retired president of the Hampton Lumber Company, write a family history. She discovers that Dan's brother is handling the business in a shady way, and her life is in danger.

SAYE, ALBERT BERRY. *Georgia: Government and History.* Evanston, Ill., Row, Peterson and Company, 1957. 448p. $2.75.

This text on Georgia government and history is designed primarily for high school students. Although emphasis is placed upon the present constitution and government, it includes the main features of the constitutional history of the state. Dr. Saye is Professor of Political Science at the University of Georgia.

SCOFIELD, DOROTHY. *The Shining Road.* New York, Longmans, Green and Co., 1957. 186p. $2.75.

Elinor, a high school senior, goes for the summer with her aunt to a Canadian island where she makes new friends and finds an interesting career. The author is a branch librarian of the Atlanta Public Library.

SCOTT, ROBERT LEE, JR. *Samburu, the Elephant.* New York, Dodd Mead, 1957. 159p. $2.75.

The American hunter, Bwana Bob, realizes his dream when he goes on a safari hunting a long-time-coveted elephant, Samburu. The book is illustrated by Frank Hubbard.

SMITH, D. F. DAVES. *Half-Breed.* New York, Exposition Press, 1956. 63p. $2.50.

A collection of lyric poetry about nature, people, and philosophy written in plain, everyday language. Miss Smith is an English teacher at the Hapeville, Georgia, High School.

STEWARD, DAVENPORT. *Caribbean Cavalier.* New York, Dutton, 1957. 253p. $3.75.

Keith Hampton sails for the new world to rescue his brother, a prisoner of the Spanish in a dungeon in St. Augustine. The time is 1739, and the locale shifts from Jamaica and Cuba to Charleston and Georgia. The story reaches its climax in the Battle of Bloody Marsh, fought on St. Simons Island, July of 1742.

STOKES, MACK B. *Major Methodist Beliefs.* Nashville, The Methodist Publishing House, 1956. 96p. 50 cents.

A statement of the beliefs of the Methodist denomination which shows how they interpret the ageless affirmations of the Bible. Dr. Stokes is Parker Professor of Systematic Theology and Associate Dean of the Candler School of Theology, Emory University.

STRAUSS, WALTER A. *Proust and Literature.* Cambridge, Mass., Harvard University Press, 1957. 260p. $4.75.

A study of Marcel Proust as a critic, in an attempt to assess the influence of other writers on Proust, or to delineate Proust's attitude toward other writers. The author is Professor of Romance Languages at Emory University.

TAYLOR, ANTOINETTE ELIZABETH. *The Woman Suffrage Movement in Tennessee.* New York, Bookman Associates, 1957. 150p. $3.50.

This study traces the development of the woman suffrage movement in Tennessee from its origin in the 1870's to the ratification of the nineteenth amendment by Tennessee in 1920. The author, a native of Columbus, Georgia, is an Associate Professor at Texas State College for Women.

TAYLOR, GERALD K., JR. *Relationships Between Land Value and Land Use in a Central Business District.* Washington, D. C., Urban Land Institute, 1957. 77p. Apply.

A research study prepared under a grant from the J. C. Nichols Foundation of the Urban Land Institute to the Georgia Institute of Technology. Mr. Taylor is a permanent staff member of the Atlanta Metropolitan Planning Commission.

THIGPEN, CORBETT H. and CLECKLEY, HERVEY M. *The Three Faces of Eve.* New York, McGraw-Hill, 1957. 308p. $4.50.

An account of the interviews between two psychiatrists and a young woman who had three separate and very different personalities. The authors, the psychiatrists who interviewed Eve White, are in the Department of Psychiatry and Neurology at the University of Georgia Medical College and are on the staff of the University Hospital in Augusta, Georgia.

TOWNSEND, ELIAS CARTER. *Risks; The Key to Combat Intelligence.* Harrisburg, Pa., Military Service Publications Co., 1955. 82p. $1.50.

A realistic approach to effective combat intelligence procedures. The author is a native of Cartersville, Georgia.

TUCKER, H. PARKS. *Prison Is My Parish.* Westwood, N. J., Revell, 1957. 191p. $2.95.

This book describes Chaplain Tucker's work among some of the toughest criminals in the country at the Atlanta Federal Penitentiary, which has more than 2,500 inmates. There are tragic personal stories of many of the prisoners, humorous incidents, and inspiring transformations. The story is told to George Burnham.

VINSON, JOHN CHALMERS. *William E. Borah and the Outlawry of War.* Athens, University of Georgia Press, 1957. 222p. $4.50.

An examination of the conduct of Senator William E. Borah as Head of the Senate Foreign Relations Committee and the policies he favored for the years 1917 to 1931 that prompted his being called the "perfect isolationist." Dr. Vinson is a member of the History Department at the University of Georgia.

WARREN, JAMES E., JR. *The Teacher of English: His Materials and Opportunities.* Denver, Colo., Alan Swallow, 1957. 95p. $2.00.

A collection of essays concerned with the teaching of the English language and its literature to American high school students. The author is Chairman of the English Department, Brown High School, Atlanta, Georgia.

WARREN, KITTRELL J. *Ups and Downs of Wife Hunting.* Emory University, Georgia, Emory University Publications, Sources and Reprints, Emory University Library Ser. 10, No. 1, 1957. 39p. 75 cents.

This humorous essay is a reprint of a rare Confederate imprint originally written in 1861 by a Georgia lawyer, soldier, and later, newspaper editor. Edited by Floyd C. Watkins, Assistant Professor of English, Emory University.

WATKINS, FLOYD C. *Thomas Wolfe's Characters; Portraits from Life.* Norman, Okla., University of Oklahoma Press, 1957. 194p. $3.75.

A searching look into Wolfe's characters to disprove misunderstandings and to show that some of his fiction is fact and is based on life in his home-town—Asheville, North Carolina. The author is an Assistant Professor of English at Emory University.

WIGGINTON, BROOKS ELLIOTT. *Trees and Shrubs for the Southern Coastal Plain.* Athens, University of Georgia Press, 1957. 154p. $2.50.

A manual dealing with plant usage in the Southern Coastal Plain, useful to both amateur and professional gardeners as well as nurserymen and park and cemetery superintendents. The author is a member of the Landscape Architecture Department at the University of Georgia.

WIGGINS, SAMUEL PAUL. *The Student Teacher in Action.* Boston, Allyn and Bacon, 1957. 217p. $2.95.

A text devoted to techniques of teaching geared to assisting the thinking, observing, and planning process of the student teacher at elementary and secondary levels.

WILLIAMS, CAROLYN WHITE. *History of Jones County, Georgia: 1807-1907.* Macon, Georgia, J. W. Burke Co., 1957. 1103p. $10.00.

A comprehensive history of one of Middle Georgia's counties—with detailed accounts of the outstanding historical events and brief family sketches. The appendix contains documents, abstracts from records, lists of county officers, roster of Jones County companies in wars, etc. Mrs. Williams lives at Round Oak, Georgia.

WILLIAMS, RALPH ROGER, editor. *Standard Georgia Practice with Forms.* Rochester, New York, Lawyers Cooperative Publishing Co., 1956-57. Vols. III through VI. $15.00 each.

A comprehensive text statement of pleading and practice in civil cases in Georgia, together with appropriate forms, including a treatment of evidence and matters of trial and appellate procedure. Volumes I and II were published in 1955.

WILLIAMS, VINNIE. *The Fruit Tramp.* New York, Macmillan, 1957. 247p. $3.50.

This novel depicts life along the 1800-mile fruit and vegetable picking circuit that stretches from Lake Okeechobee along the Appalachian shelf to Aroostook Basin in Maine—the small towns, the fields, the orchards and swamps, the wild life and the people.

WILLIAMSON, J. C. *North Georgia Baptist Association.* Dalton, Ga., The L. A. Lee Co., 1957. 131p. Apply.

The autobiography of an association of Baptists, their struggles, problems, growth, and attainments through the years from 1862 to 1956. The churches belonging to this association are located in Whitfield, Murray, and Walker counties. Dr. Williamson resides in Dalton, Georgia.

WOOD, MARIE STEVENS WALKER. *The Walker Heritage.* Macon, Ga., Merriewood Press, 1956. 274p. Apply.

A compilation of records and data relating to the genealogy of the Walker family, collateral lines, and allied families. Mrs. Wood lives in Macon, Georgia.

WOODWARD, JOHN R. *Butch, The Diary of a Dog.* New York, Twayne Publishers and Southern Publications Society, 1956. 128p. $2.75.

A dog's daily life with his master and mistress, written as if in his own diary. The author is a resident of Atlanta, Georgia.

WOOFTER, THOMAS J. *Southern Race Progress: The Wavering Color Line.* Washington, D. C., Public Affairs Press, 1957. 180p. $3.50.

Recollections and insights by one of the nation's top experts on race relations. The introduction is by Jonathan Daniels. The author is a native of Macon, Georgia.

YERBY, FRANK. *Fairoaks.* New York, Dial Press, 1957. 405p. $3.95.

The story of a vast Southern plantation and of a man who lived a lie so magnificently that in the end it came true.

Bibliography of Georgia Authors
1957-1958

THE ninth in the REVIEW's series of annual "Bibliographies of Georgia Authors," this annotated Bibliography is, as nearly as the compiler could make it, a complete and accurate record of books published by Georgia authors from November 1, 1957, to November 1, 1958. The annotations are descriptive, not critical; intended to place, not to judge the book. U. S., State, County, and City Documents, parts of books, brief analytics, and pamphlets of less than 25 pages have been omitted. Prices are given except when not supplied by publisher or when book is obtainable only on specific request, in which case the word "Apply" is used.

In determining whom to designate as Georgia authors, the compiler has included authors born in Georgia and claiming Georgia as their native state and those who have lived in Georgia for a period of five years and who did their writing here.

The compiler will welcome and appreciate readers' sending to him any additions or corrections. They may be sent to him at any time in care of the GEORGIA REVIEW. Several books inadvertently omitted from previous Bibliographies are listed here. Any books omitted from the present Bibliography will be included in the list for 1958-1959.

Acknowledgment is made to members of the staff of the Special Collections Division of the University of Georgia Library for their assistance in the preparation of this Bibliography.

ABRAHAM, JOSEPH L. *A Guide to Real Estate Sales Contracts.* 1957. 32p. *Georgia Real Estate Contracts.* 1958. 44p. *Real Estate Brokerage and Commissions in Georgia.* 1958. 16p. Atlanta, Real Estate Publications. Sold as a set of three for $6.00.

 A packet of three books, by an Atlanta real estate attorney, on many phases of the legal aspects of the real estate business.

ADAMS, CARSBIE C. *Space Flight.* New York, McGraw-Hill, 1958. 373p. $6.50.

 Traces man's efforts to travel in outer space, which have culminated, so far, in the recent American and Russian satellite launchings. Dr. Adams is a resident of Atlanta, Georgia.

AIKEN, CONRAD POTTER. *Sheepfold Hill.* New York, Sagamore Press, 1958. 62p. $2.95.
Poems in conventional and experimental verse forms. The major poem, "Crystal," expresses Aiken's philosophy "of the forever-togetherness of all flesh and all time, the searching for man's place in the universe, the attempted recovery of life's lost milestones."

ALLEN, CHARLES L. *All Things Are Possible Through Prayer.* Westwood, N. J., Revell, 1958. 128p. $2.00.
Dr. Allen, pastor of Atlanta's Grace Methodist Church, gives simple, practical answers to everyone's questions about prayer.

AUSTIN, AURELIA. *Bright Feathers.* Columbia, S. C., R. L. Bryan Co., 1958. 60p. $3.00.
A collection of lyrical poems from a former newspaper columnist and prose writer, touching on themes of love, childhood fancies, nature, and faith. The author lives in Atlanta, Georgia.

BARNETT, ALBERT EDWARD. *The New Testament, Its Making and Meaning.* Nashville, Tenn., Abingdon Press, 1958. Revised edition. 304p. $3.00.
A concise introduction to the twenty-seven books of the New Testament, offering new understanding of their vital religious message. Dr. Barnett is professor of New Testament, Candler School of Theology, Emory University.

BLISS, ALICE. *Words For Dancing.* Atlanta, Russell and Wardlaw, 1958. 28p. $2.00.
A collection of some forty poems which are in free verse with a few sonnets about people, love, nature, and small towns. The author is a native of Atlanta, Georgia.

BLOCH, CHARLES J. *States' Rights: The Law of the Land.* Atlanta, Harrison, 1958. 381p. $10.00.
A statement showing in detail what the original concept of the American government was, what has happened to it over the years by judicial interpretation, and what we may expect if present trends continue. Mr. Bloch is a resident of Macon, Georgia.

BOAL, BOBBY SNOW. *A Tree for Phyllis and Me.* New York, William R. Scott, 1957. 45p. $2.50.
A tale of the adventures of two tree-climbing friends, their tree house and their make-believe world high above the ground. Mrs. Boal is a native of Valdosta, Georgia.

BOLES, PAUL DARCY. *Parton's Island.* New York, Macmillan, 1958. 191p. $3.75.
Two teen-age boys discover an island of their own in an Alabama river and experience the joys of independence and exploration until change and the outside world encroach on their idyllic paradise.

BOWEN, ROBERT A. *Tall in the Sight of God*. Asheville, N. C., John F. Blair, Publisher, 1958. 372p. $4.95.
This historical novel traces the trials and triumphs of three generations of a family of Southern Highlanders from the Revolution through Reconstruction. Robert Bowen is a native Georgian and a graduate of the University of Georgia.

BONNER, JAMES CALVIN. *The Georgia Story*. Oklahoma City, Harlow, 1958. 492p. $3.36.
A new synthesis of Georgia materials in text book form for the senior high school and junior college levels, this book covers Georgia's history from the days of the Indians to the present. Dr. Bonner is Professor of History at Georgia State College for Women, Milledgeville, Georgia.

BRANNAN, DONIE LEONE. *My Pastor*. Atlanta, Foote and Davies, 1957. 125p. $2.50.
The life story of Dr. William Asa Duncan, who for thirty years was pastor of the First Baptist Church in East Point, Georgia. The author is a native of Camilla, Georgia.

BRAWNER, NELLIE BARKSDALE. *Through the Years*. Atlanta, Curtis Publishing Co., 1958. 200p. $4.00.
A compilation of inspirational articles, poems, prayers, and speeches intended as a reference guide for individuals and church groups. Mrs. Brawner is a resident of Atlanta, Georgia.

BRAY, VIVIAN L. *Potpourri*. Cleveland, Tenn., Pathway Press, 1957. 117p. Paper $1.00. Cloth $2.00.
A collection of poetry, favorite sermons, lectures, and a few jokes of a retired Methodist minister of the North Georgia Conference.

BROOKS, ROBERT PRESTON. *Under Seven Flags*. Athens, Georgia, University Printing Department, 1958. 88p. $2.00.
The author presents a brief account of his early life, education, teaching, and world travel.

CALDWELL, ERSKINE. *Molly Cottontail*. Boston, Little, Brown, 1958. 32p. $2.50.
Describes the experience of a lad who tried to kill a rabbit, only frightened it with the noise of the shotgun, and then made a friend and pet of the near-victim.

CARR, JAMES MCLEOD. *Glorious Ride*. Atlanta, Church and Community Press, 1958. 156p. $2.50.
Relates how a Methodist minister and great country preacher, Henry McLaughlin (1869-1950), dedicated his life to the expansion of the Rural Church Movement. The author is a resident of Atlanta, Georgia.

CARROLL, GEORGE FRANKLIN. *Mammy and Her Chillun*. New York, Comet Press, 1958. 94p. $3.00.
A portrait of a Southern Mammy, Aunt Lucy, and her stories for children. This collection contains twenty-nine stories. Mr. Carroll, a native of Atlanta, lives in Macon, Georgia.

CAYLOR, JOHN. *The Great I Am's of Jesus*. Grand Rapids, Mich., Zondervan, 1957. 86p. $2.00.
   Twelve messages based on the statements Jesus made concerning His nature and ministry. Dr. Caylor is editorial secretary of the Baptist Home Mission Board in Atlanta, Georgia.

CLARK, JOHN G. *Meditations on the Lord's Supper*. Nashville, Tenn., Broadman Press, 1958. 124p. $2.50.
   Old and new themes relating to the Lord's Supper are discussed in this book of meditations. Mr. Clark, a native Georgian and a graduate of Mercer University, died in 1955.

COLEMAN, KENNETH. *The American Revolution in Georgia, 1763-1789*. Athens, University of Georgia Press, 1958. 345p. $5.50.
   Starting with the background description of growth and change in the colony during the decade and a half before actual revolt, this book traces Georgia's participation in the struggle for independence and her transition from colony to state. Dr. Coleman is a member of the History Department at the University of Georgia.

COLEMAN, LONNIE. See: Coleman, William Lawrence.

COLEMAN, WILLIAM LAWRENCE. *The Southern Lady*. Boston, Little, Brown, 1958. 219p. $3.75.
   Set on a European bound freighter, this psychological novel tells of a Southern lady who pretends prejudice but is actually "passing" for white, and the effect she has upon her fellow passengers.

CONRAD, JACK RANDOLPH. *The Horn and the Sword*. New York, Dutton, 1957. 222p. $5.00.
   Traces the worship of the bull as a symbol of power and fertility from the stone age to modern times. Dr. Conrad, a native of Atlanta, is Head of the Department of Anthropology at Southwestern University in Memphis, Tenn.

COULTER, ELLIS MERTON, ed. *The Journal of William Stephens, 1741-1743*. Athens, University of Georgia Press, 1958. 300p. $5.00.
   Through his journal William Stephens, Secretary of the Province of Georgia, undertook to inform the Trustees on everything which happened in Georgia. This is number two of the Wormsloe Foundation Publications. Dr. Coulter is Professor Emeritus of History at the University of Georgia.

CRAIG, GEORGIA. See: Gaddis, Peggy.

DAVIS, MAGGIE H. *The Winter Serpent*. New York, McGraw-Hill, 1958. 300p. $4.50.
   The story of a ninth century Scottish girl who is sold by her stepbrother to a barbaric Viking leader. Upon her escape she searches through Ireland and England for safety only to find that real peace awaits her with the Viking husband she has been forced to wed. Mrs. Davis lives on a farm near Jonesboro, Georgia.

DERN, PEGGY. See: Gaddis, Peggy.

DERN, MRS. JOHN SHERMAN. See: Gaddis, Peggy.

DOWELL, SPRIGHT. *A History of Mercer University*. Macon, Mercer University, 1958. 412p. $4.00.

All phases of the colorful past of Mercer University, one of Georgia's leading institutions of higher learning, have been carefully recorded in this history by a former president of the university.

DREWRY, JOHN E., ed. *The What, and How of Communications: Press, Radio, Television, Periodicals, Public Relations, and Advertising As Seen Through Institutes and Special Occasions of the Henry W. Grady School of Journalism, 1957-1958*. Vol. LIX, No. 2. Athens, University of Georgia Bulletin, 1958. 214p. Paper $2.00. Cloth $3.00.

A compilation of addresses on journalistic subjects which were delivered at the several institutes, conventions, and special occasions sponsored by the University of Georgia's School of Journalism during the 1957-1958 session.

ETHRIDGE, WILLIE SNOW. *Summer Thunder*. New York, Coward-McCann, 1958. 319p. $3.95.

The story of Georgia's founding interwoven with the romance of a typical young couple of the era, through which she reveals the essential qualities that stood our early settlers in good stead, as well as interesting and little known episodes of Georgia's colonial history.

EVERHARDT, POWELL. *The Pianist's Art*. Atlanta, Privately printed, 1958. 396p. $15.00.

A comprehensive manual on piano playing for the student and the teacher, giving a complete analysis of the learning and playing processes from the very beginning to the finished performance. Mr. Everhart is a resident of Atlanta, Georgia.

FINCH, MILDRED AUSTIN. See: Austin, Aurelia.

FORD, ELIZABETH M. *Son of the Oath*. New York, Pageant Press, 1958. 100p. $2.50.

This book develops a completely new theory about the birth of Christ, based on literal historic fact and symbolic interpretation. Mrs. Ford is a resident of Atlanta, Georgia.

FORD, MARCIA. See: Radford, Ruby Lorraine.

FROST, CONNIE CURTIS. *Deep Within*. Dallas, Tex., Triangle Publishing Co., 1958. 40p. $2.00.

Nature, faith, love, and religion are the subjects dealt with in this collection of lyric poems. Mrs. Frost resides in Atlanta, Georgia.

GADDIS, PEGGY (pseud. Peggy Dern). *Beloved Intruder*. New York, Arcadia House, 1958. 220p. $2.75.

The trials and tribulations of a young television actress who fails an audition and falls in love with a man who disapproves of show business.

GADDIS, PEGGY. *Dr. Cary's Yearning.* London, Foulsham, 1957. 191p. 10s 6d.

Beth Mason, a nurse in a small backwoods community, finds herself working with a doctor who resents his obligation to work in so isolated an area.

GADDIS, PEGGY. *Dr. Henry's Secret Love.* London, Foulsham, 1958. 191p. 10s 6d.

Nurse Ellen Burke dedicates her work and love to Doctor Henry Griswold, a widower who is afraid to acknowledge his love for her.

GADDIS, PEGGY. *Dr. Ruth's Romance.* London, Foulsham, 1958. 192p. 10s 6d.

Dr. Ruth Prescott, disappointed in love, leaves the Grace Memorial Hospital to take over a general practice in an isolated town along the coast only to be snubbed by the local citizens.

GADDIS, PEGGY (pseud. Georgia Craig). *Grass Roots Nurse.* New York, Arcadia House, 1958. 224p. $2.75.

A student nurse decides to spend her last year of training at a small country hospital, and rooms with a family of ten children. She learns more from this family about life than she could get out of any nursing textbook.

GADDIS, PEGGY (pseud. Peggy Dern). *Homesick Heart.* New York, Arcadia House, 1958. 222p. $2.75.

After a lifetime of furnished rooms, Maggie McElroy, a working girl, is thrilled to inherit an entire "estate"—a run-down Georgia farm.

GADDIS, PEGGY (pseud. Georgia Craig). *A Husband for Janice.* New York, Arcadia House, 1958. 224p. $2.75.

A lively young man brings new life to a sleepy Georgia town—and love to a girl who lives there.

GADDIS, PEGGY. *Love Is Enough.* New York, Arcadia House, 1958. 223p. $2.75.

When she discovers that the young man she had thought to be penniless is an oil millionaire Jill Barclay is very upset and almost refuses to marry him.

GADDIS, PEGGY. *Nurse at Sundown.* New York, Arcadia House, 1958. 221p. $2.75.

Nursing is her profession and love is her heart's desire, and this newly graduated nurse finds both at a large island estate in Georgia.

GADDIS, PEGGY. *This Is Tomorrow.* New York, Arcadia House, 1958. 222p. $2.75.

Nurse Kelly MacIver encounters a weird family situation when she goes to Twisted Oaks, a plantation in the South Carolina low country, to care for the wife of the owner.

GATES, JAMES E. and MILLER, HAROLD. *Personal Adjustment to Business.* Englewood Cliffs, N. J., Prentice-Hall, 1958. 496p. $7.95.

A text which considers the process of adjustment to an occupation from selecting one's career and employer, through the mechanism of preparation (appearance, letter of application, interviews) to advancing. One section is devoted to self-employment. Dr. Gates is Dean of the School of Business Administration at the University of Georgia.

GORDON, ARTHUR. *Norman Vincent Peale: Minister to Millions.* Englewood Cliffs, N. J., Prentice-Hall, 1958. 311p. $4.95.

A close friend of Norman Vincent Peale traces his life from his birth in Bowersville, Ohio, through his college days and personal struggle to his position today as a leader of the Methodist Church, an author, and an advisor to people of all faiths. Mr. Gordon is a native of Savannah, Georgia.

HARRIS, KATHLEEN. See: Humphries, Mrs. Adelaide.

HARWELL, RICHARD BARKSDALE and TALMADGE, ROBERT L. *The Alma College Library: A Survey.* Chicago, American Library Association, 1958. 45p. $2.00.

A critical survey of a small Presbyterian college library in Michigan—pointing out physical, financial, and staff needs of the institution. Mr. Harwell is a native of Washington, Georgia.

HARWELL, RICHARD BARKSDALE, ed. *Cities and Camps of the Confederate States.* Urbana, Ill., University of Illinois Press, 1958. 262p. $4.50.

An English cavalry captain, Fitzgerald Ross, in the Austrian Hussars wrote, with sympathy, his impressions of the South during the Civil War. They are edited with annotations containing comments by the captain's contemporaries on the same event.

HARWELL, RICHARD BARKSDALE, ed. *The Union Reader.* New York, Longmans, 1958. $7.50.

This story of the Civil War, as seen and reported by soldiers and civilians of the North—selections from battle orders, prison narratives, songs, addresses, and humorous sketches, is arranged chronologically and touches on all phases of Union life.

HENDERSON, LE GRAND (pseud. Le Grand). *How Baseball Began in Brooklyn.* Nashville, Tenn., Abingdon Press, 1958. 58p. $2.00.

Long ago Pieter Denboom and the Indians found something that cured all war and disagreement—baseball.

HINES, NELLE WOMACK. *Such Goings On.* Macon, Ga., John W. Burke, 1958. 283p. $4.50.

This collection of stories presents a picture of old times, old costumes, and the wit and wisdom of the author's elders who lived their lives in the leisurely pace of the long ago. Mrs. Hines taught music for 41 years at Georgia State College for Women, Milledgeville, Georgia.

HINMAN, DOROTHY. *We Build Our Words.* New York, Bookman Associates, 1957. 94p. $2.50.
  Basic techniques of reading and word recognition are discussed in this book written by the director of the Hinman School in Atlanta.

HOLDEN, GENEVIEVE. *Something's Happened to Kate.* New York, Doubleday, 1958. 184p. $2.95.
  When quiet Kate Wooley falls in love with Jim Garrett, a criminal, she becomes involved with hidden jewels and murder. The author lives in Atlanta, Georgia.

HOWELL, WILLIE P. *The Country Boy.* New York, Comet Press, 1958. 183p. $3.50.
  An autobiography which tells of the author's youth in Southwest Georgia and Northern Florida and his goal to rise above his environment and to be successful. Mr. Howell is a resident of Bainbridge, Georgia.

HUMPHRIES, ADELAIDE. *Clinic Nurse.* New York, Bouregy, 1958. 224p. $2.75.
  Susan's decision not to let her socially ambitious mother run her life has dramatic results when she meets handsome and wealthy Jon Crawford at the clinic where she works.

HUMPHRIES, ADELAIDE (pseud. Kathleen Harris). *Jane Arden, Surgery Nurse.* New York, Bouregy, 1958. 223p. $2.75.
  Jane Arden, surgical nurse in a New York hospital, is not anxious to become romantically involved after the death of her fiance, but she discovers that it isn't always easy to let one's work come first.

HUMPHRIES, ADELAIDE. *The Nurse Had Red Hair.* New York, Bouregy, 1957. 219p. $2.75.
  Vacationing in a trailer camp in Florida, young Dr. Keith Markham encounters a red-headed nurse who drastically changes his plans for the future.

HURT, JOHN JETER, SR. *This Is My Story.* Atlanta, Privately Printed, 1957. 251p. $3.00.
  An inspirational autobiography of one of the South's leading Baptist ministers. Dr. Hurt is retired and lives in Atlanta, Georgia.

INGLESBY, CHARLOTTE. *Birds and Beasts of Old Savannah.* Savannah, Privately Printed, 1958. 26p. $1.00.
  Twelve photographs with descriptive notes of the birds, beasts, and legendary animals that enlivened architectural design in Savannah in days gone by.

JAMES, AVA LEACH. *Devotions for Juniors.* Grand Rapids, Mich., Zondervan, 1955. 154p. $2.00.
  A day-by-day book of one hundred and fifty devotions for young people based on one thought from the Bible. Mrs. James is the wife of Dr. Paul S. James, pastor of the Baptist Tabernacle in Atlanta.

JAMES, AVA LEACH. *More Devotions for Juniors.* Grand Rapids, Mich., Zondervan, 1956. 152p. $2.00.
Additional material for use in the daily devotionals of young people.

JEFFCOAT, GLADYS NEILL. *God's Wayside Beauty.* New York, Vantage Press, 1958. 61p. $2.00.
A collection of memories of the author's childhood days and meditations upon nature's loveliness and beauty. The author was born in Carrollton, Georgia.

JESSUP, RICHARD. *Lowdown.* New York, Dell, 1958. 159p. $.35.
The life and death of an ugly-natured singing star of the popular record field.

JESSUP, RICHARD. *Texas Outlaw.* Greenwich, Conn., Fawcett Publications, 1958. 128p. $.25.
The story of the redemption of a young outlaw who has come to a Texas town prepared to rob its bank.

JOHNSON, E. ASHBY. *The Crucial Task of Theology.* Richmond, Va., John Knox Press, 1958. 222p. $5.00.
A Presbyterian chaplain at Austin College in Sherman, Texas, explores the correlations between theology, philosophy, and modern science, and analyzes how theological notions are framed and appraised. Dr. Johnson is a native of Columbus, Georgia.

JONES, WILBUR DEVEREUX. *Lord Aberdeen and the Americas.* Athens, University of Georgia Press, 1958. 113p. $2.00.
A synthesis of Lord Aberdeen's American foreign policy, 1841-1846, this monograph treats in some detail the problems arising from the independent status of Texas, the Oregon boundary crisis, the Anglo-French intervention in La Plata, and the origins of the Mexican War. Dr. Jones is a member of the History Department at the University of Georgia.

JORDAN, G. RAY. *Prayer That Prevails.* New York, Macmillan, 1958. 150p. $3.00.
This new contribution to the Christian literature on prayer discusses the many aspects of prayer and its significance to the life of the Christian. Dr. Jordan is Professor of Homiletics and chapel preacher of the Candler School of Theology, Emory University.

KEY, WILLIAM O. *Battle of Atlanta and the Georgia Campaign.* New York, Twayne Publishers, 1958. 87p. $3.00.
A chronicle of one of the decisive battles and campaigns in the Civil War by the late William Key, veteran newspaperman of the *Atlanta Journal*, in the manner of an on-the-spot report.

KIMBALL, GARNET DAVIS. *Beauty for Ashes.* Emory University, Ga., Banner Press, 1957. 80p. $2.50.
A collection of poems dealing with the divergent themes of nature, love, children, home, and God. The author, a native of West Virginia, lives in Atlanta, Georgia.

KING, MARTIN LUTHER. *Stride Toward Freedom*. New York, Harper, 1958. 230p. $2.95.

The story of the Negroes in Montgomery, Alabama, who fought for their goals without violence by boycotting the city's segregated buses. The author is a native of Atlanta, Georgia.

KING, SPENCER BIDWELL, JR. *Ebb Tide: As Seen Through the Diary of Josephine Clay Habersham*. Athens, University of Georgia Press, 1958. 144p. $3.00.

The diary of Josephine Clay Habersham, kept in 1863 at "Avon," the mansion on the Vernon River, tells of life—happy and tragic—in the Habersham family of Savannah during wartime. Dr. King is Head of the History Department at Mercer University.

KYTLE, ELIZABETH. *Willie Mae*. New York, Knopf, 1958. 244p. $3.50.

The story of a spirited and philosophical Negro servant, Willie Mae, her childhood in Georgia, her responsibilities as a woman, her problems and the problems of her people, and her association with white employers. As told, in Willie Mae's own way of speaking, to one of her former employers.

LAWRENCE, DAISY GORDON and SHULTZ, GLADYS DENNY. *Lady From Savannah*. Philadelphia, Lippincott, 1958. 383p. $4.95.

Juliette Low, the founder of the Girl Scout movement, was a lady of gaiety and charm and self-sacrificing courage. Here her niece Daisy, who was the first registered Girl Scout, tells of the dramatic life of her famous aunt—her shy girlhood, her marriage to an Englishman of great wealth and high social position, her dignity under bitter humiliation, and her final discovery of a way of fulfillment.

LAWRENCE, JOHN BENJAMIN. *History of the Home Mission Board*. Nashville, Tenn., Broadman Press, 1958. 170p. $3.50.

First complete history of the Board as reflected in the minutes of the Board and the Southern Baptist Convention. The book is chronologically arranged and gives a background of the Baptist missionary movement abroad and in America. Dr. Lawrence, executive secretary emeritus of the Board, resides in Atlanta, Georgia.

LE GRAND. See: Henderson, Le Grand.

LEHRER, ROBERT NATHANIEL. *Work Simplification*. Englewood Cliff, N. J., Prentice-Hall, 1957. 394p. $6.95.

This study is devoted to simplification of work, explains the importance of the human factor, the background of work problems, the use of "creative thinking," relationship of work simplification to automation, electronic and integrated data processing, human engineering, and operations research. Dr. Lehrer is Professor of Industrial Engineering at Georgia Institute of Technology.

LEONARD, GEORGE B., JR., MOSKIN, J. ROBERT, and ATTWOOD, WILLIAM. *The Decline of the American Male.* New York, Random, 1958. 66p. $2.95.

The authors of this study conclude that the American male is rapidly losing his individuality due to the rise of the American woman. George B. Leonard, Jr., is an Atlantian.

LERCHE, CHARLES OLSEN, JR. *Foreign Policy of the American People.* Englewood Cliffs, N. J., Prentice-Hall, 1958. 547p. $7.50.

An analysis of foreign policy in the United States, the social, economic, and political factors which determine it, the government mechanism which carries it out and a view of essential issues in contemporary foreign policy. Dr. Lerche is a member of the Political Science Department at Emory University.

LONGSTREET, AUGUSTUS BALDWIN. *Georgia Scenes.* New York, Sagamore Press, 1957. 208p. $1.25.

A reprint of a Georgia classic that was first published in 1835 by A. B. Longstreet (1790-1870) lawyer, preacher, writer, jurist, college president, editor, and business man, born in Augusta, Georgia. This edition has an introduction by B. R. McElderry, Jr., of the University of California.

LITTLE, MRS. JAMES. See: Sibley, Celestine.

MCCULLERS, CARSON SMITH. *The Square Root of Wonderful: A Play.* New York, Houghton Mifflin, 1958. 169p. $3.00.

The return of her former husband brings much happiness to a young divorcee who is trying to make a new, secure life for herself. The play appeared on Broadway at the National Theatre in 1957. Mrs. McCullers is a native of Columbus, Georgia.

MATHEWS, JOSEPH JAMES. *Reporting the Wars.* Minneapolis, University of Minnesota Press, 1957. 322p. $6.50.

A penetrating analysis of the fundamental problem of what freedom of information really is and how nations have dealt, never satisfactorily, with the problem of truth in time of war and national crisis. Dr. Mathews is chairman of the History Department at Emory University.

MEADOWS, THOMAS BURTON. *Psychology of Learning and Teaching Christian Education.* New York, Pageant Press, 1958. 393p. $4.50.

A study that uses the textbook approach to educating people for Christian leadership and service and features an analysis of Jesus' methods in teaching. The author is a teacher at the Atlanta Bible Institute.

MEADOWS, THOMAS BURTON. *Teachers' Manual.* New York, Pageant Press, 1958. 98p. $2.00.

A manual designed to accompany the above study includes a comprehensive arrangement of objective type tests.

MARSHALL, EDISON. *Princess Sophia.* New York, Doubleday, 1958. 380p. $3.95.

A historical romance set in Alaska during the gold rush days of 1898, which tells the story of some colorful personalities who came there to find their fortunes.

MILLER, ARTHUR SELWYN. *Racial Discrimination in Private Education: A Legal Analysis.* Chapel Hill, N. C., University of North Carolina Press, 1957. 136p. $3.50.

This study presents the many and varied legal problems that will confront the administrators of private educational institutions in the future. Dr. Miller is an Associate Professor of Law at Emory University.

MONTGOMERY, HORACE, ed. *Georgians in Profile: Historical Essays in Honor of Ellis Merton Coulter.* Athens, University of Georgia Press, 1958. 387p. $6.00.

This collection of fourteen biographical essays covers a span of almost 200 years in Georgia history. These essays were written by former students of Dr. Coulter, recently retired Head of the History Department at the University of Georgia.

OLIVER, VIRGINIA KATHERINE. *Little Folks' Enchanted Hour.* New York, Pageant Press, 1957. 61p. $2.50.

Stories and poems appropriate at the quiet hours when children like to be read to before going to sleep. The author lives in Atlanta, Georgia.

PARKS, AILEEN WELLS. *James Oglethorpe: Young Defender.* Indianapolis, Bobbs-Merrill, 1958. 191p. $1.95.

A biography, for young readers, of the man who founded the first colony in Georgia for military, political, and social reasons. This is another in the Childhood of Famous Americans Series and is illustrated by Harry Hanson.

PHILLIPS, AURELIA HEATH. *Bible Meditations.* Carrollton, Georgia, Thomasson Printing Co., 1958. 56p. $2.00.

A noted Bible teacher has selected a few of her favorite lessons for the use of teachers and students of the Bible. Mrs. M. K. Phillips, founder of the Bremen Opportunity School, is a resident of Bremen, Georgia.

PLAGINOS, JANE KENT. *The Bitter Sting.* New York, Greenwich Book Publishers, 1957. 227p. $3.00.

The story of the tangled love life of Elyce Stafford, a rich, beautiful, and bored socialite whose small world is suddenly encompassed by World War II. The author, a native of Tifton, lives in Gainesville, Georgia.

POU, GENEVIEVE LONG. See: Holden, Genevieve.

POUND, MERRITT B. and SAYE, ALBERT B. *Handbook on the Constitutions of the United States and Georgia.* Athens, University of Georgia Press. 1958. Fifth Edition. 165 p. $1.25.

Contains the text of both constitutions along with analysis of the articles and amendments and a discussion of the historical background of both documents.

QUATTLEBAUM, JULIAN K. *The Great Savannah Races.* Columbia, S. C., R. L. Bryan Co., 1957. 133p. $10.00.

Through the efforts of the Savannah Motor Club, races were conducted at Savannah in 1908, 1910, and 1911. These events were international in scope and attracted entries from the major car builders of Europe and America, together with the most famous drivers of the times. The book is profusely illustrated. Dr. Quattlebaum is a resident of Savannah, Georgia.

RADFORD, RUBY LORRAINE. *Connie Dale, 4-H Leader.* New York, Bouregy, 1958. 224p. $2.75.

Connie Dale, a Four-H leader in a small Georgia town, was faced with many problems of cooking, sewing, and housekeeping, but she found herself with even more after she befriended the Murray family.

RADFORD, RUBY LORRAINE (pseud. Marcia Ford). *A Cruise for Judy.* New York, Avalon Books, 1957. 224p. $2.75.

On a South American cruise Judy Craig, the companion of a wealthy invalid, becomes involved in a kidnaping, an oil deal in the Near East, and a romance with the ship's young doctor.

RADFORD, RUBY LORRAINE (pseud. Marcia Ford). *Scout Counselor.* New York, Bouregy, 1958. 223p. $2.75.

A story for girls, depicting life in a Girl Scout camp with its problems and pleasures. The scene is laid in North Georgia.

REAGAN, AGNES LYTTON. *A Study of Factors Influencing College Students to Become Librarians.* Chicago, Association of College and Research Libraries, 1958. 110p. $2.75.

A scholarly analysis of the influences at work on the college and university campus that have caused students to choose librarianship as a life profession. Dr. Reagan is a member of the Division of Librarianship at Emory University.

RITTENHOUSE, WILLIAM H., JR. *God's P. O. W.* New York, Greenwich Book Publishers, 1957. Second Edition. 91p. $2.50.

An account of the author's conversion to the ministry while a World War II prisoner of war in a Nazi concentration camp. Dr. Rittenhouse is pastor of the Sylvan Hills Baptist Church in Atlanta, Georgia.

ROGERS, DOROTHY. *Jeopardy and a Jeep.* Rindge, N. H., Richard R. Smith, 1957. 301p. $3.95.

An account of the dangers, delights, and hazards encountered on a six month jeep trip around Africa that covered 25,000 miles. Dr. Rogers, a native of Ashburn, Georgia, is a professor of psychology at the State University of New York.

SAYE, ALBERT B., POUND, MERRITT B., and ALLUMS, JOHN F. *Principles of American Government.* Englewood Cliffs, N. J., Prentice-Hall, 1958. Third Edition. 479p. $5.95.

Includes new or expanded material on such subjects as the Congressional Committee System, the Soviet System, Supreme Court cases, the Federal Security Program, judicial procedure, and Congressional investigations.

SELL, EDWARD SCOTT. *Geography of Georgia.* Oklahoma City, Harlow, 1958. Second Edition. 175p. $2.64.

A detailed geographic study of the state of Georgia for use in elementary and junior high schools. The book is illustrated with charts, maps, and photographs. Dr. Sell is Professor Emeritus of Geography at the University of Georgia.

SIBLEY, CELESTINE. *The Malignant Heart.* New York, Doubleday, 1958. 192p. $2.95.

The murder of a popular Atlanta newspaperwoman starts a manhunt among the staff of the paper, all of whom had motives. This is a Crime Club selection.

SMITH, CLARENCE JAY, JR. *Finland and the Russian Revolution, 1917-1922.* Athens, University of Georgia Press, 1958. 251p. $4.50.

Traces the events which led to the involvement of Finland in the 1917 Revolution of her close neighbor, Russia, and its effects upon the internal affairs of the tiny country. Dr. Smith is a member of the Historical Department at the University of Georgia.

SMITH, HOWARD ROSS. *Government and Business: A Study in Economic Evolution.* New York, Ronald, 1958. 813p. $7.50.

An historical study of the revolving relationships between government and business in the United States. Emphasis is placed upon the motives underlying economic policy. Dr. Smith is Professor of Economics at the University of Georgia.

SORREL, GILBERT MOXLEY. *Recollections of a Confederate Staff Officer.* Jackson, Tenn., McCowart-Mercer, 1958. 322p. $5.00.

General Gilbert Moxley Sorrel, a native of Savannah, has recorded in his memoirs his opinions of both Southern and Yankee leaders. This edition has been edited by Dr. Bell Wiley, Professor of History at Emory University.

STELLING, MARY ELLEN. *Partial Payment.* Francestown, N. H., Golden Quill Press, 1958. 78p. $2.50.

A collection of poems expressing the author's appreciation for friends, love of things beautiful and an interpretation of the language of life.

STEPHENS, JOHN CALHOUN, ed. *Longsword, Earl of Salisbury.* New York, New York University Press, 1957. 161p. $4.00.

A reissue of a historical romance by Thomas Leland that was first published in 1762 with critical notes and comments by the editor. Dr. Stephens is a member of the English Department of Emory University.

STEVENSON, ELIZABETH, ed. *A Henry Adams Reader*. New York, Doubleday, 1958. 408p. $5.00.

Representative cross-section from the works of Henry Adams, selected by his foremost biographer, which reveals his main themes and presents the whole range of Adams' achievement as historian, biographer, novelist, poet, and philosopher.

STEWARD, DAVENPORT. *Battle-Ax of God*. New York, Dutton, 1958. 248p. $3.95.

A vigorous tale about the First Crusade and the events which led to a brave young son of a Saxon thane to leave England and join in the famous 11th century event.

STIRLING, NORA B. *Treasure Under the Sea*. New York, Doubleday, 1957. 354p. $4.50.

An account of some famous treasures buried under the sea, descriptions of attempts both successful and disastrous, to rescue them, and information about treasures still to be recovered.

SUGG, REDDING STANCIL, JR., ed. *Nuclear Energy in the South*. Baton Rouge, La., Louisiana State University Press, 1957. 151p. $3.50.

A detailed study of the ways and means of improving the position of the South in the national economy through the peaceful uses of the atom. Dr. Sugg is a member of the faculty at Georgia State College of Business Administration, Atlanta, Georgia.

TERRILL, HELEN E. and DIXON, SARA ROBERTSON. *History of Stewart County, Georgia*. Columbus, Georgia, Columbus Office Supply Co., 1958. Vol. I. 825p. $10.00.

A concise history of one of Georgia's counties—with brief biographical sketches. The book contains church and cemetery records, marriage records, wills, lists of county officers, and rosters of Stewart County companies in the Wars.

THIERY, ADELAIDE HAMLIN. *The Bitter and the Sweet*. Emory University, Ga., Banner Press, 1958. 92p. $2.00.

A collection of poems concerning life and its many ramifications.

THOMPSON, FRED BAILEY. *Animals Have Tales*. Hapeville, Ga., Hale Publishing Co., 1957. 67p. $2.00.

A collection of true stories about circus life and the "Big Top" by a former press agent of the Hagenbeck & Wallace Circus. The author is a resident of Clarkston, Georgia.

TILLEY, JOHN SHIPLEY. *Lincoln Takes Command*. Chapel Hill, N. C., University of North Carolina Press, 1958. 334p. $5.00.

This reissue of a book first published in 1941 is a critical study of the tense period that marked the road to civil war from the secession of South Carolina to the fall of Fort Sumter. The author, a native of Georgia, now practices law in Montgomery, Alabama.

TUCKER, GLENN. *High Tide at Gettysburg*. Indianapolis, Bobbs-Merrill, 1958. 395p. $5.00.

Reviews the strategies and the importance of the Civil War battle at

Gettysburg in 1863 and the battle's importance in the course of the war. The careers and the military tactics of Longstreet, Lee, Pickett and other leaders are also surveyed.

WAMBLE, HUGH. *Through Trial to Triumph.* Nashville, Tenn., Convention Press, 1958. 142p. $.60.

A panoramic view of the development of Southern Baptists from scattered beginnings in the 1700's to today's mighty denomination—special emphasis is placed on missions and education.

WEBB, JULIA CLAY BARRON. *Tall White Candle Lighted.* Emory University, Ga., Banner Press, 1958. 61p. $3.00.

A collection of forty poems, posthumously published by the daughters of the author, about home, nature, and religion.

WHITE, GOODRICH C. *The Education of the Administrator.* Nashville, Tenn., Division of Educational Institutions, Board of Education, The Methodist Church, 1957. 62p. Apply.

A compilation of talks and formal papers delivered by Chancellor White before meetings of college administrators, this little book deals with the author's beliefs about some of the problems confronting a college president.

WHITE, HELEN CHAPPELL. *Watch for the Morning.* New York, Rinehart, 1958. 192p. $3.00.

The author replies to many letters written in response to her first book "With Wings As Eagles," an account of her struggle to accept her son's death.

WILEY, BELL IRVIN. *The Common Soldier in the Civil War.* New York, Grosset and Dunlap, 1958. 444p. $5.95.

A reissue, in one volume, of the two books in which the author created the first complete life-size portraits of Johnny Reb and Billy Yank, the common soldiers of the Civil War.

WILEY, BELL IRVIN, ed. *Kentucky Cavaliers in Dixie: The Reminiscences of a Confederate Cavalryman.* Jackson, Tenn., McCowart-Mercer, 1957. 281p. $6.00.

These reminiscences of George Dallas Mosgrove give a picture of the Kentucky cavalryman at his best, pointing up his endurance, bravery, and humor. Dr. Wiley is a member of the History Department at Emory University.

WILLIS, AUBREY. *Our Greatest Enemy: Beveraged Alcohol.* New York, Exposition Press, 1958. 158p. $3.00.

From his own experiences with alcohol, the author views the degradation and horror of alcoholism. The author lives in Tifton, Georgia.

YERBY, FRANK. *The Serpent and the Staff.* New York, Dial, 1958. 377p. $3.95.

The story of a young man who fought the poverty and degradation of his New Orleans birthplace for the wealth and position which the life of a physician offered. The scene is in the South at the turn of the century.

Bibliography of Georgia Authors
1958-1959

THE tenth in the REVIEW's series of annual "Bibliographies of Georgia Authors," this annotated Bibliography is, as nearly as the compiler could make it, a complete and accurate record of books published by Georgia authors from November 1, 1958 to November 1, 1959. The annotations are descriptive, not critical; intended to place, not to judge the book. U. S., State, County, and City Documents, parts of books, brief analytics, and pamphlets of less than 25 pages have been omitted. Prices are given except when not supplied by publisher or when book is obtainable only on specific request, in which case the word "Apply" is used.

In determining whom to designate as Georgia authors, the compiler has included authors born in Georgia and claiming Georgia as their native state and those who have lived in Georgia for a period of five years and who did their writing here.

The compiler will welcome and appreciate readers' sending to him any additions or corrections. They may be sent to him at any time in care of the GEORGIA REVIEW. Several books inadvertently omitted from previous Bibliographies are listed here. Any books omitted from the present Bibliography will be included in the list for 1959-1960.

Acknowledgment is made to members of the staff of the Special Collections Division of the University of Georgia Library for their assistance in the preparation of this Bibliography.

ABBOT, WILLIAM WRIGHT. *The Royal Governors of Georgia, 1754-1775*. Chapel Hill, University of North Carolina Press, 1959. 198p. $5.00.

    This study is a political history of colonial Georgia from the time it came under the administration of the Crown until the American Revolution. Major developments under each of the royal governors are traced. Dr. Abbot, a native of Georgia, is an Associate Professor of History at the College of William and Mary.

ADAMS, MARION. *With Light Tread*. New York, Vantage Press, 1959. 40p. $2.00.

    A collection of twenty-eight poems that reflect the author's religious training and background. Mr. Adams, a native of Moultrie, Georgia, resides in Valdosta, Georgia.

AIREV, JOSEPH. *The Location of the Synthetic Fiber Industry.* New York, John Wiley, 1959. 203p. $9.75.

A study of the location pattern in North America of the rapidly growing synthetic fiber industry and of its potential in Puerto Rico and the Southern United States. The author is Associate Professor of Economics at Emory University.

ALLEN, CHARLES L. *When You Lose a Loved One.* Westwood, N. J., Revell, 1959. 61p. $1.50.

This book is designed to help you during those first hours and days when you are struggling to comprehend and accept the loneliness in your life and in your heart. The author is the minister of Grace Methodist Church, Atlanta, Georgia.

ALLEN, CHARLES L. and WALLIS, CHARLES L. *Candle, Star and Christmas Tree.* Westwood, N. J., Revell, 1959. 64p. $1.00.

A discussion of the origins of the Christmas customs and their deeper meanings. Charles Allen is a Methodist minister in Atlanta, Georgia; Charles Wallis, a Baptist, is Professor of English at Keuka College, Keuka Park, New York.

BONNER, JAMES CALVIN. *A Short History of Heard County.* Milledgeville, Ga., Privately Printed, 1959. 25p. Apply.

This brochure of a hundred copies contains a survey of the history of Heard County, Georgia, originally presented as a series of lectures given in conjunction with the adult education program at West Georgia College. Dr. Bonner is Professor of History at Georgia State College for Women, Milledgeville, Georgia.

BROKHOFF, JOHN R. *This Is Life.* Westwood, N. J., Revell, 1959. 126p. $2.00.

Vignettes of life which bring new understanding to everyday things; life in the home and in the church, the problem of life, the sins of life, and the life without end. Introduction is by Dr. Charles Allen. Dr. Brokhoff was for many years pastor of the Lutheran Church of the Redeemer in Atlanta, Georgia.

CALDWELL, ERSKINE. *Claudelle Inglish.* Boston, Little, Brown, 1959. 208p. $3.75.

A crossroads girl who sets out to make every man pay for one man's faithlessness and the success of her revenge is the theme of this story set in a small Southern town.

CALDWELL, ERSKINE. *When You Think of Me and Other Stories.* Boston, Little, Brown, 1959. 194p. $3.75.

A collection of short stories, widely varied in subject and background—the depression years, the war years, the rural South, and cities of Europe and America.

CASH, GRACE. *Lands Away: Rhymes from the Child's Everyday World.* Boston, Chapman and Grimes, 1958. 61p. $2.00.
   Read-aloud poems for children about nature, familiar animals, witches, and elves.

CASON, DURWARD VEAZEY. *Eyes That See.* Tucker, Ga. Privately Printed, 1959. 80p. Apply.
   Biography of Durward Cason, Jr., by his father, who is Secretary of the Department of Negro Work of the Georgia Baptist Convention. Mr. Cason, Jr., who was preparing for missionary work, was drowned in a boating accident in California.

CAYLOR, JOHN. *Ways of Witnessing.* Atlanta, Home Mission Board, Southern Baptist Convention, 1958. 119p. $.75.
   Ways of witnessing for Christ are discovered in the lives of home missionaries the author has chosen for biographical treatment.

CHAMPION, JOHN M. *Predicting Academic Success of Business Administration Students.* Research Paper No. 13. Atlanta. Bureaus of Business and Economic Research, School of Business Administration, Georgia State College of Business Administration. 1959. 51p. Gratis.
   A research paper designed not only for use by colleges but also by business managers, since the methodology may be used in industrial organizations. The author is Assistant Professor of Management at Georgia State College of Business Administration.

CHAPMAN, JAMES E. and WELLS, WILLIAM H. *Factors in Industrial Location in Atlanta, 1946-55.* Research Paper No. 8 Atlanta. Bureau of Business and Economic Research, School of Business Administration, Georgia State College of Business Administration. 1959. 39p. Gratis.
   A study to determine the importance and significance of the factors causing certain selected firms to locate in Atlanta over a ten-year period. The authors are on the faculty of the Georgia State College of Business Administration.

CHENEY, BRAINARD. *This Is Adam.* New York, McDowell, Obolensky, 1958. 294p. $3.95.
   The story of a Negro overseer in Georgia who risked his own safety in his loyalty to his employer. Mr. Cheney is a native of Georgia.

CLINKSCALES, BERTIE H. *The Far Horizon.* Philadelphia, Dorrance, 1958. 56p. $2.00.
   The theme of Christian hope and the love of God are woven through these poems about mountains, hills, birds, flowers, and people. Mrs. Clinkscales, a native of Georgia, now resides in South Carolina.

COLEMAN, LONNIE WILLIAM. *Sam.* New York, McKay, 1959. 245p. $3.95.
   Samuel Kendrick, a successful New York publisher, is a homosexual, but he is also involved emotionally with Addie, an unhappy married woman who understands him and returns his feelings.

COTTLE, SIDNEY and WHITMAN, TATE. *Corporate Earning Power and Market Valuation, 1935-1955.* Durham, N. C., Duke University Press, 1959. 201p. $12.50.

A comprehensive study of earning power and market valuations which seeks to develop yardsticks to provide a consistent basis for comparative analysis as a tool for management decision with respect to future capital investment as well as current operating policy.

COULTER, ELLIS MERTON, ed. *The Journal of William Stephens, 1743-1745.* Athens, University of Georgia Press, 1959. 288p. $5.00.

Through his journal William Stephens, Secretary of the Province of Georgia, undertook to inform the Trustees on everything which happened in Georgia. This is number three of the Wormsloe Foundation Publications. Dr. Coulter is Professor Emeritus of History at the University of Georgia.

CRAIG, GEORGIA. See: GADDIS, PEGGY.

DAVIS, OLIVE BELL. *Exodus:* 20. New York, Pageant Press, 1959. 280p. $3.50.

A cross section of all Southern types—rural, small town, city, and international—are portrayed in this story of Tom Tolbert, a man who breaks all of the Ten Commandments, on his rise from poverty to financial success. The author is a resident of Atlanta, Georgia.

DEMETRE, MARGARET. *Unchained Desire.* New York, Comet Press, 1959. 295p. $3.50.

A novel of race prejudice, moral degeneration, and corrupt politics in the South. Mrs. Demetre is a native of Savannah, Georgia.

DERN, MRS. JOHN SHERMAN. See: GADDIS, PEGGY.

DERN, PEGGY. See: GADDIS, PEGGY.

DREWRY, JOHN E., ed. *Are We Communicating? Press, Radio, Television, Periodicals, Public Relations, and Advertising As Seen Through Institutes and Special Occasions of the Henry W. Grady School of Journalism, 1958-59.* Vol. LX, No. 2, Ser. 1180. Athens, University of Georgia Bulletin, 1959. 222p. Paper $2.00. Cloth $3.00.

A compilation of addresses on communications delivered during the past year at the several institutes, conventions and other special occasions sponsored by the University's School of Journalism.

DUNCAN, JOHN A. *Honeymoon Haven.* New York, Vantage Press, 1959. 322p. $4.50.

A story of how a young couple spend a perfect honeymoon in a secluded cottage, finding for themselves a deep and fulfilling love.

EDGE, FINDLEY BARTOW. *Does God Want You as a Minister of Education?* Nashville, Broadman Press, 1951. 42p. $0.25.

This little booklet gives a clear view of the qualifications and work of a minister of education in a church.

EDGE, FINDLEY BARTOW. *Helping the Teacher*. Nashville, Broadman Press, 1959. 192p. $2.95.
A book for Sunday School teachers giving practical suggestions and methods. Includes selecting aims, preparing the lesson, and employing methods that are tried and true.

EDGE, FINDLEY BARTOW. *Teaching for Results*. Nashville, Broadman Press, 1956. 256p. $3.00.
A thorough treatment of the art of Christian teaching for teachers who are vitally interested in the goals of their efforts. The author is a native Georgian and is on the faculty of Southern Baptist Seminary, Louisville, Kentucky.

EMBRY, ELOISE WILLIAMS. *Hands Full of Honey*. New York, Exposition Press, 1959. 40p. $2.50.
A collection of thirty-eight poems that give deep and pleasant word pictures on religion, friends, recollections of childhood, and family life. The author lives in Macon, Georgia.

ENGLISH, MILDRED E. *College in the Country*. Athens, University of Georgia Press, 1959. 136p. $3.00.
A program for the education of adults in rural areas, with the program built specifically around their own study choices and educational trips. College in the Country represents a cooperative effort of West Georgia College and surrounding areas. Dr. English is Professor Emeritus of Georgia State College for Women, Milledgeville, Georgia.

ETHRIDGE, WILLIE SNOW. *Russian Duet: The Story of a Journey*. New York, Simon and Schuster, 1959. 313p. $3.95.
In the summer of 1958 the author and her friend Nila Magidoff took a trip to Russia in order to find Nila's mother, sister, and niece, of whom she hadn't had a word in ten years. This is the story of their riotous decidedly off-the-beaten-track adventure.

EVANS, TREVOR. *Fundamentals of Mathematics*. Englewood Cliffs, N. J., Prentice-Hall, 1959. 289p. $5.00.
Designed for remedial courses given college freshmen, this book makes mathematics easier for the poorly prepared students by means of its logical and rigorous presentation. Dr. Evans is the Chairman of the Mathematics Department at Emory University.

FAULK, LANETTE and JONES, BILLY W. *History of Twiggs County, Georgia*. Columbus, Ga., Columbus Office Supply Co., 1959. 500p. $10.00.
A comprehensive history of one of Georgia's early counties, containing early tax digests, family biographies, cemetery records, church records, natural resources, list of veterans of all wars, and extracts from newspapers. This book may be obtained from the Major-General John Twiggs Chapter, D.A.R., Dry Branch, Georgia.

FORD, MARCIA. See: RADFORD, RUBY LORRAINE.

GADDIS, PEGGY (pseud. PEGGY DERN). *April Heart.* New York, Arcadia House, 1959. 222p. $2.95.

A young girl whose foster parents are killed in an automobile accident goes to Louisiana to live with her real father and is greeted with some unexpected complications.

GADDIS, PEGGY (pseud. PEGGY DERN). *At Granada Court.* New York, Arcadia House, 1959. 220p. $2.75.

A Spanish style motel in Florida, owned and operated by a young girl and her mother, is the setting for this romance involving some of the paying guests.

GADDIS, PEGGY (pseud. PEGGY DERN). *Caribbean Melody.* New York, Arcadia House, 1959. 221p. $2.95.

A dance team encounters problems, financial and romantical, on the Caribbean island of Martinique.

GADDIS, PEGGY (pseud. GEORGIA CRAIG). *Her Alaskan Home.* New York, Arcadia House, 1959. 223p. $2.75.

Sally Perry, homesick for her Georgia home, rediscovers the beauty of her Alaskan home through the eyes of her visiting sister, Kathy.

GADDIS, PEGGY. *Homesick Heart.* London, Wright and Brown, 1959. 222p. 10s 6d.

A girl who has always lived in furnished rooms inherits an "estate"— a down-at-heels Georgia farm—with its attendant complications and compensations.

GADDIS, PEGGY (pseud. GEORGIA CRAIG). *Kerry Middleton, Career Girl.* New York, Arcadia House, 1959. 224p. $2.95.

A contented personal secretary, who has rejected the thought of marriage because of her sister's marital misfortunes, begins to have her doubts about spinsterhood when she meets a kind and intelligent man.

GADDIS, PEGGY (pseud. PEGGY DERN). *Little Love.* New York, Arcadia House, 1959. 224p. $2.75.

The broken heart of a jilted girl is mended with a new romance in a small town in the Blue Ridge Mountains.

GADDIS, PEGGY. *Mountain Nurse.* New York, Arcadia House, 1959. 223p. $2.95.

After graduating from nursing school, Julie Winston goes on a vacation to a remote area of the Blue Ridge Mountains. There, unexpectedly, she gets her first patient, a difficult young man known as the "Wayfaring Stranger."

GADDIS, PEGGY. *Nurse Gerry.* New York, Arcadia House, 1959. 223p. $2.75.

Geraldine Knight, private duty nurse, goes to the lovely Isle d'Or off the Florida coast on a case. There she finds an unusual romance.

GADDIS, PEGGY. *Nurse Hilary*. New York, Arcadia House, 1958. 222p. $2.75.
Hilary Westbrook, R.N., accepts a position as an assistant in a new home for the aged. She develops a true affection for the people there and fights determinedly against a money-conscious administration.

GADDIS, PEGGY. *Nurse Leota's Romance*. London, Foulsham, 1959. 184p. 10s 6d.
A young nurse in a Florida city contends with the antagonisms of her patient's relatives.

GADDIS, PEGGY. *Nurse Linette's Loyalty*. London, Foulsham, 1958. 184p. 10s 6d.
The jealousy of a patient's sister-in-law tries the loyalty of a young private duty nurse caring for a crotchety old man.

GADDIS, PEGGY. *Romantic Nurse Sally*. London, Foulsham, 1959. 184p. 10s 6d.
Nurse Sally finds that what she thought was going to be a vacation becomes a rewarding and romantic experience working with small children.

GADDIS, PEGGY (pseud. GEORGIA CRAIG). *Sandy*. New York, Arcadia House, 1958. 221p. $2.75.
With the new boom of tourist traffic in her home town in Georgia, Sandy Jessup persuades her aunts to open their home to overnight travelers. This action leads Sandy to a romantic encounter as well as a political problem.

GADDIS, PEGGY. *Settlement Nurse*. New York, Arcadia House, 1959. 220p. $2.95.
A nurse who has grown up in an orphanage finds happiness working in a settlement house.

GADDIS, PEGGY (pseud. GEORGIA CRAIG). *There's Always Hope*. New York, Arcadia House, 1959. 223p. $2.75.
After years of caring for her two younger sisters, Hope's life seemed empty when they married. Her impetuous decision to take a Caribbean cruise filled the new emptiness in her life.

GARRISON, KARL C. *Growth and Development*. New York, Longman's, 1959. Second Edition. 573p. $5.50.
A second edition of Dr. Garrison's summary of data relating to the physical and psychological development of infants and children; with chapters by Florene Young and Florence Heisler.

GARRISON, KARL C. and FORCE, DEWEY G. *The Psychology of Exceptional Children*. New York, Ronald Press, 1959. Third Edition. 592p. $6.00.
This edition has been extensively revised and includes new chapters on epilepsy, cerebral palsy, and cardiac conditions. Dr. Garrison is a member of the staff of the College of Education, University of Georgia.

GARRISON, WEBB BLACK (pseud. GARY WEBSTER). *Codfish, Cats and Civilization.* Garden City, N. Y., Doubleday, 1959. 263p. $3.95.

In a new approach to the study of animal ecology, Dr. Garrison invests his chapters with a wealth of history, statistics, anecdotes, and pertinent conclusions. The author is a native of Covington, Georgia.

GODLEY, MARGARET. *Historic Tybee Island.* Savannah Beach, Georgia, Savannah Beach Chamber of Commerce, 1958. 72p. $1.25.

This book traces the history of Tybee Island from the earliest mention of the Island in 1605, through five major wars, to 1958. Profusely illustrated with reproductions from various libraries, private collections, and museums.

HALLIDAY, WILLIAM ROSS. *Adventure Is Underground: The Story of the Great Caves of the West and the Men Who Explore Them.* New York, Harper, 1959. 206p. $4.50.

A doctor and experienced "caver" describes various caves in the Western United States, discusses techniques of cave exploration and relates his own and others' experiences in caves.

HARRIS, JOEL CHANDLER. *Uncle Remus—His Songs and Sayings.* New York, Heritage Press, 1959. 158p. $5.00.

A new edition of the folk stories of Joel Chandler Harris. The introduction is by Marc Connelly and the illustrations are by Seong Moy.

HARRIS, KATHLEEN. See: HUMPHRIES, ADELAIDE.

HARWELL, RICHARD B., ed. *Kate—The Journal of a Confederate Nurse.* Baton Rouge, Louisiana State University Press, 1959. 225p. $6.00.

This journal gives a close and intimate picture of life in the Confederate hospitals and behind the lines of Civil War action.

HEINZ, MAMIE W. *Growing and Learning in the Kindergarten.* Richmond, Va., John Knox Press, 1959. 157p. $3.00.

This study has two purposes: to show that children mature through satisfying experiences of adventure, exploration, and experimentation; and to show the changes that take place in the teacher as she evaluates what happens to her children. The author was born in Atlanta, Georgia.

HUBBELL, RAYNOR. *Confederate Stamps, Old Letters, and History: A Story of Three Score Years and Ten of Stamp Collecting. What It Has Done for Me and What It Could Do for You Whatever May Be Your Age.* Griffin, Ga. Privately Printed, 1959. 67p. $5.00.

Historical reminiscences and hobbies of a collector of stamps and old letters. Profusely illustrated. The author is a resident of Griffin, Georgia.

HUMPHRIES, ADELAIDE (pseud. Kathleen Harris). *Jane Arden, Head Nurse.* New York, Bouregy, 1959. 221p. $2.95.

Jane's appointment as head nurse in a children's hospital in a small Florida town brings her to a challenging and rewarding job, but hospital politics and local gossip are serious obstacles to be overcome.

HUMPHRIES, ADELAIDE. *Nurse on Horseback.* New York, Bouregy, 1959. 224p. $2.75.
A story of a young nurse whose return to her home in the West is complicated by a series of challenging and dramatic episodes.

HUTCHESON, CHRISTINE GORE. *Off the High Horse.* New York, Pageant Press, 1959. 115p. $3.00.
A collection of humorous verse by a person who has observed life as a newspaperwoman, teacher, and county welfare director. The author is a native of Marietta, Georgia.

JANUS, SIDNEY Q. *Our Story . . . Atlanta. A Panorama of Israel.* White Plains, New York. 1957. 176p. $5.00.
An interpretation in words, graphic art, and pictures of the rebirth of the State of Israel. In addition to a large pictorial section on Israel, there are also sections on the history of Jewish organizations in Atlanta and tributes to certain leading Atlanta citizens. The author has been a resident of Atlanta since 1942.

JEFFCOAT, RALEIGH. *Seven Little Karmuns Plus One.* Atlanta, Home Mission Board, Southern Baptist Convention, 1958. 26p. $0.50.
A picture storybook on evangelism in Alaska and life among the Eskimos. Mrs. John Jeffcoat is a native of Waycross, Georgia.

JOHNSON, HAROLD L. *Exploration in Responsible Business Behavior: An Exercise in Behavioral Economics.* Research Paper No. 4. Atlanta. Bureau of Business and Economics Research, School of Business Administration, Georgia State College of Business Administration. 1958. 66p. Gratis.

JONES, CARTER BROOKE. *The White Band.* New York, Funk and Wagnalls, 1959. 334p. $4.50.
A novel dealing with race violence and mob rule in the deep South. The author is a former resident of Atlanta, Georgia.

JONES, DOROTHY HOLDER. *The Wonderful World Outside.* New York, Dodd, Mead, 1959. 90p. $2.75.
The story of a teenaged orphan girl who has grown up in a dreary institution, living for the day when she will be able to leave it. When the time comes, however, she finally realizes that her fellow inmates are really her "family." This book won the Dodd-Mead 17th Summer Literary Competition. Mrs. Jones is a Decatur housewife.

JONES, RAY G. JR., and CAMPBELL, CLAUDE A. *The Development of Georgia's Tufted Textile Industry.* Research Paper No. 12. Atlanta. Bureau of Business and Economic Research, School of Business Administration, Georgia State College of Business Administration. 1959. 46p. Gratis.

A record of the economic development of a rapid growth industry reflecting the problems commonly faced by such an industry arising among small-scale local entrepreneurs. Mr. Jones is a native of Dalton, Georgia.

JORDAN, C. RAY. *You Can Preach! Building and Delivering the Sermon.* Westwood, N. J., Revell, 1958. 256p. Paper $1.75.

A new edition of Dr. Jordan's explanation of the art and science of successful preaching. The use of illustrative stories and quotations adds to the effectiveness of Dr. Jordan's methodology.

KEATS, JOHN. *Insolent Chariots.* New York, Lippincott, 1958. 232p. $3.95.

A pointed commentary on how Americans regard their automobiles and on present auto styles. Digs into the ways new car styles are evolved, and the facts behind new car styles, mammoth highways, car sales procedures, and other aspects of the automotive industry.

KEATS, JOHN. *School Without Scholars.* Boston, Houghton, Mifflin, 1958. 202p. $3.00.

Describing two imaginary schools that are at opposite poles of formal old-fashioned education and education for "life adjustment," the author picks out what elements he would and would not recommend from each, and makes other criticisms of present-day education.

KEATS, JOHN. *The Crack in the Picture Window.* Boston, Houghton, Mifflin, 1957. 196p. $3.00.

An incisive indictment of the housing developments which dot contemporary suburbia stressing the stifling effects they have on the lives and personalities of those who inhabit them. Illustrated by Don Kindler. The author is a native of Moultrie, Georgia.

KIKER, DOUGLAS. *Strangers on the Shore.* New York, Random House, 1959. 344p. $3.95.

A novel of officers and their wives in the peacetime American Navy. The main characters are: a promising young officer and his wife, who resents his career; and a young woman whose ill-starred marriage is ended a month after it begins. The author, a native of Griffin, Georgia, now lives in Alexandria, Virginia.

KIMBALL, GARNET DAVIS. *Heartstring Harmonies.* Atlanta, Banner Press, 1959. 67p. $2.50.

A collection of poems that describe the world around us—the beauties of nature and the people who populate it.

KING, JOHN H. *Three Hundred Days in a Yankee Prison.* Marietta, Ga., Continental Book Company, 1959. 114p. $6.00.

A facsimile reprint of a work first published in 1904. Dr. King was for many years the surgeon at the Confederate Soldiers Home in Atlanta, Georgia.

KNIGHT, WILLYS R. *Probing into the Economic Attitudes of College Students.* Research Paper No. 3, Atlanta, Bureau of Business and Economic Research, School of Business Administration, Georgia State College of Business Administration. 1958. 62p. Gratis.

An initial exploration into the realm of college students' economic attitudes, searching for factors underlying such attitudes, and analyzing reasons given by students. The author is Director of the Bureau of Business and Economic Research, Georgia State College of Business Administration.

LANTZ, J. EDWARD. *Reading the Bible Aloud.* New York, Macmillan, 1959. 144p. $3.50.

A guide to help the church school teacher, layman, and parent in his understanding, preparation, and actual reading of passages of Scripture. The author is a Professor of Gammon Theological Seminary, Atlanta, Georgia.

LEE, GRACE, ed. *Helping the Troubled School Child.* New York, National Association of Social Workers, 1959. 447p. $5.00.

Selected readings in school social work, 1935-1955. Miss Lee is a former classroom teacher and at present is a visiting teacher in Mitchell County, Georgia.

LEMLY, JAMES HUTTON. *Expressway Influence on Land Use and Value, Atlanta, 1941-1956.* Atlanta, Georgia State College of Business Administration, Bureau of Business Economic Research, 1958. 137p. $2.50.

This study of land value was prepared for the State Highway Department of Georgia and the United States Bureau of Public Roads.

LEONARD, GEORGE. *Shoulder the Sky.* New York, McDowell, Obolensky, 1959. 310p. $4.50.

A novel about two young flying instructors at a training base in Georgia who fall in love with the same girl. The author was born in Macon, Georgia, and grew up in Atlanta, Georgia.

LONGSTREET, AUGUSTUS BALDWIN. *Georgia Scenes.* Gloucester, Mass., Peter Smith, 1959. 198p. $3.25.

A reprint of a Georgia classic that was first published in 1835 by A. B. Longstreet (1790-1870), lawyer, preacher, writer, jurist, college president, editor, and business man, born in Augusta, Georgia. This edition has an introduction by B. R. McElderry, Jr., of the University of California.

MCCULLERS, CARSON SMITH. *The Square Root of Wonderful: A Play.* New York, Samuel French, 1958. 87p. $1.00.

The acting edition of a play that appeared on Broadway at the National Theatre in 1957. Mrs. McCullers is a native of Columbus, Georgia.

MCGILL, RALPH. *A Church, A School.* Nashville, Abingdon, 1959. 96p. $2.00.

In selections from his columns from the *Atlanta Constitution* Pulitzer Prize winner Ralph McGill expresses his views on human rights today.

McGinty, C. Lamar. *Sermon Outlines*. No. I. Westwood, N. J., Revell, 1957. 80p. $1.25.

Fifty-two clear and complete sermon outlines—one for each Sunday in the year—with Scripture texts from Genesis through Revelations. The author is a native of Georgia.

McPherson, Nenien C., Jr. *The Power of a Purpose*. Westwood, N. J., Revell, 1959. 156p. $2.50.

With abundant illustrations from life and scripture, this book challenges the reader to direct his will toward a worthy purpose and to use the power of this purpose to live victoriously day by day.

McPherson, Robert G. *Theory of Higher Education in Nineteenth-Century England*. Athens, University of Georgia Press, 1959. 135p. $2.00.

University education in England underwent a thorough transformation in the nineteenth century. The evolution is followed through an examination of outstanding authorities in English education. Dr. McPherson is a member of the History Department at the University of Georgia.

Marshall, Edison. *The Pagan King*. Garden City, N. Y., Doubleday, 1959. 380p. $3.95.

A romance about the legendary ruler of fifth century England, King Arthur, told in the first person. The author envisions a historical setting of lawlessness and strife, which was stemmed by this hero of countless myths.

Mason, David E. *The Charley Matthews Story*. Atlanta, Home Mission Board, Southern Baptist Convention, 1958. 79p. $0.50.

An account of the life of C. E. Matthews and his labors in the mission fields.

Montgomery, Horace. *Howell Cobb's Confederate Career*. Tuscaloosa, Ala., Confederate Publishing Co., 1959. 144p. $4.00.

Tenth in the series of Confederate Centennial studies, this monograph not only presents the military career of Howell Cobb, but also brings out his role in the events preceding the war. Dr. Montgomery is a Professor of History at the University of Georgia.

Moore, Edith Wyatt. *Natchez Under-the-Hill*. Natchez, Miss., Southern Historical Publications, 1958. 131p. $3.00.

A native of Georgia who has lived in Natchez since 1919 has written a history of this colorful and once notorious town that huddled beneath the bluffs in contrast to the proud and aristocratic town on top of the hill.

Moore, William Frank. *Why the Righteous May Suffer*. New York, Greenwich Books, 1959. 35p. $2.50.

In this study of deep personal significance to every Christian, the author says in his foreword, "To sufferers this is a message of knowledge and comfort; to non-sufferers, it is meant to help them to a better understanding why some loved one, or friend may be a sufferer." The author was the Baptist chaplain at Battey State Hospital, Rome, Georgia.

NEWTON, LOUIE D. *Fifty Golden Years*. Hapeville, Georgia, Longino and Porter, 1958. 92p. $0.50.
Detailing the history of the Atlanta Association of Baptist Churches from 1909 to 1958 and its emphasis on evangelism and missions. The author is pastor of the Druid Hills Baptist Church in Atlanta, Georgia.

ODUM, EUGENE P. and ODUM, HOWARD T. *Fundamentals of Ecology*. Philadelphia, Saunders, 1959. Second Edition. 546p. $7.50.
This is the second edition of Dr. Odum's concise work on ecology, designed for the college student and the layman desiring an introduction to the subject.

OGBURN, CHARLTON, JR. *Big Caesar*. Boston, Houghton, Mifflin, 1959. 118p. $2.75.
Big Caesar is a huge truck, an ancient truck, which Ronnie decides to get running again after it has been idle for years. This adventure is the turning point in the life of this young boy. The author was born in Atlanta, Georgia.

OGBURN, CHARLTON, SR. *Economic Plan and Action: Recent American Developments*. New York, Harper, 1959. 287p. $4.75.
This study of United States economic development since 1946 is based on the reports of the National Planning Association. The Full Employment Act, export of United State's Capital, farm commodities surplus, organized labor and collective bargaining, productive uses of nuclear energy, and other aspects of the economy are examined by a former counsel of the National Planning Association.

OGBURN, CHARLTON, JR. *The Bridges*. Boston, Houghton, Mifflin, 1957. 68p. $3.50.
The story of a rare understanding between a fourteen-year-old girl and her grandfather, who have a deep love for the natural wilderness of their river-bound island.

OGBURN, CHARLTON, JR. *The Marauders*. New York, Harper, 1959. 307p. $4.50.
The story of Merrill's Marauders, the 2,600 American soldiers who fought behind Japanese lines in the jungles of Burma for six months during World War II.

ORR, CLYDE, JR. *Between Earth and Space*. New York, Macmillan, 1959. 253p. $4.95.
Describes the earth's atmosphere, explains various weather phenomena, climate changes, particles in the air, and atmospheric electricity, and

discusses the effect of the atmosphere on man's social and economic existence. Dr. Orr is a research Professor of Chemical Engineering at Georgia Institute of Technology.

ORR, CLYDE, JR. *Fine Particle Measurement: Size, Surface, and Pore Volume.* New York, Macmillan, 1959. 35p. $10.50.
Information on methods currently in use in research laboratories for determining size, surface, and pore volume.

PADDOCK, LAURA HUTCHINS (pseud. AUNT LOLLIPOP). *Little Mrs. Lame Duck.* Miami, Florida, Aunt Lollipop Publications, 1959. 25p. $1.50.
A story for the kindergarten set about a one-legged duck and her friends and their troubles with Mr. Fox. Illustrated by Garland Smith. Both author and illustrator are natives of Athens, Georgia.

PARANKA, STEPHEN. *Marketing Implications of Interurban Development.* Research Paper No. 11. Atlanta, Bureau of Business and Economic Research, School of Business Administration, Georgia State College of Business Administration, 1958. 39p. Gratis.
A report analyzing the changing marketing environment and revealing the need for planning future market operations in relation to predicted population trends. The author is Associate Professor of Marketing at Georgia State College of Business Administration.

PERRY, EDMUND. *The Gospel in Dispute; the Relation of Christian Faith to Other Missionary Religions.* Garden City, N. Y., Doubleday, 1958. 230p. $3.95.
A study of the contemporary missionary activities of Judaism, Islam, Hinduism, and Buddhism and their challenge to the Christian Faith. Dr. Perry is a native of Georgia.

PHILLIPS, ULRICH BONNELL. *Life and Labor in the Old South.* New York, Grossett, 1959. 384p. $2.95.
A reprint edition of a book first published in 1929. Dr. Phillips, a native of Georgia, was considered one of America's outstanding historians.

RADFORD, RUBY LORRAINE (pseud. MARCIA FORD). *Island Nurse.* New York, Bouregy, 1959. 224p. $2.95.
A nurse is assigned to the case of an elderly cardiac patient on a secluded island.

RANGE, WILLARD. *Franklin D. Roosevelt's World Order.* Athens, University of Georgia Press, 1959. 234p. $4.50.
This book is a study of Roosevelt's thinking on international affairs during his career in public life. It traces his ideas for promoting peace among nations and for bringing about a world order. Professor Range is a member of the Political Science Department at the University of Georgia.

RIDGE, GEORGE ROSS. *The Hero in French Romantic Literature.* Athens, University of Georgia Press, 1959. 144p. $3.75.

A detailed analysis of the romantic hero that shows him as a social projection, an ideal man who reflects the intellectual currents of his era—not a series of different heroes, but an archetypal hero who assumes different forms in various works. Dr. Ridge is a member of the French Department at Georgia State College of Business Administration, Atlanta, Georgia.

RUCHTI, HELEN HOLMES. *For You.* Atlanta, Home Mission Board, Southern Baptist Convention, 1958. 72p. $0.50.

This is a series of five stories of evangelism in home missions, represented by outstanding missionary personalities. Mrs. W. C. Ruchti is the wife of the pastor of the Fifth Avenue Baptist Church in Rome, Georgia.

RUTH, CLAIRE MERRITT and SLOCUM, BILL. *The Babe and I.* Englewood Cliffs, N. J., Prentice-Hall, 1959. 215 p. $3.95.

The story of one of America's legendary heroes told by his widow. Mrs. Ruth recalls the crowded, eventful years of marriage to the Babe with warmth and affection, and has some things to say about the shabby treatment her husband received from the national game he had done so much for. Mrs. Ruth is a native Georgian.

SAYE, ALBERT B. *Election Laws of Georgia.* Athens, Institute of Law and Government, School of Law, University of Georgia, 1959. 226p. Paper $2.50.

In two sections, (A) the Statutes and (B) an analysis of these statutes, this study includes all general election laws in force up to March, 1959. The author is Professor of Political Science at the University of Georgia.

SCHOECK, HELMUT. *U. S. A.: Motive und Strukturen.* Stuttgart, Deutsche Verlags-Anstalt, 1959. 427p. $4.00.

A fresh interpretation of the American scene in its many aspects as seen by a German sociologist; designed to correct and supplement the present views of the United States held by Europeans today. Dr. Schoeck is Associate Professor of Sociology at Emory University.

SCHWARTZ, DAVID JOSEPH. *The Magic of Thinking Big.* Englewood Cliffs, N. J., Prentice-Hall, 1959. 228p. $4.95.

The author offers techniques for building confidence, poise, and resourcefulness and offers plans for achieving success. Dr. Schwartz is Professor of Marketing at Georgia State College of Business Administration, Atlanta, Georgia.

SCOTT, ROBERT LEE, JR. *Flying Tigers: Chenault of China.* Garden City, N. Y., Doubleday, 1959. 285p. $3.95.

Concentrates on the years between 1937 and 1957 during which Chenault organized and trained his famous Flying Tigers to fight against the Japanese in World War II, and, in the postwar period, created CAT airlift to supply the Communist-besieged villages of northern China and Manchuria. The author, a native of Macon, Georgia, was one of Chenault's Flying Tigers and a close personal friend of the late general.

SCOTT, WILLIAM G. *The Social Ethic in Management Literature.* Studies in Business and Economics. Bulletin No. 4. Atlanta, Bureau of Business and Economic Research, School of Business Administration, Georgia State College of Business Administration, 1959. 116p. Gratis.

This study in the shift in emphasis in management philosophy from individualism to collectivism notes trends and draws implications for management practice. The author is Associate Professor of Management, Georgia State College of Business Administration.

SCREVEN, PATRICIA. *Skidmarks to Hell.* Boston, Bruce Humphries, 1959. 209p. $3.00.

This is the tough, brutal story of an honest policeman turned bad by circumstances and love for a woman he could never marry. Miss Screven is a resident of Atlanta, Georgia.

SENTELL, PERRY, JR. *Handbook for Georgia Legislators.* Athens, Institute of Law and Government, School of Law, University of Georgia, 1958. 117p. $3.50.

A handbook designed primarily for new members of the Georgia General Assembly, the book includes information on such topics as rules, order of business, committee procedure, routes of bills, and motions, written in as clear and forthright language as the subject permits.

SHIELDS, LARRY, comp. *Laff Insurance.* New York, Vantage Press, 1957. 125p. $2.95.

A collection of jokes and cartoons concerning all phases of the insurance profession.

SMITH, LILLIAN EUGENIA. *One Hour.* New York, Harcourt, Brace, 1959. 440p. $5.00.

There are serious consequences and psychological developments in a Southern town when an eight-year-old child accuses one of the community's most respected citizens, a research scientist, of rape. The young minister of the parish to which both families belong believes in the scientist and seeks to prove his innocence, but he also develops an interest in the strange little girl with her world of fantasies. Lillian Smith is a resident of Clayton, Georgia.

STAMPOLIS, ANTHONY. *Employees' Attitudes Toward Unionization, Management and Factory Conditions: A Survey Case Study.* Research Paper No. 7. Atlanta, Bureau of Business and Economic Research, School of Business Administration, Georgia State College of Business Administration, 1958. 48p. Gratis.

A case study using the questionnaire method to investigate factors associated with union attitudes and labor-management relations. The author is Professor of Political Economy at the Georgia State College of Business Administration.

STEPHENS, JOHN C., JR., ed. *Poems of Zechariah Worrell*. Atlanta, The Library, Emory University, 1958. 55p. Apply.

A selection of verse written by an eighteenth century Methodist preacher and circuit rider in Ireland; these poems give an insight into the Reverend Worrell's personal feelings. The editor is Associate Professor of English at Emory University.

STEVENS, PATRICK M. *Voyaging to Discovery*. Lexington, Ga., The Oglethorpe Echo, 1959. 41p. $1.00.

An appeal for greater research into God's laws and a more enlightened approach to truth. The author is a resident of Union Point, Georgia.

STEWARD, DAVENPORT. *Black Spice*. New York, Dutton, 1959. 255p. $3.95.

The spice trade in exotic nineteenth century Sumatra is the background for this tale of treachery, Malay pirates, love, death, and the rescue of a beautiful American woman from her captors.

STOVER, MARY and CRAWFORD, LUCILLE LOGAN. *God Leads Me*. New York, Morehouse-Gorham, 1959. Various paging. Teachers Guide $2.00. Child's Study Leaflet $1.20. Handwork Sheets $1.35.

This is a new series of Episcopal Sunday School lessons for nursery-age children. Marian Kinney Richardson, Dean of Medicine at Emory University, supplied songs to fit the lessons. The authors reside in Atlanta, Georgia.

SUGG, REDDING S., JR. and LEACH, RICHARD H. *The Administration of Interstate Compacts*. Baton Rouge, Louisiana State University Press, 1959. 262p. $4.50.

Discusses the constitutional background of interstate compacts and the relationships between agencies formed under such compacts and the state governments and the agencies of the federal government. Dr. Suggs is Associate Professor of English at Georgia State College, Atlanta, Georgia.

THOMSON, JAMES. *The Praying Christ: A Study of Jesus' Doctrine and Practice of Prayer*. Grand Rapids, Mich., Eerdmans, 1959. 155p. $3.00.

In analyzing Jesus' teaching and habits of prayer, the Lord's Prayer and another of His prayers are studied and interpreted by a Professor of Old Testament at Columbia Seminary, Decatur, Georgia.

TOMPKINS, IVA R. *The Birdlife of the Savannah River Delta*. Atlanta, Georgia Ornithological Society, 1959. 68p. $1.50.

This study describes the habitats, habits, and general occurrence of 144 species ranging from the loons and grebes through the gulls and terns. The book is illustrated by Tompkin's photographs of sea beaches, salt marshes, and the like.

TUCKER, W. T. *Advertising Appropriations Methods in Banking.* Studies in Business and Economics. Bulletin No. 3. Atlanta, Bureau of Business and Economic Research, School of Business Administration, Georgia State College of Business Administration, 1959. 52p. $1.50.

Although this is a study of how general theories of advertising appropriations fit the banking business, the findings may be applied to other types of business. The author is Associate Professor of Marketing, Georgia State College of Business Administration.

VEASEY, PAULINE and O'HARA, ADINE L. *"What's Your Menu?"* Atlanta, Privately Printed, 1959. 164p. $3.00.

A collection of recipes for the favorite dishes and menus of the great and near-great.

WALKER, DANTON. *Danton Walker's Guide to New York Nitelife.* New York, Putnam, 1958. 224p. $2.95.

A guide to New York restaurants and night clubs in all sections of the city from Broadway and Yorkville to the Village and Harlem. The author was born in Marietta, Georgia.

WATSON, VINCENT C. *Modern Far Eastern History.* United States Armed Forces Institute. Madison, Wis., Rinehart, 1959. 122p. Apply.

A study guide designed to give the student a working knowledge of the modern history of the Far East, giving him facts upon which to base his own interpretation of current events in that area. The author is Assistant Professor of Political Science at Georgia State College.

WEBSTER, GARY. See: GARRISON, WEBB BLACK.

WHETTEN, LELAND C. *Cumulative Voting for Directors: Its Origin and Significance.* Studies in Business and Economics. Bulletin No. 2. Atlanta, Bureau of Business and Economics Research, School of Business Administration, Georgia State College of Business Administration, 1959. 47p. Gratis.

Traces the history and significance of the concept of cumulative voting, pointing out the pros and cons and discussing trends among corporate directors. The author is Professor of Accounting, Georgia State College of Business Administration.

WIGGINS, JAMES WILHELM and SCHOECK, HELMUT, eds. *Foreign Aid Reexamined; A Critical Appraisal.* Washington, D. C., Public Affairs Press, 1958. 250p. $5.00.

A collection of 13 of the papers for a symposium on culture contact in "undeveloped" countries, held under the auspices of the Department of Sociology and Anthropology at Emory University.

WIGGINS, SAM P. *Successful High School Teaching.* Cambridge, Mass., Riverside Press, 1958. 379p. $5.00.

Directed to teachers and prospective teachers, this book considers the teachers' responsibility and sets up criteria for effective education, showing how teachers can make creative contributions to the important job of educating youth.

WILEY, BELL IRVIN, ed. *Letters of Warren Akin, Confederate Congressman.* Athens, University of Georgia Press, 1959. 159p. $3.75.

The majority of these letters, written while Akin was a member of the Confederate Congress, give an insight into legislative procedures, personnel of Congress, and life in Richmond. They also show the reaction of the Akin family to the crisis of the war and personal tragedy.

WILEY, BELL IRVIN,, ed. *They Who Fought Here: A Pictorial History of the Soldier: 1861-1865.* New York, Macmillan, 1959. 273p. $10.00.

An account of the men, both Yankee and Confederate, who learned to fight by fighting—giving details of their enlistment, weapons, clothing, shelter, diversions, rations, and moral codes and their reactions in the face of danger, disease, and death. The 207 illustrations were selected by Hirst D. Milhollen from private collections, libraries, museums, and historical societies. Dr. Wiley is a member of the History Department at Emory University.

WILEY, BELL IRVIN, ed. *"This Infernal War"; The Confederate Letters of Sgt. Edwin H. Fay.* Austin, University of Texas Press, 1958. 482p. $6.00.

The war correspondence of an observant, fluent Confederate sergeant, a schoolmaster in private life, who served in the Trans-Mississippi country. Dr. Wiley, Professor of History at Emory University, was assisted by Lucy E. Fay in editing these letters.

WILLIAMS, MARY A. *Pitter, Patter, Roundabout.* New York, Vantage Press, 1959. 66p. $2.00.

Poems and stories written for little folks in simple, easily-understood language tell of the wonders about us. Mrs. Williams was born in Register, Georgia, and now lives in Statesboro, Georgia.

WILSON, ROBERT CUMMING. *Drugs and Pharmacy in the Life of Georgia, 1733-1959.* Atlanta, Foote and Davies, 1959. 443p. $6.00.

The comprehensive story of doctors, drugs, medicine, and pharmacy in Georgia. Supplements give detailed information in the above fields and several appendices present additional information on drugs. The book is being distributed through the University of Georgia Press, Athens, Georgia. The author is Dean Emeritus of the School of Pharmacy, University of Georgia.

YANCY, A. H. *Interpositionullification.* New York, Comet Press, 1959. 134p. $2.75.

The author has recreated, from the pages of his life, the world of a Negro family in Georgia during the first half of the twentieth century. The author was born in Macedonia, Georgia.

Bibliography of Georgia Authors
1959-1960

THE eleventh in the REVIEW's series of annual "Bibliographies of Georgia Authors," this annotated Bibliography is, as nearly as the compiler could make it, a complete and accurate record of books published by Georgia authors from November 1, 1959, to November 1, 1960. The annotations are descriptive, not critical; intended to place, not to judge the book. U. S., State, County, and City Documents, parts of books, brief analytics, and pamphlets of less than 25 pages have been omitted. Prices are given except when not supplied by publisher or when book is obtainable only on specific request, in which case the word "Apply" is used.

In determining whom to designate as Georgia authors, the compiler has included authors born in Georgia and claiming Georgia as their native state and those who have lived in Georgia for a period of five years and who did their writing here.

The compiler will welcome and appreciate readers' sending to him any additions or corrections. They may be sent to him at any time in care of the GEORGIA REVIEW. Several books inadvertently omitted from previous Bibliographies are listed here. Any books omitted from the present Bibliography will be included in the list for 1960-1961.

Acknowledgment is made to members of the staff of the Special Collections Division of the University of Georgia Library for their assistance in the preparation of this Bibliography.

AARON, IRA E. and COOPER, BERNICE L., eds. *Reading Skill Builder. Part Three*. Pleasantville, N. Y., Education Division, Reader's Digest Services, 1960. Teacher's edition—144 p., Student's Edition—144 p., 51 cents, each.

Carefully chosen articles from the *Reader's Digest* have been expertly adapted to the Grade 4 reading level. The editors are members of the faculty of the College of Education at the University of Georgia.

AIKEN, CONRAD POTTER. *Collected Short Stories of Conrad Aiken*. New York, World Publishing Company, 1960. 566p. $6.00.

Forty-one stories chosen by Pulitzer Prize-winner, Conrad Aiken, as his finest. Many have been unavailable for years, and twelve are new additions to Aiken's last collection of stories published ten years ago. Mr. Aiken is a native of Savannah, Georgia.

AIKEN, CONRAD POTTER. *A Reviewer's A B C.* New York, Meridian Books, 1958. 414p. $5.00.
A collection of critical addresses, essays, and lectures by Conrad Aiken from 1916 to the present, on English and American literature.

ANDREWS, ELIZA FRANCES. *The Wartime Journal of a Georgia Girl, 1864-1865.* Macon, Georgia, Ardivan Press, 1960. 396p. $5.50.
A new edition of the journal of a Washington, Georgia, girl that gives a graphic picture of life in middle Georgia during the war-torn years of 1864-65. Edited and with an introduction by Dr. Spencer Bidwell King, Jr., who is Head of the History Department at Mercer University.

ATKINSON, BUTLER M., JR. *What Dr. Spock Didn't Tell Us; or A Survival Kit for Parents: An Encyclopedic Guide to Hitherto Uncatalogued Afflictions, Aberrations, Exotic Diseases of the American Child.* New York, Simon and Schuster, 1959. 72p. $2.50.
A humorous book about children for parents. Illustrated by Whitney Darrow, Jr. The author is a native of Atlanta, Georgia.

AXLEY, LOWRY. *Holding Aloft the Torch: A History of the Independent Presbyterian Church of Savannah, Georgia.* Savannah, Pigeonhole Press, 1958. 247p. $5.00.
Two hundred years of the history of a church which survived and prospered in spite of earthquakes, hurricanes, fires, epidemics, and internal dissensions.

BARTLETT, ELIZABETH. *Behold This Dreamer.* Pacific Palisades, Calif., Privately Printed, 1959. 30p. $2.00.
A limited edition of verse by Atlanta poet Elizabeth Bartlett contains poems on the many facets of human experience.

BARTLETT, PAUL. *When the Owl Cries.* New York, Macmillan, 1960. 242p. $4.50.
Mexico, during the Revolution of 1910, is the setting for this novel about a wealthy but idealistic plantation owner, his bitter conflict with his father and his disintegrating marriage. The author is a former resident of Atlanta, Georgia.

BELL, EARL LEASTON and CRABBE, KENNETH CHARLES. *The Augusta Chronicle: Indomitable Voice of Dixie. 1785-1960.* Athens, University of Georgia Press, 1960. 273p. $5.00.
A history of the oldest newspaper in the South and accounts of some of its "big stories," from the early days of the nation through the present. The authors are residents of Augusta, Georgia.

BELL, MALCOLM, JR. *Savannah, Ahoy!* Savannah, Pigeonhole Press, 1959. 66p. $3.00.

An account of the intrepid little *Savannah*, the first steam ship to cross the far reaches of the Atlantic Ocean. The story is told against the background of Savannah in 1819, whose citizens were then creating much of the character the city retains today. The author is a native of Savannah, Georgia.

BENEFIELD, LOWELL VANCE. *Second Book of Poems.* Atlanta, Privately Printed, 1959. 100p. $3.50.

A collection of poems about children, nature, friends old and new, religion, and love. The author lives in Atlanta, Georgia.

BERND, JOSEPH L. *Grass Roots Politics in Georgia.* Atlanta, Emory University Research Committee, 1960. 172p. $3.00.

This study contains a factual history of the competition between Talmadge and Anti-Talmadge factions; election statistics by precinct and county, 1942-1954; and facts and analysis of leadership, county unit system, Negro voting, rural and urban voting habits. The book may be obtained from the author at 2597 Elizabeth Place, Macon, Georgia.

BLACK, EUGENE ROBERT. *The Diplomacy of Economic Development.* Cambridge, Mass., Harvard University Press, 1960. 74p. $3.00.

A candid examination of the economic relations between the affluent and the poorer nations in the free world, stressing the importance of diplomacy and the need for flexible economic planning. Based on lectures delivered at Tufts University. Eugene Black, a native of Atlanta, Georgia, is president of the International Bank for Reconstruction and Development.

BLACKSTOCK, WALTER. *Miracle of Flesh.* Francetown, N. H., Golden Quill Press, 1960. 55p. $2.75.

A collection of forty-one short poems about man's aspirations and lonely quest for truth. Dr. Blackstock, a native of Atlanta, Georgia, is now professor of English at High Point College, in North Carolina.

BLICKSILVER, JACK. *Cotton Manufacturing in the Southeast: An Historical Analysis.* Bulletin No. 5. Studies in Business and Economics. Bureau of Business and Economic Research, School of Business Administration, Georgia State College of Business Administration, Atlanta, Georgia, 1959. 176p. Gratis.

A study to analyze and evaluate the factors leading to the development of the southern cotton textile industry, its changing role and significance, and its possible future orientation. The author is Associate Professor of Economic History, Georgia State College of Business Administration.

BLICKSILVER, JACK and BOWDOIN, MARY H. *The Impact of Georgia Ports upon the Economy of the State*. Research Paper Series, Number 15. Bureau of Business Research. School of Business Administration, Georgia State College of Business Administration, Atlanta, Georgia. 1960. 61p. Gratis.

This study of the effects of the Georgia ports, particularly Savannah, on the economy of the State as a whole is divided into three parts: the first deals with the history of the ports, the second with the local economy and the third with the State's economy. The authors are professors at the Georgia State College of Business Administration.

BLISS, ALICE. *Ellipse of Sonnets*. Athens, McGregor's, 1960. 28p. $1.95.

A collection of poems and sonnets dedicated to the memory of Byron Herbert Reece. The edition is limited to one hundred copies. The author lives in Atlanta, Georgia.

BOURNE, GEOFFREY HOWARD, ed. *The Structure and Function of Muscle*. Volume I—Structure. New York, Academic Press, 1960. 472p. $14.00.

This book is the first volume of a proposed three-volume work on various aspects of modern research on muscle, aiming to amass material hitherto widely scattered. The editor is with the Department of Anatomy, Emory University, Atlanta, Georgia.

BOURNE, GEOFFREY HOWARD, ed. *The Structure and Function of Muscle*. Volume II—Biochemistry and Physiology. New York, Academic Press, 1960. 593p. $14.00.

Volume II deals mainly with the functional rather than the structural aspects of muscle, and will be of special interest to biochemists and physiologists, neurologists, pathologists, cardiologists, and others concerned with neuromuscular disease in humans and animals, since it provides the norms from which muscular action deviates in pathological conditions.

BOURNE, GEOFFREY HOWARD and WILSON, EILEEN M. H. *World Review of Nutrition and Diatetics*. Philadelphia, Lippincott, 1960. 272p. $12.00.

The first issue of a new international review journal evaluating papers in the nutritional field. The reviews are written by authorities. The object of the journal is "to describe the nutritional status of peoples under different geographic, climatic, and economic conditions, and to examine all available knowledge in order to find solutions wherever nutrition problems exist."

BOWDOIN, MARY H. *Georgia's Railway Freight Pattern: An Analysis of Composition and Routes, 1949-1955*. Research Paper, Number 5. Bureau of Business and Economic Research, School of Business Administration, Georgia State College of Business Administration, Atlanta, Georgia, 1958. 93p. Gratis.

Rail freight shipments to and from Georgia are presented in this study from various approaches, to ascertain trade patterns in Georgia. General findings are summarized and numerous tables are included containing detailed information on specific items.

BRANCH, JOSEPH MELTON. *Mount Vernon, 1859-1958*. Printed for the Mt. Vernon Association by *News and Farmer*, Louisville, Georgia, 1959. 48p. $1.50.
   Written for the centennial of the Association observed in 1958. The history is divided into decades and briefly describes the Georgia background for each period as a background for the history of this Baptist Association.

BRELAND, LYDIA FOSTER. *My Patchwork Quilt, and Other Poems*. New York, Exposition Press, 1959. 32p. $2.50.
   A collection of twenty-seven poems about life in its many ramifications. The author, a native of Hall County, Georgia, is currently teaching at Dawsonville, Georgia.

BROWN, ENOCH. *Wivern at My Window*. New York, Carlton Press, 1960. 56p. $2.00.
   A collection of seventy-one poems on a variety of subjects written in a strange and complex idiom. The author lives in Jefferson, Georgia.

BRYAN, MARY GIVENS. *Passports Issued by Governors of Georgia, 1785 to 1809*. Special Publications of the National Genealogical Society, No. 21. Washington, National Genealogical Society, 1959. 58p. $2.75; $1.75 to members of the Society.
   These passports, issued to westward bound families desiring to travel through Indian Territory, are not only of historical importance, but are also of great value to the genealogist, since they list heads of families by name, and include other pertinent information.

BRYANT, ALLAN and DAVIES, GENEVA, eds. *One Cup of Water*. Columbia, S. C., R. L. Bryan Company, 1960. 80p. $2.50.
   The second anthology of the Manuscript Club of Atlanta, Georgia, contains one hundred and eight poems by thirty-three poets. Varied moods and styles are represented in this collection.

BUGG, MARY COBB. See: Cobb, Mary.

BURNEY, SARAH JOE H. *Wrought of God*. Atlanta, Georgia Baptist Woman's Missionary Union, 1960. 117p. $1.25.
   A chronicle of the organization, maintenance, development and growth of the Baptist Woman's Missionary Union in Georgia, 1884-1959. The author, Mrs. Frank S. Burney, lives in Waynesboro, Georgia.

CALDWELL, ERSKINE. *Claudelle*. London, Heinemann, 1959. 179p. 15s.
   The English edition of *Claudelle Inglish*.

CALDWELL, ERSKINE. *Three by Caldwell: Tobacco Road; Georgia Boy; The Sure Hand of God*. Boston, Little, Brown, 1960. 241p., 239p., 243p. $4.95.
   The first time that these three novels of the South have appeared as a trilogy.

CALHOUN, CALFREY C. *Public Relations in Secondary-School Business Education.* Research Paper Series, Number 17. Bureau of Business and Economic Research, Georgia State College of Business Administration, Atlanta, Georgia, 1960. 56p. Gratis.

Part I: The Nature and Scope of Current Activities and Media. This study, first in a series of publications on public relations in business education, identifies and classifies a wide range of public relations activities, practices, and media used in business education, as a basis for subsequent study and evaluation. The study also contains a public relations checklist for Business Education.

CANNON, WILLIAM RANSOM. *History of Christianity in the Middle Ages.* Nashville, Abingdon Press, 1960. 352p. $4.50.

A synthetic history of Christianity from A.D. 476 to A.D. 1453, in all phases of its development, doctrinal as well as institutional, the Greek Church as well as the Latin Church. The author is Dean of the Candler School of Theology, Emory University, Atlanta, Georgia.

CARTER, THOMAS L., JR. *A Compilation of the Property Taxation Laws of Georgia.* Institute of Law and Government, School of Law, University of Georgia, Athens, 1960. 231p. $5.00, Paper, $6.00, Cloth.

This volume consists of a compilation of the general statutes of state-wide application relating to property taxation in Georgia along with notes and brief abstracts of the case law interpreting these statutes. A detailed subject index is included.

CHILDERS, JAMES SAXON. *The Nation on the Flying Trapeze: The United States as the People of the East See Us.* New York, David McKay, 1960. 284p. $4.50.

An account of a trip made for the State Department through the Far East and the Middle East. The author reveals with disturbing bluntness just what the United States is faced with in these crucial areas. Mr. Childers, former editor of the *Atlanta Journal,* is president of an Atlanta publishing firm.

CARTLEDGE, SAMUEL ANTOINE. *Basic Grammar of the Greek New Testament.* Grand Rapids, Michigan, Zondervan, 1959. 137p. $3.95.

A grammar designed to aid students in reading the New Testament in Greek. Chapter divisions largely follow the parts of speech, with paradigms given to enable determination of the form of virtually every noun or verb used in the New Testament, and the five-case system has been used in dealing with noun forms. The author is Professor of New Testament and Exegesis at Columbia Theological Seminary, Decatur, Georgia.

CHRISTOPHER, THOMAS W. *Constitutional Questions in Food and Drug Laws.* Chicago, Commerce Clearing House, 1960. 116p. $3.50.

This review provides a systematic description of the present state of Constitutional issues arising from the 1938 Federal Food, Drug, and Cosmetic Act, buttressing Federal laws, and similar state and local laws. The author is Professor of Law and Director of the Bureau of Legal Research and Service at Emory University, Atlanta, Georgia.

COBB, MARY. *Top Dog.* Garden City, N. Y., Doubleday, 1960. 235p. $3.95.

A passion for power is the dominant factor in Jessica Dabney's life. She dominates her three grown children and rules with an iron hand over the local dog-show world until the events of an all-important Atlanta dog show destroy her power. The author is a resident of Atlanta, Georgia.

COLEMAN, KENNETH. *Georgia History in Outline.* Athens, University of Georgia Press, 1960. 126p. Paper $1.75.

A concise history of Georgia from the beginning to modern times, this book presents the highlights of the state's development—political, economic, and social. It will be useful to both students and laymen interested in an over-all view of Georgia's past. The author is a Professor of History at the University of Georgia.

COULTER, ELLIS MERTON. *Georgia; A Short History.* Chapel Hill, University of North Carolina Press, 1960. Revised and enlarged edition. 537p. $6.00.

This book, first published in 1933 under the title *A Short History of Georgia,* has been brought up-to-date by the addition of a chapter and revisions in the text and the bibliography. Dr. Coulter is Professor Emeritus of History at the University of Georgia.

CRAIG, GEORGIA. See: Gaddis, Peggy.

DERN, MRS. JOHN SHERMAN. See: Gaddis, Peggy.

DERN, PEGGY. See: Gaddis, Peggy.

DICKSON, EDWARD. *Strange Autumn.* Atlanta, Colonial House Publishers, 1960. 240p. $2.95.

A romance of intrigue and pastoral love set amid the red clay hills of East Tennessee. The author is a physician residing in Atlanta, Georgia.

DODSON, SAMUEL KENDRICK. *From Darkness to Light.* New York, Greenwich Book Publishers, 1959. 110p. $2.75.

A study of spiritual meanings of light and darkness as revealed in the Scriptures.

DREWRY, JOHN E., ed. *Attaining Goals via Better Communications: Press, Radio, Television, Periodicals, Public Relations, and Advertising As Seen Through Institutes and Special Occasions of the Henry W. Grady School of Journalism, 1959-1960.* Vol. LXI, No. 2, Ser. 1193. Athens, University of Georgia Bulletin, 1960. viii, 201p. Paper $2.00. Cloth $3.00.

The 1959-60 compilation of addresses and papers delivered at the various institutes and other special occasions sponsored by the University of Georgia's School of Journalism.

DUNSON, ELEANOR ADAMS. *The Dunson Family in the South.* Atlanta, Privately Printed, 1960. 141p. $10.00.

A genealogical record of the Dunson, Rogers, Adams, Gray, and allied families of Georgia and the Southeast. The author is a resident of Atlanta, Georgia.

DUREN, JAMES A. *On Wings of the Evening.* New York, Pageant Press, 1960. 328p. $4.00.

A Civil War novel about the struggle of two suitors for the love and the hand of a beautiful Southern belle. The customs and traditions are woven into this tale based on the life of the author's grandmother. Reverend Duren is a retired Baptist minister and lives in Meigs, Georgia.

EHLERS, CARROL W. *Special Incentives for Salesmen in the South.* Research Paper Series, Number 6. Bureau of Business and Economic Research, School of Business Administration, Georgia State College of Business Administration, Atlanta, Georgia, 1958. 69p. Gratis.

A study in selected motivation procedures aimed at (1) discovering the key factors in the successful use of special incentives for salesmen in the South; (2) determining, if possible, the relative effectiveness of such programs; and (3) comparing the study with a similar study conducted at the national level.

EVERETT, EDWIN M., WALL, CHARLES A., JR., and DUMAS, MARIE. *Correct Writing, Form C.* Boston, Heath, 1960. 384p. $2.50.

This revised and enlarged edition of the authors' earlier books has been sharpened and brought up-to-date, and sectional numbers and letters have been inserted for ease in referring to various subject sections. The authors are members of the English Department at the University of Georgia.

FLANDERS, BERTRAM HOLLAND, ed. *Atlanta Poetry Gallery.* Atlanta, Franklin Printing Company, 1960. 84p. $3.00.

Fifty-four poets are represented in this first anthology compiled by the Atlanta Writers Club—the oldest and largest organization of writers in Georgia.

FLEMING, BERRY. *The Winter Rider.* New York, Lippincott, 1960. 173p. $3.50.

A strange and bewitching novel about a middle-aged novelist and a girl with a fiddle case who hitches a ride with him. Mr. Fleming lives in Augusta, Georgia, where he was born. He has written novels which deal with politics and social life in Georgia.

FORD, ELIZABETH AUSTIN. *Christmas Past in Georgia, 1697-1958.* Atlanta, Privately Printed, 1959. Unpaged. $1.00.

A book that describes observations of the Yuletide in Georgia from 1697 to Christmas, 1958, when America's satellite passed over Atlanta three times, delivering its Christmas message from President Eisenhower. The author lives in Decatur, Georgia.

FORD, MARCIA. See: Radford, Ruby Lorraine.

FORT, TOMLINSON. *Differential Equations*. New York, Holt, Rinehart and Winston, 1960. 184p. $4.75.

A college text written to be used as an introduction to the subject. In dealing with the equation of the first order and first degree, the treatment is entirely symmetrical in x and y. Provides more material than usual on the theory of the linear equation, an introduction to boundary-value problems, and the LaPlace transform. The author is a native Georgian and at present is on the faculty of the University of Miami, Miami, Florida.

FOSTER, WILLIAM OMER, SR. *James Jackson: Duelist and Militant Statesman, 1757-1806*. Athens, University of Georgia Press, 1960. 238p. $4.50.

A biography of one of Georgia's great statesmen which catches his turbulent personality and fiery disposition. The author is a native of Monroe, Georgia.

FRYE, ROLAND MUSHAT. *God, Man, and Satan*. Princeton, N. J., Princeton University Press, 1960. 184p. $3.75.

"Paradise Lost" and "Pilgrim's Progress" approached in relation to their interactions with relevant theological understandings. The author is an Associate Professor of English at Emory University, Atlanta, Georgia.

GADDIS, PEGGY. *Beloved Intruder*. London, Wright and Brown, 1959. 184p. 10s 6d.

The trials and tribulations of a young television actress who fails an audition and falls in love with a man who disapproves of show business.

GADDIS, PEGGY (pseud. Peggy Dern). *Enchanted Spring*. New York, Arcadia House, 1960. 224p. $2.95.

A judge's daughter returns to her small-town home after secretarial school and helps defend a man accused of attempted murder, whom she finds she loves.

GADDIS, PEGGY. (pseud. Georgia Craig). *The Girl Outside*. New York, Arcadia House, 1960. 224p. $2.95.

Florida is the setting for this story of eighteen-year-old Holly Tolliver, an orphan who, after the death of her benefactor, learns about the adult world fast.

GADDIS, PEGGY (pseud. Peggy Dern). *Her Day in Court*. New York, Arcadia House, 1960. 224p. $2.95.

A woman lawyer deals with a client accused of murder, and with a daredevil auto racer whose wife wanted him to break his contract and retire from the troupe.

GADDIS, PEGGY. *Her Plantation Home*. New York, Arcadia House, 1959. 224p. $2.95.

The story of a girl whose parents made sacrifices to advance her stage career.

GADDIS, PEGGY (pseud. Georgia Craig). *Island Nurse.* New York, Arcadia House, 224p. $2.95.
Nurse Eugenia Hayes accompanies her small patient to the Bahama island home of the wealthy Raiford family, and discovers a private Eden—complete with serpent.

GADDIS, PEGGY. *Nurse Hilary and Doctor Stuart.* London, Foulsham, 1960. 184p. 10s 6d.
Hilary Westbrook, R.N., accepts a position as an assistant in a new home for the aged. She develops a true affection for the people there and fights determinedly against a money-conscious administration.

GADDIS, PEGGY. *Nurse Kelly Finds Romance.* London, Foulsham, 1959. 192p. 10s 6d.
Nurse Kelly MacIver encounters a weird family situation when she goes to Twisted Oaks, a plantation in the South Carolina low country, to care for the wife of the owner.

GADDIS, PEGGY. *Nurse Melinda.* New York, Arcadia House, 1960. 224p. $2.95.
A nurse working in a children's hospital in Southern California discovers a mysterious connection between one of her patients, a little Italian boy, and an attractive Hollywood star.

GADDIS, PEGGY. *Peacock Hill.* New York, Arcadia House, 1960. 224p. $2.95.
The mountains of North Carolina are the setting of this novel about two romances.

GADDIS, PEGGY. (pseud. Georgia Craig). *Reach for Tomorrow.* New York, Arcadia House, 1960. 222p. $2.95.
When her fiancé elopes with another woman, a pretty young nurse decides to accompany an elderly lady on a world cruise in order to forget her personal troubles.

GADDIS, PEGGY. *Sara Winslow, M.D.* New York, Arcadia House, 1960. 224p. $2.95.
A woman doctor, tired of prejudice against women doctors in big city hospitals, takes a job on an island off the coast of Maryland and runs into romance and mystery.

GADDIS, PEGGY. *Shadows on the Moon.* New York, Arcadia House, 1960. 220p. $2.95.
Florida is the setting for this novel of a brother and sister and the people they come to love.

GADDIS, PEGGY. *Wedding Song.* New York, Arcadia House, 1960. 224p. $2.95.
A debutante in difficult circumstances after her father's death, takes a job as bridal consultant in a department store and becomes involved in the hopes and dreams of many people besides herself.

GAULTNEY, BARBARA F. *Simply Trusting*. Atlanta, Privately Printed, 1959. 25p. 50 cents.

A collection of twenty-two inspirational poems by a young mother who is physically sightless and crippled. Mrs. Gaultney is a resident of Forest Park, Georgia.

GILLIAM, NORRIS, JR., comp. *The Department Superintendent's Plan Book*. Atlanta, Privately Printed, 1958. 78p. $1.35.

A guide to a whole year's activities that will enable a person to become a better Sunday School Department Superintendent. The author resides in Atlanta, Georgia.

GLASS, LEMUEL PAGE. *The Little Church With the Big God*. Fairburn, Ga., Privately Printed, 1960. 199p. $3.65.

A novel with a religious theme about the joys and sorrows of the people living in a small Georgia community. The author, a retired Baptist minister, lives in Fairburn, Georgia.

GOVAN, THOMAS PAYNE. *Nicholas Biddle, Nationalist and Public Banker, 1786-1844*. Chicago, University of Chicago Press, 1959. xii, 428p. $7.50.

The public and political life of Nicholas Biddle, director of the Bank of the United States, including Biddle's fight with Jackson and the Democratic party. The author is sympathetic to Biddle's efforts to obtain recharter of the Bank, and regards Biddle as a champion of prosperity in a time of economic crisis.

HALL, JAMES WILLIAM. *Lyman Hall: Georgia Patriot*. Savannah, Pigeonhole Press, 1959. 113p. $4.00.

The story of one of the signers of the Declaration of Independence from Georgia. The author is a native of Atlanta, Georgia.

HARRIS, KATHLEEN. See: Humphries, Adelaide.

HARRIS, WALTER ALEXANDER. *Here the Creeks Sat Down*. Macon, Georgia, J. W. Burke Company, 1958. 166p. $3.00.

An ethnological study of the Creek Indians at Ocmulgee Old Fields located near the present city of Macon, Georgia. The late author was a resident of Macon, Georgia.

HART, CHARLES RANDALL. *Samuel Johnson: A Portrait*. Eton, Windsor, Shakespeare Head Press, 1960. 83p. 7s 6d.

This book is a portrait of Samuel Johnson in dramatic form, consisting of eleven episodes from the life of the great lexicographer with narrative and lyric interludes. The author is Professor Emeritus of Classics at Emory University, Atlanta, Georgia.

HARWELL, RICHARD BARKSDALE, ed. *The War They Fought*. New York, Longman, Green, 1960. 755p. $6.95.

Soldiers and civilians of both the North and the South are the eyewitness contributors to this anthology of authentic reporting of the Civil War. Originally published in two parts, *The Confederate Reader* and *The Union Reader*.

HAVERFIELD, WILLIAM M. *Buenos Dias*. Nashville, Convention Press, 1960. 94p. 50 cents.

Baptist workers and workers in Mexico are introduced through the experiences of fourteen-year-old Jerry Foster and his parents, who move to Mexico for a year. The author is a native Georgian.

HENDERSON, LEGRAND. *Augustus and the Mountains*. New York, Grosset, 1960. 128p. $1.50.

An exciting story of Augustus' adventures with the real Indians in the mountains.

HENDERSON, LEGRAND. *Augustus and the River*. New York, Grosset, 1960. 128p. $1.50.

Life on a Mississippi River shanty boat is the subject for this new adventure in the life of Augustus.

HENDERSON, LEGRAND. *Augustus Goes South*. New York, Grosset, 1960. 128p. $1.50.

Augustus and his friends from the houseboat upset the peace of the lazy Louisiana swamps hunting for buried treasure.

HENDERSON, LEGRAND. *Augustus Helps the Navy*. New York, Grosset, 1960. 128p. $1.50.

Augustus and his family are living on an old schooner on Penobscot Bay, and Augustus gets mixed up with spies and enemy submarines.

HENDERSON, LEGRAND. *How Space Rockets Began*. Nashville, Abingdon Press, 1960. 64p. $2.00.

An imaginative story of a seafaring man who brought his family back to land, rigged sails on a prairie wagon, and gradually evolved this idea into a vehicle that could reach the moon.

HENDERSON, LILLIAN, comp. *Roster of the Confederate Soldiers of Georgia, 1861-1865*. Hapeville, Georgia, Printed by Longino and Porter. Vol. I-1959, 1068p. Vol. II-1959, 1082 p. Vol. III-1960, 1013 p. Vol. IV-1960, 1026 p. Apply.

A compilation of the military service records of the Confederate soldiers from Georgia. Miss Henderson is Director of the Department of Confederate Pensions and Records of Georgia.

HENSON, ALLEN LUMPKIN. *Confessions of a Criminal Lawyer*. New York, Vantage Press, 1959. 236p. $3.95.

This biography of a well-known Southern lawyer takes the reader into the intimate councils where legal maneuvers are planned and then re-creates many dramatic courtroom scenes. Judge Henson lives in Atlanta, Georgia.

HOWARD, WILLIS E. *Listen, Are You Sure You Are Listening?* Atlanta, Foote and Davies, 1956. 83p. $2.00.

A collection of ten sermons by a former Baptist minister. Copies may be obtained from the author's widow, Mrs. Willis Howard, 237 Ansley Drive, Thomson, Georgia.

HOYT, MARGARET, and DABNEY, ELEANOR HOYT, eds. *My Heart An Altar.* Richmond, Va., John Knox Press, 1959. 189p. $3.50.

Stories, prayers, scripture readings, and suggested hymns for worship services, by two active members of Presbyterian churches in Georgia. Margaret L. Hoyt is a resident of Atlanta, Georgia, and Eleanor Hoyt Dabney resides in Smyrna, Georgia.

HOYT, MARGARET, and DABNEY, ELEANOR HOYT. *Youth Looking to Jesus.* Richmond, Va., John Knox Press, 1954. 191p. $2.75.

A collection of material designed to help those who are in charge of planning worship services for young people. The authors are residents of Georgia. Illustrations are by Virginia Templin Gailey.

HUMPHRIES, ADELAIDE (pseud. Kathleen Harris). *Flight Nurse.* New York, Bouregy, 1960. 220p. $2.95.

A Texas flight nurse's short assignment in Spain makes her realize how much she cares for the United States and her fiancé.

HUMPHRIES, ADELAIDE. *Mission Nurse.* New York, Bouregy, 1960. 224p. $2.95.

With an unexpected legacy, a young American nurse goes to South Africa to visit the mission that had been her uncle's chief concern. It is currently run by a personable Englishman. She stays.

HUMPHRIES, ADELAIDE. *Nurse Had a Secret.* New York, Bouregy, 1960. 224p. $2.95.

A young nurse takes the case of a dying professor in a Florida town and finds that she is caring for an important missile specialist.

HUMPHRIES, ADELAIDE. *Orchids for the Nurse.* London, Ward, Lock, 1959. 156p. 10s 6d.

A romance about a nurse in New England who has her choice of men. Issued in the United States in 1955.

HUNTER, EDWARD. *In Many Voices: Our Fabulous Foreign-Language Press.* Norman Park, Ga., Norman College, 1960. 190p. Cloth, $3.50. Paper, $2.00.

A study of foreign-language newspapers published in the continental United States, and their role in relation to their readers and the American community.

HURST, JOHN WILLIS, ed. *Cardiac Resuscitation.* Springfield, Ill., C. C. Thomas, 1960. 141p. $5.50.

Findings on cardiac resuscitation, based on a symposium given by the Department of Medicine of Emory University School of Medicine on October 3, 1958, at the Grady Memorial Hospital, Atlanta, Georgia.

HURT, JOHN JETER. *Sermons — Short — Medium — Long*. Atlanta, Privately Printed, 1960. 284p. $3.00.

A collection of seventy-one sermons on a variety of subjects. Dr. Hurt is a retired Baptist minister and lives in Atlanta, Georgia.

JONES, MARY SHARPE (JONES) and MALLARD, MARY JONES. *Yankees A'Coming: One Month's Experiences During the Invasion of Liberty County, Georgia, 1864-1865.* Edited by Haskel Monroe. Confederate Centennial Studies, No. 12. Tuscaloosa, Ala., Confederate Publishing Company, 1959. 102p. $4.00.

Journal kept by Mrs. C. C. Jones, Sr., and her daughter Mrs. Robert Quarterman Mallard during the invasion of Liberty County, Georgia, by Sherman's troops. Edited and with introduction by Haskell Monroe.

JONES, ROBERT TYRE, JR. *Golf is My Game*. Garden City, N. Y., Doubleday, 1960. 255p. $4.50.

First book to come from the man who is, perhaps, the world's most famous golfer. Bobby Jones tells the story of his own years of competition, his work in teaching golf, designing clubs, and organizing the Augusta National Golf Course and the Master's Golf Tournament it sponsors.

JONES, WILBUR DEVEREUX and MONTGOMERY, HORACE. *Civilization Through the Centuries*. Boston, Ginn, 1960. 883p. $8.75.

A college text, concerned primarily with the development of western civilization from earliest man to the present. The authors are Professors of History at the University of Georgia.

JORDAN, GERALD RAY. *Religion That is Eternal*. New York, McMillan, 1960. 134p. $3.00.

Messages on moral and spiritual values in a turbulent modern age. The main points are summarized at the end of each chapter. Dr. Jordan is Professor of Preaching and Chapel Preacher at the Candler School of Theology, Emory University, Atlanta, Georgia.

KEELER, CLYDE EDGAR. *Secrets of the Cuna Earthmother; a Comparative Study of Ancient Religions*. New York, Exposition Press, 1960. 352p. $6.00.

A study of the religion and sacred rites of the Cuna Indians of Central America. Dr. Keeler is Professor of Biology at Georgia State College for Women, Milledgeville, Georgia.

KIRKLAND, WILLIE SCHUMAN. *Flesh and Blood*. New York, Vantage Press, 1959. 253p. $3.95.

The early days of Georgia and Savannah are the background for this love story. Mrs. Kirkland lives in Savannah, Georgia.

LECONTE, JOSEPH (1823-1901). *Ramblings Through the High Sierras*. San Francisco, Sierra Book Club, 1960. 176p. $3.00.

A new edition of the story of the University of California's Excursion Party through the High Sierras first published in 1875. The author, a native of Liberty County, Georgia, was Professor of Philosophy and Natural History at the University of California.

LeGrand. See: Henderson, LeGrand.

Longstreet, James (1821-1904). *From Manassas to Appomatox.* Bloomington, Ind., Indiana University Press, 1960. 692p. $8.95.

Civil War memoirs by Lieutenant-General James Longstreet, a controversial figure in the Confederate Army. Reprinted with an introduction, notes and a new Comprehensive Index by James I. Robertson, Jr.

Lyde, Marilyn Jones. *Edith Wharton: Convention and Morality in the Work of a Novelist.* Norman, Okla., University of Oklahoma Press, 1959. 194p. $4.00.

An examination of the philosophical and artistic import of the novelist's work, taking into account the opinions of various literary critics, and the changes in society that have affected critical appraisals. The author is a member of the English Department at Georgia State College of Business Administration, Atlanta, Georgia.

McCarthy, David. *Killing at the Big Tree.* Garden City, N. Y., Doubleday, 1960. 192p. $2.95.

Blair McKenny, the sheriff of a small Southern town, finds his efforts to solve a murder complicated by irate townspeople who demand revenge. Mr. McCarthy is Copy Editor for the *Atlanta Journal.*

McDonald, Ellis Atkisson. *Green Leaves.* Mill Valley, California, The Wings Press, 1959. 80p. $2.50.

A collection of poems that treat with nature, religion, love, and man's relation to these three. Mrs. McDonald is a resident of Chamblee, Georgia.

McFarlane, Philip James. *House Full of Women.* New York, Simon and Schuster, 1960. 245p. $3.50.

A story of how the death of his father and brother, the growing insanity and eventual death of his mother, and the prevalent decadence of the New South affects the life of a twelve-year-old boy. The author, a native of Georgia, now resides in Boston, Massachusetts.

McGee, John Llewllyn. *Musings and Memories.* New York, Pageant Press, 1960. 64p. $2.50.

A book that tells of the struggles, trials, and tribulations of a college professor. The author is Emeritus Professor of Biochemistry at Emory University, Atlanta, Georgia.

McGowan, Gordon. *The Skipper and the Eagle.* Princeton, N. J., Van Nostrand, 1960. 214p. $5.75.

A true sea story of how, at the end of World War II, an American Coast Guard officer refitted a German three-masted bark and sailed her from Bremerhaven to New York. The author is a resident of Thomasville, Georgia.

MAJOR, JAMES RUSSELL. *Representative Institutions in Renaissance France, 1421-1559.* Madison, University of Wisconsin Press, 1960. 182p. $4.00.

A history of French representative institutions from the beginning of the reign of Charles VII until the death of Henry II just before the outbreak of the Wars of Religion. The author is an Associate Professor of History at Emory University, Atlanta, Georgia.

MARSHALL, JOHN DAVID, comp. *Of, By, and For Librarians: Further Contributions to Library Literature.* Hamden, Conn., Shoe String Press, 1960. 335p. $7.00.

This anthology brings together in convenient form some forty articles and essays from a variety of sources which should prove interesting reading for the practicing Librarian or the Library School student. The compiler, Mr. Marshall, is on the staff of the University of Georgia Libraries, **Athens, Georgia.**

MARSHALL, EDISON. *Earth Giant.* Garden City, N. Y., Doubleday, 1960. 380p. $4.50.

A novel about Hercules that follows him from his boyhood, through his mythological exploits, to his manhood and a thirteenth labor.

MARTIN, HAROLD. *Father's Day Comes But Once a Year.* New York, Putnam, 1960. 192p. $3.95.

With his four children safely grown up and out of his hair, this father indulges in some retrospective chuckles over the humorous and touching adventures of parenthood—from taking the kids to the beach to "Who Put the BB's in the Peanut Butter?"

MONTGOMERY, MARION. *Dry Lightning.* Lincoln, University of Nebraska Press, 1960. 72p. Cloth $3.00. Paper $2.00.

In the pages of this volume of poems, we encounter a young man who views himself and his surroundings in the American South with an inquiring eye. The author is an Instructor in English at the University of Georgia.

MORRIS, SCOTT, JR. *The Life and Poetry of Herbert R. Caulk.* Manchester, Ga., Privately Printed, 1960. 46p. $2.00.

A brief biographical sketch of the Georgia poet Herbert R. Caulk, who died in 1955. Sixteen of his poems are included. Mr. Morris is a resident of Moultrie, Georgia.

O'CONNOR, FLANNERY. *The Violent Bear It Away.* New York, Farrar, Straus and Cudahy, 1960. 243p. $3.75.

Set in the back country of Tennessee, this satirical but compassionate novel tells the story of an orphan who stubbornly attempts to resist the religious calling that has been prophesied for him.

ODUM, JOHN D. *Hell in Georgia.* New York, Corlies, Macy, and Company, 1960. 153p. $3.50.

A Civil War novel about the battle of Missionary Ridge in 1863. The author lives in Kingsland, Georgia.

PEEPLES, EDWIN AUGUSTUS, JR. *A Professional Storywriter's Handbook.* Garden City, N. Y., Doubleday, 1960. 282p. $4.50.

This handbook includes a general discussion of the nature of fiction and particularly of the short story. Suggestions are given the would-be writer on sources of material, developmental procedures, and editing techniques. The author is a native of Atlanta, Georgia.

PINHOLSTER, GARLAND F. *Encyclopedia of Basketball Drills.* Englewood Cliffs, N. J., Prentice-Hall, 1958. 228p. $5.85.

A collection of drills on the fundamentals of basketball plays that have proven successful. The author is a member of the faculty of Oglethorpe University, Atlanta, Georgia.

POLLOCK, ROBERT MASON and POLLOCK, EILEEN. *With Love.* By Maurice Chevalier, as told to Eileen and Robert Mason Pollock. Boston, Little, Brown, 1960. 424p. $5.00.

Internationally acclaimed as a stage and screen entertainer, Maurice Chevalier here recounts his career, his private life, and his private loves. Robert Mason Pollock is a native of Monroe, Georgia.

POPE, EDWIN. *Baseball's Greatest Managers.* Garden City, N. Y., Doubleday, 1960. 286p. $3.95.

The assistant sports editor of the *Miami Herald* presents twenty informal pieces about famous baseball managers of the past and present. The author is a native of Athens, Georgia.

POUND, MERRITT B., and ASKEW, J. THOMAS. *Georgia Government.* Oklahoma City, Okla., Harlow Publishing Company, 1959. 380p. $3.36.

The first part of this study discusses not only the government of Georgia but also that of the federal system from an historical viewpoint. The second part describes the workings of the government of Georgia with much attention to voting, election, the county, municipalities and services such as education, health and welfare, and the important legislation of 1959.

RADFORD, RUBY LORRAINE. *Crime and Judy.* New York, Avalon Books, 1960. 222p. $2.95.

A young woman, eager to help out a famous detective, gets a chance to prove her sleuthing abilities.

RADFORD, RUBY LORRAINE (pseud. Marcia Ford). *Gail's Golden Filly.* New York, Avalon Books, 1960. 224p. $2.95.

A college graduate returns to her grandfather's horse farm to find her favorite mare has been sold by mistake. She wins back her mare when she falls in love with and wins its new owner, her next-door neighbor.

REINSCH, J. LEONARD and ELLIS, ELMO I. *Radio Station Management.* New York, Harper, 1960. Second Revised Edition. 337p. $6.00.

This revised edition, of a standard manual for the trade, has been completely rewritten to cover new programming and advertising concepts for radio created by the licensing of thousands of new stations, the cutback of network radio, and the development of television during the last decade. Mr. Reinsch is executive director of Atlanta's WSB television and radio station, and Elmo Ellis is manager of programming and production at WSB.

RODDENBERRY, ROBERT S., JR. *Ancestors and Descendants of Cader Atkins Parker, 1810-1884.* Adel, Ga., The Patten Publishers, 1959. 140p. $7.50.

A biography of an early Georgia Baptist minister and a record of his descendants. Records of the Parker, Atkins, Pope, Vick, and Anthony families.

ROTON, OUIDA WADE. *Fan the Ember.* New York, Exposition Press, 1960. 56p. $2.50.

A collection of seventy-eight lyric poems with a religious theme. The author is a resident of Acworth, Georgia.

SCHWARTZ, DAVID J. *An Exploratory Analysis of the Development and Present Status of Voluntary and Cooperative Groups in Food Marketing.* Research Paper Series, Number 2. Bureau of Business and Economic Research, School of Business Administration, Georgia State College of Business Administration, Atlanta, Ga., 1957. 40p. Gratis.

A study of the history, development, advantages and disadvantages, and present status of voluntary and cooperative groups in food marketing.

SCHWARTZ, DAVID J. *The Franchise System for Establishing Independent Retail Outlets.* Research Paper Series, Number 14. Bureau of Business and Economic Research, Georgia State College of Business Administration, Atlanta, Ga., 1959. 26p. Gratis.

An exploratory study intended to explain to small business men, investors, students and others the what, why, and how of franchising independent retailers.

SCHWARTZ, DAVID J. *The Relationship of the Salesman's Wife to the Salesman's Selling Performance.* Research Paper Series, Number 16. Bureau of Business and Economic Research, School of Business Administration, Georgia State College of Business Administration, Atlanta, Ga., 1960. 31p. Gratis.

A study that attempts to determine what sales executives feel is the effect of the salesman's wife on his selling performance, and to learn what—if anything—can be done by the sales executive to motivate the salesman's wife to motivate the salesman. The author is Professor of Marketing at the Georgia State College of Business Administration.

SHOECK, HELMUT and WIGGINS, JAMES WILHELM, eds. *Scientism and Values.* Princeton, N. J., Van Nostrand, 1960. 320p. $6.50.

Twelve essays by a group of learned authors, editors, and professors who deplore the growing tendency to extend the quantitative and experimental methods of the natural sciences beyond their proper domain, into fields of human relationships. The editors are members of the faculty of Emory University, Atlanta, Georgia.

STEVENSON, MARY B. *Where Wonder Treads*. Dallas, Royal Publishing Company, 1960. 72p. $3.50.

A collection of lyric poems on the many facets of human living, containing a keen insight into everyday relationships. The author is a resident of Atlanta, Georgia.

STIRLING, NORA B. *Exploring for Lost Treasure*. Garden City, N. Y., Garden City Books, 1960. 56p. $2.50.

True stories of treasure hunts, modern and ancient, for juveniles. The illustrations are by H. B. Vestal.

SUGG, REDDING S., JR., and JONES, GEORGE H. *The Southern Regional Education Board*. Baton Rouge, Louisiana State University Press, 1960. 144p. $4.00.

The Southern Regional Education Board, an agent of sixteen states from Texas to Delaware, was conceived to formulate methods by which the Southern states could act co-operatively to improve standards of higher education. This volume sums up the achievements of the first decade of this agency which pioneered in the regional approach to higher education. Redding S. Suggs, Jr., is Associate Professor of English at Georgia State College.

SUGGS, LOUISE, ed. *Golf for Women*. Garden City, N. Y., Doubleday, 1960. 192p. $3.95.

Professional women golfers give instructions to amateur women golfers on developing techniques in every aspect of golf, from fundamentals to difficult shots and putting.

SURRENCY, ERWIN. *Guide to Legal Research*. New York, Oceana Publications, 1959. 124p. $4.50.

Intended for use in law schools, this book describes the basic features of many of the books useful to lawyers. Mr. Surrency is a native of Jesup, Georgia.

TAILFER, PATRICK. *A True and Historical Narrative of the Colony of Georgia*. Athens, University of Georgia Press, 1960. 169p. $5.00. Wormsloe Foundation Publication Number 4.

First published in 1741 under the title "A True and Historical Narrative of the Colony of Georgia in America," the text is reprinted here with the running commentary of the Earl of Egmont. Modern English usage is indicated where the language is obscure. Edited with an introduction by Dr. Clarence Ver Steeg.

TALMADGE, JOHN E. *Rebecca Latimer Felton*. Athens, University of Georgia Press, 1960. 200p. $4.50.

Nine stormy decades, a biography of Georgia's "Grandma Felton," first woman member of the Senate of the United States, author, educator, pioneer in the Temperance movement, and advocate of Women's Rights. The author is a member of the English Department of the University of Georgia.

TEAGUE, CHRISTINE. *Anybody But a Fool.* New York, Exposition Press, 1959. 157p. $3.00.

The trials and tribulations of a Georgia family are dealt with in this novel about the South and Southerners. The author is a native Georgian and now resides in Dallas, Texas.

THILENIUS, EDWARD ALBERT and KOGER, JIM. *No Ifs, No Ands, A Lot of Butts; 21 Years of Georgia Football.* Atlanta, Foote and Davies, 1960. 313p. $5.00.

The story of the private life of Coach Wally Butts, and his 21 years as head coach at the University of Georgia. The appendix contains Georgia football records from 1892 to the present. Ed Thilenius is a native of Athens, Georgia, and Jim Koger is a native of Washington, Georgia.

THOMPSON, MARY E. *The Driftwood Book.* Princeton, N. J., VanNostrand, 1960. 200p. $5.95.

Explains the mechanical aspects of and offers suggestions on the artistic use of driftwood in flower arrangements. The one hundred and twenty-eight photographs in the book are by Leonid Skvirsky of Atlanta, Georgia. Mrs. Thompson lives in Smyrna, Georgia.

THOMPSON, SALLY. *The Keener Love.* New York, McDowell, Obolensky, 1960. 309p. $3.95.

Taking up where the headlines and blurred wedding pictures leave off, this is the story behind a suicide told without generalizations and psychological embellishments. The author is a former resident of Atlanta, Georgia.

TOMLINSON, EDWARD. *Look Southward, Uncle.* New York, Devin-Adair, 1959. 369p. $6.00.

A survey of South American culture and economy and discussion of major problems in light of United States policies toward South America. The author is a native of Jesup, Georgia.

TUCKER, GLENN. *Hancock the Superb.* Indianapolis, Bobbs-Merrill, 1960. 368p. $5.00.

The biography of a Union general during the Civil War. Winfield Scott Hancock fought at Antietam, Fredericksburg, Gettysburg, Spotsylvania, the Wilderness, and Cold Harbor. Contains much information on the Army of the Potomac, its leaders and battles.

TYRE, NEDRA. *Hall of Death.* New York, Simon and Schuster, 1960. 215p. $2.95.

Murder and mystery in a reform school for girls involve the sympathetic and idealistic young English teacher. Violence before the cause of a suicide and murder are found.

VINZANT, MARION MCGINTY. *Deepstep, R. F. D.* Atlanta, Home Mission Board, Southern Baptist Convention, 1959. 69p. 50 cents.

A boy and girl from Chicago visit their grandparents in Deepstep, Georgia, for a month's visit. Through their experiences the author teaches the importance of the rural church, tithing, and missionaries. Mrs. Vinzant is a member of the faculty of Tift College, Forsyth, Georgia.

WALLACE, INEZ and MCCULLAR, BERNICE. *Building Your Home Life.* Chicago, Lippincott, 1960. 550p. $4.40.

An all-purpose homemaking book compiled by two well-known Georgia educators. Basic textbook for teachers of home economics concerned with girls of early senior high school age.

WARING, ANTONIO J., JR. *Laws of the Creek Nation.* Athens, University of Georgia Press, 1960. 27p. $1.00.

Published for the first time are fifty-six of the laws of the Creek Indians. The manuscript, dated January 8, 1825, is in the handwriting of Chilly McIntosh, clerk of the Greek National Council. This is the University of Georgia Libraries Miscellanea Publications, Number 1. The editor, Dr. Waring, is a resident of Savannah, Georgia.

WESTERFIELD, CLIFFORD. *Histology and Embryology of the Domestic Animals.* Part I. Athens, Ga., Privately Printed, 1957. 131p. $3.00.

A lecture outline and laboratory manual for college students, Part I begins with the cell, gametes, fertilization, and cleavage, and follows the development of the new organism through embryonic and fetal stages of development. Dr. Westerfield is Head of the Department of Veterinary Anatomy and Histology at the University of Georgia.

WESTERFIELD, CLIFFORD. *Histology and Embryology of the Domestic Animals.* Part II. Athens, Ga., Privately Printed, 1957. 134p. $3.00.

Part II covers muscle, blood, and nervous tissue; the blood, vascular, lymphatic, and integumentary systems and the organs of special sense. The embryological development of each system precedes the histological study.

WESTERFIELD, CLIFFORD. *Histology and Embryology of the Domestic Animals.* Part III. Athens, Ga., Privately Printed, 1958. 149p. $3.00.

Part III is comprised of the digestive, respiratory, urogenital, and endocrine systems, dealt with in the same way as Parts I and II.

WHETTEN, LELAND CARLING. *Recent Proxy Contests: A Study in Management-Stockholder Relations.* Studies in Business and Economics. Bulletin, Number 6. Bureau of Business and Economic Research, School of Business Administration, Georgia State College of Business Administration, Atlanta, Ga., 1959. 80p. Gratis.

A comprehensive inquiry into the entire field of proxy contests, showing the variety and relationships of the forces at work, and relating these forces to fundamental trends in American business corporations which affect their relations with stockholders. The author is Professor of Accounting at Georgia State College of Business Administration.

WHITING, THOMAS A. *Sermons on the Prodigal Son.* Nashville, Abingdon Press, 1959. 111p. $2.00.
Twelve brief messages on the well-known parable by the minister of the First Methodist Church in Valdosta, Georgia.

WILEY, BELL IRVIN, ed. *A Southern Woman's Story: Life in Confederate Richmond.* By Phoebe Yates Pember. Jackson, Tenn., McCowat-Mercer Press, 1959. 199p. $4.95.
The account of Phoebe Yates Pember's experiences as matron of Chimborazo Hospital in wartime Richmond. Originally published in 1879, the present edition contains an introduction by Bell Irvin Wiley and a number of Mrs. Pember's letters here published for the first time.

WILLIAMS, VINNIE. *Walk Egypt.* New York, Viking Press, 1960. 308p. $4.50.
A novel about the difficulties and strength of a young Georgia woman who becomes the support of her shiftless family after her father's death, and who, even when she finds love, must bear up under terrible sorrows. The author lives in Thomson, Georgia.

WINDHAM, DONALD. *The Hero Continues.* New York, Crowell, 1960. 191p. $3.50.
A novel of the corrupting powers of success in the commercial theater. The author is a native of Atlanta, Georgia.

WOOD, JAMES HORACE. *Nothing But the Truth.* Garden City, N. Y., Doubleday, 1960. 286p. $3.75.
An autobiographical account of how Lawyer James Wood fought a two-year battle to save his innocent client from the charge of murder.

YEARNS, WILFRED BUCK. *The Confederate Congress.* Athens, University of Georgia Press, 1960. 293p. $5.00.
A study of the Confederate Congress and its relation to the Davis administration and the war effort, describing the legislation, debates, personalities, and politics involved. An appendix gives brief biographical data on the Confederate congressmen, including their voting records on the Davis administration proposals. The author, a native of Louisville, Georgia, is a member of the History Department of Wake Forest College.

YERBY, FRANK. *Gillian.* New York, Dial Press, 1960. 346p. $3.95.
A novel about a mysterious, unpredictable, and gorgeous woman from Alabama and the men she loves and tries to destroy.

YERBY, FRANK. *Jarrett's Jade.* New York, Dial Press, 1959. 342p. $3.95.
The adventures in Scotland and the pre-Revolutionary South of a tempestuous and proud man, the founder of an American dynasty and lover and beloved of several beautiful women.

ZINN, HOWARD. *LaGuardia in Congress.* Ithaca, N. Y., Published for the American Historical Association by Cornell University Press, 1959. 288p. $5.50.

Reviews and appraises the tempestuous Congressional career of Fiorello LaGuardia, and defines LaGuardia's position in the Progressive movement. The author is Professor of History and Chairman of the Department of History and Social Sciences at Spelman College in Atlanta, Georgia.

Bibliography of Georgia Authors
1960-1961

THE twelfth in the REVIEW's series of annual "Bibliographies of Georgia Authors," this annotated Bibliography is, as nearly as the compiler could make it, a complete and accurate record of books published by Georgia authors from November 1, 1960, to November 1, 1961. The annotations are descriptive, not critical; intended to place, not to judge the book. U. S., State, County, and City Documents, parts of books, brief analytics, and pamphlets of less than 25 pages have been omitted. Prices are given except when not supplied by publisher or when book is obtainable only on specific request, in which case the word "Apply" is used.

In determining whom to designate as Georgia authors, the compiler has included authors born in Georgia and claiming Georgia as their native state and those who have lived in Georgia for a period of five years and who did their writing here.

The compiler will welcome and appreciate readers' sending to him any additions or corrections. They may be sent to him at any time in care of the GEORGIA REVIEW. Several books inadvertently omitted from previous Bibliographies are listed here. Any books omitted from the present Bibliography will be included in the list for 1961-1962.

Acknowledgment is made to members of the staff of the Special Collections Division of the University of Georgia Library for their assistance in the preparation of this Bibliography.

AIKEN, CONRAD POTTER. Selected Poems. New York, Oxford University Press, 1961. 274p. $4.75.
    A representative selection, considered by Pulitzer Prize winner Conrad Aiken as his most important poetic works since 1917. Mr. Aiken is a native of Savannah, Georgia.

ALLEN, CHARLES L. *Healing Words.* Westwood, N. J., Fleming Revel, 1961. 159p. $2.50.
    The assorted spiritual cures that are suggested in this message can be as spectacular as those accomplished by any of man's wonder drugs.

ALLEN, CHARLES L. *The Twenty-Third Psalm.* Westwood, N. J., Fleming Revel, 1961. 62p. $1.50.

The treasured "Shepherd Psalm" is here utilized to undergird and informally outline a positive and practical approach to life. Dr. Allen, a native of Georgia, is now pastor of the First Methodist Church, Houston, Texas.

BARFIELD, LOUISE CALHOUN. *History of Harris County, Georgia, 1827-1961.* Columbus, Ga., Columbus Office Supply Company, 1961. 766p. $12.00.

A record of Harris County, Georgia, from its creation in 1827 to the present day. It contains a list of county officials, census records, brief sketches of communities, individual biographies, marriage records, etc. The author is a resident of Columbus, Georgia.

BEAUMONT, CHARLES A. *Swift's Classical Rhetoric.* Athens, University of Georgia Press, 1961. 158p. $2.50.

A study of Jonathan Swift's use of ancient rhetoric in his ironic essays is number eight in the University of Georgia Monograph Series. The author is a member of the English Department at the University of Georgia.

BLACK, JOHN LOGAN. *Crumbling Defenses.* Macon, Ga., J. W. Burke Co., 1960. 133p. $4.65.

The memories and reminiscences of John Logan Black, Colonel C.S.A., have been edited and documented by Mrs. Eleanor D. McSwain of Macon, Georgia.

BLEDSOE, JOSEPH CULLIE. *An Outline of Research Methods in Education.* Athens, University of Georgia, 1959. 143p. Mimeographed $2.00.

A manual designed to aid the graduate student in the field of education. Dr. Bledsoe is Professor of Education at the University of Georgia.

BOGGUS, HOMER ALLEN. *Tears of Joy.* New York, Vantage Press, 1960. 278p. $3.95.

A novel set in South Georgia after the Civil War. Its main theme is that the power of forgiveness will always be the source of our highest good. The author is a native of Heard County, Georgia.

BONNER, JAMES CALVIN. *The Georgia Story.* Chattanooga, Tenn., Harlow Publishing Corp., 1961. 492p. $3.36.

This edition has been updated and includes events through September 1961. New illustrations and a glossary have been included. The author is head of the History Department at the Woman's College of Georgia at Milledgeville, Georgia.

BOWNE, ELIZABETH. *Gift From the African Heart.* New York, Dodd, Mead, 1961. 272p. $3.95.

The author, a Georgia girl of slave-holding ancestry, tells of her journey to the interior of Liberia to visit the grave of her husband, who had been killed in an airplane crash—a journey which brought her understanding and sympathy for the villagers she met in the back country, and a new maturity and faith with which to face her own future.

Brandeis, Donald. *The Gospel in the Old Testament.* Grand Rapids, Mich., Baker Book House, 1960. 188p. $3.95.

The author, an evangelist-at-large of the Baptist Church, points out that the Old Testament is filled with good news and that a person's spiritual life may be enlarged and deepened through an increased knowledge of the Scriptures.

Brown, Robert Kevin and Sturgess, Albert Henley. *Real Estate Primer.* Englewood Cliffs, N. J., Prentice-Hall, 1961. 249p. $7.50.

A guide that incorporates tested sales techniques and selling information that will help the real estate salesman acquire the two requisites of his profession—knowledge and skill. The authors are residents of Atlanta, Georgia.

Buckingham, Walter Samuel. *Automation: Its Impact on Business and People.* New York, Harper, 1961. 196p. $4.50.

This study gives the general reader a clear cut picture of important social and economic consequences of the new technology of automation. The author is Director of the School of Industrial Management and Professor of Economics at the Georgia Institute of Technology.

Caldwell, Erskine. *Erskine Caldwell's Men and Women.* Boston, Little, Brown, 1961. 320p. $4.50.

A collection of twenty-two short stories arranged to show life from youth to old age. This collection is edited and with an introduction by Carvel Collins.

Carlton, William Marion. Laboratory Studies in General Botany. New York, Ronald Press, 1961. 420p. $4.50.

A college manual that provides a sequence of basic exercises for the laboratory work in the first course in plant science. Dr. Carlton is Associate Professor of Botany at the University of Georgia.

Carr, James McLeod. *Working Together in the Larger Parish.* Atlanta, Church and Community Press, 1960. 105p. Paper $1.50.

A helpful guide for ministers, church workers, and the laymen who live and labor in large city parishes.

Cartledge, Groves Harrison. Presbyterian Churches and Early Settlers in Northeast Georgia. Athens, University of Georgia Printing Department, 1961. 208p. $5.00.

A compilation of historical sketches by a well-known Presbyterian minister of Northeast Georgia, who lived from 1820 to 1899. The book was compiled by Dr. Jessie Mize and Miss Virginia Louise Newton, both residents of Athens, Georgia.

Cobb, Tyrus Raymond. *My Life in Baseball, the True Record.* Garden City, N. Y., Doubleday, 1961. 283p. $4.50.

The late Georgia Peach, whose baseball record is still unchallenged, tells his fabulous story as it happened—lessons he learned the hard way; his friendship with the great; his great seasons; and his days as a manager. The author was a native of Royston, Georgia.

COOPER, J. WESLEY. *A Treasure of Louisiana Plantation Homes.* Natchez, Miss., Southern Historical Publications, 1961. 183p. $13.50.

A collection of color photographs of ante-bellum Louisiana plantation homes. A short historical sketch accompanies each photograph. The author is a native of Tifton, Georgia.

CORLEY, FLORENCE FLEMING. *Confederate City, Augusta, Georgia, 1860-1865.* Columbia, S. C., University of South Carolina Press, 1960. 130p. $6.00.

Advertisements, clippings, drawings, letters, and diaries all combine to record something of what Augusta, Georgia, was like as a place to live in during the Civil War, and how the War changed its mode of life. The author, a native of Augusta, now lives in Marietta, Georgia.

COULTER, ELLIS MERTON. *James Monroe Smith, Georgia Planter—Before Death and After.* Athens, University of Georgia Press, 1961. 294p. $5.00.

The biography of a wealthy Georgia planter whose colorful career did not end with his death but was kept alive in numerous claims and counter-claims in the settling of his estate. The author is Emeritus Head of the History Department, University of Georgia.

CRAIG, GEORGIA. See: GADDIS, PEGGY.

CULLEN, JOHN B. In collaboration with WATKINS, FLOYD C. *Old Times in the Faulkner Country.* Chapel Hill, University of North Carolina Press, 1961. 132p. $3.00.

A book about the people, the traditions and the history from which Faulkner built the "Yoknapatawpha world." Organized, edited, and completed by Floyd C. Watkins, Professor of English at Emory University, Atlanta, Georgia, who gathered his material from the conversations and letters of John Cullen.

DEBAILLOU, CLEMENS, ed. *John Howard Payne to His Countrymen.* Athens, University of Georgia Press, 1961. 61p. $2.00.

Payne's account of why he came South to gather data on the Cherokee Indians, and his arrest and imprisonment by the Georgia Guard in North Georgia is reprinted from the *Augusta Constitutionalist* of December 23, 1835. This is the University of Georgia Libraries Miscellanea Publications, Number 2. The editor, Dr. DeBaillou, is a resident of Athens, Georgia.

DERN, MRS. JOHN SHERMAN. See: GADDIS, PEGGY.

DERN, PEGGY. See: GADDIS, PEGGY.

DREWRY, JOHN E., ed. *Onward and Upward With Communications: Press, Radio, Television, Periodicals, Public Relations and Advertising as Seen Through Institutes and Special Occasions of the Henry W. Grady School of Journalism, 1960-1961.* Vol. LXII, No. 1. Athens, University of Georgia Bulletin, 1961. 226p. Paper $2.00. Cloth $3.00.

A compilation of addresses on journalistic subjects which were delivered at the several institutes, conventions, and special occasions sponsored by the University of Georgia School of Journalism during the 1960-1961 session.

ELLIS, A. L. *Common Sense Food Suggestions for Good Health, for Good Eating, for Good Cooking.* Atlanta, Privately Printed, 1961. 26p. $1.00.

A discussion of Thyroxine, Cholesterol, and fatty acids and how they can affect the eating habits of the individual. The author resides in Atlanta, Georgia.

ETKIN, ANNE LITTLE. *All at Sea.* Riverdale, Md., Seymour Etkin, 1961. 68p. $2.50.

An adventure story about the sea and boats for the junior high school student. The author is a former resident of Thomasville, Georgia.

FORBES, W. STANTON. *Scherzo.* Athens, The Berman Printers, 1961. 30p. Apply. A mirror fantasy based upon the Civil War. Copies may be purchased from the Atlanta Art Museum.

FORD, ELIZABETH AUSTIN. *Stone Mountain.* Decatur, Ga., Wommack Quality Printing Co., 1959. 70p. $1.50.

A compilation of legends, stories, poems, photographs, and maps relating to Stone Mountain. The author is a resident of Decatur, Georgia.

FORD, MARCIA. See: RADFORD, RUBY LORRAINE.

FREDERICK, MARY BARRINGTON. *Thronateeska Song.* New York, Exposition Press, 1961. 79p. $3.00.

A narrative poem of the Flint River. The author lives in Marshallville, Georgia.

FUHRMANN, PAUL TRAUGOTT. *Introduction to the Great Creed of the Church.* Philadelphia, Westminister Press, 1960. 144p. $3.00.

The story of the church creeds is the story of Christianity's centuries old and recurring struggle against forces, both within and without, that endangered the very existence of the faith. Dr. Fuhrmann is a Professor at Columbia Theological Seminary, Decatur, Georgia.

GADDIS, PEGGY (pseud. GEORGIA CRAIG). *Doctor Grant's Desire.* London, Foulsham, 1960. 184p. 10s 6d.

A student nurse decides to spend her last year of training at a small country hospital, and rooms with a family of ten children. She learns more from this family about life than she could get out of any nursing textbook.

GADDIS, PEGGY. *Doctor Hugh's Two Nurses.* London, Foulsham, 1960. 192p. 10s 6d.
   Doctor Hugh's medical career is endangered by romantic complications with two staff nurses.

GADDIS, PEGGY. *Doctor Talbot.* New York, Arcadia House, 1961. 221p. $2.95.
   Dayne Talbot, loyal, courageous, and armed with a brand new medical degree, returns to Cane Creek to clear her dead father's name of a fifteen-year-old drug-traffic scandal.

GADDIS, PEGGY. *Home for Sale.* New York, Arcadia House, 1961. 221p. $2.95.
   When a charming stranger comes to town looking for a farm, realtor Lee Folsom finds that she is more interested in romance than in realty.

GADDIS, PEGGY. *Intruders in Eden.* New York, Arcadia House, 1961. 223p. $2.95.
   The plans of Jefferson Randall for building an exclusive resort on a South Carolina island are blocked by a beautiful young girl who refuses to sell her plantation.

GADDIS, PEGGY. *Junior Prom Girl.* New York, Arcadia House, 1961. 224p. $2.95.
   Penny, a pampered 17-year-old, cannot believe that the handsome stranger is not in love with her, but with her widowed mother.

GADDIS, PEGGY. *Kerry Middleton, Career Girl.* London, Wright and Brown, 1961. 224p. 10s 6d.
   A contented personal secretary, who has rejected the thought of marriage because of her sister's marital misfortunes, begins to have her doubts about spinsterhood when she meets a kind and intelligent man.

GADDIS, PEGGY. *The Nurse and the Pirate.* New York, Arcadia House, 1961. 224p. $2.95.
   A dull cruise explodes with danger and romance when Kathy's ship is hijacked by a dashing revolutionary, and she is plunged into front-page adventure.

GADDIS, PEGGY. *Nurse Polly's Mistake.* London, Foulsham, 1960. 184p. 10s 6d.
   Nursing is her profession and love is her heart's desire, and this newly graduated nurse finds both at a large island estate in Georgia.

GADDIS, PEGGY. *Persistent Suitor.* New York, Arcadia House, 1961. 224p.
   Life had treated two sisters differently, but a danger-packed reunion proved to them that blood was thicker than they had thought.

GADDIS, PEGGY. (pseud. GEORGIA CRAIG). *Piney Woods Nurse.* New York, Arcadia House, 1961. 224p. $2.95.

Nurse Jill Barclay finds that her main problem at Harmony Grove is not her patient, but her patient's son, and a lovely gypsy girl who believes in voodoo.

GADDIS, PEGGY (pseud. PEGGY DERN). *Rozalinda.* New York, Arcadia House, 1961. 224p. $2.95.

The forthcoming visit of Rozalinda, a glamorous movie star, to her old home in the Blue Ridge mountains causes much apprehension to the family that she left behind.

GADDIS, PEGGY. (pseud. PEGGY DERN). *Wild Orchids.* New York, Arcadia House, 1961. 223p. $2.95.

Brought up in sheltered innocence by a maiden aunt in Kentucky, 19-year-old Gail Harrison loses her heart in a casual romance, and follows the man she loves to Florida—only to discover that he hardly remembers her.

HARWELL, RICHARD BARKSDALE, ed. *Robert E. Lee, A One Volume Abridgement of the Four Volume Edition by Douglas Southall Freeman.* New York, Scribner's, 1961. 624p. $10.00.

The vital message of the original has been preserved in this abridgement of one of the classics in American History. The editor is a native Georgian and is Librarian at Bowdoin College.

HEBSON, VERNA CASTLEBERRY. *Trapesin' Woman.* Atlanta, C & H Press, 1961. 170p. $3.50.

A factual story of the author's five-month trip to Europe and her encounters with the people of fifteen countries during 1958. The author is a resident of Atlanta, Georgia.

HENDERSON, LEGRAND. *Augustus Hits the Road.* New York, Grosset, 1961. 128p. $1.50.

Augustus and his family have a mix-up with gypsies, trailer camps and a counterfeiter.

HENDERSON, LEGRAND. *Augustus Rides the Border.* New York, Grosset, 1961. 127p. $1.50.

Life on the Mexican border as a goat herder is the subject for this new adventure in the life of Augustus.

HENDERSON, LEGRAND. *Augustus Saves a Ship.* New York, Grosset, 1961. 128p. $1.50.

Augustus, an involuntary stowaway, saves a ship from an enemy submarine.

HOLDEN, GENEVIEVE. *Deadlier than the Male.* Garden City, N. Y., published for the Crime Club by Doubleday, 1961. 187p. $2.95.

New Orleans is the setting for this murder mystery about a female Bluebeard. The author lives in Atlanta, Georgia.

HUFF, WILLIAM HENRY. *I'm Glad I'm Who I Am.* Stoney Creek, Va., The Millennium Press, 1960. 40p. $2.00.

A collection of poems about incidents in the life of the author, a native of Oglethorpe County, Georgia, who now lives in Chicago, Illinois.

HUMPHRIES, ADELAIDE (pseud. KATHLEEN HARRIS). *Camp Nurse.* New York, Avalon Books, 1961. 222p. $2.95.

Despite the unflattering disguises she affects at a boys' summer camp, romance finds its way to beautiful Tanis Thaler.

HUMPHRIES, ADELAIDE. *Swamp Nurse.* New York, Avalon Books, 1961. 224p. $2.95.

A society-girl-turned-nurse and a young minister work together for the poor inhabitants of the vast and hazardous Okefenokee Swamp.

JESSUP, RICHARD. *Chuka.* Greenwich, Conn. Fawcett, 1961. 160p. 35 cents.

A gunfighter helps in the desperate defense of a Colorado fort.

KEITH, EDMOND. *Christian Hymnody.* Knoxville, Tenn., Convention Press, 1956. 147p. 75 cents.

A studybook designed to train music leadership and enlarge the music ministry of the churches of the Southern Baptist Convention. The author is a resident of Atlanta, Georgia.

KEITH, EDMOND and McGLOTHEN, GAYE L. *Hymns We Sing.* Nashville, Tenn., Convention Press, 1960. 121p. $1.00.

A hymnology for teenagers that includes words and music. Mr. Keith is Associate Director, Church Music Department, Southern Baptist Convention, Atlanta, Georgia.

KNAPP, MARY GIBSON. *Fifty Year History of the Women of the Church.* Atlanta, Privately Printed, 1960. 31p. $1.00.

An historical and chronological study of the work of the women of the Presbyterian Church, written by the Historian of the Georgia Synodical.

LAWRENCE, ALEXANDER A. *A Present for Mr. Lincoln.* Macon, Ga., Ardivan Press, 1961. 321p. $4.95.

This story of Savannah, Georgia, from secession to Sherman, is told in the idiom of those who experienced and wrote about its rebellion, frustration, and defeat. The author is a native of Savannah, Georgia.

LAWRENCE, ELIZABETH. *Gardens in Winter.* New York, Harper, 1961. 218p. $4.50.

Gardening ideas and information about winter plants and blooms in all parts of the country. The book is illustrated by Caroline Dorman. The author, a native of Savannah, Georgia, lives in Charlotte, North Carolina.

LAWRENCE, JOHN BENJAMIN. *A New Heaven and a New Earth*. New York, American Press, 1960. 165p. $2.75.

An understandable interpretation of the Book of Revelations, based on forty years of study. The author is a resident of Atlanta, Georgia.

LEGRAND. See: HENDERSON, LEGRAND.

LEHRMAN, EDGAR H., trans. and ed. *Turgenev's Letters: A Selection*. New York, Knopf, 1961. 401p. $5.00.

A selection of letters and excerpts of letters from Turgenev's vast correspondence in a book intended not only for the general reader but also for the scholar. Edited and translated from the Russian, French, and German originals by the Associate Professor of Russian at Emory University.

LEMLY, JAMES H. *Non-Vehicular Benefits from Utility Use of Streets and Highways*. Atlanta, Bureau of Business Research of Georgia State College of Business Administration for the United States Department of Commerce, Bureau of Roads, 1960. 100p. Gratis.

A study made for the Federal Government so that Congress will be able to judge as to the degree of benefits which highways provide to the various groups within the nation. Dr. Lemly is a Professor at the Georgia State College of Business Administration, Atlanta, Georgia.

LINCOLN, CHARLES ERIC. *The Black Muslims in America*. Boston, Beacon Press, 1961. 276p. $4.95.

A case study of the Black Muslims, an organization of Negroes who preach black supremacy. The author is Professor of Social Philosophy at Clark College, Atlanta, Georgia.

LOMAX, LOUIS E. *The Reluctant African*. New York, Harper, 1960. 117p. $2.95.

A current study of the explosive situation in South Africa, written by a Negro reporter, a native of Valdosta, Georgia.

LONG, NATHANIEL GUY. *Financing the Church Budget*. Atlanta, Church and Community Press, 1957. 61p. $1.00.

A practical guide to church finances for the pastor and the board of stewards.

LYLE, GUY REDVERS. *The Administration of the College Library*. New York, H. W. Wilson, 1961. Third Edition. 419p. $7.00.

A revised and extended edition of a study that gives the student a simple, logical, and self-contained introduction to all aspects of library administration as they apply to college libraries. The author is Librarian at Emory University, Atlanta, Georgia.

MCCLAIN, ROY O. *If With All Your Heart*. Westwood, N. J., Fleming H. Revel, 1961. 190p. $3.00.

A book that reveals the author's awareness of the world we live in and his struggle to relate the gospel to the problems and challenges of our time. Dr. McClain is pastor of the First Baptist Church in Atlanta, Georgia.

McCULLERS, CARSON. *Clock Without Hands*. Boston, Houghton-Mifflin, 1961. 241p. $4.00.

A perceptive and colorful study of the change in Southern mores as seen in the actions and thoughts of two men and two adolescents—one a Negro. The author is a native of Columbus, Georgia.

McGRATH, FRANCES and ABERNETHY, DON. *The Pirates' House Cook Book*. Asheville, N. C., The Biltmore Press, 1961. 191p. $2.75.

A collection of authentic recipes taken from the files of the Pirates' House menus. This famous restaurant is located in Savannah, Georgia.

MALONE, HENRY THOMPSON. *The Episcopal Church in Georgia, 1733-1957*. Atlanta, published by the Protestant Episcopal Church in the Diocese of Atlanta, 1960. 334p. $2.95.

A chronological history of the Episcopal Church in Georgia, tracing its development from its settlement in Savannah in 1733 to the celebration of the Golden Anniversary of the Diocese of Atlanta in 1957.

MARSHALL, EDISON. *West With the Vikings*. Garden City, N. Y., Doubleday, 1961. 444p. $5.95.

Leif Ericson tells the story of his life and times, leading up to his discovery of North America 500 years before Christopher Columbus set foot in the New World.

MARSHALL, JOHN DAVID. *An American Library History Reader*. (Contributions to Library Literature, No. 3) Hamden, Conn., Shoe String Press, 1961. 466p. $9.00.

This anthopology presents, for the first time in book form, papers of the American Library History Round Table as well as other essays dealing with the past of American Librarianship. The compiler is Acquisitions Librarian of the University of Georgia Libraries.

MARTIN, CHARLES. *I've Seen 'Em All*. Byron, Ga., Privately Printed, 1961. 113p. $2.50.

An intimate, personal account of fifty-three years of football at the University of Georgia. Copies may be obtained from the author, Box 275, Byron, Georgia.

MILLER, JULIAN HOWELL. *A Monograph of the World Species of Hypoxylon*. Athens, University of Georgia Press, 1961. 80p. $6.50.

The result of over 25 years of study of the species of Hypoxylon and other genera in the Zylariaceae. Included are 75 plates comprising 238 photomicrographs and descriptions. The late Dr. Miller was Regent's Professor Emeritus of Plant Pathology and Plant Breeding at the University of Georgia.

MITCHELL, MARGARET. *Gone With the Wind*. New York, Macmillan, 1961. 954p. $10.00.

The twenty-fifth anniversary edition of this great Civil War novel is illustrated by Ben Stahl. A booklet entitled "Gone With the Wind and Its Author Margaret Mitchell" accompanies this edition.

MITCHELL, STEPHENS and KILBRIDE, J. B. *Real Property Under the Code of Georgia and the Georgia Decisions*. Atlanta, Curtis Printing Company, 1960. Second Edition. 786p. $20.00.

This revision of a basic reference tool in the legal profession is brought up-to-date with the addition of much new material. The authors are both residents of Atlanta, Georgia.

NEFF, LAWRENCE W. *The Hymn of Hate and the Law of Love*. Atlanta, Banner Press, 1961. 66p. $2.50.

This book of poetry is divided into two parts and each part, though written in short lyrics, builds up a theme to a climax. The author is a resident of Atlanta, Georgia.

O'CONNOR, FLANNERY, ed. *A Memoir of Mary Ann, Prepared by the Dominican Sisters*. New York, Farrar, Straus, and Cudahy, 1961. 144p. $3.50.

The appealing life story of a pious, lively child who died at the age of 12 in a Dominican home for incurable cancer cases in Atlanta, Georgia. The editor, Flannery O'Connor, is a resident of Milledgeville, Georgia.

PARKS, EDD WINFIELD. *William Gilmore Simms As Literary Critic*. Athens, University of Georgia Press, 1961. 152p. $2.75.

A study of one of the central figures in the literature of the Old South and the first American critic to emphasize the need for organic rather than comparative criticism. Dr. Parks is a member of the English Department at the University of Georgia.

PHILLIPS, ALLEN A. *Nuggets for Happiness*. Cleveland, Tenn., Pathway Press, 1959. 116p. $2.00.

An inspirational book that is a compilation of the author's writings for the past twenty-eight years. Dr. Phillips is pastor of Wesley Memorial Methodist Church, Atlanta, Georgia.

PIERCE, HUBBELL. *Murdoch*. New York, Harper, 1961. 26p. $1.95. Harpercrest. $2.19.

A storybook for the very young about a croquet-playing mouse named Murdoch and some of his unusual relatives. The author is a former resident of Atlanta, Georgia.

POPE, CLIFFORD HILLHOUSE. *The Great Snakes*. New York, Knopf, 1961. 375p. $6.95.

This story includes the natural history of the boa constrictor, the anaconda, the largest pythons, and the comparative facts about other snakes and basic information on reptiles in general. The author is a native of Washington, Georgia.

RADFORD, RUBY LORRAINE (pseud. MARCIA FORD). *Linda's Champion Cocker.* New York, Avalon Books, 1961. 220p. $2.95.

A prize-winning cocker and the love of a young veterinarian helps Linda Bernard shape her plans for a career raising champion dogs.

RADFORD, RUBY LORRAINE. *Once Upon a Spring.* New York, Avalon Books, 1961. 224p. $2.95.

Disillusioned when Hal Fulton forsakes medicine for acting, Doctor Diane Maxwell ironically falls for the author of Hal's first play. The author is a resident of Augusta, Georgia.

RADFORD, RUBY LORRAINE. *Secret of Ocean House.* New York, Abelard-Schuman, 1961. 157p. $3.00.

A mysterious house, a wrecked ship, and coded messages give three youngsters an adventurous summer. The illustrations are by Lewis Hart.

RANGE, WILLARD. *Nehru's World View.* Athens, University of Georgia Press, 1961. 139p. $3.50.

A case study of Jawaharlal Nehru's theory of international relations. This book describes his explanations of why nations behave as they do and also reforms he would like to see in the present inter-state system. Dr. Range is a member of the Political Science Department at the University of Georgia.

RICE, THADDEUS BROCKETT and WILLIAMS, CAROLYN WHITE. *History of Greene County, Georgia, 1786-1886.* Macon, J. W. Burke Co., 1961. 648p. $15.00.

A comprehensive history of one of Georgia's oldest counties with detailed accounts of the outstanding historical events and brief family sketches. Marriage records, lists of county officers, rosters of Greene County companies in wars, etc., are also included. Dr. Rice, who collected and wrote most of the material in this book, died in 1950, and Mrs. Williams, the editor, lives at Round Oak, Georgia.

RIDGE, GEORGE ROSS. *The Hero in French Decadent Literature.* Athens, University of Georgia Press, 1961. 210p. $3.75.

A detailed analysis of the decadent hero that shows him as a cultural projection of a dying society. Dr. Ridge is a member of the French Department at Georgia State College of Business Administration, Atlanta, Georgia.

RIDGE, GEORGE ROSS. *Under the Georgia Sun.* Coral Gables, Fla., Wake-Brook House, 1961. 64p. $3.00.

A collection of some fifty sonnets by an Associate Professor of French at Georgia State College of Business Administration, Atlanta, Georgia.

SCOTT, THURMAN THOMAS. *Mark of a Champion.* New York, Longmans, Green, 1961. 214p. $3.50.

A courageous and determined young boy fights desperately to keep and train the puppy he has grown to love. The author resides in Thomasville, Georgia.

SELL, EDWARD SCOTT. *Geography of Georgia.* Oklahoma City, Harlow, 1961. Third Edition. 183p. $3.20.
The third edition of this basic reference work is brought up-to-date with revisions, new statistics, and illustrations. The author is Professor Emeritus of Geography at the University of Georgia.

SMITH, HOWARD ROSS. *Democracy and the Public Interest.* Athens, University of Georgia Press, 1960. 166p. $3.00.
Number five in the series of University of Georgia Monographs, this study deals with the problems and complications of a democratic society as it seeks to safeguard the interests of the majority without inflicting penalties on minorities and special groups. Dr. Smith is Professor of Economics in the College of Business Administration at the University of Georgia.

SMITH, NANNETTE CARTER. *Sunlight and Shadow.* Atlanta, Harper Printing Company, 1960. 46p. $3.00.
The many aspects of life, both bright and dark, are reflected in this book of poems by an Atlanta poet.

STEVENSON, ELIZABETH. *Lafcadio Hearn.* New York, Macmillan, 1961. 362p. $6.95.
A full length biography of the tragic and little-known American writer who discovered Japan for most of the Western world. The author lives in Atlanta, Georgia.

TALMAGE, FRANKLIN C. *The Story of the Presbytery of Atlanta.* Atlanta, Foote & Davies, 1960. 242p. $3.00.
A history of Presbyterianism in North Georgia from 1820 to 1960, containing maps of Hopewell, Goodhope, and Atlanta Presbyteries.

TALMAGE, FRANKLIN C. *The Story of the Synod of Georgia.* Atlanta, Privately Published, 1961. 123p. $1.50.
A history of Presbyterianism in Georgia from 1733 to 1960. Dr. Talmage is former Secretary of Church Extension of the Presbytery of Atlanta, Georgia.

TEMPLE, SARAH GOBER and COLEMAN, KENNETH. *Georgia Journeys.* Athens, University of Georgia Press, 1961. 360p. $6.00.
An account of Georgia's early settlers from the founding of the colony in 1732 through 1754. This work was begun by the late Mrs. Mark Temple of Marietta, Georgia, and has been edited and completed by Dr. Coleman of the History Department at the University of Georgia.

TUCKER, GLENN. *Chickamauga: Bloody Battle in the West.* Indianapolis, Ind., Bobbs-Merrill, 1961. 448p. $6.00.

A narrative account of the historic two-day battle of Chickamauga during the Civil War. The author is a part-time resident of Georgia whose North Georgia farm is named "Filibuster Hill."

VINSON, JOHN CHALMERS. *Referendum for Isolation.* Athens, University of Georgia Press, 1961. 148p. $2.50 paper.

The defeat of Article Ten of the League of Nations Covenant is the subject of this study by Dr. Vinson of the History Department of the University of Georgia. This is University of Georgia Monographs, No. 6.

WARREN, KITTRELL J. *The Life and Public Services of an Army Straggler, 1865.* Athens, University of Georgia Press, 1961. 98p. $2.50 paper; $3.75 cloth.

This reprint of a rare Civil War book is a fictional and comic treatment of an unsoldierly Confederate deserter and straggler who preyed upon the country instead of defending it on the battle field. This reprint was edited with an Introduction by Dr. Floyd Watkins of the English Department at Emory University, Atlanta, Georgia. This is Number Three in the University of Georgia Libraries Miscellanea Publications.

WELTNER, PHILIP. *Process and Service.* Atlanta, C. L. Weltner, 1961. 136p. $4.00.

This book deals with the technical aspects of the laws of process and service and the initial steps to be taken in instigating law suits. This study by the late President of Oglethorpe University and Chancellor of the University System of Georgia, first issued in 1929, has been brought up-to-date by the author's son, Charles Longstreet Weltner of Atlanta, Georgia.

WILLIFORD, WILLIAM BAILEY. *Americus Through the Years.* Atlanta, Privately Printed, 1960. 207p. $10.00.

Americus, one of Georgia's beautiful towns, is the subject of this one hundred and twenty-five year history—from its beginning as a village of skinned-pole houses to a thriving, bustling city. The author, a native of Americus, now lives in Atlanta, Georgia.

YERBY, FRANK. *Garfield Honor.* New York, Dial Press, 1961. 347p. $3.95.

Roak Garfield, a Texas ranch hand, fights his way across America in a search for self and wealth, and uses and destroys the women who are irresistibly drawn to him.

YOUNG, JAMES HARVEY. *The Toadstool Millionaires.* Princeton, N. J., Princeton University Press, 1961. 282p. $6.00.

A general history of patent medicines in America during the free-wheeling days before federal regulations. Dr. Young is the Chairman of the History Department of Emory University, Atlanta, Georgia.

Bibliography of Georgia Authors
1961-1962

THE thirteenth in the REVIEW's series of annual "Bibliographies of Georgia Authors," this annotated Bibliography is, as nearly as the compiler could make it, a complete and accurate record of books published by Georgia authors from November 1, 1961, to November 1, 1962. The annotations are descriptive, not critical; intended to place, not to judge the book. U. S., State, County, and City Documents, parts of books, brief analytics, and pamphlets of less than 25 pages have been omitted. Prices are given except when not supplied by the publisher or when book is obtainable only on specific request, in which case the word "Apply" is used.

In determining whom to designate as Georgia authors, the compiler has included authors born in Georgia and claiming Georgia as their native state and those who have lived in Georgia for a period of five years and who did their writing here.

The compiler will welcome and appreciate readers' sending to him any additions or corrections. They may be sent to him at any time in care of the GEORGIA REVIEW. Several books inadvertently omitted from previous Bibliographies are listed below. Any books from the present Bibliography will be included in the list for 1962-1963.

Acknowledgment is made to members of the staff of the Special Collections Division of the University of Georgia Library for their assistance in the preparation of this Bibliography.

ADAMS, CARSBIE CLIFTON, and VON BRAUN, WERNHER. *Careers in Astronautics and Rocketry*. New York, McGraw-Hill, 1962. 252p. $6.95.

A general survey of the many opportunities in the field of astronautics offered by universities, governmental agencies, and industrial organizations. Dr. Adams is a resident of Atlanta, Georgia.

ADAMS, J. C. *The Bishop of Heard County Preaches*. Nashville, Tenn., Privately Printed, 1962. 160p. $2.50.

A book of sermons from Dr. Adams' fifty years as a rural pastor in the Methodist Church. The introduction is by Bishop Arthur J. Moore.

AIKEN, CONRAD POTTER. *Brownstone Eclogues and Other Poems.* Bloomington, Indiana University Press, 1962. 61p. Cloth $3.50. Paper $1.75.
A collection of poetry by Georgia's Pulitzer Prize winning poet.

ALLEN, CHARLES L. *The Life of Christ.* Westwood, N. J., Revell, 1962. 160p. $2.50. Deluxe Edition. $3.95.
This chronicle in narrative form harmonizes the four Gospel accounts and incorporates verses of Scripture. The author is pastor of First Methodist Church, Houston, Texas.

BENSON, BERRY. *Berry Benson's Civil War Book.* Athens, University of Georgia Press, 1962. 200p. $4.00.
This book is a Confederate sergeant's account of how he scouted behind enemy lines, twice escaped from prisons, and on the eve of Lee's surrender, stole through Union picket lines and headed home to Augusta, Georgia, still carrying his sharpshooter's rifle. The volume is edited by Mrs. Susan Williams Benson of Athens, a daughter-in-law of the Confederate soldier.

BIGGERS, DOROTHY L. *Across the Stream.* New York, Carlton Press, 1962. 180p. $3.00.
A novel relating the determined effort of a young man to provide educational, financial, and spiritual assistance to his family. The author lives in West Point, Georgia.

BISHER, FURMAN. *With a Southern Exposure.* New York, Thomas Nelson, 1962. 255p. $3.95.
A collection of sixty of the best sports columns written by the sports editor of the *Atlanta Journal.* The introduction is by Bing Crosby.

BLACK, EUGENE ROBERT. *Tale of Two Continents—Africa and South America.* Athens, Ferdinand Phinizy Lectures, University of Georgia, 1961. 36p. $1.00.
Two lectures, delivered at the University of Georgia on April 12 and 13, 1961, by the President of the International Bank for Reconstruction and Development.

BRANDEIS, DONALD. *A Faith for Modern Man.* Grand Rapids, Mich., Baker Book House, 1961. 129 p. $2.95.
This study is designed as a reply to those who would challenge Christianity and also for those who need to be established in the faith. The author is evangelist-at-large of the Baptist Church and lives in Atlanta, Georgia.

BRYAN, MARY GIVENS, editor. *Abstracts of Colonial Wills of the State of Georgia, 1733-1777.* Atlanta, published by the Atlanta Town Committee of the National Society, Colonial Dames of America. 1962. 158p. $5.09.

These abstracts give a picture of life in Georgia in the Colonial period and provide a valuable reference tool for the researcher in history. The book may be obtained from the editor, State Department of Archives & History, 1516 Peachtree N.W., Atlanta 9, Georgia.

BURGE, DOLLY LUNT. *The Diary of Dolly Lunt Burge, 1847-1875.* Athens, University of Georgia Press, 1962. 160p. $4.00.

A personal record of plantation life in Middle Georgia in mid-nineteenth century. The book is edited by James I. Robertson, Jr.

CALDWELL, ERSKINE. *Close to Home.* New York, Farrar, Straus & Cudahy, 1962. 216p. $3.95.

The brutal treatment of a Negro brings the question of race relations in a small town out in the open.

CALDWELL, ERSKINE. *God's Little Acre.* New York, Farrar, Straus & Cudahy, 1962. 218p. $6.50.

This edition is published nearly thirty years after the first appearance of this ribald best seller about a Georgia dirt farmer and his family. This is a special gift edition with ten portrait drawings by Milton Glasser.

CARTLEDGE, SAMUEL ANTOINE. *The Bible: God's Word to Man.* Philadelphia, Westminster Press, 1961. 143p. $3.00.

This book seeks to give some insight into the nature of the Bible and to acquaint the reader with the many areas of Biblical scholarship that can aid him in coming to a richer, fuller understanding of the meaning of the Bible. The author is Professor of New Testament and Exegesis at Columbia Theological Seminary, Decatur, Georgia.

CAUTHEN, KENNETH. *The Impact of American Religious Liberalism.* New York, Harper, 1962. 290p. $6.00.

This study deals with the conflicts among the major exponents of liberalism in the American theological tradition and evaluates the permanent values of such a movement. The author was a former member of the Christianity Department at Mercer University, Macon, Georgia.

CLARK, FRANK G. *Poems—The Uncrowned Queen.* Macon, Ga., Southern Press, 1962. 96p. $2.00.

A collection of seventy-five poems dealing with the divergent themes of nature, love, home, prayer, philosophy, service, and God. The author, former Mercer University faculty member, now lives at Norman Park, Georgia.

COMER, DAVID B., III, and SPILLMAN, RALPH R. *Modern Technical and Industrial Reports.* New York, Putnam, 1962. 425p. $7.95.

This book presents the principles and practices of writing technical, business, and industrial reports. The authors are members of the English Department at Georgia Institute of Technology.

CRAIG, GEORGIA. See: GADDIS, PEGGY..

DAVIES, GENEVA, ed. *The Measured Tread*. Atlanta, The Manuscript Club, 1962. 72p. $3.00.
  This third anthology of poems by thirty-one members of the Manuscript Club is a worthy tribute to commemorate their Silver Anniversary. Mrs. Davies is a resident of Decatur, Georgia.

DERN, MRS. JOHN SHERMAN. See: GADDIS, PEGGY.

DERN, PEGGY. See: GADDIS, PEGGY.

DICKEY, JAMES. *Drowning with Others*. Middleton, Conn., Wesleyan University Press, 1962. 96p. Paper $1.25. Cloth $3.50.
  A collection of thirty-six poems dealing with life in its phases, by a native of Atlanta.

DICKEY, JAMES. *Into the Stone and Other Poems*. New York, Scribners, 1960. 206p. $3.95.
  A prize winning collection of poems published in the *Poets of Today Series*, Number VII, edited by John Hall Wheelock. The author is a native of Atlanta.

DOUGHTIE, BEATRICE MACKEY. *Documented Notes on Jennings and Allied Families*. Atlanta, Privately Printed, 1961. 1036p. $15.00.
  A comprehensive genealogy of the Jennings and allied families in America. Included in the notes are land grants, wills, war and pension records; data from church minutes and registers; Bible, marriage, cemetery, and other valuable records. The compiler is a resident of Atlanta, Georgia.

DREWRY, JOHN E., ed. *Diagnosis and Prognosis in Journalism: Press, Radio, Television, Periodicals, Public Relations, and Advertising As Seen Through Institutes and Special Occasions of the Henry W. Grady School of Journalism, 1961-1962*. Vol. LXIII, No. 5. Athens, University of Georgia Bulletin, 1962. 185p. Paper $2.00. Cloth $3.00.
  The 1961-1962 compilation of addresses and papers delivered at the various institutes and other special occasions sponsored by the University of Georgia's School of Journalism.

ETHRIDGE, WILLIE SNOW. *There's Yeast in the Middle East*. New York, Vanguard Press, 1962. 320p. $4.50.
  An informal, lighthearted tour through the Middle East—from the land of the Hittites to the land of the Hiltonites—by a delightful, intrepid traveler. The author, a native of Georgia, now lives in Louisville, Kentucky.

FLANDERS, BERTRAM HOLLAND, ed. *Gems of Atlanta Authors Guild.* Atlanta, Atlanta Authors Guild, 1962. 70p. $3.50.

A collection of prose, poetry, and humor from thirty-eight members of the Atlanta Authors Guild. The editor is Professor Emeritus of English, Georgia State College, Atlanta, Georgia.

FLOYD, WOODROW W. *Rising Waters.* New York, Vantage Press, 1961. 165p. $3.50.

The age-old conflict between the old and the new is the theme of this novel about the construction of a dam on the Etowah River in North Carolina. The author, a native of Adairsville, Georgia, now lives in Marietta, Georgia.

FORD, MARCIA. See: RADFORD, RUBY LORRAINE.

FORT, MARION KIRKLAND, ed. *Topology of 3-Manifolds and Related Topics.* Englewood Cliffs, N. J., Prentice-Hall, 1962. 256p. $10.00.

This comprehensive survey of modern manifold topology with emphasis on the geometric aspects is the complete record of the proceedings of the 1961 Topology Institute at the University of Georgia. The editor is Head of the Department of Mathematics at the University of Georgia.

GADDIS, PEGGY (pseud. GEORGIA CRAIG). *Bahamas Nurse.* London, Foulsham, 1962. 184p. 11s 6d.

Nurse Eugenia Hayes accompanies her small patient to the Bahama island home of the wealthy Raiford family and discovers a private Eden—complete with serpent.

GADDIS, PEGGY (pseud. GEORGIA CRAIG). *Enchanted Spring.* London, Foulsham, 1961. 174p. 10s 6d.

A judge's daughter returns to her small-town home after secretarial school and helps defend a man who is accused of attempted murder, and whom she finds she loves.

GADDIS, PEGGY. *Future Nurse.* New York, Arcadia, 1962. 223p. $2.95.

The romantic adventures of a student nurse.

GADDIS, PEGGY (pseud. GEORGIA CRAIG). *The Girl Outside.* London, Wright and Brown, 1961. 176p. 10s 6d.

Florida is the setting for this story of eighteen-year-old Holly Tolliver, an orphan who, after the death of her benefactor, learns about the adult world fast.

GADDIS, PEGGY (pseud. PEGGY DERN). *Leona Gregory, R. N.* New York, Arcadia House, 1961. 224p. $2.95.

A small Florida Gulf Coast hospital is the setting for this novel of a young nurse and her romantic adventures.

GADDIS, PEGGY (pseud. GEORGIA CRAIG). *Mountain Melody.* New York, Arcadia House, 1962. 224p. $2.95.

Judge Bramblett's two granddaughters seemed as different as night and day until a young attorney from up North proves that they have at least some tastes in common.

GADDIS, PEGGY (pseud. PEGGY DERN). *Palm Beach Girl.* New York, Arcadia House, 1962. 222p. $2.95.

A romantic client poses unexpected problems for Dinah, who handles vacation details for wealthy families.

GADDIS, PEGGY. *Peacock Hill.* London, Wright and Brown, 1961. 174p. 10s 6d.

The mountains of North Carolina are the setting of this novel about two romances.

GADDIS, PEGGY. *Robin.* New York, Arcadia House, 1962. 224p. $2.95.

Robin O'Dare, adopted by a wealthy, domineering matron, finally rebels when she meets a young man in the Caribbean.

GADDIS, PEGGY (pseud. GEORGIA CRAIG). *Substitute Nurse.* New York, Arcadia House, 1962. 223p. $2.95.

A shy young nurse must either renounce her love for the handsome intern or fight for it and risk heartbreak.

GODDARD, THOMAS H. and GODDARD, JOHN H., JR. *The Mills, Cope, and Related Families of Georgia.* Philadelphia, Dunlap Printing Company, 1962. 334p. $10.00.

The Tufts, Eppinger, Obear, Goddard, Fell, Childs, Cubbedge, Lovell, Charlton, Hartridge, Cann, Mills, Cope, and Wisenbaker families are covered in this comprehensive genealogy. The authors are natives of Griffin, Georgia.

GOLLEY, FRANK B. *Mammals of Georgia: A Study of Their Distribution and Functional Role in the Ecosystem.* Athens, University of Georgia Press, 1962. 218p. $3.75.

This handbook, describing eighty species of mammals found in Georgia, will be invaluable to professional biologists in forestry and wildlife management, to students and teachers, and to laymen interested in wildlife. Dr. Golley, a member of the Zoology Department of the University of Georgia, is Director of the Institute of Radiation Ecology, Atomic Energy Commission Savannah River Operations, Aiken, South Carolina.

GRANADE, COLUMBUS. *Poems and Sayings.* Washington, Ga., Privately Printed, 1961. 171p. $3.00.

A collection of eighty-one poems by a Georgia poet who was born May 5, 1831, and died November 5, 1914. This book may be obtained from Mr. C. C. Granade, Box 488, Washington, Georgia.

GREGORIE, ANNE KING. *Christ Church, 1706-1959.* Charleston, South Carolina. The Dalcho Historical Society, 1961. 169p. $4.00.
The history of the establishment and growth of a plantation parish of the Protestant Episcopal Church in South Carolina. The author, a native of Savannah, Georgia, died on December 4, 1960.

HABERSHAM, ANNA WYLLY. *The Journal of Anna Wylly Habersham, 1864.* Darien, Georgia, The Ashantilly Press, 1961. 25p. $3.00.
A new edition of the Civil War diary of a Savannah, Georgia, girl, this winner of the 1961 Southern Books Competition award was designed and illustrated by William G. Haynes, Jr. of the Ashantilly Press.

HATCHER, GEORGE, ed. *Georgia Rivers.* Athens, University of Georgia Press, 1962. 76p. $3.00.
Written by six prominent journalists, this collection of articles on the Savannah, Ogeechee, Altamaha, St. Marys, Suwannee, Coosa, Flint, and Chattahoochee Rivers first appeared in *The Atlanta Journal and Constitution Magazine.*

HAWES, LILLA MILLS, editor. *Collections of The Georgia Historical Society,* Vol. XIII. Savannah, Georgia, The Georgia Historical Society, 1959. 154p. $3.50.
The Letter Book of Thomas Raspberry, 1758-1761, gives a picture of economics in the Colony of Georgia for that period. So far as is known, this is the earliest Georgia merchant's letter book still in existence. The original book is in the library of the Georgia Historical Society.

HAYES, MAUDE MILLER. *The John Clarence Calhoun Miller Family;* an appendix to the sketch of the Miller and Calhoun-Miller families by Florence McWhorter Miller, 1927. Hartwell, Georgia, Privately Printed, 1961. 56p. Apply.
This genealogical appendix to a book published in 1927 is a record of the John Clarence Calhoun Miller family from 1927 to 1961. The compiler lives in Hartwell, Georgia.

HAYS, THOMAS M., comp. *Public Communications Media in Georgia.* Decatur, Georgia, Selective Publications, 1961. 88p. $7.50.
A directory of public communications media in Georgia that lists newspapers, business, professional and trade periodicals, organizational journals, government publications, and radio and television broadcasting stations. The compiler is a resident of Decatur, Georgia.

HEINSOHN, LILLIAN BRITT. *Southern Plantation.* New York, Hearthside Press, 1962. 286p. $4.50.
The story of a Labrah plantation, including some of its treasured recipes. The author is a native Georgian.

HENDERSON, LEGRAND. *Augustus and the Desert.* New York, Grossett, 1960. 128p. $1.50. Library Binding, $3.18.
   Augustus and his family have many adventures in the North American desert; a reprint of an Augustus favorite.

HENDERSON, LEGRAND. *Augustus and the River.* New York, Grossett, 1962. 128p. $1.50.
   The adventures of a shanty-boat family on a trip down the Mississippi River. A reprint in the Augustus series.

HENDERSON, LEGRAND. *How Baseball Began.* Nashville, Tennessee, Abingdon, 1962. 63p. $2.00.
   About the O'Learys, their cow, their move to Boston, and the beginning of baseball.

HENDERSON, LEGRAND. *Samson Catches a Mystery.* New York, Houghton, 1962. 150p. $3.00.
   A story about an eight-year-old boy and his adventures in a haunted house. Illustrated by the author.

HENDERSON, LINDSEY P. *The Oglethorpe Light Infantry.* Savannah, Civil War Centennial Commission of Savannah and Chatham County, 1961. 58p. $1.50.
   A military history of the Oglethorpe Light Infantry, recounting the strategy and the details of battles and skirmishes in which they were engaged during the War, 1861-1865. The author is a native of Savannah, Georgia.

HICKS, ALBERTA KINARD. *Down Suwannee River with Stephen Collins Foster.* Elon College, North Carolina, Privately Printed, 1962. 31p. Apply.
   A poetic tribute to Foster and the river he made famous in song.

HOLLAND, LYNWOOD MATHIS, and MALONE, PERILLAH A. *Georgia Government.* Austin, Texas, the Steck Company, 1961. 136p. $3.68.
   An up-to-date study of the government of Georgia. Dr. Holland is a member of the Political Science Department at Emory University.

HOLLOMAN, ANN C., comp. *Hart County, Georgia—1860 Census.* Macon, Ga., Privately Printed, 1961. 82p. $2.25.
   This book, reproduced from typewritten originals, is the first census for Hart County, Georgia, and also contains the mortality schedules and the slave schedules for the County. The author is a resident of Macon, Georgia.

HUMPHRIES, ADELAIDE. *The Nurse Made Headlines.* New York, Avalon Books, 1962. 223p. $2.95.
   Cheryl Lanier's first mistake was touching the gun that had killed her wealthy patient; the second, trusting the victim's handsome nephew.

HURT, JOHN JETER. *My Fifty Favorite Stories.* Atlanta, Privately Printed, 1961. 216p. $2.75.
   A collection of the author's favorite stories from his experience as one of the South's leading Baptist ministers. Dr. Hurt, until his death, made his home in Atlanta, Georgia.

JONES, BILLY WALKER. *History of Stone Creek Baptist Church.* Columbus, Ga., Columbus Office Supply Company, 1961. 88p. $4.00.
   A comprehensive history of the Stone Creek Baptist Church, located in Twiggs County, Georgia, for the years 1808 through 1958. The author is a resident of Dry Branch, Georgia.

JORDAN, GERALD RAY. *Preaching During a Revolution: Patterns of Procedure.* Anderson, Ind., Warner Press, 1962. 192p. $3.50.
   In this book, Dr. Jordan advances new approaches for reaching people with the power of the Gospel. Dr. Jordan is Professor of Preaching, Candler School of Theology, Emory University.

JOSLIN, G. STANLEY. *The Minister's Law Handbook.* New York, Channel Press, 1962. 256p. $4.95.
   A book for pastors confronted with the legal problems involved in marriage, privilege communications, copyright, government aid, and wills. The author is a member of the faculty of the Emory University School of Law.

LANCE, THOMAS JACKSON. *Joseph Astor Sharp.* Calhoun, Georgia, North Georgia Conference Historical Society. 1961. 78p. $3.00.
   A biography of Dr. Joseph Astor Sharp, president of Young Harris College from 1839-1930. The author is a former president of Young Harris and a resident of Calhoun, Georgia.

LEGRAND. See: HENDERSON, LEGRAND.

LOMAX, LOUIS E. *The Negro Revolt.* New York, Harper, 1962. 271p. $4.50.
   A report on the nature of the reasons behind the upsurge of Negro militancy in the Civil Rights area. The author views this trend as a revolt against both established patterns of segregation and the Negro leaders who adhere to more traditional means of breaking down racial barriers. The author is a native of Valdosta, Georgia.

McGEHEE, MAUD. *To Get My Name in the Kingdom Book.* Atlanta, Franklin Printing Company, 1962. 42p. $1.00.
   A collection of poems about life, love, friends, and God. The author is a resident of Atlanta, Georgia.

McLARTY, NANCY. *Chain of Death.* Garden City, New York, published for the Crime Club by Doubleday, 1962. 192p. $2.95.

The setting of this novel is Guatemala, and the plot concerns the Communist attempt to take over the Western Hemisphere. The author is a resident of Atlanta, Georgia.

McPherson, Robert G., ed. *The Journal of the Earl of Egmont, 1732-1738.* Athens, University of Georgia Press, 1962. 460p. $7.50.

The present work is the first publication of a fundamental original source of Colonial history; the abstract of the Trustees' Proceedings for the Establishment of the Colony of Georgia.

Mariana [Foster, Marian Curtis]. *Miss Flora McFlimsey's Valentine.* New York, Lothrop, Lee, and Shepard, 1962. Unpaged. $2.00.

This new Flora McFlimsey book is a charming Valentine in itself, with a page waiting to be inscribed to the one you love. Ages 4-8.

Marshall, Edison. *The Conqueror.* Garden City, New York, Doubleday, 1962. 396p. $5.75.

A novel which tells of the strange ambition which drove and eventually destroyed history's most illustrious conqueror, Alexander the Great.

Martin, Milward Wyatt. *Twelve Full Ounces.* New York, Holt, Rinehart and Winston, 1962. 136p. $4.00.

This study records the creation and growth of the Pepsi-Cola Company. The author, a native of Eatonton, Georgia, is a Senior Vice-President of the Pepsi-Cola Company and the head of its legal department.

Mauelshagen, Carl. *Salzburg-Lutheran Expulsion and Its Impact.* New York, Vantage Press, 1962. 200p. $3.95.

A history of the inhabitants of Salzburg, Austria, from antiquity to 1731, the expulsion of the Lutheran dissenters, their trek into northern Protestant Europe and their reception. Small banks of these Salzburg refugees settled in Georgia under the leadership of Samuel Urlsperger, 1733-1741. The author, a native of Germany, is Professor Emeritus, Georgia State College, Atlanta, Georgia.

Montgomery, Marion. *The Wandering of Desire.* New York, Harper, 1962. 301p. $4.95.

A novel about the persistence and unchangeability of land despite man's efforts to possess and change it. The author is Assistant Professor English at the University of Georgia.

Muse, Helen E. *Green Pavilions: A Novel of the French and Indian War.* New York, Carlton Press, 1961. 260p. $3.00. (A Milestone Book).

This novel is the story of Jere Holliday, a Virginian, who settled in the Wilderness on the Great Lakes in the pioneer era before and during the French and Indian War of 1754-1763. The author is a teacher at the Georgia School for the Deaf at Cave Springs, Georgia.

O'CONNOR, FLANNERY. *Wise Blood*. New York, Farrar, Straus, and Cudahy, 1962. Second Edition. 232p. $4.50.

This edition brings back into print Miss O'Connor's highly acclaimed first novel, originally published in 1952, of a primitive fanatic from Tennessee who believed fervidly in his mission to preach the "Church without Christ" on street corners in Georgia.

OGBURN, DOROTHY and OGBURN, CHARLTON, JR. *Shake-speare: The Real Man Behind the Name*. New York, Morrow, 1962. 282p. $4.50.

This book contrasts Will Shaksper, who the authors claim was never known to have written anything but his name, with Edward de Vere, Earl of Oxford, whose life the Ogburns attempt to show bears an amazingly precise relationship to Shakespeare's works.

OZMENT, ROBERT V. *. . . But God Can*. Westwood, N. J., Revell, 1962. 126p. $2.50.

This book assures the reader that when he trusts God unreservedly, life will be beautiful and abundant, no mater what the circumstances. Dr. Ozment is Pastor of St. James Methodist Church, Atlanta, Georgia.

PARKS, AILEEN WELLS. *Davy Crockett, Young Rifleman*. Indianapolis, Ind., Bobbs-Merrill, 1962. 200p. $2.25.

One of the popular Childhood of Famous Americans Series, this book tells the story of the boyhood days of the young Tennessean who became a famous hunter and died in the Alamo. This edition is illustrated by Justin Pearson. The author is a resident of Athens, Georgia.

PARKS, WINFIELD EDD. *Ante-Bellum Southern Literary Critics*. Athens, University of Georgia Press, 1962. 368p. $7.50.

This study discusses the intellectual history of the South from 1785-1861, and includes all the major literary critics, exclusive of Poe. Dr. Parks is Professor of English at the University of Georgia.

PARKS, JOSEPH HOWARD. *General Leonidas Polk, C. S. A., the Fighting Bishop*. Baton Rouge, Louisiana State University Press, 1962. 408p. $7.50.

Biography of the first Episcopal Bishop of Louisiana and the Southeast and one of the leading figures of the Confederacy. The author is Head of the History Department at the University of Georgia.

PARTHEMOS, GEORGE STEVEN, ed. *Higher Education in a World of Conflict*. Athens, University of Georgia Press, 1962. 175p. $2.00.

This book originated from a conference at the University of Georgia dealing with the doctrines, strategy, and tactics of Communism and the responsibility of higher education to meet the challenges. Herein are nine lectures by a distinguished group of Americans from the fields of business, government, and education. Dr. Parthemos is Associate Professor of Political Science at the University of Georgia.

PINHOLSTER, GARLAND F. *Coach's Guide to Modern Basketball Defense.* Englewood Cliffs, N. J., Prentice-Hall, 1961. 212p. $5.35.
   This handbook presents the latest defensive trends and styles in basketball and offers new defensive ideas and variations. The author is Athletic Director and Head Basketball Coach at Oglethorpe University.

POUND, MERRTT BLOODWORTH and SAYE, ALBERT BERRY. *Handbook on the Constitutions of the United States and Georgia.* 6th edition. Athens, Georgia, University of Georgia Press, 1962. 171p. $1.25.
   This handbook contains the text of both Constitutions, with discussion of historical background and analyses of the articles and amendments, as well as an expanded chapter on civil rights and a new approach in the chapter on foreign relations.

PROCTOR, JOHN HOWARD and THORNTON, WLLIAM MCKENZIE. *A Handbook for Line Managers.* New York, American Management Association, 1961. 244p. $5.25.
   This handbook tells the supervisor—concisely and without jargon—how to identify training needs, plan training programs, conduct both "man-to-man" training and group conferences, and spark trainees' interest in acquiring new knowledge and skills. Mr. Thornton is a native of Georgia.

RADFORD, RUBY LORRAINE (pseud. MARCIA FORD). *Journey Into Danger.* New York. Avalon Books, 1962. 221p. $2.95.
   Escorting young Mrs. Carswell to Bermuda seems a lark to traveling companion Ellen Newman until both women run afoul of Communist spies. The author lives in Augusta, Georgia.

RAIFORD, MORGAN, ed. *Contact Lens Management.* Boston, Little Brown, 1962. 260p. $12.50.
   This survey was originally published as part of the International Ophthalmology Clinics Series, Vol. I, No. 2, and is in its second printing, with a Spanish edition planned. The editor and two of the contributors are associated with the Ponce de Leon Eye and Ear Infirmary in Atlanta, Georgia.

RIGDON, LOUIS T. *Georgia's County Unit System.* Decatur, Georgia, Selective Books, 1961. 112p. $2.10.
   This study is an historical appraisal of legislative apportionment formulas and the county unit system in primary nominations.

RUSK, DEAN. *Role of the Foundation in American Life.* Claremont, Calif., Claremont University College, 1961. 65p. $2.75.
   These two lectures, presenting an interesting interpretation of the significance of foundations in American life were delivered the month before Dr. Rusk was named Secretary of State in President Kennedy's cabinet. The author is a native of Georgia.

SAYE, ALBERT B., POUND, MERRITT B., and ALLUMS, JOHN F. *Principles of American Government*. Englewood Cliffs, N. J., Prentice-Hall, 1962. 469p. $5.95.

The principles, organization, and functions of American governments are presented in a concise, straightforward account in this fourth edition of a standard work.

SCOTT, ROBERT LEE, JR. *Boring a Hole in the Sky*. New York, Random House, 1961. 292p. $5.95.

Confessions of a fighter pilot who holds numerous military decorations and has flown over six million miles. The author is a native of Macon, Georgia.

SCUDDER, C. W. *Danger Ahead*. Nashville, Tenn., Broadman, 1961. 180p. $3.25.

A Christian approach to some current problems, ranging from racial to economic. The author, a former public school teacher in Georgia, is Professor of Christian Ethics at Southwest Baptist Theological Seminary.

SCUDDER, C. W. *Family in Christian Perspective*. Nashville, Tenn., Broadman, 1962. 192p. $3.50.

This book seeks to answer the question of what a family ought to be. Its purpose is to determine a family ethic from a theological perspective. The author is Professor of Christian Ethics at Southwestern Baptist Theological Seminary, Fort Worth, Texas.

SEYDELL, MILDRED. *Poetry Profile of Belgium*. Wauthier-Braine, Belgium, M. Seydell, 1960. 131p. $3.00.

A collection of French and Belgian poetry with explanatory notes in English. The author is a native of Atlanta.

SLAPPEY, PANSY AIKEN. *A Man and His City—Brown Hayes and Atlanta*. Atlanta, Southern Publications Society, 1961. 78p. $1.50.

The story of a man's passion for the protection of the heart of his city. The author lives in Atlanta, Georgia.

SMITH, BERTHENIA CROCKER and WILLINGHAM, JEAN SAUNDERS. *Bibb County, Georgia, Early Wills and Cemetery Records*. Macon, Georgia, Mary Hammond Washington Chapter, DAR, 1961. 88p. $5.00.

Complete abstracts of wills, 1822-1855, as well as burial records of persons living in the Bibb County area. The authors are residents of Macon, Georgia.

SMITH, CLARENCE JAY. *Man and Society: Problems and Historical Experience*. Athens, University of Georgia Center for Continuing Education, 1961. 149p. Apply.

This study is volume two in the *Basic Issues of Man* series, dealing with social changes.

SMITH, HERBERT ORLANDO. *These Foster Sons.* Atlanta, Alumni of Boys High School, 1961. 77p. Apply.

This collection of poems was published by the Alumni of Atlanta's old Boys High School. Professor Smith was principal of the school from 1920-1946.

SMITH, LILLIAN. *Killers of the Dream.* New York, Norton, 1961. 253p. $4.50.

This enlarged and revised edition of a book that first appeared in 1949 contains a new foreword and a new introduction which includes an interpretation of the student sit-ins and an incisive account of the new African nations and their impact on American foreign policy. The author lives in Clayton, Georgia.

SMITH, LILLIAN. *Memory of a Large Christmas.* New York, Norton, 1962. $2.95.

A Christmas reminiscence of her Southern childhood. The book is illustrated by Constance McMillan.

SMITH, SARAH QUINN. *Early Georgia Wills—Lincoln County.* Washington, Georgia, Privately Printed, 1960. 47p. $4.00.

Abstracts of wills of Lincoln County people, reflecting the early history of that county. The author lives in Washington, Wilkes County, Georgia.

STEEDMAN, MARGUERITE. *Refuge in Avalon.* Garden City, New York, Doubleday, 1962. 477p. $5.95.

A panoramic novel of the rich man of Jerusalem who claimed the body of Christ after the Crucifixion and brought the first tidings of Christianity to Britain.

STOKES, MACK B. *The Epic of Revelation.* New York, McGraw-Hill, 1961. 240p. $4.95.

An essay in Biblical theology. Dr. Stokes is Associate Dean at the Candler School of Theology, Emory University.

SUDDETH, RUTH ELGIN, OSTERHOUT, ISA LLOYD, and HUTCHESON, GEORGE LEWIS. *Empire Builders of Georgia.* Austin, Texas, the Steck Company, 1962. Third Edition. 559p. $4.50.

Designed for the general public as well as students, this book is divided into two parts: "Georgia's Role in History" and "The Treasures of Georgia." The book is illustrated and designed by Warren Hunter.

SYLVESTER, C. DOUGHTY. *Presenting a Pictorial History of Augusta, Georgia.* Augusta, Georgia, WEL-COM-IN Publications, 1962. 48p. $1.25, students and schools.

A pictorial history of Augusta, Georgia, showing floods, fires, buildings, and historic events that have occurred in the city. The book may be obtained from the author at Box 546, Augusta, Georgia.

TALMADGE, JOHN ERWIN, HAMAN, JAMES B., and BORNHAUSER, FRED. *The Rhetoric-Reader, with an appendix on grammar and syntax.* Chicago, Scott, Foresman, 1962. 526p. $4.50.

The purpose of this book is to discuss the problems a writer should be aware of and to offer solutions to these problems. It sets forth rhetorical principles and suggestions for applying them, presents examples of distinguished prose and analyzes them, and provides an appendix on syntax and grammar.

THOMPSON, CLAUDE HOLMES. *Theology of the Kerygma.* New York, Prentice-Hall, 1962. 174p. $5.35.

A study in primitive preaching. The author is Professor of Systematic Theology at the Candler School of Theology, Emory University.

VANN, SARA KATHERINE. *Training for Librarianship Before 1923.* Chicago, American Library Association, 1961. 242p. $7.00.

This study examines the education for librarianship prior to the publication of Williamson's report on training for library service in 1923.

WHITE, JESS R., ed. *Sports Rules Encyclopedia.* Palo Alto, Calif., National Press, 1961. 563p. $7.50.

This publication makes available to physical education teachers, sports program directors, and others working with sports an official comprehensive rules book for thirty-eight sports and games. The editor is Associate Professor of Health, Physical Education, and Recreation at Georgia Southern College, Statesboro, Georgia.

WHITE, ROBB. *Torpedo Run.* Garden City, New York, Doubleday, 1962. 183p. $2.95.

Mutiny and adventure aboard a Navy P-T Boat during World War II is the setting of this novel for teen-agers.

WILDER, WILLIAM MURTHA. *Wilder Families in the Southeastern United States.* Albany, Ga., A. L. Seely Company, 1951. 334p. Apply.

A genealogical record of one of the outstanding families in Georgia and the Southeast. The compiler is a resident of Albany, Georgia.

WILLIFORD, WILLIAM BAILEY. *Peachtree Street, Atlanta.* Athens, University of Georgia Press, 1962. 176p. $4.00.

This book traces the evolution of Atlanta's famous thoroughfare from an Indian trail to a village road in the 1840's, through its rebuilding after 1864, to its present concrete and steel canyon walls. The author, a native of Americus, now lives in Atlanta, Georgia.

WILLIFORD, WILLIAM BAILEY. *Williford and Allied Families.* Atlanta, Privately Printed, 1962. 284p. $15.00.

Many old photographs and well-documented research make this a valuable genealogical work of several well-known Georgia families. The author lives in Atlanta, Georgia.

WINDHAM, DONALD. *The Warm Country*. New York, Scribners, 1962. 208p. $3.50. Paper $1.65.

A collection of fourteen short stories covering a wide range of characters and settings. Introduction by E. M. Forster.

YATES, B. C. *Historic Cobb County*. Marietta, Ga., Cobb County Federal Savings and Loan Association, 1961. 35p. Apply.

This book presents the highlights of the history of Cobb County and the surrounding area from antiquity to the present day.

YERBY, FRANK GARVIN. *Griffin's Way*. New York, Dial Press, 1952. 345p. $4.95.

The story, set in 1870, concerns a beautiful Yankee nurse hired to take care of an aristocratic young Mississippian whose sanity is a casualty of war.

Bibliography of Georgia Authors

1962-1963

THE fourteenth in the REVIEW's series of annual "Bibliographies of Georgia Authors," this annotated Bibliography is, as nearly as the compiler could make it, a complete and accurate record of books published by Georgia authors from November 1, 1962, to November 1, 1963. The annotations are descriptive, not critical; intended to place, not to judge the book. U. S., State, County, and City Documents, parts of books, brief analytics, and pamphlets of less than 25 pages have been omitted. Prices are given except when not supplied by publisher or when book is obtainable only on specific request, in which case the word "Apply" is used.

In determining whom to designate as Georgia authors, the compiler has included authors born in Georgia and claiming Georgia as their native state and those who have lived in Georgia for a period of five years and who did their writing here.

The compiler will welcome and appreciate readers' sending to him any additions or corrections. They may be sent to him at any time in care of the GEORGIA REVIEW. Several books inadvertently omitted from previous Bibliographies are listed here. Any books omitted from the present Bibliography will be included in the list for 1963-1964.

Acknowledgment is made to members of the staff of the Special Collections Division of the University of Georgia Library for their assistance in the preparation of this Bibliography.

AIKEN, CONRAD POTTER. *The Morning Song of Lord Zero.* New York, Oxford University Press, 1963. 130p. $4.75.

   Twenty-three new poems comprise the first two sections of this collection. The third, fourth, and fifth sections are drawn, respectively, from "A Letter from Lio Po," "Skylight One," and "Sheepfold Hill." Mr. Aiken is a native of Savannah, Georgia.

AIKEN, CONRAD POTTER, ed. *Twentieth Century American Poetry.* New York, Modern Library, 1963. New revised edition. 410p. $1.95.

   This edition of a collection of poems by American poets is edited and has a preface by Conrad Aiken.

AIKEN, CONRAD POTTER. *Ushant.* New York, Meridian, 1962. 365p. Paper. $1.75.
  The poet's self-analytical autobiographical record in which the author is both the man on the couch talking and the observer listening to the man. This study was first published in 1952.

ALEXANDER, JOHN A. *Potidaea—Its History and Remains.* Athens, University of Geogia Press, 1963. 176p. $5.00.
  A historical archaeological study of the Corinthian colony, in Northern Greece, from its founding in 600 B.C. to its fall in 356 B.C. during the Peloponnesian War. The author is Head of the History Department at Georgia State College, Atlanta, Georgia.

ALLEN, CHARLES L. *The Lord's Prayer, An Interpretation.* Westwood, N. J., Revell, 1963. 64p. $2.00.
  Presented originally as a segment of his book, *God's Psychiatry,* Dr. Allen's interpretation is complemented in this special edition with color line sketches by Ismar David. Dr. Allen, a native of Georgia, is pastor of the First Methodist Church of Houston, Texas.

ALLEN, CHARLES L. and WALLIS, CHARLES L. *When Christmas Came to Bethlehem.* Westwood, N. J., Revell, 1963. 64p. $1.50.
  In this account the Bethlehem starlight etches "ordinary folks"—Mary, Joseph, Herod, Simeon, Anna, the Shepherds, and the Wise Men—who helped make the first Christmas.

ALLEN, ELLEN GORDON. *Japanese Flower Arrangement, a Complete Primer.* Rutland, Vt., Tuttle, 1963. Revised edition. 86p. $2.75.
  The purpose of this book is fourfold: to increase the skill of those who love to arrange flowers; to provide a more comprehensive understanding of this Japanese art; to help students where no teacher is available; and to provide a medium of instruction among the many schools of Japanese flower arrangement.

ANDREWS, P. C. *Reminiscing Meditations and Observations.* Columbus, Ga., Privately Printed, 1963. 55p. $1.00.
  The author has served twenty-six churches during his ministry and from his many and varied experiences he draws the incidents recorded in this collection.

BOWEN, JOHN MCGOWAN. *The Bowen Family.* Decatur, Ga., Bowen Press, 1962. 115p. Apply.
  A genealogical record of the McGowan, Bowen, and Brooks Families of George's Creek, Pickens County, South Carolina. Mr. Bowen is a resident of Decatur, Georgia.

BURCH, ROBERT. *A Funny Place to Live.* New York, Viking, 1962. 40p. $2.50.
   Lost in the woods and offered hospitality by many friendly creatures, Vic and Trudy still prefer their own home—just as the animals consider the children's house "a funny place to live." This book was a Junior Literary Guild Book selection for 1962.

BURCH, ROBERT. *Tyler, Wilkin, and Skee.* New York, Viking, 1963. 156p. $3.00.
   The story of life on a Georgia farm during the depression as seen through the eyes of three small brothers. The author is a native of Fayette County, Georgia.

BURNS, ROBERT W. *The Art of Staying Happily Married.* Englewood Cliffs, N. J., Prentice-Hall, 1963. 223p. $3.95.
   Dr. Burns, President of the International Convention of Christian Churches, discusses such subjects as managing the family finances, getting along with in-laws, and bringing up children. The author as pastor of the Peachtree Christian Church in Atlanta, Georgia, has married some 3,500 couples.

BYERS, EDNA HANLEY, comp. *Robert Frost at Agnes Scott College.* Decatur, Ga., McCain Library, Agnes Scott College, 1963. 75p. $2.50.
   The primary purpose of this brochure is to increase the usefulness, for scholars, of all the important records and materials in the College Library concerning Robert Frost's twenty visits to Agnes Scott. Mrs. Byers is Librarian at Agnes Scott College, Decatur, Georgia.

CALDWELL, ERSKINE. *The Bastard and Poor Fool.* London, Bodley Head, 1963. 240p. 16s.
   Electric with power to shock, Erskine Caldwell's first novels are now published in England for the first time. The locale for these stories is set amidst the world of the poor whites in Georgia.

CALDWELL, ERSKINE. *The Last Night of Summer.* New York, Farrar, Straus & Cudahy, 1963. 178p. $3.95.
   A businessman's first experience with an adulterous affair ends in tragedy for all concerned.

CANNON, WILLIAM RAGSDALE. *Journeys After St. Paul.* New York, Macmillan, 1963. 276p. $4.95.
   The personal report of an odyssey that started in 1951 and ended in 1960. The author visited every site which the New Testament tells us the Apostle Paul had been during his life time in the first century. Dr. Cannon is Dean of Candler School of Theology at Emory University, Atlanta, Georgia.

CARRINGTON, JOHN WESLEY. *Builders of Tomorrow*. Winder, Ga., Privately Printed, 1962. 97p. Apply.

A collection of poems that treat with all facets of life. The author lives in Winder, Georgia.

CAY, JOHN EUGENE. *Ward Allen: Savannah River Market Hunter*. Savannah, Ga., Pigeonhole Press, 1959. 48p. $3.50.

The story of a veteran hunter and fisherman who lived on a houseboat anchored off Pennyworth Island in the Black River, a branch of the Savannah River. The author is a resident of Savannah, Georgia.

CHAMPION, JOHN M. and BRIDGES, F. J. *Critical Incidents in Management*. Homewood, Ill., Richard D. Irwin, 1963. 300p. $10.95.

This study treats the practical problems confronted daily by executives and analyzes each situation—included are forty-eight incidents and ninety-three critiques. Both of the authors are Professors of Business Management at Georgia State College, Atlanta, Georgia.

CLUTE, ROBERT EUGENE. *The International Legal Status of Austria—1938-1955*. The Hague, Netherlands, Martinus Nijhoff, 1962. 157p. 18.75 guilders.

This study is confined to an examination of the international legal problems involved in Austria's changed status from the Anschluss of March 13, 1938, until the signing of the State Treaty on May 15, 1955. The author is a member of the Political Science Department at the University of Georgia.

CONWAY, HOBART MCKINLEY, JR., ed. *The Weather Handbook*. Atlanta, Conway Publications, 1963. 255p. $15.00.

A summary of weather statistics for principal cities throughout the United States and around the world. The editor is a resident of Atlanta, Georgia.

COULTER, ELLIS MERTON. *John Ellis Coulter, Small-Town Businessman of Tarheelia*. Athens, Privately Printed, 1962. 241p. Apply.

A biographical account of the author's father, a businessman and civic leader in the small North Carolina town of Connelly Springs. The edition is limited to 99 copies.

COULTER, ELLIS MERTON, ed. *The Journal of Peter Gordon, 1732-1735*. Athens, University of Georgia Press, 1963. 88p. $3.75.

Diary of one of the original settlers of the Colony of Georgia. Includes extended criticisms of the public policies regarding land holdings, servants, slaves, and government. Dr. Coulter is Regents' Professor Emeritus of History at the University of Georgia.

CRAIG, GEORGIA. See: GADDIS, PEGGY.

DAVIS, MAGGIE. *The Far Side of Home.* New York, Macmillan, 1963. 314p. $4.95.
A novel of the Civil War in Georgia, with scenes at Jonesboro, Atlanta, and the Battle of Kennesaw Mountain. The rural, middle-class South is well portrayed in this story set in the winter of 1863. The author is a resident of Atlanta, Georgia.

DERN, MRS. JOHN SHERMAN. See: GADDIS, PEGGY.

DERN, PEGGY. See: GADDIS, PEGGY.

DREWRY, JOHN E., ed. *Better Journalism for a Better Tomorrow: Press, Radio, Television, Periodicals, Public Relations, and Advertising As Seen Through Institutes and Special Occasions of the Henry W. Grady School of Journalism, 1962-1963.* Vol. LXIV, No. 6, Athens, University of Georgia Bulletin, 1963. 300p. Paper $2.00. Cloth $3.00.
The 1962-1963 compilation of addresses and papers delivered at the various institutes and other special occasions sponsored by the University of Georgia's School of Journalism.

EDGE, FINDLEY B. *A Quest for Vitality in Religion.* Nashville, Broadman, 1963. 251p. $3.95.
An inquiry into the nature and meaning of Christian life and what is needed to regenerate church membership. The author, a native of Albany, Georgia, is Professor of Religious Education at Southern Seminary since 1950.

EVANS, JEWELL R. *Songs for Savings.* Decatur, Ga., Bowen Press, 1962. 80p. $3.00.
A collection of thirty inspirational poems about saints, sinners, shadows, sunshine, and the South. Mrs. Evans, a native Georgian, is Church Library Consultant with the Baptist Book Store in Atlanta, Georgia.

FOLSOM, MARION B. *Executive Decision Making in Business and Government.* New York, McGraw-Hill, 1962. 137p. $4.95.
This study contains a wealth of vital facts and suggestions drawn from both proven business concepts and procedures and the best experience in government. The author, a native Georgian, is Director of Eastman Kodak Company and former Secretary of Health, Education, and Welfare.

FORD, WILLIAM HERSCHEL. *Simple Sermons About Jesus Christ.* Grand Rapids, Zondervan, 1961. 104p. $1.95.
A collection of messages on the life of our Lord, as well as His many attributes and His unique position as the Saviour from sin.

FORD, WILLIAM HERSCHEL. *Simple Sermons for Today's World.* Grand Rapids, Zondervan, 1960. 120p. $1.95.
The sermons in this collection are directed to the contemporary man whose problems are unique to the age in which he lives.

FORD, WILLIAM HERSCHEL. *Simple Sermons for Funeral Services.* Grand Rapids, Zondervan, 1962. 54p. $1.50.
A collection of sermons designed to aid the pastor in planning simple, dignified, and sincere sermons for funeral services. The author, a native of Monroe, Georgia, is pastor of First Baptist Church in El Paso, Texas.

FORD, WILLIAM HERSCHEL. *Simple Sermons on the Christian Life.* Grand Rapids, Zondervan, 1962. 116p. $1.95.
A collection of sermons that are "pep talks" for the Christian—aimed at often overlooked areas in the Christian experience.

FORD, WILLIAM HERSCHEL. *Simple Talks for Christian Workers.* Grand Rapids, Zondervan, 1961. 120p. $1.95.
A collection of anecdotes, illustrations, poems, outlines, and devotional talks for public speakers.

GADDIS, PEGGY. *Clinic Nurse.* New York, Arcadia, 1963. 221p. $2.95.
When her doctor father suffered a heart attack and had to retire, Carol Haralson went to work in the local clinic with young Dr. Drake who had interned under her father.

GADDIS, PEGGY (pseud. GEORGIA CRAIG). *Emergency Nurse.* New York, Arcadia, 1963. 224p. $2.95.
Nurse Elaine Preston had many kinds of cases to deal with in the emergency ward of a big charity hospital.

GADDIS, PEGGY (pseud. PEGGY DERN). *Holiday Nurse.* New York, Arcadia, 1963. 224p. $2.95.
A young woman whom an automobile accident has left in a coma for several years is the only patient of a pretty young nurse named Hope.

GADDIS, PEGGY. *The Nurse and the Pirate.* London, Foulsham, 1962. 184p. 11s 6d.
A dull cruise explodes with danger and romance when Kathy's ship is hijacked by a dashing revolutionary, and she is plunged into front-page adventure.

GADDIS, PEGGY. *The Nurse and the Star.* New York, Arcadia, 1963. 222p. $2.95.
Pretty nurse Kay Herrell rejects a film career for work in an island hospital where patients still believe in vodoo witchcraft.

GADDIS, PEGGY. *Nurse Ann's Dream Doctor*. London, Foulsham, 1963. 188p. 11s 6d.

A shy young nurse must either romance her love for the handsome intern or fight for it and risk heartbreak.

GADDIS, PEGGY. *Nurse at the Cedars*. New York, Arcadia, 1963. 223p. $2.95.

Although nurse Susan Merrill knew that her patient was doomed to die of an incurable heart ailment, she refused to accept the inevitable and held out hope for his recovery.

GADDIS, PEGGY. *Nurse Christine*. New York, Arcadia, 1962. 224p. $2.95.

Christine is recovering from pneumonia in Florida—but a handsome beachcomber brings complications that do not show on her chart.

GADDIS, PEGGY. (pseud. GEORGIA CRAIG). *A Nurse Comes Home*. New York. Arcadia, 1963. 219p. $2.95.

A wealthy patient of nurse Holly Lowman gives her the opportunity to return to Gate City and a responsible position at Mission Hospital helping those who cannot help themselves.

GADDIS, PEGGY (pseud. PEGGY DERN). *Orchids for a Nurse*. New York, Arcadia, 1962. 224p. $2.95.

Although nurse Gayle has an understanding with a hard-working intern, she finds the love of a wealthy patient hard to laugh off.

GADDIS, PEGGY (pseud. GEORGIA CRAIG). *Rehearsal for a Wedding*. New York, Arcadia, 1962. 222p. $2.95.

Linsay brings her Manhattan roommate along on a home-town visit. The roommate promptly sets her sights on Linsay's home-town sweetheart.

GARRISON, KARL C. *Before You Teach Teen-agers*. Philadelphia, Fortress Press, 1962. 174p. $1.50. Teachers Guide. 64p. $0.60.

A study that presents the psychological problems that must be faced by teachers of young people. Dr. Garrison is Professor of Educational Psychology at the University of Georgia.

GINN, D. PERRY and CHAMBERLAIN, EUGENE. *A Study of the Old Testament*. Nashville, Broadman, 1963. 192p. $2.75. Paper $1.00.

A text book designed to aid young people in their program of Christian education in Southern Baptist Churches. The author is a native of Atlanta, Georgia.

GRANTHAM, DEWEY W. *The Democratic South*. Athens, University of Georgia Press, 1963. 110p. $2.50.

An interpretation of the politics of the Solid South in general and the development of the Democratic party in that region in particular. The author is a native of Manassas, Georgia.

GRAVES, HENRY LEA. *A Confederate Marine.* Tuscaloosa, Ala., Confederate Publishing Co., 1963. 140p. $4.00.
This sketch of Henry Lea Graves with excerpts from the Graves family correspondence, 1861-1865, is edited by Richard Harwell. Graves was a native of Newton County, Georgia.

GREENE, REYNOLDS W., JR. *Between an Atom and a Star.* Grand Rapids, Eerdmans, 1963. 89p. $2.50.
Personal reflections on the relevancy of the Christian message today. The author is pastor of the North Decatur Methodist Church in Decatur, Georgia.

HARRIS, KATHLEEN. See: HUMPHRIES, ADELAIDE.

HARWELL, RICHARD B., ed. *Colorado Volunteers in New Mexico, 1862.* Chicago, Lakeside Press, 1962. 309p. Apply.
In the account of his military experience the author, Ovando J. Hollister, speaks as a private soldier, although he was promoted to a sergeancy before his retirement in 1863 because of injuries received in service. He died in Salt Lake City early in 1892. The editor is a native Georgian and is Librarian at Bowdoin College, Brunswick, Maine.

HIGHFILL, ROBERT DAVID. *The Magic Robe and other Poems.* New York, Exposition Press, 1962. 79p. $2.50.
A collection of poems that have as a central theme the scorn for the shortsightedness of man in facing, alone, international issues that lead to war. The author is Pollock Professor of English at Mercer University, Macon, Georgia.

HUMPHRIES, ADELAIDE. *Doctor of the Keys.* New York, Avalon Books, 1963. 224p. $2.95.
When Dr. Eric Blaine returns to the Florida Keys, Julie is dismayed to find that he still regards her as a sister and not a sweetheart.

HUMPHRIES, ADELAIDE (pseud. KATHLEEN HARRIS). *Jane Arden's Homecoming.* New York, Avalon Books, 1963. 224p. $2.95.
Jane Arden's automobile accident caused a loss of memory and no recollection of the man she was engaged to marry.

HUMPHRIES, ADELAIDE. *Lady Doctor.* New York, Avalon Books, 1963. 224p. $2.95.
Beautiful Dr. Billie Whitcomb was attracted to her mysterious next door neighbor and his lonely boy.

HURST, JOHN WILLIS, ed. *Electrocardiographic Interpretation.* New York, McGraw-Hill, 1963. 320p. $12.95.
This study brings together the interpretation of eighty cases by five

outstanding cardiologists prior to the clinical history of the patient being known. Dr. Hurst is Chairman of the Department of Internal Medicine at Emory University, Atlanta, Georgia.

JONES, GEORGE FENWICK. *The Ethos of the Song of Roland*. Baltimore, Johns Hopkins Press, 1963. 216p. $5.00.

A study that attempts to correct misinterpretations of the first great monument of French literature and one of the great epics of all times. The author, a native of Savannah, Georgia, is Professor of Foreign Languages at the University of Maryland.

JORDAN, GERALD RAY. *Christ, Communism, and the Clock*. Anderson, Ind., Warner, 1963. 128p. $1.50.

The alarming growth of Communism is discussed at great length in this study. Dr. Jordan is Professor of Homiletics and Chapel Preacher of the Candler School of Theology at Emory University, Atlanta, Georgia.

KEATS, JOHN CRESSWELL. *They Fought Alone*. Philadelphia, Lippincott, 1963. 425p. $6.95.

Recreates what took place on the island of Mindanao in the Philippines during World War II when a group of Americans and Filipinos refused to surrender to the Japanese. The author is a native of Moultrie, Georgia.

KING, GEORGE HARRIS. *Pastures for the South*. Danville, Ill., Interstate, 1963. Fourth edition. 310p. $4.25.

A high school text designed to give vocational agriculture students the "know-how" of establishing a sound grazing program. Dr. King is Director of the University of Georgia Agricultural Experiment Stations.

KING, MARTIN LUTHER. *Strength to Love*. New York, Harper, 1963. 146p. $3.50.

A collection of Baptist sermons prepared by the author for his parishioners in Montgomery and Atlanta. Dr. King is a native of Atlanta, Georgia.

KING, SPENCER BIDWELL, JR. *Georgia Voices*. Macon, Ga., Department of History, Mercer University, 1962. 187p. $3.25.

This is a history of Georgia told by Georgians and by visitors who recorded their impressions of the state and the people. Dr. King is Professor of History at Mercer University, Macon, Georgia.

LAWTON, EDWARD P. *The South and the Nation*. Fort Myers, Fla., Island Press, 1963. 215p. Cloth $4.95. Paper $2.50.

Extended from material used for an article in THE GEORGIA REVIEW entitled "Northern Liberals and Southern Bourbons," indicting the North for moral and legal injustice against the South. The author is a native of Savannah, Georgia.

LAWRENCE, ALEXANDER A. *Johnny Leber and the Confederate Major.* Darien, Ga., Ashantilly Press, 1962. 63p. $3.00.

A long short-story of a Confederate youth, whose faith ran deep, set against a background of Sherman's march past a Screven County farm and the boy's subsequent service in Wheeler's Cavalry. The author is a prominent Savannah, Georgia, lawyer.

LEWIS, JOHN RANSOM. *To Dock at Stars.* Washington, University Press of Washington, 1962. 74p. $3.50.

A collection of lyric poems in which the powerful forces of sun, sea, and storm clash—inspired by the years the author spent as a Naval officer in World War II. Dr. Lewis is a plastic surgeon in Atlanta, Georgia.

LOMAX, LOUIS E. *When the World Is Given.* Cleveland, World Publishing Co., 1963. 223p. $3.95.

This study describes what goes on at Black Muslim meetings, what is preached, the rationale of the separate Negro state they want, Malcolm X's preaching that white men are devils, and the allegations that the Muslims teach anti-Semitism. The author is a native of Valdosta, Georgia.

LOVE, ALBERT and CHILDERS, JAMES SAXON, ed. *Listen to Leaders in Business.* Atlanta, Tupper and Love, 1963. 267p. $4.75.

Top leaders in business give the reader the benefit of their valuable experience in these first-hand accounts designed to show every American how to achieve his goals. The editors are residents of Atlanta, Georgia.

LOVE, ALBERT and CHILDERS, JAMES SAXON, ed. *Listen to Leaders in Law.* Tupper and Love, 1963. 332p. $4.75.

Essays by sixteen distinguished lawyers on all aspects of the legal profession offer guidance to people entering the profession and to those already in practice.

LOVE, ALBERT and CHILDERS, JAMES SAXON, ed. *Listen to Leaders in Medicine.* Atlanta, Tupper and Love, 1963. 340p. $4.75.

Top leaders in the field of medicine tell of their own experiences and offer valuable advice to those seeking a medical career.

LOVEGREN, ALTA LEE. *The Big Difference.* Nashville, Convention Press, 1963. 82p. $0.50. Teachers Guide $0.25.

The customs and activities of boys and girls in Jordan are treated in this study for young people. The author is a native of Cedartown, Georgia.

LOTT, ROBERT E. *The Structure and Style of Azorin's El Caballero Inactual.* Athens, University of Georgia Press, 1963. 115p. $2.75.

A critical study of the significance and aesthetic structure of a key work of the noted twentieth century Spanish novelist. Dr. Lott is a member of the Modern Foreign Languages Department at the University of Georgia.

LYLE, GUY REDVERS. *The President, the Professor and the College Library.* New York, H. W. Wilson Co., 1963. 88p. $2.50.

Three talks on the college library with emphasis on the role of the president and the faculty in its development, followed by a concluding chapter containing the author's recommendations, and an appendix on college library standards. The author is Director of Libraries at Emory University, Atlanta, Georgia.

MCGILL, RALPH EMERSON. *The South and the Southerner.* Boston, Atlantic, Little, Brown, 1963. 307p. $5.00.

A look at the moral dilemma the South has lived with for 150 years— an intensely dramatic blend of history and autobiography. The author is publisher of the *Atlanta Constitution.*

MARSHALL, EDISON. *Cortez and Marina.* Garden City, N. Y., Doubleday, 1963, 461p. $5.95.

This biographical novel of Cortez begins with his boyhood in Spain and ends with his romance with the Indian princess, Marina, without whose aid he never could have conquered Mexico.

MASSEE, J. C. *Louie D. Newton—The Witness.* Decatur, Ga., Bowen Press, 1963. 40p. $1.50.

A spiritual biography of the pastor of Druid Hills Baptist Church in Atlanta, Georgia.

MEBANE, JOHN. *Books Relating to the Civil War.* New York, Yoseloff, 1963. 144p. $10.00.

A priced check list, including regimental histories, Lincolniana, and Confederate imprints, for some 4,600 items. The compiler is a former editorial writer for *The Atlanta Journal.*

MOORE, ARTHUR JAMES. *Fight On! Fear Not!* Nashville, Abingdon, 1962. 144p. $2.50.

A collection of ten forceful sermons by a retired bishop of the Methodist Church. Bishop Moore is a resident of Atlanta and St. Simons, Georgia.

MOORE, RAYBURN S. *Constance Fenimore Woolson.* New York, Twayne, 1963. 173p. $3.50.

This new volume in Twayne's United States Authors series deals with the life and times of Constance F. Woolson, in relation to her work. She is viewed not only as a local colorist but also as a contributor to the international theme and to the novel of analysis. Dr. Moore is Associate Professor of English at the University of Georgia.

MORRIS, SCOTT, JR. *Confederate Poets—Physician and Priest.* Macon, Southern Press, 1963. 51p. $1.25.

Two short essays about the life and works of Francis Orray Ticknor and Father Abram Joseph Ryan with a selection of their poems are included in this volume for high school students. The author is a resident of Moultrie, Georgia.

MYERS, T. CECIL. *Faith for a Time of Storm.* Nashville, Abingdon, 1963. 160p. $3.00.

The basic doctrines of the Christian faith are plainly set forth in twelve sermons for every man who would strengthen his faith. Dr. Myers is pastor of Grace Methodist Church, Atlanta, Georgia.

NELSON, JACK and ROBERTS, GENE. *The Censors and the Schools.* Boston, Atlantic-Little-Brown, 1963. 208p. $4.50.

A documented discussion of textbook censorship in the United States. Mr. Nelson is a staff writer for the *Atlanta Constitution*, Atlanta, Georgia.

NISBET, JAMES COOPER. *Four Years on the Firing Line.* Jackson, Tenn., McCowart-Mercer Press, 1963. 267p. $5.00.

This personal narrative by a Confederate officer from a small North Georgia community gives an honest report of his four years on the firing line. The author died in Chattanooga, May 20, 1917. This edition is edited by Dr. Bell I. Wiley of the History Department at Emory University, Atlanta, Georgia.

OGBURN, CHARLES, JR. and OGBURN, DOROTHY. *Shake-speare: The Man Behind the Name.* New York, Apollo, 1963. 282p. $1.95.

A discussion of the theory that Edward DeVere, Earl of Oxford, is the real author of the works of William Shakespeare. Mr. Ogburn is a native of Atlanta, Georgia.

OZMENT, ROBERT V. *Happy Is the Man.* Westwood, N. J., Revell, 1963. 128p. $2.50.

An inspirational book that combines psychological and spiritual insights to illuminate simple steps by which any one can attain genuine, enduring happiness. Dr. Ozment is pastor of St. James Methodist Church, Atlanta, Georgia.

PARKS, AILEEN WELLS. *Bedford Forrest, Boy on Horseback.* Indianapolis, Bobbs-Merrill, 1963. 200p. $1.69.

A new edition of the boyhood life of General Bedford Forrest, which first appeared in 1952. It is in the Childhood of Famous Americans Series and is illustrated by Gray Morrow. The author is a resident of Athens, Georgia.

PARKS, EDD WINFIELD. *Nashoba.* New York, Twayne, 1963. 326p. $3.95.
   The story of one of the most gallant and most hopeless of the Utopian communities of the early nineteenth century. In particular it is the story of Frances Wright, who attempted to institute a system by which Negro slaves could earn their freedom.

PHOENIX, OPAL CARMICHAEL. *The Carmichael Clan, Westbrook and Allied Families.* Decatur, Ga., Privately Printed, 1963. 455p. Apply.
   A genealogical record of some of the outstanding families in Georgia and South Carolina. The compiler is a resident of Decatur, Georgia.

PIDCOCK, JANE RAINAUD. *Wings, Water and Dogs.* Savannah, Pigeonhole Press, 1962. 64p. $3.50.
   A tale of hunting, dogs, and ducks on the rice plantations on the Combahee River in South Carolina's low country.

RADFORD, RUBY LORRAINE. *The Secret of Peach Orchard Plantation.* New York, Abelard-Schuman, 1963. 160p. $3.00.
   When July Baily learns of the missing heirloom necklace, she starts a summer of detective work on the old family plantation in Georgia. The author is a resident of Augusta, Georgia.

RADFORD, RUBY LORRAINE. *Secret of Ocean House.* London, Abelard-Schuman, 1963. 157p. 13s 6d.
   Three children's search for missing land grants involves them with pirate treasure and code messages.

REEVE, JEWELL B. *Climb the Hills of Gordon.* Calhoun, Ga., Privately Printed, 1962. 304p. Apply.
   A collection of stories, reminiscences, and newspaper accounts telling of life in Gordon County, Georgia. Mrs. Reeves lives in Calhoun, Georgia.

ROWDEN, MARJORIE. *Three Davids.* Nashville, Convention Press, 1963. 32p. $0.50. Teachers Guide $0.25.
   Brief text and twenty-three photographs tell this story of three boys—an American, a Jew, and an Arab in Nazareth. The author is a native of Atlanta, Georgia.

ROWLAND, ARTHUR RAY. *Reference Services.* Hamden, Conn., Shoe String Press, 1963. 295p. $7.50.
   A collection of sixty-two articles and essays on reference service, its past, present, and future, the organization and administration of this service, and the reference librarian and his work. The compiler is Librarian of Augusta College, Augusta, Georgia.

RUSK, DEAN. *The Winds of Freedom.* Boston, Beacon Press, 1963. 363p. Cloth $4.95. Paper $2.45.

Selections from speeches and statements of Secretary of State Dean Rusk for the period January 1961-August 1962. Mr. Rusk is a native of Cherokee County, Georgia.

RUBIN, LARRY. *The World's Old Way*. Lincoln, The University of Nebraska Press, 1962. 67p. $3.00.

A collection of fifty short lyrical poems about love, death, beauty, nature, and maturation. The author is a member of the English Department at Georgia Tech, Atlanta, Georgia.

SAYE, ALBERT BERRY. *Election Laws of Georgia*. Athens, University of Georgia, Institute of Law and Government, 1963. Second edition. 197p. Cloth $6.00. Paper $5.00.

In two sections, (A) the Statutes and (B) an analysis of these statutes, this study includes all general election laws in force up to January 1, 1963. The author is Professor of Political Science at the University of Georgia.

SIBLEY, CELESTINE. *Peachtree Street, U. S. A.* Garden City, N. Y., Doubleday, 1963. 239p. $4.50.

An Atlanta newspaper columnist writes about the city that rose from the ashes to become the boom town metropolis of the South. Miss Sibley uncovers many aspects of Atlanta's history, culture, and present-day city life.

SLATE, SAM J. and COOK, JOE. *It Sounds Impossible*. New York, Macmillan, 1963. 415p. $6.95.

A general history of broadcasting by two C.B.S. executives who have been in radio as writers, promoters, directors, and producers since its beginnings.

SLAYDEN, THELMA THOMPSON. *Miracle in Alaska*. New York, Fell, 1963. 260p. $3.95.

A young Protestant medical missionary is chagrined to find that in the eyes of a dying Catholic priest he is far from perfect.

STAAR, RICHARD F. *Poland, 1942-1962. The Sovietization of a Captive People*. Baton Rouge, Louisiana State University Press, 1963. 300p. $7.50.

This profile of contemporary Poland presents a grim contrast to the image of a rebellious, pro-Western nation which generally prevails in the United States. The author is Professor of Political Science at Emory University, Atlanta, Georgia.

STANLEY, BESS DORSEY, comp. *Index to United States Census of Georgia for 1820*. Savannah, Printed by Chatham Printing Company, 1963. 167p. $8.50.

An index to the earliest extant census of Georgia giving names of heads of families, followed by county of residence. Includes a brief outline of formation of counties of 1820 and a map. Except for some incomplete tax records, this is the earliest list of Georgia citizens. Mr. Stanley is a resident of Savannah, Georgia.

STIRLING, NORA B. *Up from the Sea: The Story of Salvage Operations.* Garden City, N. Y., Doubleday, 1963. 128p. $2.50.

This account of salvaging sunken ships covers the progress made in this operation during the last 400 years. The author is a native of Atlanta, Georgia.

TODD, ELIZABETH and ROBERTS, FRANCES. *Clothes for Teens.* Boston, D. C. Heath, 1963. 494p. $5.36.

A home economics text that considers problems of both boys and girls. Miss Todd resides in Athens, Georgia.

TROUP, CORNELIUS V. *Distinguished Negro Georgians.* Dallas, Royal Publishing Co., 1962. 203p. $3.95.

This book represents the first effort to compile a record of outstanding Negro citizens of any single state in the union. The author is a native of Brunswick, Georgia.

TUCKER, GLENN. *Dawn Like Thunder.* Indianapolis, Bobbs-Merrill, 1963. 487p. $6.95.

This history of the Barbary Wars covers the formative years when the United States set out to prove it had become an international power. The author is a part-time resident of Georgia whose North Georgia farm is named "Filibuster Hill."

WATKINS, FLOYD C. and WATKINS, CHARLES HUBERT. *Yesterday in the Hills.* Chicago, Quadrangle, 1963. 192p. $4.50.

The re-creation of life at the turn of the century in the settlement of Ball Ground in the Georgia hills. Its inhabitants, who seem peculiar to outsiders, emerge here with humor as seen through eyes that know them. Dr. Floyd Watkins is Professor of English at Emory University, Atlanta, Georgia.

WESBERRY, JAMES P. *Rainbow Over Russia.* Columbia, S. C., R. L. Bryan, 1963. 34p. $1.00.

A compilation of the author's newspaper column, "The People's Pulpit," which appears in forty-five county weeklies in Georgia and South Carolina. The author records his impressions of all facets of life in Soviet Russia. Dr. Wesberry is pastor of the Morningside Baptist Church, Atlanta, Georgia.

WILEY, BELL IRWIN. *The Plain People of the Confederacy*. Chicago, Quadrangle, 1963. 104p. $1.45.

A portrait of the common soldiers of the Confederacy, the folk at home, and the colored folk—all of whom constituted the backbone of the Southern Confederacy. Dr. Wiley is a member of the History Department at Emory University, Atlanta, Georgia.

WILLINGHAM, CALDER, JR. *Eternal Fire*. New York, Vanguard, 1963. 630p. $6.95.

A novel which touches upon the conflict of good and evil, love and lust in the human heart. The locale is a town in North Georgia. The author was born in Atlanta and spent his childhood in Rome, Georgia.

YOUSE, BEVAN K. *Arithmetic: A Modern Approach*. Englewood Cliffs, N. J., Prentice-Hall, 1963. 160p. $6.60.

A textbook for elementary teachers that examines and clarifies basic concepts and techniques in the teaching of mathematics. The author is Professor of Mathematics at Emory University, Atlanta, Georgia.

Bibliography of Georgia Authors

1963-1964

THE fifteenth in the REVIEW's series of annual "Bibliographies of Georgia Authors," this annotated Bibliography is, as nearly as the compiler could make it, a complete and accurate record of books published by Georgia authors from November 1, 1963, to November 1, 1964. The annotations are descriptive, not critical; intended to place, not to judge the book. U. S., State, County, and City Documents, parts of books, brief analytics, and pamphlets of less than 25 pages have been omitted. Prices are given except when not supplied by publisher or when the book is obtainable only on specific request, in which case the word "Apply" is used.

In determining whom to designate as Georgia authors, the compiler has included authors born in Georgia and claiming Georgia as their native state and those who have lived in Georgia for a period of five years and who did their writing here.

The compiler will welcome and appreciate readers' sending to him any additions or corrections. They may be sent to him at any time in care of the GEORGIA REVIEW. Several books inadvertently omitted from previous Bibliographies are listed here. Any books omitted from the present Bibliography will be included in the list of 1964-1965.

Acknowledgment is made to members of the staff of the Special Collections Division of the University of Georgia Library for their assistance in the preparation of this Bibliography.

ADAMS, J. C. *I Have Only One Life to Live*. Nashville, Methodist Publishing House. 1964. 143p. $2.50.
    A collection of inspirational sermons by a retired Methodist minister. The author, who is eighty-three, is known affectionately throughout North Georgia as "Bishop" Adams.

AIKEN, CONRAD POTTER. *The Collected Novels of Conrad Aiken*. New York, Holt, Rinehart and Winston, 1964. 575p. $7.95.
    These five novels, *Blue Voyage, Great Circle, King Coffin, A Heart for the Gods of Mexico*, and *Conversation* comprise the corpus of the author's fiction and are masterpieces of psychological novels.

AIKEN, CONRAD POTTER. *Selected Poems.* New York, World, 1964. 274p. Paper, $1.95.
A representative selection, considered by Pulitzer Prize winner, Conrad Aiken, as his most important poetic works snice 1917.

AIKEN, CONRAD POTTER. *A Seizure of Limericks.* New York, Holt, Rinehart and Winston, 1964. 50p. $2.50.
A collection of limericks, both moral and immoral, by one of America's most distinguished poets. Mr. Aiken is a native of Savannah, Georgia.

ALLEN, CHARLES L. *Prayer Changes Things.* Westwood, N. J., Revell, 1964. 128p. $2.50.
A practical spiritual counsel into man's relationship with God in many areas—faith, anxiety, freedom, and true greatness. Dr. Allen, a native of Georgia, is Pastor of the First Methodist Church of Houston, Texas.

ALTIZER, THOMAS J. J. *Mircea Eliade and the Dialectic of the Sacred.* Philadelphia, Westminster Press, 1963. 219p. $6.00.
Descriptive analysis of the work of a contemporary mystic and scholar, who believes that the era of Christian civilization has come to an end. The author is Associate Professor of Bible and Religion, Emory University, Atlanta, Georgia.

ANDERSON, VERNA HARRISON. *Petals from Life.* New York, Carlton Press, 1963. 88p. $2.00.
In this collection of inspirational poems the author gives voice to those significant experiences that have meant the most to her. The author, a native of Whigham, Georgia, is a resident of Summitville, Tennessee.

AUSTIN, AURELIA, ed. *Leaves of Life.* Atlanta, Atlanta Writers Club, 1964. 134p. $3.95.
An anthology of poetry compiled to help celebrate the fiftieth anniversary year of the Atlanta Writers Club. The editor is a resident of Atlanta, Georgia.

BLACKSTONE, WILLIAM T. *The Problem of Religious Knowledge.* Englewood Cliffs, N. J., Prentice-Hall, 1963. 175p. $3.95.
This study is concerned with twentieth-century philosophical answers to the age-old question of whether there can be true religious knowledge. The author is Associate Professor of Philosophy at the University of Georgia.

BLAIR, EMIL. *Clinical Hypothermia.* New York, McGraw-Hill, 1964. 272p. $12.50.
A textbook for students, surgeons, residents, and general practitioners, on the subnormal temperature of the body. The author, a native of Savannah, Georgia, is Assistant Professor of Surgery at the University of Maryland School of Medicine.

BONNER, JAMES CALVIN. *A History of Georgia Agriculture, 1732-1860.* Athens, University of Georgia Press, 1964. 252p. $6.00.

This book describes in detail the early land and labor systems of Georgia, the shortage of horsepower and plows, and the general lack of skill in tool mechanics and the problems they fostered, namely cotton—slaves—mules.

BONNER, JAMES CALVIN, ed. *The Journal of a Milledgeville Girl, 1861-1867.* Athens, University of Georgia Press, 1964. 140p. Paper, $3.00.

In her journal Anna Maria Green gives an intimate record of her observations and feeling in regard to people and events during the Cvil War period in Milledgeville, capital of Georgia at the time and in the path of Sherman's armies. Dr. Bonner is head of the History Department at the Woman's College of Georgia, Milledgeville, Georgia.

BUMGARTNER, LOUIS E. *José del Valle of Central America.* Durham, N. C., Duke University Press, 1963. 302p. $8.75.

This is the biography of a little-known figure, José del Valle—rancher, lawyer, statesman, author, scholar, gentleman of culture, and reluctant revolutionary. The author is Associate Professor of History at the University of Georgia.

BURCH, ROBERT. *Skinny.* New York, Viking, 1964. 126p. $3.00.

A sociable twelve-year-old boy is taken into the care of Miss Bessie, who owns the only hotel in a small Georgia town. Skinny manages to win the affection of everyone he encounters through his sincerity and innocently humorous outlook on life. The author is a native of Fayette County, Georgia.

CALDWELL, ERSKINE. *Around About America.* New York, Farrar, Straus & Cudahy, 1964. 224p. $4.50.

Extremely simple line drawings by Mrs. Caldwell are used to introduce each of the stops on this jaunt back and forth across the United States.

CARR, JULIAN SHAKESPEARE. *From the Cripple to Khrushchev.* New York, Vantage, 1963. 139p. $3.00.

A discussion of Russian politics and the personalities involved from the reign of the Czars to the present. The author is a resident of Atlanta, Georgia.

CHILDERS, JAMES SAXON and LOVE, ALBERT, ed. *Listen to Leaders in Engineering.* Atlanta, Tupper and Love, 1964. 267p. $5.95.

Top leaders in the field of engineering tell of their own experiences and offer valuable advice to those seeking an engineering career.

CHILDERS, JAMES SAXON and LOVE, ALBERT, ed. *Listen to Leaders in Science.* Atlanta, Tupper and Love, 1964. 332p. $5.95.

A group of America's most distinguished scientists discuss the achievements of science today. They deal with such subjects as microbiology, chemistry, genetics, geophysics, geology, anthropology, oceanography, and careers in science.

CHILDERS, JAMES SAXON. *A Way Home*. Atlanta, Tupper and Love, 1964. 235p. $3.95.
  The author traces the history of the Baptist movement from difficult days in Holland and England to its present form of worship. The author is a resident of Atlanta, Georgia.

CHURCH, LILLIAN. *Two Lovely Hands*. Atlanta, Privately Printed, 1964. 46p. $2.00.
  A collection of poems on a variety of subjects in a variety of forms. Mrs. Robert B. Church, Jr. is a resident of Atlanta, Georgia.

CRAIG, GEORGIA. See: GADDIS, PEGGY.

COULTER, ELLIS MERTON. *Joseph Vallence Bevan: Georgia's First Official Historian*. Athens, University of Georgia Press, 1964. 176p. $5.00.
  A young Irishman who was educated in Georgia, South Carolina, and England was appointed historian of Georgia and among other things to arrange the state archives and to write a history of Georgia. He died at the age of thirty-two. Dr. Coulter is Regents' Professor of History at the University of Georgia.

DERN, PEGGY. See: GADDIS, PEGGY.

DERN, MRS. JOHN SHERMAN. See: GADDIS, PEGGY.

DICKEY, JAMES. *Helmets*. Middletown, Conn., Wesleyan University Press, 1964. 93p. Cloth, $4.00. Paper, $1.85.
  A collection of poems that have appeared in various periodicals. The author is a native of Atlanta, Georgia.

DICKEY, JAMES. *The Suspect in Poetry*. Madison, Minn., Sixties Press, 1964. 120p. $2.00.
  General critique of contemporary American poets.

DREWRY, JOHN E., ed. *Communications Cartography: Press, Radio, Television, Periodicals, Public Relations, and Advertising as Seen Through Institutes and Special Occasions of the Henry W. Grady School of Journalism, 1963-1964*. Vol. LXV, No. 2, Athens, University of Georgia Bulletin, 1964. 237p. Paper, $2.00.
  The 1963-1964 compilation of addresses and papers delivered at the various institutes and other special occasions sponsored by the University of Georgia's School of Journalism.

EDWARDS, HARRY STILLWELL. *Eneas Africanus*. Macon, Georgia, Eneas Africanus Press, 1964. 48p. $1.00.

A new edition of the story of the travels, over eight Southern states, of an old family Negro who had been entrusted with the silver of the family and a fine racehorse, as he tried to find, again, his original home and master.

ETHRIDGE, WILLIE SNOW. *I Just Happen to Have Some Pictures.* New York, Vanguard, 1964. 191p. $4.50.
A grandmother's fond recollections of her sometimes trying adventures with her twelve irrepressible grandchildren. The author is a native of Macon, Georgia.

EVANS, EETHER. *My Country.* Nashville, Convention Press, 1964. 83p. $0.35.
A children's study book designed to be used in Southern Baptist Churches. The author lives in Decatur, Georgia.

EVERETT, EDWIN MALLARD, DUMAS, MARIE F. and WALL, CHARLES, A., JR. *An Auto-Instructional Text in Correct Writing.* New York, Heath, 1964. 402p. Paper, $4.00. Answer Booklet for the Tests. $0.80.
The revised edition of a textbook in Freshman English with auto-instructional techniques applied to the material taught in earlier editions. The authors are members of the English Department at the University of Georgia.

FISH, TALLU BRINSON JONES. *Sidney Lanier: America's Sweet Singer of Songs.* Darien, Ga., Privately Printed, 1963. 25p. Cloth, $2.50. Paper, $1.25.
A miscellaneous collection of data, tributes and poems of one of Georgia's outstanding poets. The book was designed by William G. Haynes, Jr., of the Ashantilly Press. The author is Curator of the Jekyll Island Museum, Jekyll Island, Georgia.

FORD, MARCIA. See: RADFORD, RUBY LORRAINE.

FORD, WILLIAM HERSCHEL. *Simple Sermons for Time and Eternity.* Grand Rapids, Zondervan, 1964. 120p. $1.95.
The author attempts to show in a series of sermons that the genius of the Gospel lies in its applicability to both time and eternity. The author is a native of Monroe, Georgia.

FORD, WILLIAM HERSCHEL. *Simple Sermons from the Gospel of Matthew.* Grand Rapids, Zondervan, 1963. 242p. $3.95.
A collection of thirty-one messages covering chapter-by-chapter the first book of the New Testament, which Dr. Ford calls "the Gospel of the King."

FRY, THOMAS A., JR. *Get Off the Fence!* Westwood, N. J., Revell, 1963. 127p. $2.50.
A discussion on how moral decisions, once made, form the basis for

a whole life. The author was a former pastor of the Druid Hills Presbyterian Church in Atlanta, Georgia.

GADDIS, PEGGY. (pseud. PEGGY DERN). *Betsy Moran, R.N.* New York, Arcadia, 1964. 191p. $2.95.
Nurse Betsy Moran had spent a year in the County General Hospital in Decatur, Georgia, where doctors and patients were impressed by her services.

GADDIS, PEGGY. *Everglades Nurse.* New York, Avalon Books, 1964. 192p. $2.95.
Nurse Jennie Cosgrove makes frequent trips from Pinehill Hospital into the the Everglades to visit her parents and her fiancé, school teacher John Ottwell, and finds that her beautiful step-sister has also been visiting the Glades, attracted by Jennie's handsome fiancé.

GADDIS, PEGGY. *A Nurse Called Happy.* New York, Arcadia, 1963. 223p. $2.95.
Nurse Hallie Gibson's happy disposition is taxed to the limit by the daughter of an elderly patient.

GADDIS, PEGGY. *A Nurse for Happy Valley.* New York, Arcadia, 1964. 222p. $2.95.
Luana fills in for Denise as nurse in a Georgia town and tries loyally to fight her love for Denise's sweetheart.

GADDIS, PEGGY. (pseud. GEORGIA CRAIG). *Nurse Lucie.* New York, Arcadia, 1964. 222p. $2.95.
Lucie Hatcher, recently graduated from nursing school, was delighted when she was offered a position at Guale, an agricultural empire on the Georgia Coast.

GADDIS, PEGGY. (pseud. PEGGY DERN). *Nurse with a Dream.* New York, Arcadia, 1963. 224p. $2.95.
Injured in a car accident, a spoiled, wealthy young woman creates a disturbing problem for Nurse Kyria Galanos.

GADDIS, PEGGY. *Palm Beach Girl.* London, Wright and Brown, 1964. 176p. 10s 6d.
A romantic client poses unexpected problems for Dinah, who handles vacation details for wealthy families.

GARRISON, KARL CLAUDIUS. *Educational Psychology.* New York, Appleton-Century-Crofts, 1964. Second Edition. 544p. $6.50.
A textbook for use in basic courses preparing students to become teachers. Dr. Garrison is Professor of Educational Psychology at the University of Georgia.

GODLEY, MARGARET and BRAGG, LILLIAN. *Savannah Anecdotes*. Savannah, Privately Printed, 1963. 38p. $1.25.
A collection of twelve historical tales about people and events in Savannah, Georgia. Illustrations are by Joan Rueter. The authors are residents of Savannah, Georgia.

GREEN, DONALD ROSS. *Educational Psychology*. Englewood Cliffs, N. J., Prentice-Hall, 1964. 120p. $3.95.
This study emphasizes the progressive cumulative nature of school training and the transfer of training. Dr. Green is a member of the Division of Teacher Education at Emory University, Atlanta, Georgia.

GREENBLATT, ROBERT B., ed. *The Hirsute Female*. Springfield, Ill., C. C. Thomas, 1963. 328p. $12.50.
The fifteen chapters of this book, written by thirteen contributors, encompass present day thinking in regard to genetic and physiopathologic aspects of the hirsute female. The editor is Professor and Chairman of Endocrinology at the Medical College of Georgia, Augusta, Georgia.

HARRIS, KATHLEEN. See: HUMPHRIES, ADELAIDE.

HARWELL, RICHARD BARKSDALE. *Confederate Hundred*. Urbana, Ill., Beta Phi Mu, 220a Library, University of Illinois, 1964. 58p. $5.00.
A bibliographic selection of one hundred outstanding Confederate books.

HARWELL, RICHARD BARKEDALE, ed. *Confederate Imprints in the University of Georgia Libraries*. Athens, University of Georgia Press, 1964. 68p. $2.00.
Of special interests to the bibliographer and research student, this volume lists the complete collection of Confederate imprints in the University of Georgia Libraries. Mr. Harwell, a native of Washington, Georgia, is librarian of Bowdoin College, Brunswick, Maine.

HAYNES, DRAUGHTON STITH. *The Field of a Confederate Soldier*. Darien, Ga., The Ashantilly Press, 1963. 44p. $4.00.
The fragmentary field diary of a soldier who served with the army of Northern Virginia which covers the writer's active service, March, 1862, until August, 1863.

HENDERSON, LEGRAND. (pseud. LEGRAND) *The Amazing Adventures of Archie and the First Hot Dog*. Nashville, Abingdon, 1964. 64p. $2.50.
A tall tale about a boy named Archie, who found the dollar George Washington threw across the Potomac. Caught in a flour mill fire Archie discovers the first hot dog.

HODGES, ELIZABETH JAMISON. *The Three Princes of Serendip*. New York, Atheneum, 1964. 158p. $3.95.

The travels and adventures of three brave princes, who were sent by their father to complete their education through world travel.

HODGSON, HUGH, trans. *And It Came to Pass.* Savannah, Pigeonhole Press. 1963. 27p. $2.50.

Intimate stories of the child of Bethlehem by the German author Karl Heinrich Waggerl. Illustrations by Allan Kuzmicki. Dr. Hodgson, the translator, is Regent's Professor Emeritus of Music at the University of Georgia.

HOLLAND, LYNWOOD H. *Pierce M. B Young: The Warwick of the South.* Athens, University of Georgia Press, 1964. 268p. $6.00.

A biography of the youngest Confederate general, who was also a congressman and political leader in Georgia after the Civil War. Dr. Holland is Chairman of the Department of Political Science at Emory University, Atlanta, Georgia.

HUMPHRIES, ADELAIDE. *A Feather in Her Cap.* New York, Avalon Books, 1964. 192p. $2.95.

Maggie Adams and her twin sister Rita have problems—they love the same men.

HUMPHRIES, ADELAIDE. (pseud. KATHLEEN HARRIS). *Nurse on Holiday.* New York, Avalon Books, 1964. 192p. $2.95.

The theft of a beautiful young nurse's passport in Buenos Aires leads to a visit to the dark and dashing Senor Ferrel's rancho—and a dangerous discovery for Cindy.

HUMPHRIES, ADELAIDE. *The Other Love.* New York, Avalon Books, 1964. 190p. $2.95.

A girl from Boston inherits a run-down mansion in Georgia and discovers a new way of life in the South, made more interesting by an attractive neighbor.

JESSUP, RICHARD. *The Cincinnati Kid.* Boston, Little, Brown, 1963. 154p. $3.95.

A young and able poker player is initiated into the bizarre and often brutal world of big-time gambling.

JOHNSON, HAROLD L. *The Christian as a Businessman.* New York, Association Press, 1964. 192p. $3.75.

This study of the Christian in his vocation is concerned with goals, ethics, and basic commitments. The author is Associate Professor of Economics at Emory University, Atlanta, Georgia.

JOHNSON, JAMES A., JR. *Group Therapy: A Practical Approach.* New York, McGraw-Hill, 1963. 467p. $10.95.

This volume for the layman, the student, and the therapist provides an effective, complete, and authoritative presentation of group therapy. The author is Assistant Professor of Psychiatry at Emory University, Atlanta, Georgia.

JONES, R. N. *Songs of the Family*. New York, Vantage, 1963. 214p. $3.95.
A collection of prose and poetry about the joys of a family life and the anxieties of rearing five children. The author is a resident of Decatur, Georgia.

JONES, WILBUR DEVEREUX. *The Confederate Rams at Birkenhead*. Tuscaloosa, Ala., Confederate Publishing Company, 1961. 124p. $4.00.
A little known chapter in Anglo-American relations. Dr. Jones is Professor of History at the University of Georgia.

JORDAN, GERALD RAY. *Life Giving Words*. Anderson, Ind., Warner, 1964. 112p. $1.50.
Twenty-six words from the prayer of Jesus are discussed in this study for people of all religious denominations. Dr. Jordan is Professor of Homilectics and Chapel Preacher of the Candler School of Theology at Emory University, Atlanta, Georgia.

JULIAN, ALLEN PHELPS. *McArthur: The Life of a General*. New York, Duell, Sloan and Pearce, 1964. 172p. $3.95.
This biography presents the life of General Douglas McArthur from battlefield leader to Army Chief of Staff. The author is Director of the Atlanta Historical Society.

KEITH, EDMUND D. and MCELRATH, HUGH. *Sing from Your Hearts*. Nashville, Convention Press, 1964. 102p. $1.00.
A church study-course book for teenage choir members of the great Christian hymns and gospel songs—their origin and meanings. Mr. Keith is Associate Director, Church Music Department, Southern Baptist Convention, Atlanta, Georgia.

KING, MARTIN LUTHER. *Why We Can't Wait*. New York, Harper & Row, 1964. 178p. $3.50.
This study presents the arguments for the nonviolent protest as a weapon in the civil rights struggle. The author is a native of Atlanta, Georgia.

KING, SPENCER BIDWELL, JR. *Georgia Voices: Society and Thought to 1860*. Macon, Ga., Department of History, Mercer University, 1964. Volume Two. 187p. $3.25.
This is second in a proposed three-volume history of Georgia told by Georgians and by visitors who recorded their impressions of the state and people. Copies may be obtained from the Mercer College Book Store. Dr. King is Professor of History at Mercer Univeristy, Macon, Georgia.

KIRBY, ULA. *"And Gladly Teache - - ."* New York, Carlton Press, 1961. 191p. $3.50.
   The story of the struggles of a widow to educate her four children and fulfill her promise to her deceased husband. The author, a native of Appling County, Georgia, lives in Douglas, Georgia.

KIRKPATRICK, DOW, ed. *The Doctrine of the Church.* Nashville, Abingdon, 1964. 224p. $3.00.
   Sponsored by the World Methodist Council to stimulate discussion among Methodists throughout the world, these eleven essays examine the Biblical and historical bases for a doctrine of the church.

KOBS, RUTH LOWRY. *A Guide to Making and Understanding Japanese Flower Arrangements.* Columbus, Ga., Imagin-Ad, 1964. 44p. $2.00.
   A guide to the form of Japanese flower arrangement popularly called Ikebana, photographs by Brady B. Bynum. The author is a native of Columbus, Georgia.

LANOUE, FRED. *Drownproofing.* Englewood Cliffs, N. J., Prentice-Hall, 1963. 112p. $3.95.
   Downproofing is a new technique that keeps swimmers afloat indefinitely. With this revolutionary concept of water safety anyone, young or old, even the non-swimmer, can be virtually insured against the tragedy of drowning. The author is Professor of Physical Education and Head Swimming Coach at the Georgia Institute of Technology, Atlanta, Georgia.

LATTIMORE, RALSTON B., ed. *The Story of Robert E. Lee.* Philadelphia, Eastern National Park & Monument Association, 1964. 96p. $3.00.
   A biography of Lee as told in his own words and those of his contemporaries. The author, a native of Savannah, Georgia, is Park Superintendent at Fort Pulaski National Monument, Cockspur Island, Georgia.

LEGRAND. See: HENDERSON, LEGRAND.

LEWIS, JOHN RANSOM. *The Surgery of Scars.* New York, McGraw-Hill, 1963. 201p. $16.00.
   This monograph deals with the mechanism of scar-tissue formation, the problems caused by the overgrowth of scar tissues, and the complications of the scars. The author is a physician in Atlanta, Georgia.

LUMPKIN, GRACE. *Full Circle.* Boston, Western Islands, 1962. 312p. $4.00.
   A novel about life in the Communist Party in America. The author is a native of Milledgeville, Georgia.

LUPER, HAROLD LEE and MULDER, ROBERT L. *Stuttering: Therapy for Children.* Englewood Cliffs, N. J., Prentice-Hall, 1964. 225p. $4.95.

A study on the cause of stammering and stuttering in children and suggested therapy to be used by the professional and layman.

McCULLERS, CARSON and ALBEE, EDWARD. *The Ballad of the Sad Cafe.* New York, Houghton Mifflin and Atheneum, 1963. 150p. Cloth, $4.50. Paper, $1.75.
This play is an adaptation of Carson McCuller's novella, which appeared first in 1951.

McCULLERS, CARSON SMITH. *Sweet as a Pickle and Clean as a Pig.* Boston, Houghton, 1964. 31p. $2.75.
A collection of poems which capture the moods and memories of childhood. Illustrations by Rolf Gerad. The author is a native of Columbus, Georgia.

McDANIEL, EARL WADSWORTH. *Collision Phenomena in Ionized Gases.* New York, Wiley, 1964. 775p. $17.50.
A textbook for first year graduate students that deals with the experimental and theoretical aspects of atomic collisions and atomic transport phenomena, and gaseous electronics. The author is Professor of Electrical Engineering at Georgia Institute of Technology, Atlanta, Georgia.

MARSHALL, EDISON. *Lost Colony.* Garden City, N. Y., Doubleday, 1964. 438p. $5.95.
A historical novel about Sir Walter Raleigh's colonists, who settled Roanoke Island, off North Carolina, in 1587, and then disappeared.

MARSHALL, GEORGE OCTAVIUS, JR. *A Tennyson Handbook.* New York, Twayne, 1964. 291p. $6.00.
This handbook presents the basic information about each of Tennyson's poems and plays published in a volume during the poet's lifetime. A chronological table is included for quick reference to significant dates in the poet's life and career. Dr. Marshall is Associate Professor of English at the University of Georgia.

MATHEWS, MARCIA M. *Richard Allen.* Baltimore, Helicon Press, 1963. 151p. $3.95.
A biography of the founder of the African Methodist Episcopal Church, who was also the first American Negro to seek recognition for his people as a minority group. The author is a resident of Atlanta, Georgia.

MAXWELL, GILBERT. *Tennessee Williams and Friends.* New York, World, 1964. 320p. $5.95.
An intimate, anecdotal biography of a successful playwright by a man who knew him from his earliest days as a struggling author in New York. The author is a native of Washington, Georgia.

MERUCCI, ANGELO. *Yesterday's Success—Tomorrow's Challenge*. New York, Pageant Press, 1962. 94p. $2.50.
This study presents in compact form a complete manual of the multifaceted business of selling. The author is a resident of Decatur, Georgia.

MONTGOMERY, HORACE. *Johnny Cobb: Confederate Aristocrat*. Athens, University of Georgia Press, 1964. 104p. $3.00.
A biographical sketch of the son of Howell Cobb during the Civil War years. Dr. Montgomery is Professor of History at the University of Georgia.

MONTGOMERY, MARION HOYT, JR. *Darrell*. Garden City, N. Y., Doubleday, 1964. 227p. $4.50.
A child, dying of leukemia, and a compassionate if somewhat eccentric young man, make a pledge to ride to Atlanta, Georgia, on a motorcycle. The author is Assistant Professor of English at the University of Georgia.

MOORE, EDWIN. *Communion*. New York, Pageant Press, 1962. 91p. $2.50.
A collection of lyrical verse that relates human feelings to the changing world of nature. The author is a native of Washington, Georgia.

MORRIS, SCOTT, JR. *John Thomas Pound: Confederate Soldier*. Macon, Ga., Southern Press, 1964. 45p. $2.00.
A biographical sketch of a Confederate soldier from Talbot County, Georgia. Included are four letters from the soldier to his family. The author is a resident of Moultrie, Georgia.

ODUM, HOWARD WASHINGTON, 1884-1954. *Folk, Region, and Society*. Chapel Hill, N.C., University of North Carolina Press, 1964. 480p. $8.00.
A collection of previously published essays in the field of sociology selected by the author's former students and colleagues. The essays were arranged and edited by Katharine Jocher. The late Dr. Odum was a native of Washington, Georgia.

OLIPHANT, JOYCE. *A Study Guide for Student X-Ray Technicians*. Springfield, Ill., C. C. Thomas, 1963. 168p. $5.50.
Based on many years of successful teaching this guide consists of self-testing questions on every phase of x-ray technology. The author is a member of the staff of the Macon Hospital, Macon, Georgia.

PARKS, EDD WINFIELD. *Edgar Allan Poe as Literary Critic*. Athens, University of Georgia Press, 1964. 128p. $3.00.
Edgar Allan Poe was one of the first major critics to develop and refine his critical theories through magazine articles and book reviews. Dr. Parks is Professor of English at the University of Georgia.

PARKS, EDD WINFIELD. *Henry Timrod.* New York, Twayne, 1964. 158p. $3.50.
A biography and critical evaluation of the neglected South Carolina poet, Henry Timrod. Dr. Parks is Professor of English at the University of Georgia.

PRESTON, JANEF NEWMAN. *Upon our Pulses.* Francestown, N. H., The Golden Quill Press, 1964. 95p. $3.00.
A collection of poems on a variety of subjects. The author is Assistant Professor of English at Agnes Scott College, Decatur, Georgia.

RADFORD, RUBY LORRAINE. (pseud. MARCIA FORD) *Love Finds the Way.* Avalon Books, 1964. 190p. $2.95.
As apprentice to a handsome young archaeologist, auburn-haired Carol Addison finds mystery as well as relics in an old Indian mound in Florida.

ROBERTS, GUY. *Mount Carmel.* New York, Pageant, 1964. 390p. $5.00.
A novel, set in ancient Israel, that centers about the eternal struggle to reconcile the ways of man to the way of God. The author is Professor of Psychology at Georgia Southwestern, Americus, Georgia.

RUSKIN, GERTRUDE MCDARIS. *John Ross, Chief of an Eagle Race.* Decatur, Ga., Privately Printed, 1963. 85p. $2.20.
A biography of John Ross, Cherokee chief from 1828 until his death in 1866. The author is a resident of Decatur, Georgia.

RUTLAND, EVA. *The Trouble with Being a Mama.* Nashville, Abingdon, 1964. 143p. $2.95.
A Negro mother tells of the frustrations, anxieties, and joys of bringing up four lovely, lovable, and trouble making youngsters. The author, a native of Atlanta, Georgia, lives in Sacramento, California.

SHOECK, HELMUT and WIGGINS, JAMES W., ed. *The New Argument in Economics: The Public Versus the Private Sector.* New York, Van Nostrand, 1963. 265p. $5.95.
Twelve distinguished scholars—each an expert in his field—subject to critical examination all the major arguments currently advanced in favor of a further enlargement of the public, governmentally controlled or directed sector of the economy, at the expense of private initiative. The editors are Professors of Sociology at Emory University, Atlanta, Georgia.

SEIGLER, O. M. *Heartfelt Religion.* New York, American Press, 1963. 99p. $2.75.
A selection of sermons by a retired Baptist minister. The introduction is by Dr. Louie D. Newton. The author lives in Atlanta, Georgia.

SHADGETT, OLIVE HALL. *The Republican Party in Georgia from Reconstruction through 1900.* Athens, University of Georgia Press, 1964. 210p. $6.00.

First published account of the Republican Party in Georgia. Four appendices include lists of Republican members of Congress from Georgia, presidential electors, delegates to Republican national conventions, and state central committee heads. Dr. Shadgett is a member of the Political Science Department at Georgia State College, Atlanta, Georgia.

SHAPIRO, DAVID and MAHOLICK, LEONARD T. *Opening Doors for Troubled People*. Springfield, Ill., C. C. Thomas, 1963. 136p. $4.75.

This monograph describes in detail a four year research project in which the community served as a laboratory. The authors are connected with the Bradley Center, Inc., Columbus, Georgia.

SHARKEY, ROBERT P. *Money, Class, and Party: An Economic Study of Civil War and Reconstruction*. Baltimore. Johns Hopkins University Press, 1959. 346p. Cloth, $5.50. Paper, $4.00.

This study examines the financial policies of the national government in the period 1862-1870, and disagrees with the Charles Beard interpretation of the "Second American Revolution." The author, a native of Atlanta, Georgia, is Administrative Assistant to the President of Johns Hopkins University.

SIBLEY, CELESTINE. *Christmas in Georgia*. Garden City, N. J., Doubleday, 1964. 95p. $2.50.

A collection of five short stories about Christmas, with a Georgia setting, for readers of all ages. The book is illustrated by Atlanta artist Scarlett Rickenbaker. The author is a resident of Atlanta, Georgia.

SKANDALAKIS, JOHN E. and GRAY, STEPHEN W. *Smooth Muscle Tumors of the Alimentary Tract: Leiomyomas and Leimyosarcomas*. Springfield, Ill., C. C. Thomas, 1962. 484p. $17.50.

This monograph provides surgeon, internist, general practitioner, and radiologist with an understanding of the natural history and behavior of these benign and malignant neoplastic diseases. The authors are Professors of Anatomy at Emory University, Atlanta, Georgia.

SMITH, LILLIAN EUGENIA. *Our Faces—Our Words*. New York, Norton, 1964. 125p. Cloth, $3.75. Paper, $1.50.

Monologues and photographs present a portrait of the fight for freedom—told in the words and faces of Negroes and Whites.

SPALDING, HUGHES. *The Spalding Family*. Atlanta, Privately Printed, 1963. 185p. Apply.

A history of how the pioneer Catholic Spalding family in America originated in Maryland and spread to Kentucky, Georgia, and other states in the years from 1658 to 1963. The author is a resident of Atlanta, Georgia.

SPARKS, LAMAR. *Living Water.* Boston, Christopher, 1964. 185p. $3.95.
A religious book for children based on the truths in the life of Christ. The author is a native of Macon, Georgia.

STEGEMAN, JOHN F. *These Men She Gave.* Athens, University of Georgia Press, 1964. 179p. $4.75.
The story of the impact of the Civil War on a town and a community, this book gives a dual account of happenings on the home front and on the battlefields, from Mechanicsville to Appomattox. The author is a physician in Athens, Georgia.

STOFFEL, JOSEPH F. *Explosives and Homemade Bombs.* Springfield, Ill., C. C. Thomas, 1962. 104p. $5.50.
A book devoted to the problem of homemade explosives and designed to acquaint law enforcement personnel with such material that they may be required to handle, investigate, and dispose of in the course of their normal police duties. The author is a retired Major A.U.S. and lives in Columbus, Georgia.

STOKES, MACK B. *Our Methodist Heritage.* Nashville, Graded Press, 1963. 128p. $1.00.
A history of the Methodist movement from the days of John and Charles Wesley to the present. Dr. Stokes is Associate Dean at the Candler School of Theology, Emory University, Atlanta, Georgia.

TORRANCE, ELLIS PAUL. *Education and the Creative Potential.* Minneapolis, University of Minnesota Press, 1963. 167p. $4.50.
Describes recent developments in research about creativity in children and proposes changes in our educational methods which will make greater use of the creative potential. The author, a native of Milledgeville, Georgia, is Director of Educational Research at the University of Minnesota.

TURNER, HENRY ASHBY, JR. *Stresemann and the Politics of the Weimar Republic.* Princeton, N. J., Princeton University Press, 1963. 287p. $6.00.
Using information drawn from Stresemann's private papers, the book focuses on his domestic policy while he was chancellor of the Republic. The author is a native of Atlanta, Georgia, is Assistant Professor of History at Yale University.

TYRE, NEDRA. *Everyone Suspect.* New York, Macmillan, 1964. 215p. $3.95.
Horne Browning, an eighty-year-old semi-recluse, takes on a case which appears to be unsolvable—the murder of a pretty, young college student. The author is a resident of Atlanta, Georgia.

WALLACE, ROBERT B., JR. *Dress Her in White and Gold.* Atlanta, The Georgia Tech Foundation, 1963. 426p. $5.00.
An illustrated biography of Georgia Tech from its beginning in 1888 to the present day.

WAMBLE, G. HUGH. *The Shape of Faith*. Nashville, Broadman, 1962. 88p. $1.00.

An introduction to seven major American evangelical denominations—Episcopal, Congregational, Lutheran, Christian or Disciples of Christ, Methodist, Presbyterian, and Baptist. The author is a native of Cairo, Georgia.

WESLEY, CECIL COBB. *History Street*. Chicago, Windfall Press, 1964. 110p. $2.75.

A book of poems about the unfathomable reaches of time and its relation to the individual. The author is Editorial Assistant of the *Georgia Magazine* published in Decatur, Georgia.

WHITE, ROBB. *The Survivor*. Garden City, N. J., Doubleday, 1964. 216p. $3.50.

A navy lieutenant, who has rather grandiose ideas of wartime heroism, learns that bravery comes from the wellsprings of human nature and that a great deal of it is simple physical endurance.

WILEY, BELL IRVIN. *Embattled Confederates*. New York, Harper & Row, 1964. 290p. $10.00.

This is a book primarily about people. Southerners—and their activities during the war period—are vividly portrayed in words and picture. Illustrations have been compiled by Hirst D. Milhollen, Curator of Photographs, Library of Congress. Dr. Wiley is Professor of History at Emory University, Atlanta, Georgia.

WINDHAM, DONALD. *Emblems of Conduct*. New York, Scribners, 1964. 210p. $4.50.

Vignettes of autobiography that gradually build a picture of a gentle, quiet, perceptive boy growing up in a woman-dominated, poverty threatened household in Atlanta, Georgia.

WRIGHT, NATHALIA. *Horatio Greenough, the First American Sculptor*. Philadelphia, University of Pennsylvania Press, 1963. 382p. $8.50.

Greenough, who lived from 1805 to 1852, was the first American to devote himself from the outset of his career to the profession of sculpture and the first to set forth at any length the concept of functionalism in Architecture. The author, a native of Athens, Georgia, is a Professor of English at the University of Tennessee, Knoxville, Tennessee.

YARBROUGH, BIRD and YARBROUGH, PAUL, eds. *Taylors Creek*. Pearson, Ga., Press of the Atkinson County Citizen, 1963. 300p. $10.50.

A story of the community of Taylors Creek, located in Liberty County, Georgia, and its people through 200 years. Sketches of early settlers and their descendants are included.

YERBY, FRANK. *The Old Gods Laugh.* New York, Dial, 1964. 408p. $4.95.
   A modern romance set against the background of revolutionary upheaval in a Caribbean country. The author is a native of Augusta, Georgia.

ZEIGLER, HARMON. *Interest Groups in American Society.* Englewood Cliffs, N. J., Prentice-Hall, 1964. 343p. $9.00.
   This study analyzes the role played by pressure groups and their effect on the American political scene. Dr. Zeigler is Assistant Professor of Political Science at the University of Georgia.

Bibliography of Georgia Authors 1964-1965

THE sixteenth in the REVIEW's series of annual "Bibliographies of Georgia Authors," this annotated Bibliography is, as nearly as the compiler could make it, a complete and accurate record of books published by Georgia authors from November 1, 1964, to November 1, 1965. The annotations are descriptive, not critical; intended to place, not to judge the book. U. S., State, County, and City Documents, parts of books, brief analytics, and pamphlets of less than 25 pages have been omitted. Prices are given except when not supplied by publisher or when book is obtainable only on specific request, in which case the word "Apply" is used.

In determining whom to designate as Georgia authors, the compiler has included authors born in Georgia and claiming Georgia as their native state and those who have lived in Georgia for a period of five years and who did their writing here.

The compiler will welcome and appreciate reader's sending to him any additions or corrections. They may be sent to him at any time in care of the GEORGIA REVIEW. Several books inadvertently omitted from previous Bibliographies are listed here. Any books omitted from the present Bibliography will be included in the list for 1965-1966.

Acknowledgment is made to members of the staff of the Special Collections Division of the University of Georgia Library for their assistance in the preparation of this Bibliography.

ADEN, JOHN M., ed. *The Critical Opinions of John Dryden: A Dictionary.* Nashville, Vanderbilt University Press, 1963. 290p. $7.50.

  A dictionary of critical opinions drawn from all of Dryden's works except poetry and drama. Arrangement is alphabetical by subjects and chronological within subjects. The author is a native of Atlanta, Georgia.

AIKEN, CONRAD POTTER. *Cats and Bats and Things with Wings.* New York, Atheneum, 1965. Unpaged. $4.29.

  A collection of poetry for children by the winner of the Pulitzer and the Bollingen awards for poetry. The author is a native of Savannah, Georgia. The drawings are by Milton Glaser.

ALLEN, CHARLES LIVINGSTONE. *The Ten Commandments.* Westwood, N. J., Revel, 1965. 64p. $2.00.

A practical and realistic application of the Ten Commandments to life in today's world. Dr. Allen, a native Georgian, is pastor of the First Methodist Church, Houston, Texas.

ALTIZER, THOMAS J. J. *Oriental Mysticism and Biblical Eschatology.* Philadelphia, Westminster Press, 1961. 218p. $4.95.

Discusses the significance of Christian and Buddhist principles for modern man who the author believes has lost his faith. Dr. Altizer is a member of the faculty at Emory University, Atlanta, Georgia.

ANDERSON, CHARLES ROBERT. *Emily Dickinson's Poetry: Stairway of Surprise.* New York, Holt, Rinehart and Winston, 1960. 334p. $5.95.

An intensive study of Emily Dickinson's poetry, including the full text of over one hundred of her best poems. The author, a native of Macon, Georgia, is Professor of American Literature at Johns Hopkins University, Baltimore, Maryland.

ANDERSON, C. EUGENE. *Financial Hero: R. J. Taylor of Macon.* Macon, Ga., Southern Press, 1964. 178p. $10.00.

A biographical sketch of successful business man and leading citizen of Macon, Georgia. The late author was a resident of Macon, Georgia.

AVERITT, JACK NELSON. *Georgia's Coastal Plain.* West Palm Beach, Fla., Lewis Historical Publishing Co., 1965. Three Volumes. Apply.

The two volumes of formal history cover the development of the coastal region of Georgia from earliest settlements to the present day. The third volume consists of contemporary biographies of inhabitants of the region. Dr. Averitt is Chairman, Division of Social Sciences, Georgia Southern College, Statesboro, Georgia.

BAINE, RODNEY M. *Thomas Holcroft and the Revolutionary Novel.* Athens, University of Georgia Press, 1965. 132p. $3.00.

A critical study of Thomas Holcroft, England's first revolutionary novelist, and his contribution to English literature. The author is a member of the English Department at the University of Georgia.

BEATTY, FREDERIKA. *William Wordsworth of Dove Cottage.* New York, Twayne, 1964. 320p. $6.00.

A study of the poet's most productive decade, June 1797-May 1807. The author is a native of Darien, Georgia, is an Associate Professor of English at Hunter College, New York City.

BEAUMONT, CHARLES A. *Swift's Use of the Bible.* Athens, University of Georgia Press, 1965. 104p. Paper, $2.50.

A comprehensive documentation of the use of Biblical material in Swift's works. The author is a member of the English Department at the University of Georgia.

BELL, LOIS HENDRIX. *Only the Whippoorwill.* Smyrna, Ga., The Print Shop, 1965. 58p. Apply.

A collection of poems about life in its many ramifications. The author, a native of Cherokee County, Georgia, is a resident of Cobb County, Georgia.

BENSEN, WALTER. *Hindenburg's Soldier.* New York, Vantage, 1965. 177p. $3.50.

The memoirs of a young German artillery officer in World War I who tells how the war looked from the other side. The author is a resident of Athens, Georgia.

BLACKSTONE, WILLIAM T. *Francis Hutcheson and Contemporary Ethical Theory.* Athens, University of Georgia Press, 1965. 96p. Paper, $2.75.

This systematic analysis of Hutcheson's ethical theory gives proper historical position to the British philosopher who made significant contributions to the theory of utilitarianism. Dr. Blackstone is Head of the Department of Philosophy and Religion at the University of Georgia.

BOSKOFF, ALVIN and ZEIGLER, HARMON. *Voting Patterns in a Local Election.* Philadelphia, Lippincott, 1964. 154p. $1.45.

This study's primary aims are to locate and assess the importance of status, influence process, and commitment to the community for the behavior of voters. Dr. Boskoff is a Professor at Emory University and Dr. Zeigler is a Professor at the University of Georgia.

BRAMBLETT, AGNES COCHRAN. *With Lifted Heart.* Boston, Brandon, 1965. 64p. $3.00.

A collection of poems on love, life, and friends by the Poet Laureate of Georgia.

BROILES, ROLAND DAVID. *The Moral Philosophy of David Hume.* The Hague, Netherlands, Martinus Nijhoff, 1964. 97p. $3.00.

This study is primarily concerned with Hume's arguments concerning the respective roles of reason and passion in moral decisions. The author is an Assistant Professor of Philosophy at the University of Georgia.

BROUGHER, WILLIAM E. *Baggy Pants and Other Stories.* New York, Vantage Press, 1965. 163p. $3.00.

A collection of short stories that treat with the foibles of human nature. The late author was a resident of Atlanta, Georgia.

BROWN, ROBERT KEVIN. *Real Estate Economics: An Introduction to Urban Land Use.* Boston, Houghton Mifflin, 1965. 388p. $7.50.

A textbook, designed for the college level, with emphasis on the evolving patterns of land use in real estate and development. The author is a Professor at Georgia State College, Atlanta, Georgia.

BURCH, ROBERT. *D. J.'s Worest Enemy.* New York, Viking, 1965. 142p. $3.00.

A young boy, at odds with both his family and friends, eventually discovers that he is the prime offender. Set in rural Georgia.

BURCH, ROBERT. *The Traveling Bird.* New York, McDowell, Obolensky, 1959. 42p. $2.50.

A little boy and his pet parakeet, Caesar, conduct a successful search for a puppy. The author is a native of Fayette County, Georgia.

BURKETT, WILLIAM R. JR. *Sleeping Planet.* Garden City, N. Y., Doubleday, 1965. 297p. $4.95.

A science fiction story of extraterrestial warfare set in the 25th century. The author is a native of Augusta, Georgia.

CADE, JOHN BROTHER. *Holsey, the Incomparable.* New York, Pageant Press, 1963. 221p. $4.00.

A biography of Lucius Henry Holsey, born a slave in 1842, who assisted in the founding and organization of the colored Methodist Episcopal Church in America. The author is a native of Elbert County, Georgia.

CALDWELL, ERSKINE. *In Search of Bisco.* New York, Farrar, Straus and Giroux, 1965. 219p. $4.95.

An account of the author's recent travels through the Deep South in search of a childhood Negro friend named Bisco, revealing the genesis of racial hatred in the region.

CARNEY, H. STANTON. *From Adam to Me.* Grand Rapids, Eerdman's, 1965. 300p. $4.50.

In this study, divided into five parts, the author puts the teachings of the Bible into his own words. The author is a resident of Atlanta, Georgia.

CHARLES, A. ALDO. *College Law for Business.* Cincinnati, South-Western Publishing Co., 1963. Sixth Edition. 506p. $3.84.

This edition of a basic textbook on business law includes a thorough revision of text material involving addition of legal concepts and principles heretofore not included, revision of end-of-chapter materials, and expansion of glossary. The late Dr. Charles was Professor of Business Law at the University of Georgia.

CLECKLEY, HERVEY MILTON, M. D. *The Mask of Sanity.* St. Louis, C. V. Mosby, 1965. Fourth Edition. 510p. $9.75.

This is a new edition of a study that appeared first in 1941. This attempt to clarify some of the issues involved in the "psychopathic personality" will aid all those who are seeking a solution to this distressing social disease. Dr. Cleckley is Clinical Professor of Psychiatry, Medical College of Georgia, Augusta, Georgia.

COCHRAN, JEAN D. *Augusta-Richmond County Public Library Since 1949.* Augusta, Ga., Privately Printed, 1964. 48p. Cloth, $2.00. Paper, $1.00.

A fifteen year history of the public library system in Augusta and Richmond County, Georgia. Miss Cochran is Librarian of the Augusta Public Library, Augusta, Georgia.

COOPER, BEN GREEN. *Corny Cookin'*. Mableton, Ga., Privately Printed, 1965. 32p. $1.00.

An essay and a collection of recipes of all the good things man has learned to make from maize. This book may be obtained from the author at P.O. Box 233, Mableton, Georgia.

COOPER, BEN GREEN. *Greenhurst's Kitchen.* Mableton, Ga., Privately Printed, 1964. 25p. $1.00.

A collection of Mrs. Carrie W. Green's recipes and some from her friends, Dalton, Georgia's best cooks of yesteryear.

COOPER, BEN GREEN. *Savannah's Cookin'*. Mableton, Ga., Privately Printed, 1965. 32p. $1.00.

Traditional Savannah recipes collected by a somewhat prodigal son who loves crab, shrimp, fish, oysters, and the traditional fatted lamb.

COULTER, ELLIS MERTON. *Georgia Waters.* Athens, Georgia Historical Quarterly, 1965. 208p. Apply.

These studies of Tallulah Falls, Madison Springs, Scull Shoals, and the Okefenokee Swamp first appeared in the *Georgia Historical Quarterly*. They have been indexed and a bibliography has been added. The edition is limited to 199 copies.

COULTER, ELLIS MERTON. *Old Petersburg and the Broad River Valley of Georgia.* Athens, University of Georgia Press, 1965. 236p. $6.00.

The author describes life among the Petersburgers and the Broad River Valley settlers: the types of businesses and trade, political and social aspects, and the important part that religion and education played in the lives of early Georgians. Dr. Coulter is Regents' Professor Emeritus of History at the University of Georgia.

CRAIG, GEORGIA. See: GADDIS, PEGGY.

DANIEL, MARY HELEN. *My Gift*. New York, Exposition Press, 1965. 102p. $3.50.
A collection of poems, about family and friends, that covers a wide range of emotional experience in the fields of philosophy and nature. The author is a resident of Macon, Georgia.

DARDEN, GORDON WALLACE. *Dardens of Williams Creek*. Athens, Privately Printed, 1963. 50p. Apply.
A record of the Dardens, including their antecedents and descendants, who moved from Virginia to Wilkes County, Georgia. Mr. Darden lives in Athens, Georgia.

DAUGHTRY, NANCY MARGARET G. *Bit O'Stone Mountain and Bits O'Nature*. Atlanta, Privately Printed, 1965. 62p. $1.50.
A naturalist with a discerning eye, a love of beauty, and a sense of humor takes young and old on a nature walk.

DAVIDSON, WILLIAM H. *Pine Log and Greek Revival*. Alexander City, Ala., Outlook Publishing Co., 1964. 396p. $12.50.
A pictorial and historical guide book of ante-bellum and post-bellum houses in Troup and Harris counties in Georgia and Chambers County in Alabama. The author lives at West Point, Georgia.

DAVIS, OLIVE BELL. *Between Two Novels*. New York, Olympic Press, 1965. 106p. $3.50.
A collection of short stories, poems, and monologs on a variety of subjects. The author is a resident of Atlanta, Georgia.

DERN, PEGGY. See: GADDIS, PEGGY.

DICKEY, JAMES. *Buckdancer's Choice*. Middleton, Conn., Wesleyan University Press, 1965. 80p. Cloth, $4.00. Paper, $1.85.
A collection of poems that penetrate into areas of life that we too often evade or deny. Mr. Dickey is a native of Atlanta, Georgia.

DOBBS, WAYNE and PINHOLSTER, GARLAND F. *Basketball's Stunting Defenses*. Englewood Cliffs, N. J., 1964. 208p. $5.35.
This illustrated coaching guide explains game-winning variations on the man-for-man and zone defenses that are designed to stop any offensive threat—from an individual sharpshooter to a potent fast break, from pattern offense to a big pivotman. Dobbs is Head Basketball Coach at Brewton-Parker College in Mount Vernon, Georgia, and Pinholster is Head Basketball Coach at Oglethorpe College, Atlanta, Georgia.

DREWRY, JOHN E., ed. *Higher Ground for Journalism: Press, Radio, Television, Periodicals, Public Relations, and Advertising as Seen through Institutes and Special Occasions of the Henry W. Grady School of*

Journalism, 1964-1965. Vol. LXVI. No 3, Athens, University of Georgia Bulletin, 1965. 246p. Paper, $2.00. Cloth, $3.00.

The 1964-1965 compilation of addresses and papers delivered at the various institutes and other special occasions sponsored by the University of Georgia's School of Journalism.

DUNCAN, POPE ALEXANDER. *Hanserd Knollys-Seventeenth Century Baptist.* Nashville, Broadman Press, 1965. 61p. $0.95.

A study of the life and times of Knollys, including the major ideas of his writings and showing the relation between Baptists of his times and other religious groups.

DUNCAN, POPE ALEXANDER. *The Pilgrimage of Christianity.* Nashville, Broadman, 1965. 128p. $1.50.

A concise survey of Christian history from the time of the Apostles to the present day. Dr. Duncan is Dean of Brunswick Junior College, Brunswick, Georgia.

ETHRIDGE, WILLIE SNOW. *Lady, You Can't Hardly Get There from Here.* New York, Vanguard, 1965. 185p. $4.95.

Describes the maelstrom of confusion, schedules, nonschedules, and "ticket-tape" encountered in a career as lecturer, author, wife, mother, and grandmother. The author is a native of Georgia.

FICKETT, AMANDA SCHIELKE. *Friedrich Heidmann Family Tree, 1844-1964.* Athens, Privately Printed, 1965. Unpaged. $6.00.

Traces the thirteen children of Friedrich and Rebecca Heidemann through seven generations. Mrs. Fickett is a resident of Athens, Georgia.

FORD, WILLIAM HERSCHELL. *Simple Sermons for Times Like These.* Grand Rapids, Zondervan, 1965. 135p. $2.50.

A collection of inspirational sermons with challenging messages to unbelievers and Christians alike. The author is a native of Monroe, Georgia.

FOSTER, MARIAN CURTIS. See: MARIANA.

GADDIS, PEGGY. *Bayou Nurse.* New York, Arcadia, 1964. 192p. $2.95.

Apprehensive about returning to the Bayou country to care for an austere aunt, Lindsay Mallory, R.N., finds life further complicated by a young doctor who questions her credentials as a nurse.

GADDIS, PEGGY. *Hill-Top Nurse.* New York, Arcadia, 1964. 189p. $2.95.

The unexpected return of a beautiful cousin threatens to destroy Nurse Lib Rainey's romance and peace of mind.

GADDIS, PEGGY. *The Listening Nurse.* New York, Arcadia, 1965. 192p. $3.25.
Nurse Martia Stapleton forswears love after the death of her fiancé—but then she meets a young geriatrics doctor, on Florida's Gulf Coast, who sees her as a perfect nurse and an ideal woman.

GADDIS, PEGGY. (pseud. PEGGY DERN). *Nurse Angela.* New York, Arcadia, 1965. 190p. $3.25.
Angela Dennard, R.N., finds life in a hospital on an exclusive Caribbean island can be complicated not by her elderly patients but by the younger members of the staff.

GADDIS, PEGGY. *Nurse in Flight.* New York, Arcadia, 1965. 191p. $3.25.
Nurse Joyce Bramblett discovers that private duty nursing in Miami Beach can be filled with excitement and romance.

GADDIS, PEGGY. (pseud. PEGGY DERN). *Nurse in the Shadows.* New York, Arcadia, 1965. 191p. $3.25.
Assigned to care for a young invalid who lives near the Florida coast, Registered Nurse Leona Ramsey becomes involved in a tragedy which touches the life of everyone close to her patient.

GADDIS, PEGGY. (pseud. GEORGIA CRAIG). *The Nurse Was Juliet.* New York, Arcadia, 1965. 192p. $3.25.
Mountain-bred Juliet Cochran, the daughter of two doctors, returns to her home town to help her mother run the family clinic. A murder, a trial, and a romance create a drastic change in her serene existence.

GALLAWAY, MARIAN. *The Director in the Theatre.* New York, Macmillan, 1963. 386p. $6.00.
This study emphasizes the role of the director as he deals with actors, the public, backers, and commercial help. The author, a native of Savannah, Georgia, is Assistant Professor of Speech at the University of Alabama, Tuscaloosa, Alabama.

GARRISON, KARL CLAUDIUS. *Psychology of Adolescence.* Englewood Cliffs, N. J., Prentice-Hall, 1965. Sixth Edition. 487p. $7.95.
This new and enlarged edition, using the biological concept of individual development, pictures the adolescent as a unified personality growing and developing in accordance with his genetic constitution and the environmental forces that have affected him from birth.

GARRISON, KARL CLAUDIUS and FORCE, DEWEY G., JR. *The Psychology of Exceptional Children.* New York, Ronald, 1965. Fourth Edition. 571p. $7.00.
This edition has been extensively revised and up-dated and is primarily for students of education and psychology. Dr. Garrison is Professor Emeritus of Education at the University of Georgia.

GAULTNEY, BABRARA F. *Of Such Is the Kingdom.* Forest Park, Ga., Speed Quick Press, 1965. 126p. $1.50.

A representative selection of devotional thoughts taken from the author's family and friends.

GAULTNEY, BARBARA F. *No Thought for the Morrow.* Forest Park, Ga., Copy Art Press, 1962. 34p. $1.00.

The story of how a Christian family accepted and loved a handicapped child. The author is a resident of Forest Park, Georgia.

GILDEN, BERT and GILDEN, KATYA (pseud. K. B. GILDEN). *Hurry Sundown.* Garden City, N. Y., Doubleday, 1965. Two Volumes. 1135p. $7.95.

A long novel concerned with the struggle of two young ex-GI farmers to hang onto their small Georgia farms against the onslaught of a big corporation. The authors lived at Cedar Point in McIntosh County, Georgia, for many years while writing their novel.

GILMER, GEORGE ROCKINGHAM. *Sketches of Some of the First Settlers of Upper Georgia.* Baltimore, Genealogical Publishing Co., 1965. 463p. $12.50.

Originally published in 1855 with a revised and corrected edition published in Americus, Georgia, in 1926. This is a reprint of the 1926 edition with an added index supplied by the Georgia Department of Archives and History. This is an authoritative source book for genealogists and local historians.

GOLDGAR, BERTRAND A. *The Curse of Party: Swift's Relations with Addison and Steele.* Lincoln, Neb., University of Nebraska Press, 1961. 198p. $4.00.

This book examines the personal and public relationships between Swift and Addison and Steele. The author, a native of Macon, Georgia, is an Assistant Professor at Lawrence College, Appleton, Wisconsin.

GORDON, AMBROSE, JR. *The Invisible Tent: The War Novels of Ford Madox Ford.* Austin, Texas, University of Texas Press, 1964. 153p. $6.00.

A study that examines the seven books written by Ford between the approach of World War I and the ending of nineteen-twenties. The author, a native of Savannah, Georgia, is Assistant Professor of English at the Univeristy of Georgia.

GRANTHAM, DEWEY W. *The Democratic South.* New York, Norton, 1965. 109p. Paper, $1.25.

An interpretation of the politics of the Solid South in general and the development of the Democratic party in that region in particular. The book was published in 1963 by the University of Georgia Press. The author is a native of Manassas, Georgia.

GREEN, JAMES L. *Metropolitan Economic Republics.* Athens, University of Georgia Press, 1965. 240p. $4.00.

In this case study of regional economic growth the author develops a metropolitan regional economic model, discusses its basic structure, and illustrates its use through a specific situation, the Atlanta Metropolitan complex. Dr. Green is a Professor of Economics in the College of Business Administration at the University of Georgia.

GREER, MICHAEL. *Interior Design.* Garden City, N. Y., Doubleday, 1962. 256p. $13.95.

A collection of 124 photographs illustrating some of the work of Michael Greer, past President of the National Society of Interior Designers. The author, a native of Monroe, Georgia, is a member of the Faculty of New York's School of Interior Design.

HAMBIDGE, MARY C., ed. *Practical Applications of Dynamic Symmetry by Jay Hambidge.* New York, Devin-Adair, 1965. 128p. $4.95.

A reissue of a classic work on design that has long been unavailable. This edition has been arranged and edited by the author's widow. Mrs. Hambidge, Head of the Weavers of Rabun, lives near Clayton, Georgia.

HARDWICK, RICHARD. *The Plotters.* Garden City, N. Y., Doubleday, 1965. 192p. $3.50.

An ambitious company man finds his world crumbling when a seedy character, who was once his college roommate, rakes up the past for blackmail purposes. The author is a resident of St. Simons Island, Georgia.

HARRIS, JOEL CHANDLER. *Uncle Remus.* New York, Shocken, 1965. 198p. Cloth, $3.95. Paper, $1.75.

A new edition of a children's classic that first appeared in print in 1880. The introduction is by Stella Brewer Brooks and the illustrations are by A. B. Frost.

HARRIS, KATHLEEN. See: HUMPHRIES, ADELAIDE.

HICKS, ALBERTA KINARD. *Foley, Florida's Indian Trails and Log-Cabin Days on Finhollowaw River.* Elon College, North Carolina, Primitive Publications, 1962. 32p. $1.00.

A collection of poems about life and death in the early days of the state of Florida.

HICKS, ALBERTA KINARD. *Okefenokee Wonderland.* Elon College, North Carolina, Primitive Publications, 1965. 31p. $1.00.

A poetic tribute to the Okefenokee Swamp—the Land of Trembling Earth. The author lives on R.F.D. No. 3, Monticello, Georgia.

HODGES, LUCILLE. *A History of Our Locale: Mainly Evans County, Georgia.* Macon, Ga., Southern Press, 1965. 324p. $10.00.

An account of the formation of Evans County, a description of the land area, information on pioneer families, churches, towns, post offices, schools and organizations, cemetery records, and other pertinent information is included in this county history. The author is a resident of Claxton, Georgia.

HOLDEN, GENEVIEVE. *Don't Go in Alone.* Garden City, N. Y., Doubleday, 1965. 192p. $3.50.
A police captain, in Atlanta, Georgia, investigates the disappearance of four women, each of whom has ventured alone into a vacant building. The author lives in Atlanta, Georgia.

HUMPHRIES, ADELAIDE (pseud. KATHLEEN HARRIS). *Jane Arden, Space Nurse.* New York, Avalon Books, 1962. 221p. $2.95.
A young nurse experiences intrigue, danger, and love at Cape Canaveral.

HUMPHRIES, ADELAIDE. *Nurse Barbara.* New York, Avalon, 1965. 192p. $3.25.
A vacationing nurse from Florida and a young lawyer from Cincinnati are trapped by floods in a deserted farmhouse, and a romance blossoms as they take charge of survival and rescue plans for the other people marooned with them.

HUMPHRIES, ADELAIDE (pseud. KATHLEEN HARRIS). *Nurse on the Run.* New York. Avalon, 1965. 191p. $3.25.
Nurse Deborah McGarthy, hiding on a small Caribbean island until she can be cleared of the theft of a pearl necklace from a patient's yacht, finds herself a job as a mate on a fishing boat and a home with an elderly doctor and his housekeeper.

HUTCHENS, ELEANOR NEWMAN. *Irony in Tom Jones.* Tuscaloosa, Ala., University of Alabama Press, 1965. 190p. $5.95.
This study examines the oblique and subtle techniques Fielding used to achieve irony in his works. The author is a Professor of English at Agnes Scott College, Decatur, Georgia.

HYMAN, MAC. *Take Now Thy Son.* New York, Random House, 1965. 240p. $4.95.
This posthumous novel by the author of *No Time for Sergeants* is the tragic story of a man who holds too rigidly to his ideals and cannot unbend—particularly where his only son is concerned.

JACKSON, ESTHER MERLE. *The Broken World of Tennessee Williams.* Madison, Wis., University of Wisconsin Press, 1965. 208p. $5.75.
This critical study is concerned primarily with an analysis of the form and an exploration of the ideas underlying the dramatic work of a major American playwright. The author is Professor and Chairman of the Department of Speech and Drama at Clark College, Atlanta, Georgia.

JOHNSTON, DOROTHY F. *Medical–Surgical Nursing.* St. Louis, C. V. Mosby, 1965. 135p. $3.50.

An illustrated workbook for the practical nursing student whereby she may enhance her understanding of the medical-surgical patient and his care. The author was formerly Director, Athens, School of Practical Nursing, Athens, Georgia.

JONES, BILLY WALKER and ADKINS, ESTHER POOL. *History of Ebenezer Missionary Baptist Association, of Georgia, 1814-1964.* Dry Branch, Ga., Privately Printed, 1965. 256p. Cloth, $6.00. Paper, $4.00.

An historical account of the Ebenezer Association, its churches, and its ministers. Mr. Jones is a resident of Dry Branch, Georgia, and Mrs. Adkins is a resident of Irwinton, Georgia.

JONES, CHARLES COLCOCK, JR. *The History of Georgia.* Spartanburg, S. C., The Reprint Co., 1965. Two Volumes. $17.50 each.

This history, covering the aboriginal, colonial, and revolutionary epochs, is considered by leading authorities as the outstanding work on these periods of Georgia history. The two-volume set was published in 1883.

KAISER, FRANCES E. ed. *Translators and Translations: Services and Sources in Science and Technology.* New York, Special Libraries Association, 1965. Second Edition. 214p. Paper, $14.50.

Covers 128 languages and eleven areas of science based on data from questionnaires to translators and translation projects. The editor is Assistant Science-Technology Librarian, Georgia Institute of Technology, Atlanta, Georgia.

KEATS, JOHN. *The Sheepskin Psychosis.* Philadelphia, Lippincott, 1965. 190p. $3.95.

A well-known critic of our contemporary culture takes a crack at the "Myths and Realities of College Today." The author is a native of Moultrie, Georgia.

KILLIAN, LEWIS and GRIGG, CHARLES. *Racial Crisis in America.* Englewood Cliffs, N. J., Prentice-Hall, 1964. 144p. $4.50.

This book issues a sober warning to optimistic Americans of both races that conflict, not consensus will dominate the Negro's struggle for first-class citizenship. Mr. Killian is a native of Georgia and is a member of Faculty of Florida State University, Tallahassee, Florida.

KING, SPENCER BIDWELL, JR. *Rebel Lawyer.* Athens, University of Georgia Press, 1965. 104p. $3.00.

The letters of Lieutenant Theodorick W. Montfort, 1861-1862, have been edited by Dr. King with full and descriptive notes. Dr. King is a Professor of History at Mercer University, Macon, Georgia.

LAWTON, EDWARD P. *A Saga of the South.* Ft. Myers Beach, Fla., Island Press, 1965. 318p. $7.50.
A family chronicle of several prominent Georgia families—the Lawtons, the Basingers, the Starrs, and the Joneses. The author is a native of Savannah, Georgia.

LOFTIS, JOHN CLYDE. *The Politics of Drama in Augustan England.* New York, Oxford University Press, 1963. 173p. $4.80.
A study of late 17th and early 18th century playwrights whose works show concern with national politics. The author, a native of Atlanta, Georgia, is Associate Head of the English Department at Stanford University in California.

MCMENEMY, JIM. *Bunkhouse Yarns.* New York, Pageant Press, 1964. 64p. $2.75.
A collection of improbable western tales told by a character named Saddlesoap Smith. The author, a native of Atlanta, lives in New York City.

MACON, ALTHEA JANE, comp. *John and Edward Tuck of Halifax County, Virginia, and Some of Their Descendants.* Macon, Ga. Southern Press, 1964. 216p. $10.00.
A compilation of data relating to the Tuck family of Virginia and its descendants. The compiler is a resident of Brunswick, Georgia.

MANN, CAROLYN BECKNELL. *The Guide to Atlanta—Places and Pleasures—A Necessity for the Elegant and Refined.* Atlanta, Becknell-Mann Associates, 1965. 48p. Paper, $1.00.
A guidebook that is loaded with comments and descriptions of all the sights, services, places, and things that distinguish Atlanta from other cities. The author is a resident of Atlanta, Georgia.

MANN, HAROLD WILSON. *Atticus Greene Haygood: Methodist Bishop, Editor, and Educator.* Athens, University of Georgia Press, 1965. 262p. $6.00.
This biography evaluates Bishop Haygood's contributions to education, to race relationships in a difficult time, and to the orientation of the Southern Methodist Church. Dr. Mann is a native Georgian and is Professor of History at Radford College in Virginia.

MARIANA (FOSTER, MARIAN CURTIS). *The Journey of Bagwell Putt.* New York, Lothrop, Lee, and Shepard, 1965. 40p. $3.50.
The tale of the journey of an old, authentic museum doll and how she is followed by some of the tiny characters that live in the museum. This charming book was first published in 1945 and in a very limited edition.

MARSHALL, JOHN DAVID, ed. *Mark Hopkin's Log and Other Essays by Louis Shores.* Hamden, Conn., Shoe String, 1965. 383p. $9.00.

The editor has selected forty-four essays and articles concerned with books, libraries, and readers and arranged them by subjects. Dr. Shores is Dean of the School of Library Science at Florida State University. Mr. Marshall is Head of Acquisitions, University of Georgia Library, Athens, Georgia.

MAXWELL, WILLIAM BULLOCH. *The Mysterious Father: A Tragedy in Five Acts, 1807.* Athens, University of Georgia Press, 1965. 80p. Paper, $2.50.

This is the first play written and published in the state of Georgia by a native playwright, the only known copy of which is in the University of Georgia Libraries' Rare Book Collection. The play is edited by Gerald Kahan, a Professor in the Speech and Drama Department at the University of Georgia.

MEBANE, JOHN. *Treasure at Home.* New York, A. S. Barnes, 1964. 268p. $8.50.

Based on a column published in the combined Sunday edition of the *Atlanta Journal* and the *Atlanta Constitution* under the byline of Harold Heartman this study deals with a wide variety of articles called "collectibles," all of which are available to those of more modest means.

MONTGOMERY, MARION. *Stones from the Rubble.* Memphis, Tenn., Argus Books, 1965. 62p. $3.95.

A collection of poems about the many facets of life and its problems. The author, a member of the English Department at the University of Georgia, lives in Crawford, Georgia.

MOORE, WALTER L. *Outlines for Preaching.* Nashville, Broadman, 1965. 80p. $1.50.

This collection of outlines for sermons varies from evangelism, Christian growth, and social problems to stewardships. The author is Pastor of the Vineville Baptist Church, Macon, Georgia.

MYERS, T. CECIL. *Thunder on the Mountain.* Nashville, Abingdon, 1965. 176p. $3.00.

A collection of sermons that interpret the Ten Commandments in the light of today's moral needs. Dr. Myers is Pastor of Grace Methodist Church, Atlanta, Georgia.

NEELY, FRANK HENRY. *The Manager, a Human Engineer.* Atlanta, Privately Printed, 1965. 87p. $3.50.

This study deals with the public and human relations that confront managers in all types of businesses and gives practical guides to the solution of many problems. The author is a resident of Atlanta, Georgia.

NEWTON, CHARLOTTE. *Church Library Manual.* Athens, Privately Printed, 1965. 42p. $1.00.

A simple, definite guide that can be adapted for use in any church library of any denomination. The manual is available from the author, 892 Prince Avenue, Athens, Georgia.

O'CONNOR, FLANNERY. *Everything That Rises Must Converge.* New York, Farrar, Straus and Giroux, 1965. 269p. $4.95.

A collection of nine short stories by one of America's most gifted contemporary writers. Miss O'Connor was working on this collection at the time of her recent death.

OGBURN, CHARLTON, JR. *The Gold of the River Sea.* New York, Morrow, 1965. 534p. $6.95.

A young American, unhappy in the world of business and finance, experiences great exhilaration during an eventful journey through Brazil. The author is a native of Atlanta, Georgia.

OZMENT, ROBERT V. *Putting Life Together Again.* Westwood, N. J., Revell, 1965. 128p. $2.50.

This study gives practical suggestions on how to recover from despair and defeat. The author is Pastor of St. James Methodist Church, Atlanta, Georgia.

OZMENT, ROBERT V. *There's Always Hope.* Westwood, N. J., Revell, 1964. 64p. $2.00.

That no life is hopelessly lost or beyond redemption is the main theme of these twenty-nine chapters that deal with man's need for a spark of hope in a dark and dreary world.

PARKS, EDD W. and PARKS, AILEEN W., eds. *The Collected Poems of Henry Timrod.* Athens, University of Georgia Press, 1965. 216p. $7.50.

This book is a variorum edition of Timrod's major poetry, arranged as nearly as possible in chronological order. The editors have included a biographical and critical introduction. Dr. Parks is a Professor of English at the University of Georgia. His wife, Aileen, has written several historical novels.

POSEY, WALTER BROWNLOW. *Religious Strife on the Southern Frontier.* Baton Rouge, La., Louisiana State University Press, 1965. 112p. $4.00.

The story of the incredible and wonderful competition among the various religious denominations on the Kentucky, Tennessee, and Lower Mississippi Valley frontier. The author is Head of the Department of History at Agnes Scott College, Decatur, Georgia.

POU, GENEVIEVE LONG. See: HOLDEN, GENEVIEVE.

PRICE, EUGENIA. *The Beloved Invader.* New York, Lippincott, 1965. 248p. $4.50.

Little did Anson Dodge, Jr., realize when he came to St. Simons Island, Georgia, after the Civil War that the Island and its people would play a dramatic part in his life. The author is a part time resident of St. Simons Island, Georgia.

RADFORD, RUBY LORRAINE. *Juliette Low, Girl Scout Founder.* Champaign, Ill., Garrard, 1965. 80p. $1.98.

An illustrated biography of Daisy Low, founder of the Girl Scouts, for Brownie-aged Scouts. The author is a resident of Augusta, Georgia.

RAYMOND, JOHN F. *The Marvelous March of Jean Francois.* Garden City, N. Y., Doubleday, 1965. 61p. $3.25.

The story of the adventures of the Emperor Napoleon's little drummer boy.

REDDICK, DEWITT CARTER. *Journalism and the School Paper.* Boston, D. C. Heath, 1963. Fifth Edition. 437p. $4.32.

A high school text used for many years throughout the country to instruct students interested in newspaper work. The author, a native of Savannah, Georgia, is Director of the School of Journalism, University of Texas, Austin, Texas.

REESE, GUSSIE, Comp. *This They Remembered.* Washington, Ga., Washington Publishing Co., 1965. 200p. $5.00.

This book was compiled and published by members of the Oglethorpe County Chapter No. 1292, United Daughters of the Confederacy of Lexington, Georgia, as their Centennial project.

RIDGE, GEORGE ROSS. *The Black Beatitudes.* Francestown, N. H., Golden Quill Press, 1964. 54p. $3.00.

An American song of Zarathustra written by the poet when he was seventeen. The author is a member of the English Department, Georgia State College, Atlanta, Georgia.

SANDERS, BETTY FOY. *Favorite Recipes of Georgia's First Lady.* Atlanta, Privately Printed, 1965. 25p. Apply.

A collection of favorite recipes that have been served at the Governor's mansion featuring Georgia products.

SEBBA, GREGOR. *Bibliographia Cartesiana, a Critical Guide to the Descartes Literature, 1800-1960.* New York, Heinman, 1965. 510p. $20.00.

Clarification of Descartes studies over their historical and topical range as well as a systematic analytical survey of Cartesian literature published during the last 160 years. Dr. Sebba is Professor of Liberal Arts, Graduate Institute of the Liberal Arts, Emory University, Atlanta, Georgia.

SHEETS, HERCHEL H. *Places Christ Hallowed.* Nashville, Tenn., The Upper Room, 1965. 125p. Apply.

This study describes some of the places connected with the earthly life and ministry of Jesus Christ. The author is a Pastor of the Methodist Church in Canton, Georgia.

SHUMATE, FRANCES. *From My Window.* New York, Vantage, 1965. 78p. $2.50.
A collection of poetry on nature, mankind, faith, freedom, and peace. The author lives in Atlanta, Georgia.

SIMMS, HOYT P. *Some Answers and Reasons.* Valdosta, Ga., Southern Stationery and Printing Co., 1965. 32p. $0.30.
A study of the basic tenets of the Primitive Baptist faith. Elder Simms is a resident of Decatur, Georgia.

SNELLING, LAURENCE. *The Return of Lance Tennis.* New York, Holt, 1965. 189p. $4.50.
The story of a young man who pursues a life of irresponsibility and inertia while appearing to be an industrious and dedicated artist. The author is a native of Brunswick, Georgia.

SPALDING, HUGHES. *The Spalding Family.* Atlanta, Privately Printed, 1965. Volume Two. 291p. Apply.
A history of how the pioneer Catholic Spalding family in America originated in Maryland and spread to Kentucky, Georgia, and other states in the years 1658 to 1965. The author is a resident of Atlanta, Georgia.

SPRING, SAMUEL. *Metal Cleaning.* New York, Reinhold, 1963. 234p. $9.75.
This study is concerned with the best and most economic methods to remove soil and grime from the surface of metals. The author is Vice President and Technical Director of Oxford Chemical Corporation, Atlanta, Georgia.

STEVENS, MILDRED TAYLOR. *Family Letters and Reminiscences.* Macon, Ga., Southern Press, 1961. 395p. $10.00.
A collection of letters, photographs, newspaper clippings, and sketches of the author's family. Mrs. Stevens lives in Macon, Georgia.

STIRLING, NORA B. *Who Wrote the Classics?* New York, John Day, 1965. 250p. $4.95.
Discusses the lives, personalities, and styles of ten classics, including Shakespeare, Jane Austin, Edgar Allan Poe, Charles Dickens, the Brontës, Mark Twain and others. The author is a native of Atlanta, Georgia.

TIMBERLAKE, RICHARD HENRY, JR. *Money, Banking, and Central Banking.* New York, Harper, 1965. 352p. $6.95.
This study presents the logic of monetary and banking theories and gives enough historical background to clarify the framework of contemporary monetary and banking institutions. The author is Professor of Finance at the University of Georgia.

WAGNON, DANIEL SYDNEY. *Israel and the Lord's Return*. Macon, Ga., Southern Press, 1963. 203p. Apply.

This book examines the fate of Israel in the light of Scriptural teachings as revealed in God's Holy Word. The author is a resident of Macon, Georgia.

WARREN, JAMES. *Altars and Destinations*. Atlanta, Privately Printed, 1964. 25p. Apply.

A collection of twenty poems about God.

WARREN, JAMES. *Trembling Still for Troy*. Atlanta, Privately Printed, 1965. 30p. Apply.

Poems based on Grecian themes by the Head of the Department of English, The Lovett School, Atlanta, Georgia.

WARREN, MARY BONDURANT, ed. *1800 Census of Oglethorpe County, Georgia*. Athens, Privately Printed, 1965. $2.25. Mimeographed.

The only extant census of 1800 within the State of Georgia; all others were destroyed during the War of 1812. Mrs. Warren lives at 927 Hill Street, Athens, Georgia.

WEBB, LESTER A. *Captain Alden Partridge and the United States Military Academy*. Northport, Ala., American Southern Publishing Co., 1965. 250p. $7.50.

This study exposes the cruel injustice done Captain Partridge, the true "Father of West Point." The author, a retired army colonel, resides in Oglethorpe County, Georgia.

WELLS, DAVID F. and DAVIS, GERALD. *Readings in Modern European History*. Dubuque, Iowa. William C. Brown, 1965. 445p. $5.75.

A compilation of some of the basic writings of the great intellects of all times who have influenced the course of history in Europe since 1660. The authors are Associate Professors of History at Georgia State College, Atlanta, Georgia.

WHEELER, RAYMOND. *Earth Moods Under the Stars*. East Point, Ga., Lettercraft Press, 1965. 68p. $1.50.

A collection of verse that explores the beauty in timeless subjects of nature, nostalgia, love, and death. The author resides in Atlanta, Georgia.

WHITE, JANE F. *Teaching Typewriting*. Portland, Maine, J. Weston Walch, 1964. 170p. Apply.

This illustrated study gives many current methods and teaching procedures in the area of typewriting. The author is a member of the faculty of the Division of Business, Georgia Southern College, Statesboro, Georgia.

WIGGINS, ROBERT ALONZO. *Ambrose Bierce*. Minneapolis, University of Minnesota Press, 1964. 48p. Paper, $0.65.
A critical appraisal of Bierce with biographical and bibliographical information included.

WIGGINS, ROBERT ALONZO. *Mark Twain: Jackleg Novelist*. Seattle, University of Washington Press, 1964. 141p. $5.00.
Twain's artistic decline has been variously explained and excused but Wiggins refuses to praise a bad novel merely because it was written by Mark Twain. The author is a native of Columbus, Georgia.

WILKINSON, STANNYE. *Our Town, Franklin, Georgia*. Franklin, Ga., Privately Printed, 1965. 48p. Paper, $2.00.
A brief illustrated history of the town and residents of Franklin, the county seat of Heard County, Georgia. The author lives in Franklin, Georgia.

WILLIAMS, NELLIE LOWMAN. *Sunset Glory*. Atlanta, Privately Printed, 1964. 46p. Apply.
A pot pourri of poetry. The author is a resident of Atlanta, Georgia.

WILLIAMS, VINNIE. *I Resign You, Stallion*. New York, Viking, 1965. 288p. $4.95.
A story of horses and men in a horse-loving Southern community. The author is a resident of Thomson, Georgia.

WINDHAM, DONALD. *Two People*. New York, Coward-McCann, 1965. 252p. $4.95.
Although the relationship between an American businessman and a young Italian is unconventional, its effect on each is important enough to override the immoral aspects. The author is a native of Atlanta, Georgia.

WOOD, VIRGINIA S. *1805 Georgia Land Lottery*. Cambridge, Mass., Greenwood Press, 1964. 393p. $8.95.
Transcribed and indexed by Virginia S. Wood and Ralph V. Wood. The body of this book consists of a transcription of all data in the original 1805 Land Lottery manuscript, which is located at the Georgia Department of Archives and History in Atlanta, Georgia. Mrs. Wood, a native of Georgia, resides in Cambridge, Massachusetts.

WRIGHT, DAVID MCCORD. *Growth and Economy; Principles of Economics*. New York, Scribners, 1964. 398p. Paper, $5.25.
This text presents a comprehensive introduction to the underlying principles of our economic system and the factors important to its growth and maintenance in a changing world. Dr. Wright is Professor of Economics and Director, Georgia Institute of Economic Understanding at the University of Georgia.

WRIGHT, NATHALIA. *American Novelist in Italy; the Discoverers: Alston to James*. Philadelphia, University of Pennsylvania Press, 1965. 288p. $6.50.

A study of the effect which traveling in Italy had on thirteen American authors who wrote during the years, 1804-1870. The author, a native of Athens, Georgia, is a Professor of English at the University of Tennessee, Knoxville, Tennessee.

WYNES, CHARLES E., ed. *The Negro in the South Since 1865*. University, Ala., University of Alabama Press, 1965. 252p. $6.95.

A collection of selected essays in American Negro history. The editor is a member of the History Department at the University of Georgia.

YERBY, FRANK. *An Odor of Sanctity*. New York, Dial, 1965. 398p. $6.95.

Story of Spain in the 10th century that tells of a young Visigoth noble named Alaric who eventually finds his place in history as San Alarico, Christian saint of Seville. The author is a native of Augusta, Georgia.

Index

Aaron, Ira E., 71, 149
Abbot, William Wright, 129
Abercrombie, Thomas Franklin, 43
Abernethy, Don, 182
Abraham, Joseph L., 17, 113
Adams, Carsbie Clifton, 1, 113, 187
Adams, J. C., 187, 219
Adams, Marion, 129
Aden, John M., 237
Adkins, Ester Pool, 248
Aiken, Conrad Potter, 1, 2, 29, 43, 67, 97, 114, 149, 150, 173, 188, 203, 204, 219, 220, 237
Airev, Joseph, 130
Alciatore, Jules C., 43, 53
Alexander, Henry Aaron, 67
Alexander, John A., 204
Alexander, Thomas B., 17
Allen, Catherine Louise, 83
Allen, Charles Livingstone, 18, 29, 53, 54, 68, 97, 98, 114, 130, 173, 188, 204, 220, 238
Allen, Ellen Gordon, 204
Allen, Rossie C., 54
Allums, John F., 14, 63, 125, 199
Altizer, Thomas J. J., 220, 238
Anderson, C. David, 88
Anderson C. Eugene, 238
Anderson, Charles Robert, 238
Anderson, Thomas, 29
Anderson, Verna Harrison, 220
Andrews, Eliza Frances, 150
Andrews, Marshall, 2
Andrews, P. C., 204
Asher, Erna Fromme, 44
Askew, J. Thomas, 165
Atkinson, Butler M., Jr., 150
Aultman, Ruth W., 11
Austin, Aurelia, 114, 220
Averitt, Jack Nelson, 238
Axley, Lowry, 150

Baine, Rodney M., 238
Baker, Woolford Bales, 83
Barber, Sadie Pike, 84
Barfield, Louise Calhoun, 174
Barker, Lillian, 18
Barnett, Albert Edward, 114
Barragan, Maude, 54
Barrow, Elfrida De Renne, 84
Bartlett, Elizabeth, 150
Bartlett, Paul, 150

Bayne, Charles J., 2
Bealor, Alex W., III, 98
Beard, Donald E., 44
Beardslee, William A., 93
Beatty, Frederika, 238
Beaumont, Charles A., 174, 239
Beeson, Leola Selman, 84
Bell, Alice, 44
Bell, Earl Leaston, 150
Bell, Laura Palmer, 84
Bell, Lois Hendrix, 239
Bell, Malcolm, Jr., 151
Benfield, Lowell Vance, 18, 151
Bensen, Walter, 239
Benson, Berry, 188
Benton, Bonnie Higdon, 68
Bernd, Joseph L., 151
Biggers, Dorothy L., 188
Birdsong, George L. F., 68
Bisher, Furman, 188
Bixler, Harold Hench, 2, 30
Black, Eugene Robert, 151, 188
Black, John Logan, 174
Blackford, Launcelot Minor, 54
Blackshear, Perry Lynnfield, 68
Blackstock, Walter, Jr., 2, 44, 68, 151
Blackstone, William T., 220, 239
Blair, Emil, 220
Blake, William Morgan, 30
Blankenship, George H., 98
Bledsoe, Joseph Cullie, 71, 174
Blicksilver, Jack, 151, 152
Bliss, Alice, 114, 152
Bloch, Charles J., 114
Boal, Bobby Snow, 114
Boggus, Homer Allen, 174
Boland, Frank Kells, Sr., 2
Boles, Paul Darcy, 54, 84, 98, 114
Bonner, James Calvin, 115, 130, 174, 221
Bornhauser, Fred, 201
Boskoff, Alvin, 239
Bourne, Geoffrey Howard, 152
Bovee, Arthur Gibbon, 54
Bowdoin, Mary H., 152
Bowen, Eliza A., 2
Bowen, John McGowan, 204
Bowen, Robert A., 115
Bowers, Edgar, 84
Bowne, Elizabeth, 174
Boyce, Kathryn, 98
Boykin, Mrs. B. M., 75

Boylston, Elsie Reid, 44
Bragg, Lillian Chaplin, 7, 98, 225
Bramblett, Agnes Cochran, 54
Branch, Joseph Melton, 153
Brandeis, Donald, 175, 188
Brannan, Donie Leone, 115
Brannen, John R., 18
Brawner, Nellie Barksdale, 115
Bray, Colquitt C., 68
Bray, Vivian L., 115
Breland, Lydia Foster, 153
Bridges, F. J., 206
Britton, Beverly, 74
Broach, Claude U., 18
Brohoff, John R., 130
Broiles, Roland David, 239
Brookes, Stella Brewer, 2
Brooks, Robert Preston, 30, 84, 115
Brougher, William E., 239
Brown, Calvin Smith, 30, 44, 70, 84
Brown, Enoch, 153
Brown, Inez Marguerite, 68
Brown, Marel, 2, 44, 98
Brown, Robert Henry, 84
Brown, Robert Kevin, 175, 240
Brown, Wendell H., 68
Brunetti, George, 68
Bryan, Dora, 69
Bryan, Ferrebee Catherine, 68
Bryan, Mary Givens, 84, 98, 153, 188
Bryan, Thomas Conn, 44
Bryant, Allen, 18, 153
Buckingham, Walter Samuel, 175
Bugg, Mary Cobb. See Cobb, Mary
Bumgartner, Louis E., 221
Bunting, James Whitney, 44, 55
Burch, Robert, 205, 221, 240
Burge, Dolly Lunt, 189
Burgess, Jackson, 98
Burkett, William R., Jr., 240
Burleigh, Thomas D., 38
Burney, Sarah Joe H., 153
Burns, Robert W., 205
Bushee, James, Jr., 45
Byers, Edna Hanley, 205

Cade, John Brother, 240
Caldwell, Erskine, 3, 18, 30, 45, 55, 69, 85, 99, 115, 130, 153, 175, 189, 205, 221, 240
Calhoun, Calfrey C., 154
Callaway, Timothy Walton, 69
Campbell, Alice Ormond, 3, 18
Campbell, Claude A., 137
Campbell, Marie, 3
Campbell, William T., 45
Candler, Charles Howard, 3
Cannon, William Ragsdale, 19, 154, 205
Cantey, Robert C., 99

Carlton, William Marion, 175
Carnahan, David Hobart, 54
Carney, H. Stanton, 240
Carr, James McLeod, 115, 175
Carr, Julian Shakespeare, 221
Carrington, John Wesley, 206
Carroll, George Franklin, 115
Carter, Thomas L., Jr., 154
Carter, Virginia L., 85
Cartledge, Groves Harrison, 175
Cartledge, Samuel Antoine, 154, 189
Cash, Grace, 3, 30, 131
Cason, Durward Veazey, 131
Cate, Margaret Davis, 69
Cauthen, Kenneth, 189
Cay, John Eugene, 206
Caylor, John, 55, 116, 131
Center, Stella Stewart, 45
Chambliss, Rollin, 55
Champion, John M., 131, 206
Chandos, Dane, 3
Chapman, James E., 131
Chapman, Paul Wilbur, 3, 4, 45
Charles, A. Aldo, 99, 240
Cheatham, Elliott Evans, 99
Cheney, Brainard, 131
Childers, James Saxon, 154, 212, 221, 222
Chivers, Thomas Holley, 55
Christian, Mary, 55
Christopher, Thomas Wildon, 69, 104, 155
Church, Lillian, 222
Clark, Faye, 45
Clark, Frank G., 189
Clark, John G., 116
Clay, Lucius DuBignon, 4
Cleckley, Hervey M., 19, 69, 99, 109, 240
Clinkscales, Bertie H., 131
Clute, Robert Eugene, 206
Cobb, Mary, 155
Cobb, Tyrus Raymond, 175
Cochran, Jean D., 241
Cochran, Leonard H., 99
Codington, Arthur, 31
Coleman, Kenneth, 116, 155, 185
Coleman, Lonnie. See Coleman, William Lawrence
Coleman, William Lawrence, 19, 31, 46, 69, 116, 131
Collings, Henrietta, 69
Collins, Thomas, 85
Colquitt, Joseph C., 85
Comer, David B., III, 189
Conrad, Jack Randolph, 116
Conway, Hobart McKinley, Jr., 206
Cooper, Ben Green, 241
Cooper, Bernice L., 149
Cooper, George W., 4
Cooper, James B., 4

Cooper, J. Wesley, 99, 176
Cope, Channing, 4
Copeland, Edna Arnold, 4
Corder, Loyd, 70
Corley, Florence Fleming, 176
Cotsakis, Roxane, 31
Cottle, Charles Sidney, 56, 132
Coulborn, William A. L., 19
Coulter, Ellis Merton, 5, 19, 70, 85, 116, 132, 155, 176, 206, 222, 241
Covey, Elizabeth D., 100
Covey, Fred, 100
Crabbe, Kenneth Charles, 150
Craig, Georgia. See Gaddis, Peggy
Cranford, Mary Poole, 31, 56
Crawford, Lucille Logan, 145
Cullen, John B., 176
Cussler, Margaret, 31
Cuttino, George Peddy, 70

Dabney, Eleanor Hoyt, 161
Dameron, Mrs. W. C., 70
Daniel, Mary Helen, 242
Daniels, Mose, 5
Darden, Gordon Wallace, 242
Daughtry, Nancy Margaret G., 242
Davidson, William H., 242
Davies, Geneva, 31, 153, 190
Davis, Gerald, 254
Davis, Maggie H., 116, 207
Davis, Olive Bell, 132, 242
Davis, Wiley H., 104
Davis, William Columbus, 19, 20
Davis, William E., 85
Day, Enid, 20
DeBaillou, Clemens, 176
DeGive, Mary L., 31
Demetre, Margaret, 132
Dern, Mrs. John Sherman. See Gaddis, Peggy
Dern, Peggy. See Gaddis, Peggy
DeSosa, Margaret Ohlman, 20
Dewey, Maybelle Jones, 31
Dickey, James, 190, 222, 242
Dickson, Edward, 155
Dinsmore, Wayne, 45
Dixon, Sara Robertson, 127
Dobbs, Wayne, 242
Dodd, Ed, 70
Dodd, Hubert, 86
Dodd, Robert L., 56
Dodson, Samuel Kendrick, 155
Dokos, Cosmas J., 86
Donahue, Cheney Bradshaw, 86
Donaldson, George Warren, 32
Doughtie, Beatrice Mackey, 100, 190
Dowell, Spright, 32, 117
Drake, Julian R., 32

Drewry, John Eldridge, 5, 20, 32, 46, 56, 70, 86, 100, 177, 132, 155, 177, 190, 207
Dumas, Marie Frances, 57, 156, 223
Duncan, Amon O., 5
Duncan, John A., 132
Duncan, Pope Alexander, 243
Dunn, C. W., 69
Dunson, Eleanor Adams, 156
Duren, James A., 156
Dyer, John Perry, 20
Dykes, Nobie Beall, 100

Edge, Findley Bartow, 132, 133, 207
Edge, Sarah Simms, 70
Edmonds, Richard W., 86
Edwards, H. Griffin, 56
Edwards, Harry Stillwell, 223
Edwards, Lillie Trice, 32
Ehlers, Carrol W., 156
Eidson, John Olin, 20
Elliot, Charles Newton, 6, 20, 46, 56
Ellis, A. L., 177
Ellis, Elmo I., 165
Elton, Maude Lay, 32
Embry, Eloise Williams, 133
English, Mildred E., 133
English, Thomas H., 46
Equen, Murdock, 100
Ethridge, Willie Snow, 6, 32, 86, 117, 133, 190, 223, 243
Etkin, Anne Little, 177
Eubanks, John Evans, 20
Evans, Esther, 223
Evans, Jewell R., 207
Evans, Trevor, 133
Everett, Edwin Mallard, 57, 70, 156, 223
Everhardt, Powell, 117

Farber, Evan Ira, 100
Faulk, Lanette, 133
Fay, Eliot Gilbert, 46, 71
Fenster, Samuel Benjamin, 71
Fersen, Nicholas, 57
Fickett, Amanda Schielke, 243
Finch, Mildred Austin, 86. See also Austin, Aurelia
Fish, Tallu Brinson Jones, 223
Fitch, Frank W., Jr., 4
Flanders, Bertram Holland, 71, 156, 191
Fleming, Berry, 6, 33, 46, 101, 156
Floyd, Woodrow W., 191
Folger, John K., 86
Folsom, Marion B., 207
Forbes, William Stanton, 71, 177
Force, Dewey G., 135
Ford, Elizabeth Austin, 156, 177
Ford, Elizabeth M., 117

Ford, Marcia, 46, 57. *See also* Radford, Ruby Lorraine
Ford, William Herschel, 207, 208, 223, 243
Fort, John, 21
Fort, Marie Johnson, 33
Fort, Marion Kirkland, 191
Fort, Tomlinson, 21, 157
Foster, Edith, 33
Foster, Marian Curtis, 21, 33, 47, 57, 71, 101
Foster, Marian Curtis. *See* Mariana
Foster, William Omer, Sr., 157
Fowler, Grady, 87
Frederick, Mary Barrington, 177
Frost, Connie Curtis, 117
Fry, Thomas A., Jr., 223
Frye, Roland Mushat, 157
Fuhrmann, Paul Traugott, 177
Fuller, Ellis Adams, 57

Gabrielsen, Bramwell W., 21
Gabrielsen, Milton, 21
Gaddis, Peggy, 6, 7, 21, 33, 47, 57, 58, 71, 87, 101, 117, 118, 134, 135, 157, 158, 177, 178, 179, 191, 192, 208, 209, 224, 243, 244
Gaillard, Peyre, 87
Gallaway, Marian, 244
Gann, Ernest Kellogg, 47
Garnett, Christine, 71
Garrett, Constance, 7
Garrett, Franklin M., 58
Garrison, Karl Claudius, 34, 71, 87, 135, 209, 224, 244
Garrison, Webb Black, 136
Gassman, McDill McCown, 34
Gates, James Edward, 119
Gaultney, Barbara F., 159, 245
Gholson, Juluis, 28
Gibboney, Charles H., 47
Gibson, Count Dillon, 101
Gibson, Frank Kenneth, 101
Gibson, Robert E., 87
Gildea, Florence, 87
Gilden, Bert, 245
Gilden, Katya, 245
Gilliam, Norris, Jr., 159
Gilman, Glenn. *See* Gilman, Glendell William
Gilman, Glendell William, 88
Gilmer, George Rockingham, 245
Ginn, D. Perry, 209
Ginsberg, Paul, 58
Glass, Lemuel Page, 159
Gnann, Pearl Rahn, 88
Goddard, John H., Jr., 192
Goddard, Thomas H., 192
Godfrey, Caroline Hardee, 88, 101
Godley, Margaret Walton, 7, 136, 225

Goglia, Mario J., 79
Goldgar, Bertrand A., 245
Golley, Frank B., 192
Goodyear, William E., 44
Gordon, Ambrose, Jr., 245
Gordon, Arthur, 8, 119
Gordon, Hugh Haralson, Jr., 58
Gosnell, Cullen Bryant, 21, 72, 88, 101
Govan, Gilbert E., 34, 88
Govan, Thomas Payne, 159
Graham, Lorah Harris, 8
Granade, Columbus, 192
Grant, Daniel T., 88
Grantham, Dewey W., 209, 245
Graves, Henry Lea, 210
Gray, John Stanley, 34, 58, 71
Gray, Macy Bishop, 102
Gray, Stephen W., 232
Green, Claud B., 102
Green, Donald Ross, 225
Green, Gardner Leland, 8
Green, James L., 246
Green, Thomas F., Jr., 102
Greene, Reynolds W., Jr., 210
Greenblatt, Robert B., 225
Greer, Michael, 246
Gregorie, Anne King, 193
Griffin, John, 94
Griffith, Louis T., 22
Grove, Dorothy Haverty, 22
Gutzke, Manford George, 88

Habersham, Anna Wylly, 193
Hall, James William, 159
Hall, Robert H., 104
Halliday, William Ross, 136
Ham, Tom, 47
Haman, James B., 201
Hambidge, Mary C., 246
Hammer, Jane Ross, 34
Hammock, Ted L., 101
Hanson, Wesley Turnell, Jr., 58
Hardin, L. S., 90
Hardman, Thomas Colquitt, 22
Hardwick, Richard, 246
Hargrett, Lester, 22
Hargrove, Clara Nell, 28
Harley, William McDonald, 102
Harper, Carl H., 102
Harris, Joel Chandler, 58, 102, 136, 246
Harris, Kathleen. *See* Humphries, Mrs. Adelaide
Harris, Lucien, Jr., 22, 83
Harris, Pierce, 34
Harris, Seale, 72
Harris, Walter Alexander, 159
Hart, Charles Randall, 159
Hart, John Fraser, 72

Hartridge, Walter C., 10
Harwell, Richard Barksdale, 8, 22, 47, 59, 72, 89, 102, 119, 136, 159, 179, 210, 225
Harwin, Brian. See Henderson, LeGrand
Hatcher, George, 193
Haverfield, William M., 160
Hawes, Lilla Mills, 47, 72, 85, 98, 103, 193
Hayes, John Alexander, 73
Hayes, Maude Miller, 193
Haygood, William Converse, 89
Haynes, Draughton Stith, 225
Hays, Thomas M., 193
Hebson, Verna Castleberry, 179
Heinsohn, Lillian Britt, 193
Heinz, Mamie W., 136
Henderson, LeGrand, 8, 35, 59, 89, 119, 160, 179, 194, 225
Henderson, Lillian, 160
Henderson, Lindsey P., 194
Henry, Inez, 89
Henson, Allen Lumpkin, 160
Henson, Jean, 8
Hervey, Harry, 9
Hewlett, John Henry, 22
Hicks, Alberta Kinard, 194, 246
Hicky, Daniel Whitehead, 23
Highfill, Robert David, 210
Hines, Nelle Womack, 119
Hinman, Dorothy, 89, 120
Hodges, Elizabeth Jamison, 225
Hodges, Lucille, 246
Hodgson, Hugh, 226
Hoffman, John Leon, 9
Holcomb, Walt, 23, 73
Holden, Genevieve, 48, 59, 89, 120, 179, 247
Holland, Lynwood Mathis, 9, 21, 23, 194, 226
Holleran, Cecil James, 35
Holley, Joseph Winthrop, 89
Hollingsworth, Clyde Dixon, 59
Holloman, Ann C., 194
Horkan, Nelle Irwin, 103
Hoskins, Robert N., 92
Houser, Harriet H., 73
Howard, Annie Hornady, 73
Howard, Willis E., 160
Howell, Willie P., 120
Hoyt, Margaret, 161
Hubbell, Raynor, 136
Hudson, Charles J., Jr., 23, 48
Huff, William Henry, 180
Humphries, Adelaide, 48, 49, 59, 73, 89, 90, 103, 120, 136, 137, 161, 180, 210, 194, 226 247
Hunter, Edward, 161
Hunter, Hall. See Marshall, Edison
Hurt, John Jeter, 120, 162, 195
Hurst, John Willis, 161, 210

Hutchens, Eleanor Newman, 247
Hutcheson, Christine Gore, 137
Hutcheson, George Lewis, 27, 200
Hutchings, Florence Sheaver, 103
Huxford, Folks, 73
Hyman, Mac, 60, 247

Inglesby, Charlotte, 120
Isley, Doris Natelle, 90

Jackson, Esther Merle, 247
Jacob, Peyton, 73
Jacobs, Thornwell, 23, 73
James, Ava Leach, 120, 121
Janus, Sydney Q., 137
Jeffcoat, Gladys Neill, 121
Jeffcoat, Raleigh, 137
Jenkins, Sara Lucille, 9, 23, 35, 49
Jenkins, William Franklin, 74
Jessups, Richard, 74, 90, 103, 121, 180, 226
Jones, Billy Walker, 133, 195, 248
Jones, Carter Brooke, 137
Jones, Charles Colcock, Jr., 248
Jones, Clayton, 24
Jones, Dorothy Holder, 137
Jones, George Fenwick, 211
Jones, George H., 167
Jones, Houston G., 90
Jones, Mary Sharpe, 162
Jones, R. N., 227
Jones, Ray G., Jr., 137
Jones, Robert Tyre, Jr., 162
Jones, Wilbur Devereux, 104, 121, 162, 227
Jones, William Powell, 90
Johnson, E. Ashley, 121
Johnson, Harold L., 103, 137, 226
Johnson, James A., Jr., 226
Johnson, Malcolm, 23
Johnston, Dorothy F., 248
Johnston, Edith Duncan, 9
Jordan, Arna R., 60
Jordan, Gail, pseud. See Gaddis, Peggy
Jordan, Gerald Ray, 24, 74, 121, 138, 162, 195, 211, 227
Joslin, G. Stanley, 195
Julian, Allen Phelps, 227

Kaiser, Frances E., 248
Kane, Harnett, 89
Kaye, Jack, 9
Kearns, William H., Jr., 74
Keats, John, 138, 211, 248
Keeler, Clyde Edgar, 90, 162
Keeler, O. B., 49
Keith, Edmond D., 180, 227
Kelley, Evelyn Ownes, 104
Kelly, George Lombard, 24, 35, 74
Kennedy, Harvey J., 104

Kennedy, Joseph A., 49
Key, William O., 121
Keyes, Kenneth S., Jr., 24
Kiefer, Adolph, 21
Kiker, Douglas, 104, 138
Kilbride, J. B., 183
Killens, John O., 60
Killian, Lewis, 248
Kilpatrick, William Heard, 24
Kimball, Garnet Davies, 90, 121, 138
King, Frank P., 90
King, George Harris, 211
King, John H., 138
King, Martin Luther, 122, 211, 227
King, Spencer Bidwell, Jr., 122, 211, 227, 248
Kirby, Ula, 228
Kirkland, Willie Schuman, 162
Kirkpatrick, Dow, 228
Knapp, Mary Gibson, 180
Knight, Henry, 91
Knight, Willys R., 139
Knox, James, 74
Kobs, Ruth Lowry, 228
Koger, Jim, 168
Kytle, Elizabeth, 122

Lamar, Dolly Blount, 35
Lamkin, Augustus F., 24
Lancaster, Lane W., 72, 101
Lance, Thomas Jackson, 195
Lanoue, Fred, 228
Lantz, J. Edward, 139
Lattimore, Ralston B., 228
Lawrence, Alexander A., 36, 104, 180, 212
Lawrence, Daisy Gordon, 122
Lawrence, Elizabeth, 180
Lawrence, John Benjamin, 74, 75, 122, 181
Lawton, Edward P., 211, 249
Leckie, George G., 60
LeConte, Joseph, 162
Ledbetter, Elizabeth O'Connor, 9
Lee, Edna L. Mooney, 10, 36, 49
Lee, Grace, 139
Lee, Harry, 36
LeGrand. *See* Henderson, LeGrand
Leher, Robert Nathaniel, 122
Lehrman, Edgar H., 181
Lemly, James Hutton, 60, 91, 139, 181
Leonard, George B., Jr., 123, 139
Lerche, Charles Olsen, Jr., 91, 123
Leverett, E. Freeman, 104
Lewis, John Ransom, 212, 228
Lightle, Burnette, 10
Lincoln, Charles Eric, 181
Lindsay, Perry, pseud. *See* Gaddis, Peggy
Lipscomb, Lamar Rutherford, 104
Little, Mrs. James. *See* Sibley, Celestine

Livingwood, James W., 34, 88
Lobsenz, Amelia Freitag, 24
Lochridge, Betsy Hopkins, 91
Loftis, John Clyde, 249
Lomax, Louis E., 181, 195, 212
Long, Margaret, 10, 49
Long, Nathaniel Guy, 49, 181
Longstreet, Augustus Baldwin, 75, 123, 139
Longstreet, James, 163
Lott, Robert E., 212
Love, Albert, 212, 221, 222
Lovegren, Alta Lee, 212
Lowman, Mrs. George S., 75
Lowance, Kathleen, 36
Lumpkin, Grace, 228
Lunceford, Alvin Mell, 91
Luper, Harold Lee, 228
Lyde, Marilyn Jones, 163
Lyle, Guy Redvers, 181, 213

McAllister, Elva Sinclair, 36, 50
McCarthy, David, 163
McClain, Roy O., 105, 181
McClung, Barbara Adair, 60
McCullar, Bernice, 169
McCullers, Carson, 25, 75, 123, 139, 182, 229
McCumber, W. E., 105
McDaniel, Earl Wadsworth, 229
McDonald, Ellis Atkisson, 163
McFarlane, Philip James, 163
McGee, John Llewllyn, 163
McGehee, Maud, 195
McGill, Ralph Emerson, 10, 60, 139, 213
McGinty, C. Lamar, 140
McGowan, Gordon, 163
McGrath, Frances, 182
McKinney, Charles D., Sr., 60
McLarty, Nancy, 195
McLemore, Henry, 50
McMahan, Chalmers A., 10
McMenemy, Jim, 249
McMurray, J. May, 25
McPherson, Nenien C., Jr., 140
McPherson, Robert Grier, 140, 196
McRae, Kevin, 75
McVaugh, Rogers, 39

Mackay, Robert, 10
Macon, Alethia Jane, 105, 249
Maholick, Leonard T., 232
Major, James Russell, 164
Mallard, Mary Jones
Malone, Eva Earnshaw, 75
Malone, Henry Thompson, 91, 182
Maloof, Louis J., 10, 75
Mann, Carolyn Becknell, 249
Mann, Harold Wilson, 249

Mann, Lucille Abbey, 61
Mariana, 25, 196, 249. See Foster, Marian Curtis
Marshall, Edison, 11, 25, 36, 50, 61, 91, 92, 105, 123, 140, 164, 182, 196, 213, 229
Marshall, George Octavius, Jr., 229
Marshall, John David, 164, 182, 250
Martin, Charles, 182
Martin, Edwin Thomas, 36
Martin, Harold H., 92, 164
Martin, Milward Wyatt, 196
Martin, Sidney Walter, 11
Martof, Bernard S., 92
Mason, David E., 140
Mason, Lucy Randolph, 50
Massee, J. C., 213
Mathews, Joseph James, 123
Mathews, Marcia M., 229
Mauelshagen, Carl, 196
Maxwell, Edna Stephens, 11
Maxwell, Gilbert, 11, 229
Maxwell, James Quillian, 11
Maxwell, Sue, 11
Maxwell, William Bulloch, 250
Maynard, Louise, 11
Meade, Richard H., 30
Meadows, John Cassius, 37, 61
Meadows, Thomas Burton, 123
Means, Alexander, 12
Mebane, John, 213, 250
Mell, Edward Baker, 61
Menaboni, Athos, 12
Menaboni, Sara, 12
Melton, James, 61
Merucci, Angelo, 230
Miller, Arthur Selwyn, 124
Miller, Harold, 119
Miller, Julian Howell, 182
Miller, Paul W., 12
Millis, Walter, 25
Mills, Charles, 37
Mitchell, Addie Stokes, 12
Mitchell, Margaret, 61, 183
Mitchell, Stephens, 183
Mize, Jessie Julia, 92
Mize, Leila Ritchie, 92
Mobley, Major D., 6, 92
Monsees, Casey F., 92
Montgomery, Horace, 12, 124, 140, 162, 230
Montgomery, James Stuart, 12
Montgomery, Marion, 164, 196, 230, 250
Moore, Arthur James, 37, 50, 213
Moore, Edith Wyatt, 140
Moore, Edwin, 230
Moore, Harriet Mahaffey, 92
Moore, Mavis Garey, 25, 50
Moore, Rayburn S., 213

Moore, Walter Lane, 25, 250
Moore, William Frank, 140
Morehouse, Ward, 12, 50
Morenus, Constance Gay, 51
Morgan, Beatrice Payne, 105
Morgan, Mary Frances, 37
Morris, Joe Lawrence, 75, 76
Morris, Joseph Scott, Jr., 61, 164, 214, 230
Mosteller, James D., 61
Murphey, Arthur G., Jr., 105
Muse, Helen E., 196
Myers, T. Cecil, 214, 250

Nadler, Charles Elihu, 105, 106
Neely, Frank Henry, 250
Neff, Lawrence Wilson, 50, 183
Nelson, Jack, 214
Newton, Charlotte, 251
Newton, Louie DeVotie, 106, 141
Nicholson, Mrs. Madison G., 106
Nisbet, James Cooper, 214
Norris, Jack Clayton, 62
Norris, Robert A., 37

O'Callaghan, Golda Larkin, 11
O'Connor, Mary Flannery, 37, 76, 164, 183, 197, 251
Odum, Eugene Pleasants, 62, 141
Odum, Howard T., 141
Odum, Howard Washington, 26, 230
Odum, John D., 164
Odum, Mamie Ozburn, 62
Ogburn, Charles, Jr., 214
Ogburn, Charlton, Sr., 76, 141
Ogburn, Charlton, Jr., 141, 197, 251
Ogburn, Dorothy S., 76, 197, 214
Ogburn, William Fielding, 76
O'Hara, Adine L., 146
Oliphant, Joyce, 230
Oliver, Virginia Katherine, 106, 124
Olney, Clarke, 51
O'Quinn, Allen. See Quinter, Al
Orr, Clyde, Jr., 141, 142
Orr, Dorothy, 12
Osborn, Stellanova, 13, 62, 76, 106
Osterhout, Isa Lloyd, 27, 200
Outlaw, Nell Warren, 13, 37, 106
Outler, Albert Cook, 62, 76, 77
Ozment, Robert V., 197, 214, 251

Paddock, Laura Hutchins, 142
Palmer, Charles F., 77
Paranka, Stephen, 142
Park, Hugh, 62
Parks, Aileen Wells, 13, 38, 62, 124, 197, 214, 251
Parks, Edd Winfield, 13, 26, 38, 51, 77, 106, 183, 197, 215, 230, 231, 251

Parks, Joseph Howard, 197
Parthemos, George Steven, 197
Patten, Maxie Sneed, 13
Paulk, William E., Jr., 77, 92
Peeples, Edwin Augustus, Jr., 165
Pendley, Evelyn Hoge, 62
Pepper, Evelyn Hoge, 62
Pepper, Henry C., 77
Perkerson, Medora Field, 38
Perry, Edmund, 142
Peters, Harold Seymour, 38
Pfuetze, Paul E., 62
Phillips, Allen A., 183
Phillips, Aurelia Heath, 124
Phillips, Ulrich Bonnell, 142
Phoenix, Opal Carmichael, 215
Pidcock, Jane Rainaud, 215
Pierce, Alfred Mann, 26, 107
Pierce, Hubbell, 183
Pinholster, Garland F., 165, 198, 242
Plaginos, Jane Kent, 124
Poats, Rutherford Mell, 63
Pollock, Eileen, 165
Pollock, Robert Mason, 165
Pope, Clifford Hillhouse, 92, 106, 183
Pope, Edwin, 77, 165
Posey, Walter Brownlow, 51, 107, 251
Posner, Jack, 93
Pou, Genevieve Long. *See* Holden, Genevieve
Pound, Jerome B., 13
Pound, Merritt Bloodworth, 14, 26, 38, 63, 124, 125, 165, 198, 199
Preston, Janet Newman, 231
Price, Eugenia, 252
Proctor, John Howard, 198
Puckett, James, 26
Purdy, Ken, 61
Putnam, Peter, 39
Pyron, Joseph H., 39

Quattlebaum, Julian K., 125
Quattlebaum, M. M., 26
Quinter, Al, 77

Radford, Ruby Lorraine, 78, 93, 107, 125, 142, 165, 184, 198, 215, 231, 252. *See also* Ford, Marcia
Raiford, Morgan, 198
Range, Willard, 39, 63, 142, 184
Rankin, Robert S., 72, 101
Raymond, John F., 252
Reagan, Agnes Lytton, 125
Rece, Ellis Heber, 93
Reddick, DeWitt Carter, 252
Redfearn, Daniel H., 78
Reece, Byron Herbert, 13, 14, 39, 78
Reese, Gussie, 252

Reeves, Jewell B., 215
Reinsch, J. Leonard, 165
Respess, John L., Jr., 39
Rice, Thaddeus Brockett, 184
Ridge, George Ross, 143, 184, 252
Rigdon, Louis T., 198
Rittenhouse, William H., Jr., 125
Roberts, Guy, 231
Roddenberry, Robert S., Jr., 166
Rogers, Dorothy, 125
Rogers, Ernest, 14, 93
Rogers, Rachael Emmeline, 78
Rogers, Wallace, 83
Roton, Ouida Wade, 166
Rowden, Majorie, 215
Rowland, Arthur Ray, 215
Rubin, Larry, 216
Ruchti, Helen Holmes, 143
Rusk, Dean, 198, 215
Ruskin, Gertrude McDaris, 231
Ruth, Claire Merritt, 143
Rutherford, Vada, 26
Rutland, Eva, 231

Sanders, Betty Foy, 252
Saye, Albert Berry, 14, 38, 63, 107, 124, 125, 143, 198, 199, 216
Schoeck, Helmut, 143, 146, 166, 231
Schwartz, David Joseph, 143, 166
Scofield, Dorothy, 107
Scott, Harold George, 93
Scott, Robert Lee, Jr., 63, 78, 108, 143, 199
Scott, Thurman Thomas, 184
Scott, William G., 144
Screven, Patricia, 144
Scruggs, Anderson M., 27
Scudder, C. W., 199
Sears, William, 26, 51, 93
Sebba, Gregor, 78, 252
Seigler, O. M., 231
Sell, Edward Scott, 14, 126, 185
Sentell, Perry, Jr., 143
Seydell, Mildred, 199
Shadgett, Olive Hall, 231
Shapiro, David, 232
Sharkey, Robert P., 232
Sheets, Herschel H., 252
Sherrod, Robert Lee, 63, 64
Shields, Larry, 144
Shuler, Edward Leander, 64
Shulman, Arnold, 104
Shultz, Gladys Denny, 122
Shumate, Frances, 253
Sibley, Celestine, 126, 216, 232
Simmons, Ernest P., 2
Simms, Hoyt P., 253
Skandalakis, John E., 232
Slappey, Pansy Aiken, 199

Slate, Sam J., 216
Slayden, Thelma Thompson, 216
Smith, Berthenia Crocker, 199
Smith, Clarence Jay, Jr., 93, 126, 199
Smith, Daisy Frances Daves, 108
Smith, Herbert Orlando, 200
Smith, Howard Ross, 126, 185
Smith, James Harry, 38
Smith, Lillian Eugenia, 14, 64, 78, 144, 200, 232
Smith, Nannette Carter, 27, 185
Smith, Sarah Quinn, 200
Smith, Virginia Field, 94
Snelling, Laurence, 253
Sorrel, Gilbert Moxley, 126
Spalding, Hughes, 232, 253
Sparks, Lamar, 233
Spillman, Ralph R., 189
Spring, Samuel, 253
Stacy, James, 39
Stampolis, Anthony, 144
Standard, Diffee William, 64
Stanley, Bess Dorsey, 216
Starr, Richard F., 216
Steedman, Marguerite, 200
Steele, Harold Clyde, 78
Stegeman, John F., 233
Stelling, Mary Ellen, 126
Stephens, John C., Jr., 145
Stephens, John Calhoun, 126
Stephens, Leila, 94
Stephenson, Diane D., 100
Stevens, Mildred Taylor, 253
Stevens, Patrick M., 145
Stevenson, Elizabeth, 14, 94, 127, 185
Stevenson, Mary B., 94, 167
Steward, Davenport, 14, 40, 51, 64, 94, 108, 127, 145
Stirling, Nora B., 127, 167, 217, 253
Stoffel, Joseph F., 233
Stokes, Mack B., 108, 200, 233
Stokes, Thomas L., 27
Stover, Mary, 145
Strauss, Walter A., 108
Strobel, Philip A., 64
Stuckey, H. P., 27
Sturgess, Albert Henley, 175
Suddeth, Ruth Elgin, 27, 51, 200
Sugg, Redding Stancil, Jr., 127, 145, 167
Suggs, Louise, 51, 167
Surrency, Erwin Campbell, 94, 167
Swanson, Ernst, 94
Sweigert, Ray Leslie, 79
Sydnor Charles Sackett, 40
Sylvester C. Doughty, 200

Tailfer Patrick, 167
Talmage, Franklin C., 185
Talmadge, Herman Eugene, 79
Talmadge, John Erwin, 22, 167, 201
Tankersley, Allen P., 27, 79
Tankersley, Charles W., 27
Tate, William, 52
Taylor, Antoinette Elizabeth, 108
Taylor, Gerald K., 108
Teague, Christine, 168
Temple, Sarah Gober, 185
Terrill, Helen E., 127
Thiery, Adelaide Hamlin, 127
Thigpen, Corbett H., 109
Thilenius, Edward Albert, 168
Thomas, Ray Hilman, 45
Thompson, Cicero L., 95
Thompson, Claude Holmes, 201
Thompson, Fred Bailey, 127
Thompson, Mary E., 168
Thompson, Sally, 168
Thompson, Thelma, 40
Thomson, James, 145
Thornton, William McKenzie, 198
Tilley, John Shipley, 127
Timberlake, Richard Henry, Jr., 253
Todd, Elizabeth, 217
Tomlinson, Edward, 168
Tompkins, Iva R., 145
Torrance, Ellis Paul, 233
Townsend, Ellis Carter, 109
Travis, Robert Jesse, 95
Troup, Cornelius V., 217
Tucker, Glenn, 79, 95, 127, 168, 185, 217
Tucker, H. Parks, 109
Tucker, W. T., 146
Turner, Henry Ashby, Jr., 233
Tyre, Nedra, 40, 52, 64, 168, 233

Vance, Henry C., 95
Vandiver, Jewell, 64
Vann, Sara Katherine, 201
Van Royen, Edith, 79
Van Royen, Russell G., 79
Vanstory, Burnette, 95
Veasey, Pauline, 146
Veatch, C. L., 4
Vinson, Dora, 14
Vinson, John Chalmers, 79, 109, 186
Vinzant, Marion McGuity, 169

Wade, John D., 70
Wagnon, Daniel Sydney, 254
Walker, Danton MacIntyre, 79, 95, 146
Walker, George Fuller, 40
Wall, Charles Augustus, Jr., 57, 156, 223
Wallace, Inez, 169
Wallace, Robert B., Jr., 233
Wamble, G. Hugh, 128, 234
Ware, Louise, 27

Ware, Sarah Pollard, 79
Waring, Antonio J., Jr., 169
Warren, James E., Jr., 109, 254
Warren, Kittrell, J., 109, 186
Warren, Mary Bondurant, 254
Wasson, Woodrow Wilson, 40
Watkins, Charles Hubert, 217
Watkins, Floyd C., 109, 217
Watson, Vincent C., 146
Watt, Nell Hodgson, 65
Webb, Julia Clay Barron, 128
Webb, Lester A., 254
Webster, Gray. *See* Garrison, Webb Black
Weens, H. Stephen, 44
Wells, David F., 254
Wells, William H., 131
Weltner, Philip, 186
Wesberry, James P., 217
Wesley, Cecil Cobb, 234
West, John Quinn, 79W
West, Lulameade, 41
West, Robert Hunter, 80
Westerfield, Clifford, 169
Wheeler, Raymond, 254
Whetten, Leland Carling, 146, 169
White, Goodrich C., 128
White, Helen Chappell, 52, 80, 128
White, Jane F., 254
White, Jess R., 201
White, Mary Culler, 80
White, Robb, 52, 65, 95, 201, 234
White, Walter Francis, 80
Whiting, Thomas A., 170
Whitman, William Tate, 56, 132
Whittemore, Myrtle, 52
Whittle, Connie R., 85
Wiggins, James Wilhelm, 146, 231
Wiggins, Robert Alon, 20, 255
Wiggins, Samuel Paul, 110, 146
Wigginton, Brooks E., 15, 110
Wilcox, Gerald Erasmus, 65
Wilder, William Murtha, 201
Wiley, Bell Irvin, 41, 80, 95, 128, 147, 170, 218, 234
Wilkes, Thomas G. E. *See* Wilcox, Gerald Erasmus
Wilkins, Bobby E., 80

Wilkinson, Stannye, 255
Williams, Carolyn White, 110, 184
Williams, Eleanor, 15
Williams, Mary A., 147
Williams, Nellie Lowman, 28, 52, 80, 255
Williams, Preston H., 15, 28
Williams, Ralph Roger, 80, 110
Williams, Vinnie, 110, 170, 255
Williamson, J. C., 110
Williford, William Bailey, 186, 201
Willingham, Calder, 15, 28, 41, 81, 218
Willingham, Jean Saunders, 199
Willis, Aubrey, 96, 128
Wilson, Eileen M. H., 152
Wilson, Pauline Park, 28
Wilson, Robert Cumming, 147
Windham, Donald, 15, 170, 202, 234, 255
Wingo, Caroline Elizabeth, 65
Winters, Margaret Campbell, 96
Wood, James Horace, 170
Wood, Marie Stevens, 52, 81, 110, 255
Wood, Virginia, 41
Wood, William Thomas, 81
Woodall, Bess Grey, 96
Woodward, John R., 111
Woofter, Thomas Jackson, 111
Worsley, Etta Blanchard, 41
Wright, David McCord, 255
Wright, Nathalia, 234, 256
Wynes, Charles E., 256
Wynn, William T., 15

Yancy, A. H., 147
Yarbrough, Bird, 234
Yarbrough, Paul, 234
Yates, B. C., 202
Yearns, Wilfred Buck, 170
Yerby, Frank Garvin, 15, 28, 41, 52, 65, 81, 96, 111, 128, 170, 186, 202, 235, 256
Young, Eleanor M., 28
Young, Ida, 28
Young, James Harvey, 186
Youse, Bevan K., 218

Zeigler, Harmon, 235
Zim, Howard, 171